Dynamics of Emigration

MAKING SENSE OF HISTORY
Studies in Historical Cultures
General Editor: Stefan Berger
Founding Editor: Jörn Rüsen

Bridging the gap between historical theory and the study of historical memory, this series crosses the boundaries between both academic disciplines and cultural, social, political and historical contexts. In an age of rapid globalization, which tends to manifest itself on an economic and political level, locating the cultural practices involved in generating its underlying historical sense is an increasingly urgent task.

Recent volumes:

Volume 43
Dynamics of Emigration: Émigré Scholars and the Production of Historical Knowledge in the 20th Century
Edited by Stefan Berger and Philipp Müller

Volume 42
Transcending the Nostalgic: Landscapes of Postindustrial Europe beyond Representation
Edited by George S. Jaramillo and Juliane Tomann

Volume 41
The Geopolitics of Rudolf Kjellén: Territory, State and Nation
Edited by Ragnar Björk and Thomas Lundén

Volume 40
Analysing Historical Narratives: On Academic, Popular and Educational Framings of the Past
Edited by Stefan Berger, Nicola Brauch, and Chris Lorenz

Volume 39
Postwar Soldiers: Historical Controversies and West German Democratization, 1945–1955
Jörg Echternkamp

Volume 38
Constructing Industrial Pasts: Heritage, Historical Culture and Identity in Regions Undergoing Structural Economic Transformation
Edited by Stefan Berger

Volume 37
The Engaged Historian: Perspectives on the Intersections of Politics, Activism and the Historical Profession
Edited by Stefan Berger

Volume 36
Contemplating Historical Consciousness: Notes from the Field
Edited by Anna Clark and Carla L. Peck

Volume 35
Empathy and History: Historical Understanding in Re-enactment, Hermeneutics and Education
Tyson Retz

Volume 34
The Ethos of History: Time and Responsibility
Edited by Stefan Helgesson and Jayne Svenungsson

Volume 33
History and Belonging: Representations of the Past in Contemporary European Politics
Edited by Stefan Berger and Caner Tekin

For a full volume listing, please see the series page on our website:
http://berghahnbooks.com/series/making-sense-of-history

DYNAMICS OF EMIGRATION

Émigré Scholars and the Production of Historical Knowledge in the 20th Century

Edited by Stefan Berger and Philipp Müller

berghahn
NEW YORK · OXFORD
www.berghahnbooks.com

First published in 2022 by
Berghahn Books
www.berghahnbooks.com

© 2022 Stefan Berger and Philipp Müller

All rights reserved. Except for the quotation of short passages
for the purposes of criticism and review, no part of this book
may be reproduced in any form or by any means, electronic or
mechanical, including photocopying, recording, or any information
storage and retrieval system now known or to be invented,
without written permission of the publisher.

Library of Congress Cataloging-in-Publication Data
Names: Berger, Stefan, editor. | Müller, Philipp (Historian), 1974– editor.
Title: Dynamics of emigration : émigré scholars and the production of
   historical knowledge in the 20th century / edited by Stefan Berger and
   Philipp Müller.
Other titles: Émigré scholars and the production of historical knowledge in the
   20th century
Description: New York : Berghahn Books, [2022] | Series: Making sense of
   history ; 43 | Includes bibliographical references and index.
Identifiers: LCCN 2022016545 (print) | LCCN 2022016546 (ebook) |
   ISBN 9781800736092 (hardback) | ISBN 9781800736108 (ebook)
Subjects: LCSH: Historiography—History—20th century. | Historians. |
   Exiled scholars—History—20th century. | Learning and scholarship—
   History—20th century.
Classification: LCC D13 .D96 2022 (print) | LCC D13 (ebook) |
   DDC 907.2—dc23/eng/20220513
LC record available at https://lccn.loc.gov/2022016545
LC ebook record available at https://lccn.loc.gov/2022016546]

British Library Cataloguing in Publication Data

A catalogue record for this book is available from the British Library

ISBN 978-1-80073-609-2 hardback
ISBN 978-1-80073-610-8 ebook

https://doi.org/10.3167/9781800736092

Contents

Introduction. Dynamics of Émigré Scholarship in the Age
of Extremes 1
Stefan Berger and Philipp Müller

Chapter 1. 'A Private Perch': Cosmopolitanism, Nostalgia
and Commitment in the Émigré Historian's Persona 23
Jo Tollebeek

Chapter 2. The Émigré Historian: A Scholarly Persona? 45
Herman Paul

Chapter 3. The Long Arm of the Dictator: Cross-Border
Persecution of Exiled Historians 58
Antoon De Baets

Chapter 4. Nativism and the Spectre of Antisemitism in
the Placement of German Refugee Scholars, 1933–1945 74
Joseph Malherek

Chapter 5. Defending Objectivity: Paul Oskar Kristeller and the
Controversy over Historical Knowledge in the United States 94
Iryna Mykhailova

Chapter 6. Émigré Historians and the Postwar Transatlantic
Dialogue 109
Philipp Stelzel

Chapter 7. Between Integration and Institutional
Self-Organisation: Polish Émigré Scholarship in the
United States, 1939–1989 124
Kai Johann Willms

Chapter 8. The Unlikely Careers of Laura Polanyi (1882–1959) as a Historian: The Intersections of Exile, Gender, Class and Age 139
Judith Szapor

Chapter 9. 'From *Geistesgeschichte* to Public History': The Years of Emigration of the Hungarian Historian Béla Iványi-Grünwald, Jr. 156
Vilmos Erős

Chapter 10. Building New Networks: Russian Émigré Scholars in Yugoslavia 173
Branimir Janković

Chapter 11. Networking in Santa Barbara, Writing History: Dimitrije Đorđević and the Comparative History of Balkan Nations 188
Michael Antolović

Chapter 12. António Sérgio and José Ortega y Gasset: History, Theory and Experiences of Exile 205
Sérgio Campos Matos

Chapter 13. Émigré Portuguese Historians in France, 1945–1974: New Methods of Thinking and Writing Portuguese History 224
Christophe Araujo

Conclusion. New Perspectives on Émigré Scholarship and What Remains to be Done 237
Stefan Berger and Philipp Müller

Index 251

INTRODUCTION

Dynamics of Émigré Scholarship in the Age of Extremes

STEFAN BERGER AND PHILIPP MÜLLER

Introduction

Stanisław Aronson recalls the onset of political violence and the consequences for his life as follows: 'One moment I was enjoying an idyllic adolescence in my home city of Lodz, and the next we were on the run'.[1] Stanisław Aronson, a Polish Jew, born in 1925, now living in Tel Aviv, found himself more than once 'at the sharp end of European history', as he puts it, and warns retrospectively against the power of deliberately spreading lies, which for him is what preceded discrimination and persecution and at the same time concealed disastrous consequences for him and his family.[2] 'I would only return to my empty home five years later, no longer a carefree boy but a Holocaust survivor and Home Army veteran living in fear of Stalin's secret police, the NKVD.'[3]

    The extremes of the twentieth century have undoubtedly encouraged and promoted flight and migration, which are by no means matters of the past. Forced migration is – unfortunately – still part of current political events. This book takes the timeliness of the topic as an opportunity to recall refugee scholars in general and émigré historians in particular. Above all, however, the book advances research questions on émigré scholarship. At the centre of the book is the question of the dynamics of emigration and its repercussions for scholarship. First, we ask about concrete consequences of

---

Notes for this section begin on page 15.

persecution for the lives of intellectuals and scholars. How did researchers who emigrated appropriate their new social and institutional environment and – sometimes completely unknown – academic scene? What considerations and policies shaped the organisations that brokered on their behalf and supported them? What role did the micropolitics of scholars play in all these processes? A further important element is the persona of the scholars: how did the personae of scholars change in this context? How did émigré scholars deal with various if not inconstant and contradictory (self-) images? In what kind of active self-fashioning were they engaged, and what role did gender play in this process? Finally, the question arises as to how dynamics of migration prompted new historical concepts and questions: which ideas remained untouched? Which notions, questions, and the spectrum of themes and questions, altered and evolved?

Scholarship in Exile: Historiographical Reflections with Special Emphasis on Historians

In our contemporary globalised world, scholars move around different countries with considerable ease. Never before in the history of the historical and related academic professions has it been so easy to spend time abroad during one's studies and again, later, during the dissertation or postdoctoral phases, and later still, when established as visiting professors or fellows at centres of advanced study in different parts of the world. Transnational biographies of historical scholars are increasingly common in a profession that is no longer contained by national boundaries,[4] even if it would be dangerous to underestimate the continued significance of those borders.[5] The contemporary permeability of national scholarly boundaries has led to an increase in the phenomenon of voluntary emigration for many reasons: scholarly advancement, better pay, improved research opportunities, the desire to learn more about other academic cultures, or simply the offer of a job. Such migration is, however, by no means restricted to the contemporary age. It was found already in the nineteenth century. Thus, for example, Ludwig Riess, a pupil of Leopold von Ranke, taught at Tokyo Imperial University between 1887 and 1902, leaving a deep legacy of historicism in the Japanese historical profession.[6] Especially in the intense decades of globalisation around 1900, which arguably have not yet been surpassed in the first decades of the twenty-first century, voluntary scholarly migration was a common phenomenon, resembling the contemporary situation. In between lies the twentieth century, characterised in its first half by hypernationalisms that, combined with racism, led to two world wars, civil wars and genocides on a hitherto unprecedented scale. In its second half, the Cold War ideological conflict led to innumerable wars in which the capitalist US and the Communist Soviet Union sought to dominate a world politics characterised by the institutionalisation of the nation-state principle on a global scale in the wake of decolonisation.

Although the phenomenon of exile scholarship is an ancient one that can be traced back many centuries, the question emerges whether the twentieth century was the one in which enforced exile was a particularly frequent experience. Ideologies such as nationalism, fascism and communism forced many scholars into exile, where they sometimes established diaspora historiographies that often had a transgenerational impact on scholarly traditions. One particularly prominent example among many is the exile and subsequent diaspora historiography of the Baltic states during the Cold War of the twentieth century. It forged alternative national histories of Estonia, Latvia and Lithuania to the ones that were written under the Soviet rule between the end of the Second World War and the regained independence of the Baltic states in the early 1990s.[7]

Voluntary migration might have, at times, amounted to a self-imposed exile, but it was quite distinct from the exile situations that were the consequence of brute force and often denied scholars any choice in the matter of migration. Never before did so many historians have to leave their homelands if they wanted to avoid persecution, imprisonment and death than in the twentieth century. And the 'crimes against history' continue, of course, into the twenty-first century and our present. When the International Federation of Human Rights, one of the oldest human rights organisations in the world, founded in 1922, reported these crimes and spoke out against 'history producers' in Russia, it adopted a concept and a book title by Antoon De Baets, who has been the most important historian to date in highlighting the contemporary and ongoing persecution of historians around the world.[8] Naturally, force is an expandable concept. Is, for example, economic force not also a force? If historians cannot get jobs in their home countries are they not forced to migrate if they want to continue to be historians? There is also the vexed question of political or methodological bias that excludes historians from making a career in their native countries. One of the greatest British social historians of the post-Second World War era, George Rudé, spoke of his own professional existence in Australia as one of exile. Even if he described it as 'one of the most pleasant', there clearly was a feeling of being exiled from the place that was at once his homeland and one of the main focuses of his scholarship; another focus being France, with his studies on eighteenth- and nineteenth-century radicalism.[9] In the field of exile historiography, it certainly makes sense to differentiate between different types of exile.[10] Yet it also seems reasonable not to draw the lines too narrowly but instead to look at all situations in which historians found themselves confronted with a situation in which they moved from one country that was familiar to them to another that was, at least at first, alien to them. It would appear that those situations were particularly frequent in the twentieth century, given the political nature of historical thinking and its abundant ideological instrumentalisation in the age of extremes.

If the writing of history eschewed antiquarianism and was, in Friedrich Nietzsche's sense, 'critical history writing'[11] – that is, connected to a present and its search for possible futures – then historians following such a path often lived dangerously, for their work amounted to interventions in political debates that had contemporary relevance. If their writing was part and parcel of a counter-discourse that was opposed to those in power, they were likely to feel the wrath of those to whom they spoke of an unwanted history. Hence, the history of exile historiographies has often been connected to a history of engaged history writing in which the historians saw themselves as contributing to public political debates to which the past was relevant.[12] The borderline between historians and politicians could be a narrow one. Thus, Marian Kukiel was Professor of History at the Polish University in Exile during the Second World War, but he was also the Minister for War in the Polish government in exile. Claudio Sánchez-Albornoz and Lluís Nicolau d'Olwer were both historians but also worked in government; in Albornoz's case as head of the Spanish government in exile, between 1959 and 1971, and in d'Olwer's case as ambassador of the government in exile in Mexico.[13] Many German scholars exiled by National Socialism volunteered their services during the Second World War to the American Office for War Information, the Board of Economic Warfare, and the Office of Strategic Services (OSS). Hajo Holborn, a pupil of Friedrich Meinecke, who had to leave his professorship of history at Berlin's Hochschule für Politik in 1933 and successfully established himself as professor of history at Yale University between 1934 and 1969, even became President of the American Historical Association between 1967 and 1969 and was head of the Department of Research and Analysis at the OSS during the Second World War. Thereafter, he frequently advised different American governments on questions relating to Germany, and after 1960, he was the Director of the American Council on Germany.[14] In this part of the story of exile historiographies, the exiled historians found themselves in exile for a political reason.

However, another story of exile historiography is completely unrelated to a tradition of engaged history writing and instead has to do with the persecution of historians not because of their historical work or their civic engagement or a connection between the two, but because of ethnic, racial, religious, class or gender discriminations regardless of what historians wrote or said. Hans Rothfels, to give just one example, was a deeply conservative German historian in the interwar period who championed a form of

'*Volksgeschichte*' that was deeply nationalist and even racist.[15] His political outlook would have been compatible with the National Socialists had he not been a Jew – at least in the eyes of the National Socialists. Hence, he reluctantly left National Socialist Germany for the United States in 1938 to embark on a very successful career at the University of Chicago, before returning, after 1945, to West Germany, where his conservatism influenced the postwar West German historiography for decades to come.

Religion is a marker of exclusion in Islamic nation states of the contemporary era just as it was in Protestant nation states of the nineteenth century. For Islamist historians, it is thus impossible to imagine a non-Muslim historian employed at the universities of the Islamic Republic of Iran,[16] just as many Protestant historians in nineteenth- century Germany or Britain found it impossible to imagine a Catholic or Jewish historian as a respected member of the historical profession.[17]

University education is a privilege largely enjoyed by middle-class people, and class remains an important exclusionary factor for the recruitment of historians. In many parts of the West, it was unthinkable until well into the twentieth century to use either the language of class or deal with topics that highlighted the existence of class differences or social movements built around constructions of class identities. The exclusion of Gustav Mayer from the historical profession is a case in point.[18] Mayer, one of the most important early labour historians in Germany, had to flee the National Socialists after 1933 and experienced not only exclusion within Germany but also exile. Here, however, we are already back with questions of power, engagement and exclusion discussed in the previous paragraph.

Another prominent exclusionary factor was gender. The professionalisation of history writing in the nineteenth century was characterised by the systematic exclusion of women from the profession.[19] Whilst, over the last forty years women have been slowly catching up in the West, they remain discriminated against in many other parts of the world. When Western universities began to admit women again from the last third of the nineteenth century onwards, history became a popular subject, and hence exile was a fate that women historians shared with their male colleagues. Among the refugees from National Socialist Germany, for example, were also women historians such as Emmy Heller and Lucie Varga. Their fate in exile was by no means uniform – some were more successful than others in establishing themselves in their new surroundings. Yet, their struggle was clearly characterised by another dimension that was lacking from the struggle of their male colleagues: gender discrimination.[20]

Class, gender and religious exclusions in themselves, however, rarely produced situations of exile, as these tended to be exclusions preventing the recruitment of workers, women and members of religious minorities of even becoming historians in the first place – in most cases. Ethnic/racial discrimination did produce a significant exile community because of regime changes that introduced such ethnic exclusions, most notably the National Socialist regime in Germany. And indeed, much exile historiography has focused on the emigration of racially discriminated scholars from central Europe/the German lands in the 1930s.[21]

Indeed, the dictatorships of the twentieth century and their racially or politically motivated persecution of historians has taken centre stage in the historiography of exiled historians to date.[22] Both fascist and communist dictatorships and their dealings with historians they regarded as oppositional have been studied widely. Italian fascism produced relatively few exiles, as most historians attempted to arrange themselves within the regime, which was, in any case, willing to tolerate a certain diversity of opinion within the academy.[23] Thus, for example, Benedetto Croce was able to publish his national history of Italy under fascism, despite the fact that it was a thinly veiled critique of the fascist view of Italian history.[24] However, the fascist state could also turn murderous, as was the case with the brothers Rosselli, who had joined the Resistance and were killed by fascist thugs in exile in France in 1937.[25] Others, like the socialist Gaetano Salvemini or the lapsed communist Franco Venturi, were forced into exile, where they upheld different national master narratives than the fascist ones.[26]

The situation in National Socialist Germany was not altogether different. Here also only a minority of historians were dismissed by the regime, whilst the majority made their peace with the fascists.[27] The minority consisted of those deemed Jewish by the National Socialists and those who were Social Democrats, Communists, or otherwise politically opposed to the National Socialist regime, like Felix Gilbert.[28] When Francoism was finally established in Spain, following a bloody civil war between 1936 and 1939, many liberals and left-wing academics left the universities and went into exile in other European or, often, Latin American countries.[29] Around one third of all university professors at Spanish universities lost their jobs after 1939. Among historians, the exodus included Rafael Altamira, Pere Bosch Gimpera, Claudio Sánchez-Albornoz and Américo Castro.[30] Javier Malagón even claimed that Spanish history was the most pressing issue amongst the many exiled intellectuals that the Spanish Civil War produced.[31]

The communist regimes in the twentieth century were at least as thorough in uprooting scholars that were ideologically opposed to them and less willing to accommodate other views than their fascist counterparts. They produced large exile communities. Many so-called 'bourgeois' historians left the Soviet Union in the years after the successful Bolshevik October revolution in 1917.[32] They settled in Paris, Berlin and especially in Prague, where they set up a whole host of institutions, such as the Russian University in Prague, the Kondakov Institute, the Russian Historical Archive Abroad and the Russian Library (later renamed Slav Library).[33] The Soviet Union put considerable energy into building up its own historical expertise and completely remoulded the historical profession in the 1920s.[34] In the 1930s, many of those first-generation communist historians were purged by Stalin and ended up as victims in the Gulag or they were killed in the prisons of the Soviet state that they had helped to legitimate through their historical writing.[35]

In Communist Eastern Europe after 1945, we can observe similar patterns. 'Bourgeois' historians went into exile using existing networks that often comprised of historians of their own nationality who already were abroad, whilst a new generation of communist historians were often trained by those who had returned from exile during the Second World War.[36] Many journalists, philosophers, linguists, novelists, poets and diplomats who were exiled from Communism during the Cold War turned to history as a result of having become exiles. Hence we can see that the experience of exile encourages in exiles a turn to history in the search for explanations about their own fate.[37]

Such a turn to history produced a range of historical institutions. Exiles from Communist Eastern Europe were particularly diligent institution-builders: the Polish Instytut Historyczny in Rome, the Collegium Carolinum in Munich, the Harvard-Ukrainian Research Institute, the Archive of Czechs and Slovaks Abroad in Chicago, the Bakhmeteff Archive at Columbia University, the Polish Institute and Sikorski Museum in London, the Museum of Russian Culture in San Francisco, and the Polish Institute of Arts and Sciences in America were just some of the most prominent exile institutions that brought together historians and scholars from other disciplines to promote scientific work and build bridges with the scientific communities of their host countries. Exiled historians also founded scientific journals that became successful platforms for research on the countries they had been exiled from; for example, *The Polish Review*, published by the Polish Institute for Arts and Sciences in America. They founded publishing houses that became hubs of exile scholarship presenting alternative interpretations to the ones peddled by Marxist-Leninists behind the Iron Curtain.[38]

Yet, as the Ukrainian exiles in Canada during the Cold War demonstrated, all scholarly exile undertakings benefited enormously from lively interaction with their host societies, in that it allowed for the modernisation of concepts and methods.[39] It is interesting to observe that the refugees from National Socialism, although hugely influential in their host countries (e.g. in the US and Britain), were far less active as institution-builders. They concentrated more on fitting into the existing institutions of their host countries, where they were often hugely successful.[40]

After the Communists took over power in China in 1949, the historical profession, like other humanities disciplines, was also completely transformed. Many non-communist historians either joined the Kuomintang in Taiwan or left for other shores,[41] especially the United States, which, as one of the biggest academic markets and one that was relatively open to foreign talent, took a huge share of exiled scholars, including historians in the twentieth century.[42]

The huge influx of exiled scholars from fascist and right-wing dictatorships in Europe and from the Communist Soviet Union saw the setting up of a whole host of institutions meant to help the exiles: the Academic Assistance Council was founded in Britain in 1933 and became the Society for the Protection of Science and Learning in 1936. The Comité de Savants in France, the Notgemeinschaft Deutscher Wissenschaftler im Ausland in Switzerland, and the Emergency Committee in Aid of Displaced German Scholars, later extended to Emergency Committee in Aid of Displaced Foreign Scholars, served the same purpose.[43]

Whilst the writing of exile historiography to date has largely focused on the twentieth century, a trend that this current volume is following, a broader chronological look might yield interesting results. Thukydides famously claimed that his twenty years of living in exile made him a more insightful historian.[44] The Jewish-Spanish historian Salomo Ibn Verga, the chronicler of Jewish persecution, had to leave Spain for Portugal in the late fifteenth century and eventually was allowed to leave Portugal for the Ottoman empire, but he died en route to his new place of exile.[45] The turbulent years of the English civil war and its aftermath saw a number of historians exiled at different points in their lives.[46] Upheaval often produced situations of exile. The European nineteenth century is often described as a century of revolutions.[47] Starting with the 'great French revolution' of 1789, the nineteenth century saw many revolutionary uprisings in different parts of Europe, for political and nationalist reasons, of which the 1848 revolutionary cycle was particularly prominent.[48] Revolutions produced upheavals in which historians were uprooted from their professional positions and forced into exile or where they lost their jobs. Jules Michelet, for example, could stay in France, but he lost his position as keeper of the national archives and professor at the Collège de France for supporting the revolution of 1848. He had to earn a living by publishing a series of popular books together with his wife on everything from the sea to love and the mountains.[49]

As a historian in Paris, he had been deeply influenced by his contact with the Polish exiled poet Adam Mickiewicz, who also wrote history. Michelet's works on Polish history and some of his concepts were directly inspired by Mickiewicz, who in turn was deeply influenced by Michelet's historical works. Paris in the 1830s and 1840s was a key hub for exiles, and they often rubbed shoulders with French academics and intellectuals in those years.⁵⁰ Another earlier example of a nineteenth-century exile is Germaine de Stael, who produced her work under the impact of a double exclusion from professional recognition and integration – that is, as an exile who had to flee revolutionary France in the 1790s and as a woman. It was from this position that she wrote her insightful history of the German lands.⁵¹ Political persecution produced many exile histories. This was as true of socialism in the nineteenth century as it was for communism in the twentieth. Louis Blanc and Karl Marx are two famous examples of socialist/communist historians who penned their histories in exile.⁵² In the twentieth-century, Arthur Rosenberg and Boris Souvarine were two examples of historians who used their exile situation in order to rethink constructively their Marxist approaches and reconsider the future perspectives for revolutionary change. As a result, they left the Communist Party and reoriented themselves politically in their new host countries.⁵³

With communism, much of the writing on exile scholarship and refugee historians has focused on the northern transatlantic world (i.e. Europe and North America). Yet the phenomenon was a global one, with strong relevance to Latin America, Asia and Africa. During the course of the twentieth century, a succession of right-wing dictatorships in Latin America exiled scores of left-of-centre historians for political reasons. Sometimes, like in the case of Emilio Ravignani and José Luis Romero, two Argentinian historians fleeing from Peronism, they found new academic homes in neighbouring countries – in Ravignani's and Romero's case in Uruguay, from where they could develop powerful positions as institution-builders and constructivists of historical master narratives.⁵⁴ Exiled scholars, of course, served as important institution-builders elsewhere, and one of the most famous examples is the New School in New York, which would not have come into being and would have looked very different without the influx of refugees from Central Europe.⁵⁵ In Europe before the First World War, Pavel Vinogradoff's establishment of the École Russe de Hautes Études Sociales in Paris is another example of successful institution-building by exiled historians.⁵⁶

Returning to Latin America, Mario Sznajder and Luis Roniger have argued convincingly that the politics of exile was, almost throughout the whole of the twentieth century, an important means of institutional exclusion practised by most Latin American governments to silence unwelcome voices, including those coming from history writing.⁵⁷ But, as the cases of Argentina and Uruguay underline, the same governments that put scholars into exile could also receive scholars fleeing from elsewhere if they fitted the particular political framework of the receiving country. It is intriguing to observe how in some Latin American countries, like Argentina and Uruguay, this history of exile, and mutual scholarly relations through exile, is a continuous one from the interwar period to the end of the twentieth century.⁵⁸

In Latin America, the topic of exile historiography has a political immediacy, as the contexts of dictatorships are often recent and the legacies both of those who chose exile and those forced into exile are contentious and the subject of acrimonious contemporary debate.[59]

Elsewhere, the writing of Black history and the many black African diasporas across the globe has become the subject of intense debate.[60] In Southern Africa, exile histories have constructed the experience of exile, and in particular the experience of living in 'the camp', as a crucial foundational experience for the construction of a post-apartheid South Africa.[61] And 'refugee historians' from Burundi, living in Tanzania, played a crucial role in producing historical narratives that were vital in forging collective identity among Burundian refugees.[62]

National insurrections in postcolonial situations in Africa and Asia frequently led to exile, yet the same is true for Europe. Here many historians who had sided with nationalist uprisings against multinational empires in the nineteenth century were forced into exile after these uprisings had failed. Thus, for example, Poland saw two major uprisings, in 1831 and 1862, in which nationalists sought to re-establish Poland on the map of Europe, from where it had vanished in multiple treaties that partitioned the Polish lands between Prussia, Russia and the Habsburg empire in the late eighteenth century. Joachim Lelewel, the archetype of the radical romantic historian,[63] had to leave his native Warsaw after 1831 for his part in the uprising. He settled in Paris and later in Brussels, from where he continued to write a succession of history books on the Polish lands, aimed at keeping awake the Polish historical consciousness and defining the Polish lands, especially at the border with the Russian empire.[64]

Writing national historical master narratives from a position of exile was quite a common phenomenon, as exiled historians remained vexed and fascinated by their former homelands, and they often wanted to contest either imperial, colonial or alternative master narratives. A fully-fledged Basque national historical narrative, for example, only emerged in exile after 1939: in close association with leading exiled politicians, Basque historians constructed a nationalist narrative that aimed at distancing the Basque country from Spain.[65] Teaching and writing outside of their old homeland in new surroundings, exiled historians often inspired students of history in their new countries to specialise in the histories of their homelands. Thus refugee historians from National Socialism in both Britain and the United States taught a generation of British and American historians the history of Germany and central Europe, thus contributing to a flowering of this subject in English-language historiography after the Second World War.[66]

Regardless of such success stories, the situation of the exiled historian is always connected to uprooting experiences that are deeply alienating. Contrary to Plutarch's famous thesis, they have rarely been a blessing in disguise. Contributions of refugee historians to scholarship were made against the odds.[67] It is intriguing to reflect on the fact that historians of ancient historiography have frequently stressed how the experience of exile was fundamental to the quality of ancient Greek historical writing.[68] This set a trend that can also sometimes be found in modern historiography despite the plain and simple fact that exiled historians were violently extracted from one country and transplanted into another. As a consequence, exiled historians often developed an acute sense of space that could produce a longing for the 'lost homeland', or, alternatively, an overriding desire to integrate themselves as quickly as possible into the new space they were transplanted to, their new 'homeland'. Often it produced a mixture of the two. In any case, the memory of the old homeland and the memory of the transition from the old to the new often haunted exiled scholars for many decades, if not for their entire lifetime.[69]

Where the hankering after the space they lost was dominant, exiled historians delved deep into their memories and in some respects came to live in the past. The anti-communist historians that fled revolutionary Russia after 1917 are a case in point. Wherever they eventually settled, they primarily mixed among other Russian exiles and protracted their pre-revolutionary concerns as historians into the post-1917 period, largely ignoring the caesura.[70] In their habitus as in their scholarly concerns they literally lived in a past that no longer had any meaning outside of their closed exile circles. Where they had an impact on the historical profession in their host countries, they prolonged pre-1917 research traditions as well as political commitments (strong anti-Communism). They lost touch with the post-1917 Soviet historiography and its developments that they regarded as politically illegitimate and scholarly humbug. We can find a similar unwillingness to engage with the new host countries among prominent Chinese exile scholars from Communism, such as Ping-Ti Ho.[71] To what extent exiled historians were willing to learn from their new environment depended on how they perceived the quality of the academic world they entered in relation to the one that they came from. Thus, for example, many German scholars emigrating from National Socialist Germany had a very high opinion of German scholarship and did not rate the scholarship in many of the places they settled. If anything, they saw their mission in introducing German 'Wissenschaftlichkeit' into their new surroundings. Hans Rothfels' habitus at the University of Chicago would fit that pattern perfectly, as it would be hard to argue that he ever became integrated into the American academic culture that he despised. His success at Chicago was based on the high reputation of German scholarship in the US and on the willingness of Chicago-based scholars to adopt the German habitus, which did not really make it a happier place.[72]

Yet exile also often produced in the exiled historian an acute desire to look for explanations of why they found themselves in exile, which often had to do with the fact that their 'cause' had lost in power struggles, forcing them to leave. Reinhart Koselleck once observed that the losers in historical conflicts write the more innovative history, as they tend to search more deeply for the reasons for their defeat, whilst the victors write a facile and teleological history ending up in their own victory.[73] The obsession with defeat producing exile has, by contrast, resulted in many excellent histories. The rethinking of history that resulted from situations of exile frequently involved conceptual innovation. Thus, for example, exiles from the Soviet Union in the interwar period established the concept of Eurasianism in order to distance themselves from those who had argued in favour of Russia modernising and catching up with the West. Westernisation, according to them, was the root cause for the destruction of the Romanov empire, with liberals and socialists/communists all attached to those Westernising tendencies. Instead, Eurasianists justified Russia's difference to the West and saw it located firmly in the East, where it allegedly had an imperial mission that was aimed at establishing an alternative to the path of Western modernisation.[74] Another example of conceptual innovation in exile is Henri Pirenne, who spent time in enforced exile as a prisoner of war in Germany during the First World War. Here, Pirenne, an ardent admirer of the German historical sciences before the First World War, developed a criticism of the strong ethnonationalist foundations of some of the German scholarship he had come to admire. He came to realise how this had also influenced his own thinking on national history; for example, in his famous history of Belgium, which was in fact first published in German in 1899. In the interwar period, he systematically de-ethnicised this history in subsequent editions of the work to be published in French.[75]

If historians stayed alert to their new surroundings and were willing to learn from them, they could also often draw from the historiographical traditions of their home countries to shed new light on the histories of their countries of origin. Thus, a generation of historians exiled from National Socialist Germany and growing up in the United States picked up theoretical pre-occupations of US historians (e.g. the progressive tradition of US American historical writing) and developed from those traditions perspectives on the history of Germany that were highly original and that in turn influenced German historians in the Federal Republic of Germany. Hans Rosenberg, for example, had to leave National Socialist Germany in 1936 and continued his career at Brooklyn College in New York and the University of California in Berkeley. After 1945, he returned to several visiting professorships at West German universities before resettling in West Germany in 1970, and his physical presence in the country from where he once had to emigrate increased his influence on the postwar generation of West German historians. Rosenberg's concepts, such as 'the Great Depression' or 'Bonapartist rule', were integrated into German '*Gesellschaftsgeschichte*' as it developed in the 1970s and 1980s.[76] Refugee historians from National Socialist Germany remained emotionally highly involved with German affairs. It is no coincidence that the role of the German resistance to National Socialism was a topic that was close to their heart, as it allowed them to construct notions of 'another Germany' that had remained 'decent' in the face of the German descent into barbarism.[77]

An interesting phenomenon in the study of exile historiographies is that of 'second-generation exile' – that is, historians who either fled as children or were born to exiles already in the new homeland.[78] Growing up with exile often produced an intense interest in the homeland of their parents' generation. In their training as historians they therefore specialised in the histories of those countries from where their parents originated. If we take, for example, the historians Wilma and Georg Iggers, who had both fled their native countries – Czechoslovakia and Germany, respectively – they retained in their scholarship a lifelong concern with the Bohemian lands (in Wilma's case) and with the history of Germany (in Georg's case). Wilma Iggers' *Women of Prague* and Georg Iggers' *The Conception of German History* are good examples of how second-generation exiles remained focused on the histories of their origin, which was an attempt to retain and revitalise old bonds of belonging and explain why they had been ruptured. The Iggers are also a good example of how exile did not only influence scholarship but also ways of life and political engagement. Their struggle against the ongoing discrimination of black people in the United States, against the Vietnam War and against the blind anti-Communism in the West were examples of political commitments that were related to the experience of early dislocation produced by exile.[79]

Some studies in the historiography of exile have focused on 'internal exile' – that is, the banishment of historians from their former places of work, usually in metropolitan centres, to the peripheries of academia or outside of academia altogether. In the vast empire of Russia/the Soviet Union, historians could be banished from Moscow and St. Petersburg to the far east or some other remote part of the empire, where their influence was limited.[80] In the communist worlds of the twentieth century, it was a common phenomenon to demote historians who had not been willing to tow the party line and make them work in factories or other non-academic jobs as a form of punishment. Sometimes they could return from there to re-occupy positions in academia, whilst at other times they simply disappeared. The Italian fascists practised 'confino' to silence antifascists, who were sent to remote islands or villages where they were de facto imprisoned and their voices remained unheard.[81] 'Internal exile' has also been used as a term of description for those scholars who felt at a distance to dictatorial regimes but did not speak up against them. Withdrawing into their scholarship was seen as a form of 'internal exile'. However, this concept is highly problematical, as it was used in the aftermath of dictatorships to veil the fact that many scholars simply arranged themselves with dictatorships and sought to protect their way of life and their position in the academy by going along with dictatorships.

Foremost among the questions that historians of exile historiography have tackled are those about their impact, both on their countries of origin and on their countries of residence. Often historians became bridge-builders between the two. They could uphold alternative histories to the ones that were produced in their countries of origin, thereby resisting attempts by dictatorial regimes to streamline history into one uncontested and homogeneous storyline. They could also inspire a new generation in their new home countries through the methods, theoretical insights and subject areas they brought with them from their countries of origin. Thus, for example, the Renaissance scholar Hans Baron brought his phenomenal knowledge of Italian Renaissance archives first to Britain and then to the United States and inspired a huge revival of Renaissance studies in both countries, especially in the United States, where he eventually settled.[82]

Yet one should not glorify most historians' experience of exile. They often struggled economically. If they could find jobs as historians at all, they were often jobs that were poorly paid and had huge teaching loads, making it difficult to continue research careers.[83] As Ragnar Björk has shown for Scandinavia, the process of re-embedding exiled historians from National Socialism was a difficult one that rarely succeeded.[84] The internationalism of historical studies that found expression, above all, in the world history congresses, organised from the late nineteenth century to the present day, has not helped much either, as it was organised through its national affiliates, hence making the nation state and its historical profession the building block of transnationalism, thereby leaving exiled historians without representation.[85] Within exile historiography, there is a clear bias towards studying those who made it in their new homelands, who managed to continue their careers and were successful. These historians did not only leave more material behind, but they were also often influential, in both their new homeland and in their country of origin. Hence the writing on exile historiography has tended to underestimate the catastrophe that exile meant to the overwhelming number of exiles and highlighted instead the few cases where exile produced, in Peter Burke's words, a 'double deprovincialization' of historical writing.[86] Burke's impressive attempt to see a 'silver lining' in the experience of exile by highlighting the exiles' ability to distance themselves from their own research traditions, to engage with new research traditions in their host countries, to move towards comparison and to mediate between different scholarly traditions and act as bridge- builders is certainly pointing to vital elements of the experience of scholarly exile, but it is referring to those 'who made it' against the backdrop of many more who did not.

The cases that are selected in this volume speak to many of the historiographical themes that are identified above as key ones in the history of historiography on émigré scholarship. We focus on some of the key countries in which historians have been exiled in the twentieth century, especially Germany, but also Russia, Poland, Hungary, the Iberian Peninsula and Serbia. Both Eastern and Western Europe are prominently represented in this volume. We have also selected individuals who are either not very well known in the existing literature on émigré scholars, or we have provided new perspectives on individuals about whom much has been written already. Overall, the contributions in this volume fit neatly into the historiography of émigré scholarship and provide tantalising new facets to the picture of transfers, adaptations and reinventions that mark the experience of exiled scholars in many parts of the world.

The editors of this volume would like to express their deep gratitude to the Fritz-Thyssen-Stiftung, whose financial support made the project possible and led to this publication.

Notes

1. Aronson, 'I survived the Warsaw Ghetto'.
2. Ibid.
3. Ibid.
4. On historians, see, for example Munro and Reid, *Clio's Lives*, where the transnational elements of historians' biographies are a prominent theme. For the neighbouring discipline of geography, see Marcus, *Transnational Geographers in the United States*. On the importance of crossing cultural borders in historiography, see the contributions in Fuchs and Stuchtey, *Across Cultural Borders*. With regard to journeys to foreign archives and libraries see Müller, 'Doing Historical Research'; idem, *Geschichte machen*, 257–317.
5. Berger, *The Past as History*, chapter 6 acknowledges the weakening of national(ist) traditions in professional history writing but also that considerable remaining linkages get stronger if we consider historical writing outside of the universities and academies of contemporary Europe. For an overview of global contemporary developments, see Maissen and May, *National History and New Nationalism in the Twenty-First Century*.
6. Mehl, 'Japan und die preussisch-deutsche Geschichtswissenschaft'; Jagno, *Deutsch-japanischer Wissensaustausch als lokale Praxis*.
7. Tamm, 'Displaced History?'.
8. On the report, see https://www.fidh.org/en/region/europe-central-asia/russia/russia-history-producers-attacked-as-regime-attempts-to-control [accessed 1 Oct. 2021]. See also De Baets, *Crimes against History*; De Baets has been the key person behind the Network of Concerned Historians: http://www.concernedhistorians.org/content/home.html [accessed 1 Oct. 2021].
9. Friguglietti, 'A Scholar "in Exile"'.
10. For conceptual discussions, see De Baets, 'Exile and Acculturation'.
11. Nietzsche, *Unzeitgemässe Betrachtungen, Zweites Stück*.
12. Berger, *The Engaged Historian*.

13. Mandelíčková and Goddeeris, 'Living in the Past', 405 f.
14. Gilbert, 'Hajo Holborn', 3–8.
15. On Rothfels, see Eckel, *Hans Rothfels*; Walther, 'Eine kleine Intervention', 11–16; Harvey, 'Hans Rothfels and the Paradoxes of Cosmopolitan Conservatism'. On Volksgeschichte, see Oberkrome, *Volksgeschichte*.
16. Aghaie, 'Islamist Historiography in Post-Revolutionary Iran'.
17. On the dominance of Protestantism and its exclusion of Catholicism within the academic culture of Imperial Germany, see Vom Bruch, *Wissenschaft, Politik und öffentliche Meinung*.
18. Mayer, *Erinnerungen*.
19. Smith, *The Gender of History*.
20. Epstein, 'Fashioning Fortuna's Whim', 301 ff.
21. Stelzel, *History after Hitler*; Frank, *Double Exile*; Ritter, 'Meinecke's Protégés'; Ritter, *German Refugee Historians*; Eakin-Thimme, *Geschichte im Exil*; Lehmann and Sheehan, *An Interrupted Past*; Epstein, *A Past Renewed*; Alter, *Out of the Third Reich*; Mitchell, *Fleeing Nazi Germany*; Rürup, 'Vertreibung'.
22. Tortarolo, 'Historians in the Storm'.
23. Goetz, *Der freie Geist und seine Widersacher*.
24. Rizi, *Benedetto Croce and Italian Fascism*.
25. Morgan, 'Reclaiming Italy?'.
26. Tortarolo, 'Salvemini'; Totarolo, 'Historians in Exile'.
27. Schönwälder, *Historiker und Politik*.
28. Lehmann, *Felix Gilbert as Scholar and Teacher*.
29. Boyd, *Historia Patria*. See also Kamen, *The Disinherited*.
30. Pasamar, *Apologia and Criticism*, chapter 3.
31. Malagón, 'Los Historiadores'.
32. Chinyaeva, *Russians Outside Russia*; Raeff, *Russia Abroad*; Rhinelander, 'Exiled Russian Scholars in Prague'.
33. Mandelíčková and Goddeeris, 'Living in the Past', 404.
34. Byrnes, 'Creating the Soviet Historical Profession'; see also: Banerij, *Writing History in the Soviet Union*; Enteen, *The Soviet Scholar-Bureaucrat*.
35. Barber, *Soviet Historians in Crisis*.
36. Zadencka, Plakans and Lawaty, *East and Central European History Writing in Exile*. Antoon De Baets counted 156 historians from East Central and Eastern European countries, excluding the Soviet Union, who were exiled by the newly established communist regimes after the Second World War. See De Baets, 'Exile and Acculturation', 328.
37. Stolarik, 'Slovak Historians in Exile in North America, 1945–1992', found 21 exiled Slovak historians, but only a handful of them were already historians before they were exiled. The rest became historians as a result of their exile experience.
38. Mandelíčková and Goddeeris, 'Living in the Past', 406–8.
39. Kravchenko, 'Ukrainian Historical Writing in Canada after the Second World War'.
40. See for relevant archival documentation: Hammel and Grenville, *Refugee Archives*.
41. Wang, 'Between Marxism and Nationalism'. See also Unger, *Using the Past*.
42. Leff, *Well Worth Saving*; Coser, *Refugee Scholars in America*.
43. Palmier, *Weimar in Exile*; Katz, 'The Acculturation of Thought'.
44. Bowersock, 'The Personality of Thucydides'.
45. Cohen, *A Historian in Exile*.
46. MacGillivray, *Restoration Historians and the English Civil War*.
47. Evans, *The Pursuit of Power*, chapter 1.
48. Evans and Von Strandmann, *The Revolutions in Europe*.
49. Petitier, *Jules Michelet*.
50. Kramer, *Threshold of a New World*. See there, pp. 185–98 on the relationship between Mickiewicz and Michelet.

51. Berger, 'An Introduction'.
52. Loubère, *Louis Blanc*; Sperber, *Karl Marx*.
53. Kessler, *Grenzgänger des Kommunismus*; Roche, *Boris Souvarine et la Critique Sociale*.
54. Buchbinder, 'Argentine Historians in Exile'.
55. Krohn, *Wissenschaft im Exil*.
56. Gutnov, 'L'École Russe'; Holdsworth, *Professor Sir Paul Vinogradoff*.
57. Sznajder and Roniger, *The Politics of Exile in Latin America*.
58. Lastra, 'Los Retornos del Exilio en Argentinia y Uruguay'.
59. Jensen, 'Exilio e Historia Reciente'. Also Jensen, 'La Historiografía'.
60. Wright, *Black History and Black Identity*.
61. Williams, 'Silence, Voices, and "the Camp"'.
62. Sommers, *Fear in Bongoland*.
63. Carr, *The Romantic Exiles*.
64. Stobiecki, 'National History'. On Lelewel see Kanka, *Joachim Lelewel*; on nineteenth-century Polish exiles, including historians, compare Marchiewicz, 'Continuities and Innovations'.
65. Aggirreazkuenaga, 'Reinterpreting the Basque Past in Exile'.
66. One example among many of such an inspiring refugee historian was Francis L. Carsten. See Alter, 'Refugees from Nazism and Cultural Transfer to Britain', 83–85. On the manifold interconnections between British and German historiography that were often enriched by experiences of exile, see Stuchtey and Wende, *British and German Historiography* as well as Berger, Lambert and Schumann, *Historikerdialoge*.
67. De Baets, 'Plutarch's Thesis'; an updated version with the same title can be found in De Baets and Berger, *Writing History in Exile*, 27–38.
68. Dillerey, 'Exile', chapter 3.
69. Creet and Kitzmann, *Memory and Migration*.
70. Raeff, *Russia Abroad*.
71. Fan, 'The Anger of Ping-Ti Ho'.
72. Eckel, *Rothfels*, 215.
73. Koselleck, 'Erfahrungswandel', 42, 52.
74. Wiederkehr, *Die eurasische Bewegung*.
75. Schöttler, 'After the Deluge'.
76. On Rosenberg, see Winkler, 'Ein Erneuerer'.
77. Lamberti, 'The Search for the "Other Germany"'.
78. Daum, Lehmann and Sheehan, *The Second Generation*.
79. See their double biography: Iggers, *Two Lives in Uncertain Times*.
80. Martin, *Dissident Histories in the Soviet Union*.
81. Garofalo, Leake, and Renga, *Internal Exile in Fascist Italy*.
82. Schiller, 'Made "Fit for America"', 345–60.
83. On the hardships of exile, see also Goddeeris, 'The Temptation of Legitimacy', 395–405. On the more general repercussions, see also Rose, *The Dispossessed*.
84. Björk, 'Re-embedding the Historian', 49–64.
85. Erdmann, *Toward a Global Community*, 162–79.
86. Burke, 'Silver Lining', 39–48. See also Burke, *Exiles and Expatriates*.

Bibliography

Aggirreazkuenaga, Joseba. 'Reinterpreting the Basque Past in Exile: Scholars, Narratives and Agendas', in Antoon De Baets and Stefan Berger (eds), *Writing History in Exile: Storia della Storiografia – History of Historiography* 69(1) (2016), 65–82.

Aghaie, Kamran Scot. 'Islamist Historiography in Post-Revolutionary Iran', in Touraj Atabaki (ed.), *Iran in the Twentieth Century: Historiography and Political Culture* (London: I.B. Tauris, 2010), 233–64.

Alter, Peter. 'Refugees from Nazism and Cultural Transfer to Britain', in Stefan Manz and Panikos Panayi (eds), *Refugees and Cultural Transfer to Britain* (London: Routledge, 2013), 83–85.

———. *Out of the Third Reich: Refugee Historians in Post-War Britain*. London: I.B. Tauris, 1998.

Aronson, Stanisław. 'I Survived the Warsaw Ghetto: Here are the Lessons I'd Like to Pass On', *The Guardian*, 5 September 2018.

Banerij, Arup. *Writing History in the Soviet Union: Making the Past Work*. London: Routledge, 2008.

Barber, John. *Soviet Historians in Crisis, 1928–1932*. London: Palgrave MacMillan, 1981.

Berger, Morroe. 'An Introduction to the Life and Thought of Madame de Staël', in Germaine de Staël (ed.), *Politics, Literature and National Character* (New Brunswick: Transaction, 2000), 1–92.

Berger, Stefan. *The Past as History: National Identity and Historical Consciousness in Modern Europe*. Basingstoke: Palgrave MacMillan, 2015.

Berger, Stefan (ed.). *The Engaged Historian: Perspectives on the Intersections of Politics, Activism and the Historical Profession*. Oxford: Berghahn Books, 2019.

Berger, Stefan, Peter Lambert and Peter Schumann (eds). *Historikerdialoge: Geschichte, Mythos und Gedächtnis im deutsch-britischen kulturellen Austausch 1750–2000*. Göttingen: V&R, 2003.

Björk, Ragnar. 'Re-embedding the Historian: German Language Refugee Scholars in Scandinavia, 1933–1945', in Antoon De Baets and Stefan Berger (eds), *Writing History in Exile: Storia della Storiografia – History of Historiography* 69(1) (2016), 49–64.

Bowersock, G.W. 'The Personality of Thucydides'. *The Antioch Review* 25 (1965), 135–46.

Boyd, Carolyn P. *Historia Patria: Politics, History, and National Identity in Spain 1875–1975*. Princeton, NJ: Princeton University Press, 1997.

Buchbinder, Pablo. 'Argentine Historians in Exile: Emilio Ravignani and José Luis Romero in Uruguay (1948–1954)', in Antoon De Baets and Stefan Berger (eds), *Writing History in Exile: Storia della Storiografia – History of Historiography* 69(1) (2016), 101–10.

Burke, Peter. 'Silver Lining: On Some Intellectual Benefits of Exile', in Antoon De Baets and Stefan Berger (eds), *Writing History in Exile: Storia della Storiografia – History of Historiography* 69(1) (2016), 39–48.

———. *Exiles and Expatriates in the History of Knowledge, 1500–2000*. Waltham: Brandeis University Press, 2017.

Byrnes, Robert F. 'Creating the Soviet Historical Profession, 1917–1934', *Slavic Review* 50 (1991), 297–308.

Carr, E.H. *The Romantic Exiles*. New York: Octagon Books, 1975.

Chinyaeva, Elena. *Russians Outside Russia: The Emigré Community in Czechoslovakia 1918–1938*. Munich: Oldenbourg, 2001.

Cohen, Jeremy. *A Historian in Exile: Solomon ibn Verga, Shevet Jehuda, and the Jewish-Christian Encounter*. Philadelphia: University of Pennsylvania Press, 2017.

Coser, Lewis A. *Refugee Scholars in America: Their Impact and Their Experiences*. New Haven: Yale University Press, 1984.

Creet, Julia, and Andreas Kitzmann (eds). *Memory and Migration: Multidisciplinary Approaches to Memory Studies*. Toronto: University of Toronto Press, 2011.

Daum, Andreas W., Hartmut Lehmann, and James J. Sheehan (eds). *The Second Generation: Émigrés from Nazi Germany as Historians*. Oxford: Berghahn Books, 2016.

De Baets, Antoon. *Crimes against History*. London: Routledge, 2018.

———. 'Plutarch's Thesis: The Contribution of Refugee Historians to Historical Writing (1945–2010)', in Shula Marks, Paul Weindling and Laura Wintour (eds), *In Defence of Learning – Plight, Persecution and Placement of Academic Refugees, 1933–1980s* (Oxford: Oxford University Press, 2011), 211–24.

———. 'Exile and Acculturation: Refugee Historians since the Second World War'. *International History Review* 28 (2006), 316–349.
Dillerey, John. 'Exile: The Making of the Greek Historian', in Jan Felix Gaertner (ed.), *Writing Exile: The Discourse of Displacement in Greco-Roman Antiquity and Beyond* (Leiden: Brill, 2007), 51–70.
Eakin-Thimme, Gabriela Ann. *Geschichte im Exil: Deutschsprachige Historiker nach 1933*. Munich: MPress, 2005.
Eckel, Jan. *Hans Rothfels: Eine intellektuelle Biographie im 20. Jahrhundert*. Göttingen: Wallstein, 2005.
Enteen, G.M. *The Soviet Scholar-Bureaucrat: M. N. Pokrovskii and the Society of Marxist Historians*. University Park: The Pennsylvanian State University Press, 1978.
Epstein, Catherine. *A Past Renewed: A Catalog of German-Speaking Refugee Historians in the United States after 1933*. Cambridge: Cambridge University Press, 1993.
———. 'Fashioning Fortuna's Whim: German-Speaking Women Emigrant Historians in the United States', in Sibylle Quack (ed.), *Between Sorrow and Strength: Women Refugees from the Nazi Period* (Cambridge: Cambridge University Press, 1995), 301–24.
Erdmann, Karl Dietrich. *Toward a Global Community: The International Historical Congresses and the International Committee of Historical Science, 1898–2000* (Oxford: Berghahn Books, 2005), 162–79.
Evans, Richard J. *The Pursuit of Power: Europe 1815–1914*. London: Penguin, 2019.
Evans, R.J.W., and Hartmut Pogge von Strandmann (eds). *The Revolutions in Europe 1848–1949: From Reform to Reaction*. Oxford: Oxford University Press, 2000.
Fan, Xin. 'The Anger of Ping-Ti Ho: The Chinese Nationalism of a Double Exile', in Antoon De Baets and Stefan Berger (eds), *Writing History in Exile: Storia della Storiografia – History of Historiography* 69(1) (2016), 147–60.
Frank, Tibor. *Double Exile: Migrations of Jewish-Hungarian Professionals through Germany to the United States, 1919–1945*. Oxford: Peter Lang, 2009.
Friguglietti, James. 'A Scholar "in Exile": George Rudé as a Historian of Australia'. *French History and Civilization* 1 (2006), 3–12.
Fuchs, Eckhardt, and Benedikt Stuchtey (eds). *Across Cultural Borders: Historiography in Global Perspective*. Lanham/Maryland: Rowman & Littlefield, 2002.
Garofalo, Piero, Elizabeth Leake, and Dana Renga. *Internal Exile in Fascist Italy: History and Representations of Confino, Manchester*. Manchester University Press, 2019.
Gilbert, Felix, and Hajo Holborn. 'A Memoir'. *Central European History* 3 (1970), 3–8.
Goddeeris, Idesbald. 'The Temptation of Legitimacy: Exile Politics from a Comparative Perspective'. *Contemporary European History* 16(3) (2007), 395–405.
Goetz, Helmut. *Der freie Geist und seine Widersacher: Die Eidverweigerer an den italienischen Universitäten im Jahre 1931*. Frankfurt am Main: Campus, 1993.
Gutnov, D.A. 'L'École Russe de Hautes Études Sociales de Paris'. *Cahiers du Monde Russe* 43 (2002), 375–410.
Hammel, Andrea, and Anthony Grenville (eds). *Refugee Archives: Theory and Practice*. Amsterdam: Rodopi, 2007.
Harvey, John L. 'Hans Rothfels and the Paradoxes of Cosmopolitan Conservatism', in Axel Fair-Schulz and Mario Kessler (eds), *German Scholars in Exile* (Lanham: Lexington Books, 2001), 51–84.
Holdsworth, W.S. *Professor Sir Paul Vinogradoff, 1854–1925*. London: The British Academy, 1926.
Iggers, Wilma, and Georg Iggers. *Two Lives in Uncertain Times: Facing the Challenges of the Twentieth Century as Scholars and as Citizens*. Oxford: Berghahn Books, 2006.
Jagno, Reik. *Deutsch-japanischer Wissensaustausch als lokale Praxis in der Meiji- und Taishō-Zeit. Das Beispiel des Kōtō Gakkō-Lehrers Georg Würfel*. Berlin: Wissenschaftlicher Verlag, 2020.

Jensen, Silvina. 'Exilio e Historia Reciente: Avances y Perspectivas de un Campo en Construcción'. *Aletheia* 1 (2011), 1–21.

———. 'La Historiografía del Último Exilio Argentino: Un Territorio en Construcción', in X Jornadas Interescuelas/Departamentos de Historia. Escuela de Historia de la Facultad de Humanidades y Artes, Universidad Nacional del Rosario. Retrieved 7 August 2020 from https://www.aacademica.org/000-006/483.

Kamen, Henri. *The Disinherited: Exile and the Making of Spanish Culture, 1492–1975*. London: Penguin, 2007.

Kanka, August Gerald. *Joachim Lelewel: Poland's Romantic Historian*. Detroit, 1955.

Katz, Barry. 'The Acculturation of Thought: Transformations of the Refugee Scholar in America'. *The Journal of Modern History* 63 (1991), 740–52.

Kessler, Mario. *Grenzgänger des Kommunismus: Zwölf Porträts aus dem Jahrhundert der Katastrophen*. Berlin: Karl Dietz Verlag, 2015.

Koselleck, Reinhart. 'Erfahrungswandel und Methodenwechsel: Eine historisch-anthropologische Skizze', in Christian Maier and Jörn Rüsen (eds), *Historische Methode* (Munich: Oldenbourg, 1988), 13–61.

Kramer, Lloyd S. *Threshold of a New World: Intellectuals and the Exile Experience in Paris, 1830–1848*. Ithaca: Cornell University Press, 1988.

Kravchenko, Volodymyr. 'Ukrainian Historical Writing in Canada after the Second World War', in Antoon De Baets and Stefan Berger (eds), *Writing History in Exile: Storia della Storiografia – History of Historiography* 69(1) (2016), 111–28.

Krohn, Claus-Dieter. *Wissenschaft im Exil: Deutsche Sozial- und Wirtschaftswissenschaftler in den USA und die New School for Social Research*. Frankfurt am Main: Campus Verlag 1987.

Lamberti, Marjorie. 'The Search for the "Other Germany": Refugee Historians from Nazi Germany and the Contested Historical Legacy of the Resistance to Hitler'. *Central European History* 47 (2014), 402–29.

Lastra, María Soledad. 'Los Retornos del Exilio en Argentinia y Uruguay: Una Historia Comparada de las Políticas y Tensiones en la Recepción y Asistencia en las Posdictaturas (1983–1989)', PhD thesis. Universidad Nacional de la Plata, 2014. Retrieved 7 August from http://www.memoria.fahce.unlp.edu.ar/tesis/te.1002/te.1002.pdf.

Leff, Laurel. *Well Worth Saving: American Universities' Life-and-Death Decisions on Refugees from Nazi Europe*. New Haven: Yale University Press, 2019.

Lehmann, Hartmut. *Felix Gilbert as Scholar and Teacher*. Washington D.C.: German Historical Institute, 1992.

Lehmann, Hartmut, and James Sheehan (eds). *An Interrupted Past: German-Speaking Refugee Historians in the United States*. Cambridge: Cambridge University Press, 1991.

Loubère, Leo A. *Louis Blanc: His Life and His Contribution to the Rise of French Jacobin-Socialism*. Westport: Greenwood Press, 1980.

MacGillivray, Royce. *Restoration Historians and the English Civil War*. The Hague: Martinus Nijhoff, 2012.

Maissen, Thomas, and Niels F. May (eds). *National History and New Nationalism in the Twenty-First Century: A Global Comparison*. London: Routledge, 2021.

Malagón, Javier. 'Los Historiadores y la Historia en el Exilio', in José Luis Abellán (ed.), *El Exilio Español de 1939* (Madrid: Taurus, 1978), 247–353.

Mandelíčková, Monika, and Idesbald Goddeeris. 'Living in the Past: Historians in Exile', in Ilaria Porciani and Lutz Raphael (eds), *Setting the Standards: Institutions, Networks and Communities of National Historiography* (Basingstoke: Palgrave MacMillan, 2012), 394–411.

Marchiewicz, Krysztof. 'Continuities and Innovations: Polish Emigration after 1849', in Sabine Freitag (ed.), *Exiles from European Revolutions: Refugees in Mid-Victorian England* (Oxford: Berghahn Books, 2003), 103–20.

Marcus, Alan P. (ed.). *Transnational Geographers in the United States: Navigating Autobiographies in a Global Age*. Lanham: Lexington Books, 2016.

Martin, Barbara. *Dissident Histories in the Soviet Union: From Destalinization to Perestroika*. London: Bloomsbury, 2019.

Mayer, Gustav. *Erinnerungen: Vom Journalisten zum Historiker der deutschen Arbeiterbewegung*. Hildesheim: Olms, 1993.

Mehl, Margaret. 'Japan und die preussisch-deutsche Geschichtswissenschaft', in Gerhard Krebs (ed.), *Japan und Preussen* (Munich: Iudicium, 2002), 233–47.

Mitchell, Allan. *Fleeing Nazi Germany: Five Historians Migrate to the America*. Bloomington: Trafford, 2011.

Morgan, Philip. 'Reclaiming Italy? Antifascist Historians and History in "Justice and Liberty"', in Stefan Berger, Mark Donovan and Kevin Passmore (eds), *Writing National Histories: Western Europe since 1800* (London: Routledge, 1999), 150–60.

Müller, Philipp. 'Doing Historical Research in the Early Nineteenth Century: Leopold Ranke, the Archive policy, and the Relazioni of the Venetian Republic'. *Storia della Storiografia* 56 (2009), 80–103.

———. *Geschichte machen: Historisches Forschen und die Politik der Archive*. Göttingen: Wallstein, 2019.

Munro, Doug, and John G. Reid (eds). *Clio's Lives: Biographies and Autobiographies of Historians*. Canberra: Australian National University Press, 2017.

Nietzsche, Friedrich. *Unzeitgemässe Betrachtungen, Zweites Stück: Vom Nutzen und Nachtheil der Historie für das Leben*. Leipzig: F.W. Fritzsch, 1874.

Oberkrome, Willi. *Volksgeschichte: Methodische Innovation und völkische Ideologisierung in der deutschen Geschichtswissenschaft, 1918–1945*. Göttingen: Vandenhoeck & Ruprecht, 1993.

Palmier, Jean-Michel. *Weimar in Exile: The Anti-Fascist Emigration in Europe and America*. London: Verso, 2006.

Pasamar, Gonzalo. *Apologia and Criticism: Historians and the History of Spain*, 1500–2000. Berne: Peter Lang, 2010.

Petitier, Paule. *Jules Michelet – Histoire d'un Historien*. Paris: Champion, 2006.

Raeff, Marc. *Russia Abroad: A Cultural History of the Russian Emigration 1919–1939*. Oxford: Oxford University Press, 1990.

Reinhard, Rürup. 'Die Vertreibung von Wissenschaftlerinnen und Wissenschaftlern aus den deutschen Universitäten und anderen westlichen Einrichtungen seit dem Beginn der NS-Herrschaft', in Dirk Schumann (ed.), *Forschen im 'Zeitalter der Extreme': Akademien und andere Forschungseinrichtungen im Nationalsozialismus und nach 1945* (Göttingen: Wallstein, 2020), 43–59.

Rhinelander, L. Hamilton. 'Exiled Russian Scholars in Prague: The Kondakov Seminar and Institute', *Canadian Slavonic Papers* 16 (1974), 331–52.

Ritter, G.A. 'Meinecke's Protégés: German Emigré Historians Between the Two World Wars'. *Bulletin of the German Historical Institute Washington* 39 (2006), 23–38.

Ritter, G.A. (ed.). *German Refugee Historians and Friedrich Meinecke: Letters and Documents 1910–1977*. Leiden: Brill, 2010.

Rizi, Fabio Fernando. *Benedetto Croce and Italian Fascism*. Toronto: University of Toronto Press, 2003.

Roche, Anne (ed.). *Boris Souvarine et la Critique Sociale*. Paris: La Découverte, 1990.

Rose, Isaac (ed.). *The Dispossessed: An Anatomy of Exile*. Amherst: University of Massachusetts Press, 2005.

Schiller, Kay. 'Made "fit for America": The Renaissance Historian Hans Baron in London Exile 1936–1938', in Stefan Berger, Peter Lambert and Peter Schumann (eds), *Historikerdialoge: Geschichte, Mythos und Gedächtnis im deutsch-britischen kulturellen Austausch 1750–2000* (Göttingen: Vandenhoeck & Ruprecht, 2003), 345–60.

Schönwälder, Karen. *Historiker und Politik: Geschichtswissenschaft im Nationalsozialismus*. Frankfurt am Main: Campus, 1992.

Schöttler, Peter. After the Deluge: The Impact of the Two World Wars on the Historical Work of Henri Pirenne and Marc Bloch', in Stefan Berger and Chris Lorenz (eds),

Nationalizing the Past: Historians as Nation-Builders in Nineteenth and Twentieth Century Europe. (Basingstoke: Palgrave MacMillan, 2010), 404–25.

Smith, Bonnie G. *The Gender of History: Men, Women and Historical Practice.* Cambridge, MA: Harvard University Press, 1998.

Sommers, Marc. *Fear in Bongoland: Burundi Refugees in Urban Tanzania.* Oxford: Berghahn Books, 2001.

Sperber, Jonathan. *Karl Marx: A Nineteenth-Century Life.* New York: Norton, 2013.

Stelzel, Philipp. 'The Second-Generation Émigrés' Impact on German Historiography', in Andreas W. Daum (ed.), *The Second Generation: Émigrés from Nazi Germany as Historians* (New York: Berghahn Books, 2015), 287–303.

———. *History after Hitler: A Transatlantic Enterprise.* Philadelphia: Pennsylvania Press, 2019.

Stobiecki, Rafal. 'National History and Imperial History: A Look at Polish-Russian Historiographical Disputes on the Borderlands in the Nineteenth and Twentieth Centuries', in Tibor Frank and Frank Hadler (eds), *Disputed Territories and Shared Pasts: Overlapping National Histories in Modern Europe* (Basingstoke: Palgrave MacMillan, 2011), 125–51.

Stolarik, Mark. 'Slovak Historians in Exile in North America, 1945–1992'. *Human Affairs* 6 (1996), 34–44.

Stuchety, Benedikt, and Peter Wende (eds). *British and German Historiography 1750–1950: Traditions, Perceptions and Transfers* (Oxford: Oxford University Press, 2000).

Sznajder, Mario, and Luis Roniger. *The Politics of Exile in Latin America.* Cambridge: Cambridge University Press, 2009.

Tamm, Marek. 'Displaced History? A New "Regime of Historicity" among the Baltic Historians in Exile (1940s to 1960s)', in Antoon De Baets and Stefan Berger (eds), *Writing History in Exile: Storia della Storiografia – History of Historiography* 69(1) (2016), 129–46.

Tortarolo, Edoardo. 'Historians in Exile: Franco Venturi in Paris in the 1930s', in D.K. Adams and M. Vaudagna (eds), *Transatlantic Encounters: Public Uses and Misuses of History in Europe and the United States* (Amsterdam: Amsterdam University Press, 2000), 89–118.

———. 'Historians in the Storm: Émigré Historiography in the Twentieth Century', in Matthias Middell and Lluis Roura (eds), *Transnational Challenges to National History Writing* (Basingstoke: Palgrave MacMillan, 2013), 377–403.

———. 'Salvemini: An Italian Historian as Political Refugee', in Antoon De Baets and Stefan Berger (eds), *Writing History in Exile: Storia della Storiografia – History of Historiography* 69(1) (2016), 83–100.

Unger, Jonathan (ed.). *Using the Past to Serve the Present: Historiography and Politics in Contemporary China.* Armonk, NY: M.E. Sharpe, 1993.

Vom Bruch, Rüdiger. *Wissenschaft, Politik und öffentliche Meinung: Gelehrtenpolitik im wilhelminischen Deutschland (1890–1914).* Husum: Mathiesen Verlag, 1980.

Walther, Peter T. 'Eine kleine Intervention und ein bescheidener Vorschlag in Sachen Rothfels', *Hans Rothfels und die Zeitgeschichte, Historisches Forum* 1 (2004), 11–16.

Wang, Edward Q. 'Between Marxism and Nationalism: Chinese Historiography and the Soviet Influence, 1949–1963'. *Journal of Contemporary China* 9 (2000), 95–111.

Wiederkehr, Stefan. *Die eurasische Bewegung: Wissenschaft und Politik in der russischen Emigration der Zwischenkriegszeit und im postsowjetischen Russland.* Cologne: Böhlau, 2007.

Williams, Christian A. 'Silence, Voices, and "the Camp": Perspectives on and from Southern Africa's Exile Histories'. *Humanity* 3 (2012), 65–80.

Winkler, Heinrich August. 'Ein Erneuerer der Geschichtswissenschaft: Hans Rosenberg, 1904–1988'. *Historische Zeitschrift* 248 (1989), 529–55.

Wright, W.D. *Black History and Black Identity: A Call for a New Historiography.* Westport: Praeger, 2002.

Zadencka, Maria, Andrejs Plakans and Andreas Lawaty (eds). *East and Central European History Writing in Exile, 1939–1989.* Leiden: Brill, 2015.

CHAPTER 1

'A Private Perch'

Cosmopolitanism, Nostalgia and Commitment in the Émigré Historian's Persona

Jo Tollebeek

The lives of émigré scholars, and particularly refugee scholars, inevitably revolve around exile and return, loss and recovery. That was no different for the historians who were forced to leave Nazi Germany in the 1930s: abandoning the country of their birth left deep scars that ran throughout their biographies. This begs the question of whether their departure, and in many cases flight, also influenced their work as historians. Which identity formed the starting point for their writing? How did they deal with a history that they were only able to understand as a disruption of a better order? What role and responsibilities did they assign to themselves as historians? In short: to which scholarly persona did the dynamics of emigration lead? And, as a corollary to this, does this persona also learn something of the ambitions and agonising with which *every* historian is familiar, of his or her professional identity?[1]

Two historians are at the heart of this narrative. Georg G. Iggers, born in 1926, and Peter Gay, born in 1923, were both members of what is described as the 'second generation' of historians who fled Germany.[2] The first generation, a group that included Felix Gilbert, Hajo Holborn, Hans Rothfels, Paul Oskar Kristeller and Helene Wieruszowski, reached their safe haven abroad in adulthood, in many cases after having already held academic posts in Germany. By contrast, the second generation arrived in the United States, England or elsewhere at a younger age and therefore developed as historians

Notes for this section begin on page 39.

outside Germany.³ As well as Iggers and Gay, this 'Generation Exodus' also included Klemens von Klemperer, Walter Z. Laqueur, George L. Mosse and Fritz Stern.⁴ They were in many respects a diverse group.⁵

Iggers left Hamburg after the '*Anschluss*' in 1938 to begin a new life in the United States. Gay did not flee Berlin until 1939, after the '*Kristallnacht*', first travelling to Cuba – away from the German nightmare that had revealed the full horror of the pogrom – before also reaching the United States in 1941. Iggers studied in Richmond, Chicago and New York (at the New School of Social Research, where quite a number of refugee scholars had found a new professional home),⁶ while Gay studied in Denver and at Columbia. Following a number of earlier appointments, in 1964 Iggers obtained a position at the State University of New York in Buffalo, where efforts would be made to build an alternative university in the years that followed. He achieved renown in the field of intellectual history and the study of historiography. Gay, for his part, pursued his academic career, in which he would publish mostly on the cultural history of the eighteenth to the twentieth century, at Columbia and Yale.

These two historians are joined in this chapter by Eric J. Hobsbawm, who, born in 1917, was of the same generation.⁷ Unlike Iggers and Gay, Hobsbawm was not a refugee historian who had found a new safe haven in a foreign land. In fact, he arrived in London in 1933 as a British citizen; the widespread notion that he was a foreigner stemmed mainly from the politically motivated suggestion that he was 'not quite British', and his ideas therefore suspect.⁸ Hobsbawm was moreover not a refugee: when he left Berlin for England, his motivations were not political – escaping the threat emanating from the Nazi regime – but economic.⁹

However, the deep significance of those Berlin years in Hobsbawm's biography, short though that period may have been, creates a bond between him, Iggers and Gay. As Hobsbawm himself later stressed, Berlin marked the birth of an all-encompassing and passionate political engagement. As a pupil of the Prinz-Heinrichs-Gymnasium in Schöneberg in the dying years of the Weimar Republic, he bore witness to a battle between national socialists and communists that was so fundamental that it made engagement without commitment impossible. In other words, Berlin was the place where Hobsbawm was able to become himself. He arrived in London with a lifelong mission, which made his experiences in Berlin in 1933 the pivotal time of his life. For him too, the city became a fixed point of reference, a place from which the triumphant national socialists had driven out the resistance. It turned Hobsbawm – not least in his own self-image – into a 'refugee', who subsequently studied at the left-wing Cambridge University, received an appointment at Birkbeck College at the University of London and later, as an emeritus, also went on to lecture at the New School of Social Research in

New York, which was already mentioned. He achieved considerable fame for his work in the field of labour history.

Iggers, Gay and Hobsbawm also shared the desire (or the urge) to reflect on the events that had shaped their lives and, to a greater or lesser extent, on the work in which those events had played a decisive role. All three wrote autobiographies,[10] each of which revealed the highly individual nature of this work. Hobsbawm himself made this observation both explicit and general: 'Every historian', he said in 1993, 'has his or her lifetime, a private perch from which to survey the world'.[11] The autobiography laid bare a professional identity that was in essence a personal one.

In *Interesting Times* (2002), Hobsbawm reconstructed his long journey through the twentieth century, from Mitteleuropa to Manhattan. It created a link between his autobiography and his most successful book, *Age of Extremes* (1994), in which he presented a historical overview of the twentieth century. In *My German Question* (1998), Gay focused on the six years – from 1933 to 1939 – he spent living under the Nazi regime in Berlin, a perspective he shared with other refugee historians such as Raul Hilberg, Gerda Lerner and Susan Groag Bell, all of whom also published autobiographies. In *Two Lives in Uncertain Times* (2006), Iggers described his dual role as a scholar and an activist. He published this work together with his wife, Wilma Abeles, who was herself also a member of the second generation of refugee historians: born in 1921, she fled to Canada from Czechoslovakia after the conclusion of the Munich Agreement in 1938, before going on to study in the United States a few years later.[12] As a historian, she published works focusing mainly on the history of the Jews in Bohemia. She shared with her peers a strong awareness of her status as an émigré historian.[13]

Hybrid Identities

The case of Wilma Iggers makes clear how complex the identity of these émigré historians could be. She had grown up in Bohemia, in a community of secularised Jews, but identified mainly with the German bourgeoisie. Whilst there, she learned Czech, the language of a group with which she felt great solidarity during the rise of National Socialism. This was the baggage she took with her to North America, where her identity was shaped further. Her husband's identity was similarly layered; Georg Iggers, too, was Jewish, and in a more explicit way than Wilma. At the same time, he too naturally felt equally German; when he arrived in the United States in 1938, still as Georg Gerson Igersheimer, he had no desire to 'Americanise' his name. In the decades that followed, he became an American but never lost his strong associations with Central Europe.

Peter Joachim Fröhlich was another with a similar hybrid identity. He too had grown up in a secularised Jewish milieu, in which the identification with German culture predominated, despite the fact that his father had been born in Poland, in Upper Silesia. After his flight from Berlin, he became an American, including in name and with total conviction, changing without hesitation from 'Fröhlich' to 'Gay'. This hybrid identity was even clearer in Hobsbawm's case. Born in Alexandria, he was the son of a British father who was himself the son of a Polish Jew who had emigrated to London and whose name had been changed by a British civil servant from 'Obstbaum' to 'Hobsbaum'. He therefore shared a Mitteleuropa Jewish heritage with Iggers and his wife and with Gay. His Anglophile mother was originally from Vienna, where the family would move immediately after the Great War. A decade later, in 1931, Hobsbawm – now an orphan – moved to Berlin, before arriving in London two years later, taking with him a lasting affinity with the culture of Central Europe. Many of the émigré historians had multiple identities.

This multiplicity was recognised and often emphasised by the émigré historians. It resulted in cosmopolitanism becoming second nature to many of them, providing a lookout tower from which they were afforded a wide-ranging view and which cast the limitations of a nationalist or parochial approach to the past, for example, into sharp relief.[14] This cosmopolitanism also lent the personae of the émigrés a degree of freedom and detachment. The diaspora had brought loss but had also created the opportunity to adopt an open and generous perspective on past and contemporary civilisation.

Hobsbawm once again appeared to be the most prominent embodiment of this. An enthusiastic traveller and notable polyglot, from the 1960s onwards especially he built a global network of contacts, including in Latin America. Rather than the unadventurous and routine milieu of academic historians (a group, as he wrote in his autobiography, that was even duller than an assembly of insurance company executives),[15] he preferred to inhabit the global village that was opening up before his eyes, drawing on the old image of the wandering Jew: 'the ancestral Jewish experience of moving from place to place among strangers.'[16] It lent breadth to his work and forced him to adopt a synthetic writing that combined to shape his significance as a historian, including far beyond Europe. Hobsbawm's cosmopolitanism explained his global impact.[17]

Insider/Outsider

But the multiplicity of their identities also made things difficult for the émigré historians. They rarely felt at home anywhere; they were insiders but at the same time always remained outsiders. The young Hobsbawm shared in the German culture to the full whilst in Vienna and Berlin, but, despite this, at school he was always seen as '*der Engländer*', 'the English boy', always the outsider. It made him an expat. Yet when he arrived in England, he was once again a foreigner in a strange land, an immigrant from Central Europe. This was also how he experienced it: he hankered after the exciting political struggle but also after the modernist cultural experiments that had made his Berlin years so lively, in a London where nothing seemed to happen – except on the jazz scene, which he had just discovered. It said a great deal that whilst in London he continued to write his diary notes in German.[18] Hobsbawm remained 'someone who does not wholly belong to where he finds himself'.[19]

The first generation of émigré historians to leave Germany for the United States generally integrated well. Dietrich Gerhard, who had obtained his doctorate in Berlin under Friedrich Meinecke, lauded his reception at Harvard in 1935; he was surprised not least by the wide knowledge of European intellectual life he found there.[20] Holborn, who had enjoyed a miraculous career in Germany, also had no difficulty climbing the academic ladder in the United States, eventually even being elected president of the American Historical Association.[21] The art historian Horst Woldemar Janson, who had studied under Erwin Panofsky in Hamburg, also quickly adapted to the American academic culture after his flight in 1935.[22] But of course, there were also less successful examples, if only because the émigrés could also encounter antisemitism in the United States.[23]

Gay, too, was to find that integrating in the New World was not without its problems. There was no shortage of goodwill on his part: after his flight from Germany and a long sojourn in Havana, he was keen to become an American as quickly as possible and immediately applied for US citizenship.[24] He also abhorred those who were sneeringly referred to by his father as '*Beiunskis*', a name reserved for Jewish refugees who constantly complained that everything was better in their country of origin – 'at home'.[25] Iggers and his wife also rapidly found their feet in the United States. At the same time, however, these émigré historians were always Europeans to their new compatriots, people with their own history who, conversely, also had to overcome a culture shock, for example, brought on by American 'consumerism'.[26] They rarely belonged to the mainstream. Just how difficult things could be was illustrated by the story of Henry Huttenbach, who arrived in the United States via Italy and England and who for many long years felt himself to be a *déraciné*.[27]

The 'insider/outsider' dichotomy, which (often) typified the identity of these émigré historians, could, however, also be used – at several levels – to clarify their professional position. Hobsbawm did this explicitly when he was invited to open the academic year at the Central European University in Budapest in 1993. He had arrived, he said, as a British citizen but also as the grandson of a Jew from Warsaw, and therefore: 'I come to you as an outsider who is also, in an oblique way, an insider.'[28]

Could this not perhaps be translated into more epistemic terms? Ethan Katz has argued that the attitude of 'displaced historians' such as Mosse and Gay reflected the 'dialectic' complexity of German history.[29] That history had indeed exhibited two faces; there had been 'two Germanies': the 'Germany of Bismarck and Schlieffen' and the 'Germany of Goethe and Humboldt'. For these refugees, the first of these Germanies evoked an immediate connection, a direct touch, a sort of painful intimate knowledge; the second allowed for a slightly more distanced view. There was the historian as an outsider, who placed history in perspective; but there was also always the insider, whose knowledge went further and deeper. It was for this reason, according to Jeremy D. Popkin, that Gay and other refugee historians always presented themselves in their autobiographies as individuals who had had to live through the past, in all its chaos and probability: they recalled 'how much of past experience exists as a kind of penumbra to history, a zone of the past where historical narrative does not shine its beams'.[30]

Insider and outsider, intimacy and remoteness, experience and interpretation: the refugee historians cast the tensions within the persona of the historian into sharp relief. They referred back to Jules Michelet, who had claimed whilst in the Musée des Monuments français to have felt 'the dead through the marble (of their graves)', in a form of direct contact.[31] But they also provided a reminder that historiography is about what is distant and past, about a land that is alien and lost.

The Longing for Restoration

For many of these émigré historians, that land that had become alien and lost existed in their memory as a world in which different groups had lived together in unquestioned harmony: the world of the past had been one of natural diversity. Hobsbawm, for example, recalled the Vienna of his childhood as a multinational and multicultural city, a city that had grown thanks to the arrival of large groups of migrants from the polyglot region, which surrounded it.[32] Similarly, Wilma Iggers consistently described the Bohemian community in which she had grown up as a multiethnic and multilingual world, in which Germans and Czechs had lived together and in which differing religions had peacefully coexisted.[33]

The position of the Jews warranted particular attention here. Both Hobsbawm and Gay emphasised their integration into the culture in which they lived, and they acted accordingly. Hobsbawm described himself as a 'non-Jewish Jew', which was translated by his friend Elise Marienstras as 'being Jewish meant for him simply the fact that he had Jewish parents'. Many people were therefore surprised that at his self-directed funeral, in 2012, he arranged for a reading of the Jewish '*Kaddish*'. The only way they were able to explain this was by recalling the promise made by the young Hobsbawm to his mother, that he would never do anything that might suggest he was ashamed of being a Jew.[34]

Gay, too, who in his autobiography also highlighted the 'ethnic mix' of 1930s Berlin, did nothing to push his Jewish identity to the fore. A religious Jewishness was something alien to him: his parents had declared him officially '*konfessionlos*', the 'village atheist' that he would remain for the rest of his life. Gay also shared with his parents an 'uncompromising rejection of any tribal identification' in relation to his Jewishness. Instead, even more so than in the case of Hobsbawm, this was replaced by a Jewish assimilation. According to Gay, the Berlin Jews were Germans and had therefore not hesitated to venture into the public arena, even when an unmistakably antisemitic mood had taken hold of society.[35] Others endorsed this, with Mosse, for example, stressing that there had been a symbiotic relationship during his childhood between Jews and Germans, and that the Jews had enjoyed to the full the fruits of the classic '*Bildung*'.[36] The experiences of the young Gay were no different until 1938, when he was denied access to the Goethe Gymnasium secondary school.

This does not, of course, mean that other Jews did not choose a different stance. Georg Iggers recounted in his autobiography that the growing antisemitism in the 1930s had led him to emphasise his Jewish identity even more: having grown up in a highly acculturated family, after 1933 he had embraced an orthodox and Zionist Jewishness, with an entirely individual complex of social and cultural associations and a radical desire for a different world – '*Eretz Yisrael*'. This had given rise to a schism: 'I increasingly felt that I was Jewish, not German, although earlier I had seen no conflict between the two.'[37] Later, too, in the United States, Iggers would continue to nurture a distinctive Jewish identity.

For Wilma Iggers and Gay, such a distinction was merely incidental. They were concerned with the interaction, with a diversity that had not ruled out communal living, but which on the contrary had given it a character all of its own, and in a natural way. As they both experienced, however, that peaceful coexistence had come to an end in the 1930s. Nationalism, obsessions with racial purity and brutal violence had ripped apart communities which had for so long been bound together. For Wilma Iggers, the end of her multiethnic and multilingual world was even stamped with a diplomatic seal, when the First Czech Slovak Republic was abolished in Munich in

1938 after being forced by Nazi Germany to relinquish Sudetenland, which was inhabited principally by Germans. Diversity had been forced to make way for a drive towards hegemony and homogeneity.

Gay and his parents had for their part suddenly become Jews, not of their own volition but because the Nazis had forced them – 'by decree' – to do so.[38] The Nazis had first distinguished and later segregated the Jews from other Germans, to the point where they had had to disappear from a society in which they had hitherto been so strongly integrated – leave in an exodus or be exterminated in the gas chambers. However, in *My German Question*, Gay not only aimed his barbs at 'the gangsters' who had conquered the country in 1933; his autobiography was also an apology directed towards his mainly American Jewish critics, who denounced him for having waited until after the '*Kristallnacht*' before leaving Germany. Jews such as Gay, so the criticism ran, had not been 'Jewish enough'. The critics cited Gershom Scholem, the Zionist who had argued as early as the beginning of the 1920s that the notion of a German-Jewish symbiosis was 'sheer self-delusion'. This was a standpoint that Gay occasionally fiercely rebutted: he refused to be locked into an identity that ruled out or was deemed to be irreconcilable with other identities.[39]

Hobsbawm shared this rejection of Zionism, which he perceived as a Jewish nationalism. During his Berlin years, anti-nationalism had become a constant element in his political engagement, and later the rise and success of the nationalist ideology became a theme in his work (*Nations and Nationalism since 1780* was published in 1990). According to Hobsbawm, together with the Iggers and Gay, the nationalists had brought an end to the prevailing 'diversity in unity'. They represented the interference of history in a natural order. The émigré historians shared an almost utopian desire for restoration. Georg Iggers spent his whole life fascinated by a quest for a global language that could be more easily learned than Esperanto.[40]

Trauma and Reconciliation

That longing lent the work of the émigré historians a nostalgic character, bathing the lost world of the past in the moonlight of memory. It was a feeling that contrasted with the cosmopolitanism described above. The openness and breadth inherent in that cosmopolitanism had disappeared in the enveloping nostalgia, not conservative in nature but in which a familiar, closed universe nonetheless dominated. Wilma Iggers wrote full of nostalgia in her autobiography about the idyllic setting in which she had spent her childhood and youth: her Bohemian village, the farm, the house, the garden, her extended family. She was happy, she recorded, to have grown up in Tomáš

Masaryk's Republic – 'very attached to our corner of the world'.[41] That same emotion ran through her academic work, which was thematically also shaped by nostalgia: 'All of my scholarly work . . . rests on my love for, and my curiosity about the world from which I came.'[42] For many years, she collected texts about the Jews in the Czech lands, and in 1995 she published *Women of Prague*, an anthology of portraits of Czech and German women, Jewish and non-Jewish, intended to illustrate the ethnic diversity and social change in her country of origin.

Gay's memoir of his years in Berlin also, as he acknowledged himself, carried 'a melancholy tone'.[43] But in his case, too, the nostalgia went further and extended to his scholarly work. In 1968, he published his renowned study of German culture in the interwar period, *Weimar Culture* (the subtitle used the dichotomy 'insider/outsider'), which evoked a world characterised by creativity and a breaking with traditions and conventions. But the excitement that accompanied this, Gay continued, was also associated with anxiety, fear and a rising sense of doom. The Weimar culture was 'a dance on the edge of a volcano'. Ultimately, it disappeared, surviving only in exile. This prompted Gay in his autobiography to describe his book about the Weimar culture as 'an elegy for a failed experiment'. As he himself acknowledged, it lent his work 'an unmistakable air of mourning'.[44]

Even those who had spent less time in Berlin, such as Hobsbawm, spoke about the Weimar culture and its decline with nostalgia. The hard, objectifying tone that dominated in *Interesting Times*[45] was notably softened in these passages. For Hobsbawm, Berlin always remained an essential *lieu de mémoire*. When he returned to the city for the first time in around 1960, he found that – unlike the Vienna of his childhood years – it had changed beyond recognition; the Allied bombardments had reduced much of the city to rubble, and little restoration had yet been carried out. But the city remained rooted in his memory: 'I was not to return to Berlin for some thirty years, but I never forgot it and never will.'[46]

At the same time as Hobsbawm, Gay also returned to Berlin for the first time since his flight in 1939. The account of that return illustrates how complex the confrontation with their German past could be for the refugees, with its 'forms of dissociation from Germany but also the desire to reconnect'.[47] Gay had been to Europe several times in the 1950s but had always avoided visiting Germany. He finally did so in 1961, albeit still with great hesitation, together with his wife Ruth Slotkin, who was herself born in the United States but from an Eastern European Jewish family.[48] 'The return of the native' proved to be a failure: Gay found that he still felt so much hatred and abhorrence towards Germany (emotions that have also been described by Stern, for example)[49] that it spoiled the visit. The emotional frustration only disappeared when he was able, with a sense of relief, to leave Germany again.⁵⁰ It was only through his friendship with Karl Dietrich Bracher that Gay was able to 'unfreeze' and visit Germany again.⁵¹ But his distrust never disappeared completely.

What Gay and his wife experienced in Berlin in 1961 was the brutishness with which history – a painful history – was able to confront them: 'Contemporary history raw and ugly had caught up with us.' It was a history characterised by violence, expulsions and destruction, which had now returned and seemed as if it could never be defeated: 'Yet even today', admitted Gay in 1998, 'when I hear German spoken in an American restaurant or airport, I cannot suppress a slight tensing up and the question, What are they doing here?'⁵² Gay presented history to his readers as something traumatising: more than half a century after the collapse of Hitler's Thousand Year Reich, he, like every surviving refugee, was to a certain extent still one of its victims.⁵³

Traumatic history is history that does not fade. Even whilst still in Havana, Gay knew that Nazi Berlin would continue pursuing him and would never let him rest ('will haunt me to the day I die'). For years, he was neither able nor willing to talk about the events, but they were nonetheless always present: 'Berlin seemed far away, but that was an illusion; for years I would pick fragments of it from my skin as though I had wallowed among shards of broken glass.' The long silence, broken for the first time only in 1945, had a troubled history that could be silenced and even buried, but not expunged. What Gay teaches us is that there can be such a thing as too much history: a past that surprises through its stubbornness, that cannot simply be dismissed, that is impossible to escape – a past that demands an analytic endeavour from the historian.⁵⁴

For other refugee historians, the confrontation with their German past was less troublesome, including for Georg Iggers. He first went back to visit Germany in 1952, almost fifteen years after he had fled the country. He found it to be an *'unheimische'* experience; conversations with friends and relatives frequently avoided mention of the terrible events from the past, and it became clear that many had still not been held to account for their responsibility in the Third Reich. But when he spent a sabbatical in Göttingen in 1961–1962, Iggers found 'a better Germany', despite the unease that had once again preceded his visit ('How am I going to know which of the people I meet are murderers?'). He returned regularly in the years that followed, and in 1990 bought an apartment there; from that time onwards, Iggers and his wife divided their time between Amherst and Göttingen. In the mid-1990s, Georg reapplied for and was granted German citizenship.⁵⁵

Where Gay presented history as a traumatic experience, Iggers portrayed it as a process of reconciliation. His re-naturalisation bore testimony to his longing to be reunited with the country of his birth. At the same time, he sought a reconciliation between Germans and Jews. He also devoted his efforts to facilitating dialogue between the parties on the two sides of the Iron Curtain during the Cold War in the hope, despite the ideological differences, of bringing about cooperation. In 1966, Iggers and his wife travelled to East Germany.[56] Two years previously Georg had visited Prague. Now he travelled to Czechoslovakia from East Germany with Wilma, her first visit to the country of her birth – now under Communist rule – since 1938.[57] The frequent visits to Göttingen made it possible to intensify these efforts, and so the émigré historian was able to fulfil a role that every historian could fulfil: putting right the wrongs done in the past, the mistakes of history – not by seeking retribution or revenge but by building bridges and bringing peace.

The longing for the restoration of a lost world, in which different communities had coexisted in unquestioned unity, turned the work of the émigré historians into a nostalgic undertaking. History had disrupted the old order. Gay and Georg Iggers made clear what this meant for the persona of the historian: it was the historian's task to acknowledge the trauma to which that disruption had led, in order to be able to repair the fractures of history – its schism, its discord, its exclusion.

The Values of the Enlightenment

These émigré historians were more aware than others of the fragility of the once acquired order: they knew that society could be derailed and destroyed at any moment. In *Weimar Culture*, Gay described a culture that had glittered for a short, dizzying, fragile moment but which had rapidly fractured and fallen apart. History was constantly portrayed as a catastrophe in this perspective. For the historian, this implied a need to contribute to maintaining what was human and valuable; the historian had to stand up for the values of the Enlightenment.

In the period 1966–1969, in other words at the same time that his book about the Weimar culture appeared, Gay published a major study, *The Enlightenment: An Interpretation*, which sought to correct the picture presented by Carl Becker in his 1932 publication *The Heavenly City of the Eighteenth-Century Philosophers*.[58] For Gay, the *philosophes* were not advocates of a naïve belief in Reason and progress, nor had they replaced Christianity with a secular religion. Rather, they had developed a nuanced vision of the role of emotions, understood the historical process in all its complexity and above all attempted to fashion a scientific view of the world that was anchored not in an abstract rationalist philosophy but in a sceptical empiricism. This interpretation drew criticism,[59] but for Gay the programme of the *philosophes* represented a permanent mission. In the closing paragraph of his book, he argued that: 'Our recognition of human irrationality, self-centeredness, stupidity beyond the philosophes' most pessimistic appraisals demands not surrender to such forces, but battle against them'.[60]

The book thus constituted a call to activism. Gay held to the social-democratic opinions inherited from his father throughout his life. Georg Iggers was of similar mind, describing himself as an 'American liberal'.[61] To this he coupled a strong political engagement, akin to that of Hobsbawm.[62] The present was linked to the past: his own experiences in the antisemitic Germany of the 1930s enabled him to recognise the injustice that black people were forced to undergo in postwar America.[63] Iggers did not hesitate, and joined in the battle against segregation and discrimination. His engagement in the Civil Rights Movement made clear that he was not interested in a 'sterile objectivity' but was willing to take action in the cause of greater social justice.[64]

In his years spent teaching at black colleges in Little Rock and New Orleans, between 1950 and 1963, Iggers did indeed throw himself into the battle against racial segregation, including through the National Association for the Advancement of Colored People.[65] In the subsequent years, he was active in the Peace Movement and in the resistance to what was perceived as the imperialist Vietnam War. Time and again he referred to the Enlightenment programme, which he believed should be universal and inclusive: for him it was about 'the belief in the dignity of all human beings and the commitment to create a world in which humans using their reason can free themselves from arbitrary authority'.[66]

Hobsbawm also explicitly threw his weight behind the Enlightenment programme with its universal reach. As he said in 1994, it was 'one of the few things that stands between us and an accelerated descent into darkness', an echo from the closing passages of *The Enlightenment*, in which Gay had renewed his faith in the programme he had described: 'The cure for the shortcomings of enlightened thought lies not in obscurantism but in further enlightenment.'[67] But Hobsbawm went further, from the Enlightenment to Communism. It was something that had inspired him earlier, in his Berlin years, when he had joined the Sozialistischer Schülerbund. Whilst there, he had embraced the notion of world revolution. As he wrote in the *New Statesman* in 1961, that could never be a moderate revolution.[68]

This led, as is known, to his lifelong involvement with the Communist Party, which Hobsbawm had joined in Cambridge. Neither the disillusion brought on by a trip to the Soviet Union in 1954–1955, nor the crisis of 1956, nor even the conflicts with the Party leadership (in which Hobsbawm always remained an outsider) caused him to give up this membership.[69] The October Revolution in 1917 continued to hold the prospect of a better world for him, in a far more universal way than Communist China did.

Hobsbawm continued to defend this standpoint even after the fall of the Soviet Union. Whilst he acknowledged that the material and moral ruin of the Soviet empire had demonstrated that the revolutionary programme was an illusion, he was not willing to abandon the values on which that programme was based.[70] They were the values of the Enlightenment.

Historiography and Morality

The defence of these enlightened values was not just a matter of ideology and political struggle, however. It also demanded intellectual support, in which attention had to be focused on the writing of history itself. This proved not to be a simple task. Composing a reflection on the position of the historian and his role in society was a difficult and laborious undertaking. At its heart were the concerns about a moral relativism: would taking historical thinking too far not lead to a dangerous negation of the idea 'that there are unchangeable human rights that are valid at all times?'[71]

This reflection unfolded in a historiographical landscape that was itself unstable. The changes could be interpreted in different ways. In *Interesting Times*, Hobsbawm described the development of historiography in the twentieth century as a protracted struggle between historical traditionalists and advancing modernists, in which the latter succeeded in promoting social history (in all its variants) to the historiographical mainstream.[72] In this regard, at least, he was on the side of the victors. The Marxist/Communist Party Historians' Group, the journal *Past & Present*, 'history from below' or 'grassroots history': Hobsbawm was pivotal in them all.[73]

While Hobsbawm claimed victory in the historiographical struggle, others worried about the relationship between historiography and morality. Georg Iggers, who by the way felt great sympathy for social history (after the fashion of the *Annales* historians or the Bielefeld School), was one such. His study of the Saint-Simonists had confronted him with the problem of the authoritarian political philosophy but also with the growing distrust towards the Enlightenment-led belief in progress. A subsequent project with Hayden White on the decline of the idea of progress was never completed. But 1968 saw the publication of Iggers' great work *The German Conception of History* (with a German edition following in 1971), which presented a critical analysis of the intellectual construction of German historiography since Herder. A few years earlier, in 1964, Mosse had already shed light on the mystical elements in German thinking in *The Crisis of German Ideology*.[74]

Iggers' book developed a critique of the German historical tradition as this had taken form in historism ('*Historismus*'): he criticised its exclusive focus on politics and the power of the State, its rejection of the notion of progress and its anti-normative emphasis on the individuality of each historical period, its social conservatism and its nationalism. All these assumptions, masked by claims to scholarly objectivity, had transformed historism into the gravedigger of the heritage of the Enlightenment; of democracy, of the belief in the ability to shape society and in progress, of universal human rights, of cosmopolitanism. To his critics, Iggers denied that he wished to draw a direct line from Herder to Hitler; but the exile from Hamburg was clear that historism had rendered the German population open to national socialism.[75]

The German Conception of History was the heroic attempt – sometimes a genuine struggle – by a refugee historian to lay bare the intellectual roots and thus also the moral order of the regime with which he had been brutally confronted in the 1930s. As Catherine Epstein rightly commented, the book was less a genealogy of the Holocaust than a diagnosis of the failure of liberalism in Germany.[76] Iggers' frame of reference remained the Enlightenment. From the 1980s, he began adopting an ever more global perspective of history, especially in his studies on the history of historiography, in which Asia acquired an increasingly prominent place.[77] Here, too, steps were taken: the comparative perspective gradually made way for a transnational approach, which in turn was superseded by a transcultural stance.[78]

Gay occasionally leaned towards the much-criticised historism, especially with regard to the idea that every historical episode can only be understood and judged from the basis of the norms that prevailed at the time. That was precisely the reason why Gay reacted with such irritation to his American Jewish critics and their accusations regarding his late departure from Germany. They were judging and condemning him on the basis of knowledge gained after the fact and were applying norms that had formed as a product of that knowledge. However, as *My German Question* put it, 'the road to Auschwitz was never straight or foreseeable.'[79] Historical understanding requires an insight into the specificity of every period (*'Jede Epoche ist . . .'*).

Yet Gay also demanded clear opinions from the historian. He praised his friend Bracher because in his work on the Weimar Republic and on National Socialism he had managed to combine 'scrupulous historical scholarship' with a 'compelling commitment to decency'. He added a caveat to his own aversion to an ahistorical, overly normative historiography: 'Yet none of this respect for complexity, I must insist, has compromised my willingness to recognize and condemn pure villainy when I see it'.[80] There was thus no question of an opposition between historiography and morality or, going a step further, between historiography and politics. The political naivety that Gay saw in the historism of Meinecke made him extremely critical.

The values that Gay wished to see upheld in historiography and other intellectual disciplines were the enlightened values of decency and dignity but also rationality. He had little time for the tradition of Nietzsche and Heidegger, in which this rationality was subverted. The more recent forms of this irrationalism drew no greater appreciation, including from Iggers: the social criticism of the Frankfurter Schule and the disciplinarian thinking of Michel Foucault, so different from the thinking in terms of emancipation that characterised Gay's own major study *The Bourgeois Experience: Victoria to Freud* (1984–1998), were alien to them. They held a very different opinion of Freud, to whom Gay (who had himself undergone analysis) dedicated a biography in 1988. Freud was not regarded as an intellectual peer of Nietzsche but rather as the 'last *philosophe*', who had developed a science of the human and offered Gay the opportunity to rid himself of the poison that Nazi Germany had placed within him.[81]

The historian was thus also expected to hold opinions that were independent – independent of the everyday customs of the society or culture he was describing. But Gay went a step further in distancing himself from historism. In his work, he stripped figures that were dear to him – Voltaire, Hume and Freud, for example – of their historical specificity by engaging in a timeless dialogue with them or joining with them in the battle against those who uphold barbarism and mendacity. Gay turned them into 'allies in the party of humanity'.[82]

Hobsbawm would sign up to this ethical project in his own way. In the – in many ways surprising – coda to his autobiography, this man who had always been so engaged called upon historians to be cautious: 'History needs distance', and 'History needs mobility'.[83] This had to be understood in the context of the evolution that took place in the later work of this émigré historian: the activism-based social history was now transformed into a reaction against identity-based historiography. Hobsbawm increasingly fought against the use of the past to create a particular identity and to exclude others who had a different identity. 'History', he spelled out in his lecture in Budapest as cited earlier, 'is the raw material for nationalist or ethnic or fundamentalist ideologies, as poppies are the raw material for heroin addiction'.[84] Hobsbawm expected the historian not to identify with the powerful elites but rather with the 'untypical minorities', who would always remain without power. 'The political project of the left is universalist', as he put it.[85]

A denouncement of historism, a resistance against irrationalism, a rejection of an identity-based dogma: the émigré historians sought a historiography that did not exclude morality – and by extension, politics – but which by contrast would allow it to reinforce the values of the Enlightenment that they so admired.[86] This was a historiography that was both rooted in time and outside of time: a position that was not tied to a here and now but was of all times. At the same time, these émigré historians also broadened the persona of the historian in another way: at a time when specialism was also enjoying a boom in historiography, the historian presented himself as a public intellectual. For Gay and Hobsbawm, this was also a self-portrait.

This once again brought forth the image of an outsider, this time with respect to the discipline of history. Gay had no time for academic rituals, scholarly conferences and footnotes. Hobsbawm regretted never having been offered a professorship at Cambridge or Oxford (he was far too left-wing for that), but also spoke with pride about teaching at institutes – Birkbeck College and the New School of Social Research – which were renowned for their radicalism and heterodoxy.[87] Moreover, as he had known since the publication of his first major work, *Primitive Rebels*, in 1959, he possessed street credibility (he himself also used the term 'a ghetto reputation'), which was much more important for his development as a historian than any official recognition by an academic establishment.[88] Self-fashioning naturally played an important role here, but the image was confirmed by the way in which these historians approached their teaching. Both Gay and Iggers enjoyed receiving students in their homes, delivering seminars that had much more the air of a salon or a political meeting than of an academic gathering.[89]

Coda

At the end of their joint autobiography, Wilma Iggers concluded that academic endeavour and the associated scholarly contacts had always been more important for her husband than for herself.[90] That was confirmed by the (gendered) role division in the writing of *Two Lives in Uncertain Times*: Georg mainly edited the passages dealing with professional and public life, while Wilma focused mainly on the personal history. But the way in which Georg also constructed his own identity as an (émigré) historian shows how difficult it is to maintain such a distinction. Hobsbawm's image of 'a private perch' did indeed neatly encapsulate the extent to which the professional identity of these historians was in essence also a personal one.

The émigré historians wrestled with dualities to a greater extent than their colleagues who had not been forced to leave – or flee – their country of origin. Their identities were hybrid and difficult to pin down, which meant that as well as being insiders they also always remained outsiders, while their writing combined intimacy and remoteness. They were fully aware that the world filled with natural diversity in which they had lived before their departure or flight was lost forever. It made them nostalgic, but also forced them to live with a traumatic surfeit of history and to seek pathways to reconciliation. The universal values of the Enlightenment were seen as a way of helping them deal with their catastrophic history. But the activism this spawned also implied a difficult reflection on the relationship between historiography, morality and politics.

But were these not also the challenges that faced *every* historian? Had they also not become nomads with no fixed identity? Were they also not gripped by a past that was gone but continued to live on without ever allowing itself to be completely captured? And were they also not expected to impart a more visible social dimension to their academic work? All this made the émigré historians into almost iconic figures: their persona served as a model.

Notes

1. On the significance of the 'persona' of the historian, see the recent publication by Algazi, 'Exemplum and Wundertier', 8–32 and Paul, *How To Be a Historian*.

2. On Iggers: Fillafer, 'Georg G. Iggers' (see also 'Franz Fillafer im Gespräch mit Georg Iggers', 84–99 and Porciani, 'Intervista a Georg Iggers', 97–117). On Gay: Dietle and Micale, 'Peter Gay', 1–23 and especially Williamson, 'Peter Gay (1923–2015)', 4–18.

3. The literature on the émigré historians from Germany is very extensive. See, e.g., Lehmann and Sheehan, *An Interrupted Past*; Keßler, *Deutsche Historiker im Exil*; Eakin-Thimme, *Geschichte im Exil* and Stelzel, *History after Hitler*, to be complemented with biographical studies (e.g. Molho, 'Besuch in Deutschland', 427–67). For the second generation, see especially Daum, Lehmann and Sheehan, *The Second Generation*, particularly the introduction by Daum, 'Refugees from Nazi Germany', 1–52; and the biographical compendium by Daum and Föhr, 'Biographies', 339–453; see also Daum, 'The Second Generation', 116–21. General introductions are provided in the *Writing the Nation* series: Mandelíčková and Goddeeris, 'Living in the Past', 394–411 and Tortarolo, 'Historians in the Storm', 377–403.

4. Laqueur, *Generation Exodus*.

5. That is illustrated for example in Epstein, 'The Second Generation', 143–51.

6. Krohn, *Intellectuals in Exile*.

7. For Hobsbawm, see the recently published monumental biography: Evans, *Eric Hobsbawm*.

8. That is emphasised in Evans, 'Eric Hobsbawm's Dangerous Reputation'.

9. On the refugee historians in England, see, e.g., Alter, *Out of the Third Reich*.

10. For more general information on the historian as an autobiographer, see Popkin, *History, Historians, & Autobiography*.

11. Cited in Kettle and Wedderburn, 'Eric Hobsbawm Obituary'.

12. Gabler, 'Wilma Iggers'.

13. See, e.g., Iggers, 'Refugee Women from Czechoslovakia in Canada', 121–28.

14. For a general discussion on this 'deprovincialization', see Burke, *Exiles and Expatriates*.

15. Hobsbawm, *Interesting Times*, 298.

16. Hobsbawm, *Interesting Times*, 310.

17. See, e.g., Ascherson, 'Eric Hobsbawm'.

18. Evans, 'Eric Hobsbawm's Dangerous Reputation'.

19. Hobsbawm, *Interesting Times*, 416.

20. Skinner and Ritter, *German Refugee Historians and Friedrich Meinecke*, 182.

21. Pflanze, 'The Americanization of Hajo Holborn', 170–79.

22. Sears and Schoell-Glass, 'An Émigré Art Historian and America', 219–42.

23. See Greenberg, '"Uphill Work"', 94–101 and Epstein, 'Schicksalgeschichte', 116–35.
24. Gay, 'At Home in America', 31–42.
25. Gay, 'The German-Jewish Legacy – and I', 203–10, especially 206.
26. Iggers, 'An Autobiographical Approach to the German-Jewish Legacy', 221–26, especially 223. For comparable examples in England: Snowman, *The Hitler Émigrés*.
27. Huttenbach, '*Le Déraciné*', 313–20.
28. Hobsbawm, 'Outside and Inside History', 1–9 (quotation on 1).
29. Katz, 'Displaced Historians', 135–55.
30. Popkin, *History, Historians, & Autobiography*, 221–45, in particular 244–45.
31. See, e.g., Haskell, *History and Its Images*, 252–53.
32. Hobsbawm, *Interesting Times*, 10.
33. Iggers and Iggers, *Two Lives in Uncertain Times*.
34. Hobsbawm, *Interesting Times*, 20–25 and Evans, *Eric Hobsbawm*, 9–10, 629 and 652–53.
35. Gay, *My German Question*, 14, 48–50 and 52.
36. See Katz, 'Displaced Historians', 142–43.
37. Iggers, *Two Lives in Uncertain Times*, 23 and 26–29 (quotation on 29) and Iggers, *Refugee Historians from Nazi Germany*, 2–3.
38. Gay, *My German Question*, 47–48.
39. Gay, *My German Question*, 111–13 and 123–24.
40. Fillafer, 'Georg G. Iggers', 456.
41. Iggers, *Two Lives in Uncertain Times*, 15.
42. Iggers, *Two Lives in Uncertain Times*, 169 (cf. 200, where her academic work is described as an 'extended mishpochology').
43. Gay, *My German Question*, x (cf. 170).
44. Gay, *My German Question*, 200–1.
45. See the comment in Cronin, 'Memoir, Social History and Commitment', 220.
46. Hobsbawm, *Interesting Times*, 43–44 and 77.
47. Daum, 'The Second Generation', 117.
48. Slotkin was herself also the author of a number of studies on the German and Eastern European Jews. See the short necrology of Fox, 'Ruth Gay, Author of Books About Jewish Life, Dies at 83'.
49. See Aschheim, *Beyond the Border*, 57–58.
50. Gay, *My German Question*, 1–20.
51. Gay, *My German Question*, 193.
52. Gay, *My German Question*, 6-7.
53. Gay, *My German Question*, 21.
54. Gay, *My German Question*, 154–55, 159, 172 and 181.
55. Iggers, *Two Lives in Uncertain Times*, 91–101 (quotation op 100), 137–38, 168–69, 176 and 181–84.
56. Iggers, *Two Lives in Uncertain Times*, 139–40 and 143–67.
57. Iggers, 'History and Social Action', 89–90.
58. For the intellectual context of the book, see, e.g., Leeman, 'Discovering a Lost Intellectuals' Project', 13–36; de Dijn, 'The Politics of Enlightenment', 785–805 and Smith, 'Reluctant Return', 210–28.
59. Among others, Leith, 'Peter Gay's Enlightenment', 157–71.
60. Gay, *The Enlightenment*, 567–68.
61. Iggers, *Two Lives in Uncertain Times*, 90.
62. See Iggers, 'The Historian', 277–99.
63. Among others, Iggers, *Two Lives in Uncertain Times*, 37: 'I at once identified with the blacks.'
64. Iggers, *Two Lives in Uncertain Times*, 201.
65. More generally, see: Edgcomb, *From Swastika to Jim Crow*.

66. Iggers, *Two Lives in Uncertain Times*, 125–26.
67. Hobsbawm, 'Barbarism', 253–65 (quotation on 254) and Gay, *The Enlightenment*, 567.
68. Hobsbawm, 'Thomas Paine', 1.
69. Hobsbawm, *Interesting Times*, 217 for an explanation (his own) of this lasting faith in the party, in part based on his Central European background. For an interesting commentary and a comparison with the German historian Jürgen Kuczynski, himself also an author of an autobiography, *'Ein Linientreue Dissident'*; Popkin, *History, Historians, & Autobiography*, 206, 209–11 and 219–20.
70. Hobsbawm, *Interesting Times*, 55–56 and 127.
71. Iggers, *Two Lives in Uncertain Times*, 97.
72. Hobsbawm, *Interesting Times*, 285–97.
73. See, e.g., Evans, *Eric Hobsbawm*, 309–15 (on the Marxist/Communist Party Historians' Group).
74. On Mosse and the close link between his life and work: Plessini, *The Perils of Normalcy*.
75. See, e.g., Iggers, 'History and Social Action', 91.
76. Epstein, 'The Second Generation', 149–50.
77. See, e.g., Qineng and Peng, 'Georg G. Iggers', 233–46.
78. Iggers, 'History and Social Action', 91 and 94.
79. Gay, *My German Question*, 111.
80. Gay, *My German Question*, 196–97 and 203.
81. Gay, *My German Question*, 203.
82. This theme is discussed further in Williamson, 'Peter Gay', 4–18 cf. Leith, 'Peter Gay's Enlightenment', 157.
83. Hobsbawm, *Interesting Times*, 415–16.
84. Hobsbawm, 'Outside and Inside History', 5.
85. Cited in Evans, *Eric Hobsbawm*, 553.
86. See also the discussions that are reconstructed in Tortarolo, 'Objectivity and Opposition', 59–70.
87. Hobsbawm, *Interesting Times*, 298–300. Also cf. Georg Iggers' description of the atmosphere and approach of the progressive State University of New York in Buffalo in *Two Lives in Uncertain Times*, 109–11.
88. Hobsbawm, *Interesting Times*, 302–3.
89. See, e.g., the description of a seminar that Georg Iggers provided together with Peter Heller, a literature researcher who had fled Vienna in 1938, on the Weimar culture and the exile literature, in the living room of his house in Amherst, with Gay and Carl E. Schorske among others as guests: Iggers, *Two Lives in Uncertain Times*, 122–23.
90. Iggers, *Two Lives in Uncertain Times*, 200.

Bibliography

Algazi, G. 'Exemplum and Wundertier: Three Concepts of the Scholarly Persona'. *Low Countries Historical Review* 131(4) (2016), 8–32.

Alter, Peter (ed.). *Out of the Third Reich: Refugee Historians in Post-War Britain*. London and New York: Bloomsbury, 1998.

Ascherson, Neal. 'Eric Hobsbawm: A Life in History by Richard J. Evans – Review'. *The Guardian*, 10 February 2019.

Aschheim, Steven E. *Beyond the Border: The German-Jewish Legacy Abroad*. Princeton and Oxford: University Press, 2007.

Burke, Peter. *Exiles and Expatriates in the History of Knowledge, 1500–2000* (The Menahem Stern Jerusalem Lectures). Waltham, MA: University Press of New England, 2017.

Cronin, James E. 'Memoir, Social History and Commitment: Eric Hobsbawm's Interesting Times'. *Journal of Social History* 37(1) (2003), 219–31.

Daum, Andreas W. 'The Second Generation: German Émigré Historians in the Transatlantic World, 1945 to the Present'. *Bulletin of the German Historical Institute* (51) (2012), 116–21.

———. 'Introduction: Refugees from Nazi Germany as Historians: Origins and Migrations, Interests and Identities', in Andreas W. Daum, Hartmut Lehmann and James J. Sheehan (eds), *The Second Generation: Émigrés from Nazi Germany as Historians* (New York and Oxford: Berghahn, 2016), 1–52.

Daum, Andreas W., and Sherry L. Föhr. 'Biographies', in Andreas W. Daum, Hartmut Lehmann and James J. Sheehan (eds), *The Second Generation: Émigrés from Nazi Germany as Historians* (New York and Oxford: Berghahn, 2016), 339–453.

Daum, Andreas W., Hartmut Lehmann and James J. Sheehan (eds). *The Second Generation: Émigrés from Nazi Germany as Historians*. New York and Oxford: Berghahn, 2016.

de Dijn, Annelien. 'The Politics of Enlightenment: From Peter Gay to Jonathan Israel'. *The Historical Journal* 55(3) (2012), 785–805.

Dietle, Robert L., and Mark S. Micale. 'Peter Gay: A Life in History', in Robert L. Dietle and Mark S. Micale (eds), *Enlightenment, Passion, Modernity: Historical Essays in European Thought and Culture* (Palo Alto, CA: Stanford University Press, 2000), 1–23.

Eakin-Thimme, Gabriela A. *Geschichte im Exil: Deutschsprachige Historiker nach 1933*. Munich: Peter Lang, 2005.

Edgcomb, Gabrielle S. *From Swastika to Jim Crow: Refugee Scholars at Black Colleges*. Malabar, FL: Krieger, 1993.

Epstein, Catherine. 'Schicksalgeschichte: Refugee Historians in the United States', in Hartmut Lehmann and James J. Sheehan (eds), *An Interrupted Past: German-Speaking Refugee Historians in the United States After 1933* (Washington and Cambridge: Cambridge University Press, 1991), 116–35.

———. 'The Second Generation: Émigré Historians of Modern Germany in Postwar America', in Andreas W. Daum, Hartmut Lehmann and James J. Sheehan (eds), *The Second Generation: Émigrés from Nazi Germany as Historians* (New York and Oxford: Berghahn, 2016), 143–51.

Evans, Richard J. 'Eric Hobsbawm's Dangerous Reputation'. *The Guardian*, 17 January 2019.

———. *Eric Hobsbawm: A Life in History*. London: Little Brown, 2019.

Fillafer, Franz L. 'Franz Fillafer im Gespräch mit Georg Iggers'. *Sozial.Geschichte: Zeitschrift für historische Analyse des 20. und 21. Jahrhunderts* 19(1) (2004), 84–99.

———. 'Georg G. Iggers: A Brief Biography', in Q. Edward Wang and Franz L. Fillafer (eds), *The Many Faces of Clio: Cross-cultural Approaches to Historiography. Essays in Honor of Georg G. Iggers* (New York and Oxford: Berghahn, 2007), 455–63.

Fox, Margalit. 'Ruth Gay, Author of Books About Jewish Life, Dies at 83'. *The New York Times*, 11 May 2006.

Gabler, Andrea. 'Wilma Iggers'. Retrieved March 2019 from http://www.fembio.org/biographie.php/frau/biographie/wilma-iggers/

Gay, Peter. *The Enlightenment: An Interpretation* (Vol. 2: The Science of Freedom). London: Random House, 1973.

———. 'At Home in America'. *The American Scholar* 46(1) (1977), 31–42.

———. 'The German-Jewish Legacy – and I: Some Personal Reflections'. *American Jewish Archives* 40(2) (1988), 203–10.

———. *My German Question: Growing Up in Nazi Berlin*. New Haven and London: Yale University Press, 1998.

Greenberg, Karen J. '"Uphill Work": The German Refugee Historians and American Institutions of Higher Learning', in Hartmut Lehmann and James J. Sheehan (eds), *An Interrupted Past: German-Speaking Refugee Historians in the United States After 1933* (Washington and Cambridge: Cambridge University Press, 1991), 94–101.

Haskell, Francis. *History and Its Images: Art and the Interpretation of the Past*. New Haven and London: Yale University Press, 1993.

Hobsbawm, Eric. 'Barbarism: A User's Guide', in Eric Hobsbawm (ed.), *On History* (New York: New Press, 1997), 253–65.

———. 'Outside and Inside History', in Eric Hobsbawm (ed.), *On History* (New York: New Press, 1997), 1–9.

———. 'Thomas Paine', in Eric Hobsbawm (ed.), *Uncommon People: Resistance, Rebellion and Jazz* (New York: New Press, 1998).

———. *Interesting Times: A Twentieth-Century Life*. London: Abacus, 2002.

Huttenbach, Henry R. 'Le Déraciné: Finding New Roots in Exile'. *American Jewish Archives* 40(2) (1988), 313–20.

Iggers, Georg G. 'An Autobiographical Approach to the German-Jewish Legacy'. *American Jewish Archives* 40(2) (1988), 221–26.

———. *Refugee Historians from Nazi Germany: Political Attitudes Towards Democracy*. Washington: United States Holocaust Memorial Museum, 2006.

———. 'History and Social Action Beyond National and Continental Borders', in Andreas W. Daum, Hartmut Lehmann and James J. Sheehan (eds), *The Second Generation: Émigrés from Nazi Germany as Historians* (New York and Oxford: Berghahn, 2016), 82–96.

———. 'The Historian as an Engaged Intellectual: Historical Writing and Social Criticism – A Personal Retrospective', in Stefan Berger (ed.), *The Engaged Historian: Perspectives on the Intersections of Politics, Activism and the Historical Profession* (New York and Oxford: Berghahn, 2019), 277–99.

Iggers, Wilma A. 'Refugee Women from Czechoslovakia in Canada: An Eyewitness Report', in Sibylle Quack (ed.), *Between Sorrow and Strength: Women Refugees of the Nazi Period* (New York: Cambridge University Press, 1995), 121–28.

Iggers, Wilma, and Georg Iggers. *Two Lives in Uncertain Times: Facing the Challenges of the 20th Century as Scholars and Citizens* (Studies in German History 4). New York and Oxford: Berghahn, 2006.

Katz, Ethan. 'Displaced Historians, Dialectical Histories: George L. Mosse, Peter Gay and Germany's Multiple Paths in the Twentieth Century'. *Journal of Modern Jewish Studies* 17(5) (2008), 135–55.

Keßler, Mario (ed.). *Deutsche Historiker im Exil (1933–1945): Ausgewählte Studien*. Berlin: Metropol, 2005.

Kettle, Martin, and Dorothy Wedderburn, 'Eric Hobsbawm Obituary: Historian in the Marxist Tradition with a Global Reach'. *The Guardian*, 1 October 2012.

Krohn, Claus-Dieter. *Intellectuals in Exile: Refugee Scholars at the New School for Social Research*. Massachusetts: University Press, 1993.

Kuczynski, Jürgen. *'Ein Linientreue Dissident': Memoiren 1945–1989*. Berlin: Aufbau-Verlag, 1992.

Laqueur, Walter. *Generation Exodus: The Fate of Young Jewish Refugees from Nazi Germany*. Hanover, NH: Brandeis University Press, 2001.

Leeman, Merel. 'Discovering a Lost Intellectuals' Project: George Mosse and Peter Gay on Myth and Mind in History', in Carolina Rodriguez-Lopez and José M. Feraldo (eds), *Reconsidering a Lost Intellectuals' Project: Exiles' Reflections on Cultural Differences* (Newcastle upon Tyne: Cambridge Scholars Publishers, 2012), 13–36.

Lehmann, Hartmut, and James J. Sheehan (eds). *An Interrupted Past: German-Speaking Refugee Historians in the United States After 1933*. Washington and Cambridge: Cambridge University Press, 1991.

Leith, James A. 'Peter Gay's Enlightenment'. *Eighteenth-Century Studies* 5(1) (1971), 157–71.

Mandelíčková, Monika, and Idesbald Goddeeris. 'Living in the Past: Historians in Exile', in Ilaria Porciani and Jo Tollebeek (eds), *Setting the Standards: Institutions, Networks and Communities of National Historiography* (Basingstoke: Palgrave, 2012), 394–411.

Molho, Anthony. 'Besuch in Deutschland: Paul Oskar Kristeller in America'. *I Tatti Studies in the Italian Renaissance* 19(2) (2016), 427–67.

Paul, Herman (ed.). *How To Be a Historian: Scholarly Personae in Historical Studies, 1800–2000*. Manchester: Manchester University Press, 2019.

Pflanze, Otto P. 'The Americanization of Hajo Holborn', in Hartmut Lehmann and James J. Sheehan (eds), *An Interrupted Past: German-Speaking Refugee Historians in the United States After 1933* (Washington and Cambridge: Cambridge University Press, 1991), 170–79.

Plessini, Karel. *The Perils of Normalcy: George L. Mosse and the Remaking of Cultural History*. Wisconsin: Wisconsin University Press, 2014.

Popkin, Jeremy D. *History, Historians, & Autobiography*. Chicago and London: University of Chicago Press, 2005.

Porciani, Ilaria. 'Attraverso molti confine: Intervista a Georg Iggers, storico indipendente'. *Passato e Presente* 64(23) (2004), 97–117.

Qineng, Chen, and Jian Peng. 'Georg G. Iggers and the Changes in Modern Chinese Historiography', in Q. Edward Wang and Franz L. Fillafer (eds), *The Many Faces of Clio: Cross-cultural Approaches to Historiography. Essays in Honor of Georg G. Iggers* (New York and Oxford: Berghahn, 2007), 233–46.

Ritter, Gerhard A., and Alex Skinner (ed.). *German Refugee Historians and Friedrich Meinecke: Letters and Documents, 1910–1977* (Studies in Central European Histories 49). Leiden and Boston: Brill, 2010.

Sears, Elizabeth, and Charlotte Schoell-Glass. 'An Émigré Art Historian and America: H.W. Janson'. *The Art Bulletin* 95(2) (2013), 219–42.

Smith, Helmut Walser. 'Reluctant Return: Peter Gay and the Cosmopolitan Work of a Historian', in Andreas W. Daum, Hartmut Lehmann and James J. Sheehan (eds), *The Second Generation: Émigrés from Nazi Germany as Historians* (New York and Oxford: Berghahn, 2016), 210–28.

Snowman, Daniel. *The Hitler Émigrés: The Cultural Impact on Britain of Refugees from Nazism*. London: Chatto & Windus, 2002.

Stelzel, Philipp. *History after Hitler: A Transatlantic Enterprise*. Philadelphia: University of Pennsylvania Press, 2018.

Tortarolo, Edoardo. 'Objectivity and Opposition: Some Émigré Historians in the 1930s and Early 1940s', in Q. Edward Wang and Franz L. Fillafer (eds), *The Many Faces of Clio: Cross-cultural Approaches to Historiography. Essays in Honor of Georg G. Iggers* (New York and Oxford: Berghahn, 2007), 59–70.

———. 'Historians in the Storm: Émigré Historiography in the Twentieth Century', in Matthias Middell and Lluis Roura (eds), *Transnational Challenges to National History Writing* (Basingstoke: Palgrave Macmillan, 2013), 377–403.

Williamson, Georg S. 'Peter Gay (1923–2015)'. *Central European History* 49(1) (2016), 4–18.

CHAPTER 2

The Émigré Historian
A Scholarly Persona?

HERMAN PAUL

Introduction

To what extent can the émigré historian be considered a scholarly persona? That is to say, to what degree can the émigré historian, living and working in hybrid spaces between cultures, be regarded as a specimen of a distinct type of historian, different from others, characterised by habits or working manners of which we can say: these are typical of émigré historians? Although the question has seldom been raised in this particular form, the sheer amount of studies devoted to, for instance, German émigré historians in the United States suggests that there is something special about émigrés that makes them more interesting objects of study than, say, historians who spent their entire careers in stable cultural contexts. Already in the 1920s, the American sociologist Robert E. Park commented on this special aura of the émigré, whom he described as 'a man living and sharing intimately in the cultural life and traditions of two distinct peoples', 'a man on the margins of two cultures and two societies', navigating between the not always reconcilable demands of his 'old self and the new'.[1] Even if Park's gendered language bears the marks of its time, his fascination with cultural hybridity has clearly endured, also among historians of historiography. Yet few of them have straightforwardly raised the question with which I started: To what extent can the émigré historian be considered a scholarly persona?

Notes for this section begin on page 54.

The short version of the answer I am going to develop in this chapter takes the form of a 'no, but'. There are few meaningful senses in which we can speak about 'the' émigré historian, in the singular, as representing a distinct scholarly persona, mainly because émigrés' experiences in different times and places were too diverse to allow for gross generalisation. Even if we zoom in on the first generation of German émigré historians in the United States, as I will do in this chapter, the ways in which these historians dealt with their cultural in-betweenness were too diverse to fit the mould of a single scholarly persona. If at all they represented a distinct type of historian, it was merely because of their *bildungsbürgerliche* background, visible in foreign language proficiency, knowledge of Beethoven and Wagner, and ability to quote Goethe or Schiller from memory – a cultural capital that struck some of their American colleagues and students as distinctively European.[2]

However, at the same time, if this postwar generation of German-American historians illustrates anything, it is that issues of professional identity were never far away. Even if these German-American émigré historians did not constitute a persona themselves, their ongoing negotiations with historiographical traditions on both sides of the Atlantic offer an interesting glimpse on how historians tried to mediate between different personae – by contrasting them, by combining them, or by trying to steer a middle course between them. More importantly, from their positions overseas, émigré historians like Hajo Holborn, Hans Rothfels, Hans Rosenberg and Felix Gilbert – all former students of Friedrich Meinecke in Berlin – developed a keen eye for what was distinctive about German historical studies. Interestingly, this did not merely turn them into observers of German scholarly personae; some of them also began to analyse these models through other, social and institutional lenses than had been customary in their home country before the war.

Existing Scholarship

Given current interest in hybridity and in-betweenness, not only among cultural theorists but also among historians of migration, one might expect that scholarship on forced migration of German historians into the English-speaking world would display a lively interest in how Hajo Holborn, Felix Gilbert and their contemporaries manoeuvred between the old world of German historical scholarship and the new world of American higher education. One might expect that social and scholarly exchanges would be treated not as one-way traffic or as a transfer from one country to another, but, as Mitchell G. Ash and Alfons Söllner put it, 'as interactive processes embedded in cultural settings that are themselves fluid enough to change'.[3]

Although this is exactly what some newer studies on second-generation émigrés try to do – Andreas Daum's work comes to mind[4] – most existing scholarship on first-generation German émigré historians in the United States has been written from a decidedly German perspective. The question that has dominated the existing literature, even if written in English, is how émigré historians related to, continued to draw on, or contributed to changes in German historiographical traditions. Wolfgang J. Mommsen, to mention only one example, consistently raises the question of the extent to which German émigrés 'remained within the Rankean paradigm'. With a similar focus, Michael H. Kater depicts Hans Rosenberg as 'the father of modern German social history' and thereby as a healthy corrective to the 'tight network of nationalist historians' that had dominated pre-war German historical studies.[5] In associating individuals with historiographical paradigms or schools, these research foci are indebted to a long tradition of thinking about historiography primarily in terms of 'approaches'. Like many other studies on European or American historiography, existing literature on German-American émigré historians shows an overwhelming interest in how 'approaches', characterised by distinct topics and/or methodologies, developed over time.

Although there is nothing wrong with this type of historiographical research, there are, generally speaking, two good reasons for supplementing this perspective with one that revolves around issues of professional identity. What does it mean to be a historian, at a given time and place? What demands does historical teaching or research make on the self (intellectually, emotionally, physically)? And how does this translate into activities that fill historians' calendars? One reason for raising these questions is that they bring into view not only historians' work – their published output – but also their day-to-day activities, their working habits, their teaching styles, their public service and outreach; in short, historians' professional identities as shaped on a daily basis in classrooms, libraries, faculty clubs and conference rooms. Another reason for focusing on such professional identities is that these may prove to be a missing link between existing scholarship on historical methods, institutions, biographies and the political subtexts of historical studies. Although I cannot substantiate this second claim here – I have done that elsewhere[6] – the first point seems highly pertinent to the study of émigré historians. If these émigrés were intermediaries between academic cultures, then what did this in-betweenness do with their professional identities?

Scholarly Personae

If I approach these questions through the prism of scholarly personae, I single out one element of a cluster of overlapping things: professional self-images, formative practices, daily routines, embodied working practices and exemplary figures. Scholarly personae is a technical term for models of how to be a historian. Often, though not always, these models are ideal-typical ones, sharply defined in contrast to each other, not because actual differences between historians are as large as these schematic distinctions suggest, but for heuristic reasons, to bring out as clearly as possible the differences between available modes of being a historian.[7]

Let me give some examples from nineteenth-century German historical studies – a world that cast a long shadow over the discipline in which the émigré historians to whom I will turn in a moment had been socialised in the 1920s and 1930s. German historians in the 1890s had quarrelled intensely over 'old' and 'new' ways of doing history, epitomised, they claimed, by Leopold von Ranke and Karl Lamprecht, respectively. The qualifier 'they claimed' is important: the Ranke attacked by Lamprecht and vigorously defended by Georg von Below and others did not exactly fit the historical Ranke. It was an image, created for polemical reasons, that highlighted some of Ranke's alleged habits and virtues – his thoroughness and commitment to political history writing in particular – at the cost of others.[8] This was hardly new. Since at least the 1840s, Ranke's name had served as a symbolic representation of aesthetic 'pleasure in history' (an aestheticism that distinguished itself from 'moralism' as embodied by Friedrich Christoph Schlosser) and as an epitome of Protestant impartiality (over against the Catholic dogmatism attributed to Johannes Janssen). Likewise, in the 1860s and 1870s, Georg Waitz and Heinrich von Sybel had frequently been played off against each other, as models of philological '*Wissenschaftlichkeit*' and patriotically-inspired history teaching, respectively. In all these cases, the names of Ranke, Schlosser, Janssen, Waitz and Sybel had not primarily served as proper names, referring to concrete individuals, but generic names, denoting types of historians – as Carl von Noorden noted when he observed as early as 1862, right after Schlosser's death, that the name of the deceased had acquired symbolic meanings that no longer did justice to the historical Schlosser.[9]

Whether or not scholarly personae were named after high-profile members of the profession, it is important to underline that precisely as ideal-typical models, personae were hardly ever fully embodied by individual historians. Personae rather served as coordinates on imaginary maps of the discipline, allowing historians to position themselves or their colleagues in the field under reference to familiar points of orientation. Although some managed to identify with a single persona, most historians preferred to steer a course between several personae – between Ranke and Janssen, for instance, as was the case for many Catholic historians around 1900, or between Ranke and Treitschke, as Dietrich Schäfer and other early twentieth-century political historians tried to do. Scholarly personae, in short, were not necessarily models for imitation. In most cases, they served as ideal-typical models in relation to which historians could position themselves — by dissociating themselves from some models, by combining several of them, or even by introducing new ones, from other countries or neighbouring fields.[10]

The *Émigré* Historian

This brings us to German-American émigré historians, whose replacement in a world different from pre-war German historical studies made them encounter personae unlike the Rankes, Treitschkes and Lamprechts from their youth. What struck them in the new world, judging by their letters and later autobiographical accounts, was the near omnipresent model of the historian as an undergraduate teacher, especially at colleges without much of a research culture. Teaching fifteen hours a week to a student population largely consisting of poor Jewish, Irish and Italian emigrants, as in Rosenberg's case, required a different type of academic than that bred by German universities before the war.[11] Also, in more research-friendly environments, émigrés encountered the historian as a 'grant hunter' — a term that Gerhard Masur's German-language memoirs kept in English so as to bring out the distinctively American features of a scholar always in search of new research money.[12] In the Second World War, moreover, German émigré historians became acquainted with yet another type of academic: the scholar in civil or military service; for instance, at the Office of Strategic Services, where both Gilbert and Holborn were employed for a number of years.[13] None of these professional identities had a clear equivalent in pre-war Germany.

Unsurprisingly, perhaps, German émigrés responded quite differently to these new models of professional identity. Some adapted relatively well, as did Gilbert, who loved his undergraduate teaching job at Bryn Mawr College. In Holborn's case, adaptation was even so successful that he became the first non-American-born president of the American Historical Association. Others responded more ambiguously, describing themselves, as Dietrich Gerhard did in a letter to Meinecke's widow, as 'a kind of scholarly hawker, carrying his bundle from continent to continent — an image that your husband, for all his tolerance, would surely have shaken his head at'.[14] Rosenberg, too, saw himself as moving back and forth between two worlds, depicting himself as 'a mediator and interpreter of the conflicting valuations, real and fancied, of different national cultures'.[15] In the realm of academic duty, this meant that Rosenberg devoted himself fully to educating young Americans at Brooklyn College but remained a little too German (as he put it) to give up on serious historical research:

> My outlook is no longer that of an emigrant. By degrees I have acquired the mentality of an immigrant who has taken roots in the land of his adoption. . . . At the same time, however, I do not consider it a disloyal attitude if I endeavour in a humble and restrained way, to remain faithful to what I value as the fruitful kernel of the German university tradition which, however gleamed or perverted in recent years, has made no trifling contribution to the common treasures of western civilization.[16]

Of course, there were also scholars whose hearts had remained in the 'Heimat'. In their letters, they complained about 'intellectual isolation' ('*wissenschaftliche Einsamkeit*') or gave expression to a 'longing for Germany' ('*Sehnsucht nach Deutschland*') that made them eager to return – as Hans Rothfels managed to do by accepting a call from the University of Tübingen in 1951.[17] Add to this that the first-generation émigrés developed very different scholarly profiles – with Gilbert, for instance, displaying little interest in politics but Rothfels and especially Holborn breathing new life into the nineteenth-century model of the historian as 'political educator of his people' – and it should be clear that they were a 'very heterogeneous crowd' indeed.[18]

In order to understand these differences, we have to take into account at least three variables. One is the émigrés' personal and professional backgrounds, which had been different enough to make them occupy a wide range of positions in pre-war German historical studies. As Mommsen puts it: 'They all came from the German '*Bildungsbürgertum*'. Otherwise, they were of different intellectual, philosophical and political persuasions.'[19] Secondly, in their adopted land, the émigrés encountered American historical studies in a variety of incarnations. As a research fellow at Chicago's Newberry Library, Hans Baron met other colleagues and engaged in different practices than Holborn at Yale or Gilbert at Bryn Mawr. Last but not least, not all émigrés were as eager or able to integrate in American academia as Holborn was. Gustav Mayer hardly spoke English, whereas Rothfels' biographer, Jan Eckel, relates that he has searched in vain for correspondence or other evidence of Rothfels maintaining more than superfluous contacts with American colleagues.[20]

What does this tell us about the émigré historian as a scholarly persona? As long as we take a scholarly persona to be a recognisable model of how to be a scholar, characterised by distinctive virtues, skills, habits or other dispositions, it should be clear that German émigré historians were too diverse to conform to a single persona. Although Robert Park, the Chicago sociologist, tried to transform the émigré into a persona – a 'new type of personality' that he called the 'marginal man' – this generalisation does not hold against empirical evidence.[21] Instead of clinging to a single persona, émigré historians navigated the conflicting demands of multiple personae – just as quite a few struggled, more generally, with social roles and expectations that were different than they were used to. (Gerhard Masur, to mention only one example, was quite astonished at the answer he received to his inquiry as to who would polish his shoes and take his clothes to the launderette: 'You do that yourself'.[22])

Perhaps the only sense in which German historians did represent a single type of scholar was that they were all '*Bildungsbürger*', with language skills, a cosmopolitan outlook and a cultural education that made them appear in American eyes as distinctively European. As Carl E. Schorske remembered:

> My own experience leads me to think that the émigrés . . . contributed less to the development of us natives as scholarly professionals than is usually assumed and much more to our cultural formation. They contributed to making intellectuals out of us young academics by broadening our horizons and multiplying our awareness of the existential implications of ideas – philosophical and literary, as well as social and political.[23]

However, the scholar as a culturally educated citizen hardly qualifies as a scholarly persona: cultural capital is compatible with a range of virtues, skills and working habits.

Perceptive Observers

Still, even if émigré historians did not represent a single persona, their transatlantic experiences certainly increased their *fascination* for historians' professional identities. This is the second, more positive argument I would like to make. On average, émigré historians were perceptive observers of scholarly habits and practices. In their letters, we find them commenting on 'the ins and outs of American college "business" [*Betrieb*]', with its heavy teaching loads and broad survey courses, which made considerable demands on historians used to more specialist teaching.[24] Others observed the lack of foreign language proficiency among American students or found themselves surprised by the 'grantsmanship' of scholars keen on acquiring research money.[25]

If these are observations on American academic life, often more elaborate were the reflections that émigré historians offered on German historical studies. Although their interest in German historiography often dated back to their years of study with Meinecke, war and forced migration fuelled this interest by lending urgency to critical reflection on the state of German historiography. To some extent, historiography courses offered a means for such reflection, also because American students, trying to make sense of a continent ravaged by war, were increasingly interested in studying the intellectual world of the Weimar Republic.[26] Rothfels taught such a historiography course in Chicago, with classes on Ranke and Meinecke, whereas Helene Wieruszoswki (another student of Meinecke) joined Friedrich Engel-Jánosi's historiography course at Johns Hopkins University.[27]

More important, however, was that Gilbert and others critically assessed the strengths and weaknesses of German historiography in journals like *The American Historical Review*. One belief that gained ground, even among Meinecke's students, was that '*Ideengeschichte*' or history of ideas as practised by their former teacher – 'an elitist-esoteric history of political ideas and doctrines that in many respects disguised the reality of historical life', as one émigré would put it – no longer sufficed.[28] Writing in 1947, Gilbert diagnosed that 'even before the Nazi period German historiography had become slightly obsolete in its exclusive concentration on political and intellectual history with its attendant neglect of problems arising out of a study of social and economic developments'.[29] Consistent with this criticism, Gilbert tried to do justice to economic factors in understanding intellectual life in postwar Germany. Advocating democracy 'at a time of economic misery and governmental weakness', he warned, may well have detrimental effects. Likewise, Gilbert believed that a resurgence of nationalist sentiments was primarily due to 'a widening of the gap' between Germany's Eastern and Western zones.[30]

Interestingly, this rediscovery of social and economic realities in which the life of the mind was embedded had implications for how émigré historians positioned themselves vis-à-vis existing scholarly personae. Continuing a tradition of mapping historical studies by drawing schematic contrasts between embodied models of historical scholarship, some émigrés followed Meinecke in contrasting Ranke (understood as an epitome of traditional political and intellectual history) with Jacob Burckhardt, of whom Gilbert declared in 1947: 'Burckhardt is increasingly emerging as a quite unique and powerful figure.'[31] As a later commentator would note, Burckhardt was an attractive alternative to Ranke because he allowed historians 'to encompass revolutionary discontinuity within their historicist premises. He never succumbed to the implicit glorification of national power politics. His dark tonalities provided the appropriate mood music for the project of German repentance . . . .'[32] Others, more radical in their reorientation, placed their hopes in the social sciences instead and contrasted their ideal of the historian as a democratically committed social scientist (embodied by Karl Dietrich Bracher, among others) with what Rosenberg disapprovingly called 'Ranke and the historical establishment'.[33]

Rosenberg himself, however, went even further. Writing to the American Department of State, after a few weeks of guest lecturing in Berlin in 1950, he eloquently lamented the 'mental isolation' of German historians, or what he called in more elaborated form their

> widespread narrowness of outlook, the prevalence of immaturity of political judgement and of a harmful spirit of political parochialism, the lack of insight into the complexities of social processes, the often amazing ignorance and

naiveté with reference to matters economic and technological, the staleness and inflexible conventionalism in the choice of research topics, the clinging to the 'old stuff' in teaching.[34]

Rosenberg was enough of a social and economic historian to realise that such deficiencies were not primarily caused by professors socialising their students into old-fashioned modes of thought but by social and institutional factors. According to Rosenberg, the administrative structure of German academia had been a key factor in keeping non-conformist tendencies at bay: 'Since these gentlemen [i.e. German professors] are used to replenish their ranks by cooptation down to the point of designating, not infrequently, their own successors their grip will not easily be broken.'[35] In the same 1950 letter to the American Department of State, Rosenberg argued that 'the attenuation of external pressures and material difficulties' in postwar Berlin made reorientation on social science models quite unlikely: people without income or proper housing have other things to do than reconsider their intellectual habits. This meant that, for Rosenberg, historians' working manners were not a product of intellectual choices: he saw them as developing under the 'force of circumstances' at least as much as through 'personal inclination'.[36]

This added an interesting twist to how German historians used to speak about scholarly personae. In the Wilhelmine and Weimar periods, personae had conventionally been defined in terms of virtues and vices. Although the 1920s had witnessed some attempts at redescribing these categories of virtue and vice in psychological language,[37] a focus on individual character traits, partly determined by personal inclination, partly shaped by examples one chose to follow, had continued to dominate historians' discourse. Rosenberg, by contrast, understood personae not as models with which one could choose to align but as embodiments of historiographical habits that had been decisively shaped by social and institutional factors. This anticipated a line of thinking, developed more fully in the second half of the century, that depicted nineteenth-century historiography not as a world populated by virtuous individuals but as a social reality determined by bourgeois conventions, middle class interests and powerful state protection.[38]

Conclusion

So, to what extent did German émigré historians in the United States constitute a scholarly persona? This chapter has argued that the first generation of German émigrés was too diverse, in terms of the kind of historian they wanted to be, to be reducible to a single persona. A historiographical equivalent to Park's 'marginal man' did not exist. At the same time, émigré historians turned out to be dedicated observers of scholarly personae, especially in Germany. While continuing the established habit of schematically juxtaposing historiographical models, historians like Rosenberg added a new dimension to the existing discourse by emphasising the social and institutional embeddedness of scholarly personae. The case examined in this chapter therefore suggests that it is more fruitful to study how émigré historians positioned themselves vis-à-vis competing personae in their field, and through what prisms they interpreted such personae, than to force these émigré historians themselves into the mould of a single persona.

On a larger canvas, this implies that hybridity and cultural in-betweenness should not be reified into distinct identities. As illustrated by the émigrés discussed in this chapter, there are many different ways in which scholars can live and work between cultures. Depending on cultural background, host environment and personal capacity for adaptation, among other factors, in-betweenness can take on a host of different forms. It therefore makes sense to regard cultural hybridity not as constitutive of a distinct 'émigré identity' but as a starting point for investigations into identities that are made, lost, challenged and/or transformed under influence of mobility or forced migration.[39]

Notes

1. Park, 'Human Migration and the Marginal Man', 892.
2. Barkin, 'German Émigré Historians in America', 155.
3. Ash and Söllner, 'Introduction', 12.
4. Daum, 'Refugees from Nazi Germany as Historians', 1–52, esp. 29–31.
5. Mommsen, 'German Historiography', 32–66, at 56 (see 57, 59, 60); Kater, 'Refugee Historians in America', 80, 92.
6. Paul, 'A Missing Link in the History of Historiography', 1011–28.
7. Paul, 'Scholarly Personae', 1–14.
8. Henz, *Leopold von Ranke*, 385–462.
9. Paul, 'The Virtues of a Good Historian', 681–709.
10. Paul, 'The Virtues and Vices of Albert Naudé', 327–38.
11. Rosenberg, 'Rückblick auf ein Historikerleben', 17.
12. Masur, *Das ungewisse Herz*, 267.
13. Katz, 'German Historians in the Office of Strategic Services', 137–38.
14. Dietrich Gerhard to Antonie Meinecke, 18 September 1954, in Ritter, *German Refugee Historians*, 205.
15. Rosenberg to Harry D. Gideonse, 31 January 1947, in Ritter, *German Refugee Historians*, 386.
16. Rosenberg to Harry D. Gideonse, 31 January 1947, in Ritter, *German Refugee Historians*, 386.
17. Hans Baron to Walter Goetz, 15 October 1954, in Ritter, *German Refugee Historians*, 316; Helene Wieruszowski to Friedrich Meinecke, 16 February 1947, in Ritter, *German Refugee Historians*, 328.

18. As Gay put it in a slightly different context in his 'Reflections on Hitler's Refugees', 117. The phrase 'political educator of his people' was used by Schnabel, among others: Berger, *The Search for Normality*, 57.

19. Mommsen, 'German Historiography', 41.

20. Ritter, *German Refugee Historians*, 105; Eckel, *Hans Rothfels*, 219–20.

21. Park, 'Human Migration', 892.

22. Masur, *Ungewisse Herz*, 263.

23. Schorske, 'The Refugee Scholar', 144.

24. Hans Rosenberg to Friedrich Meinecke, 4 December 1947, in Ritter, *German Refugee Historians*, 395.

25. Hans Baron to Walter Goetz, 15 October 1954, Ritter, *German Refugee Historians*, 313; Masur, *Ungewisse Herz*, 267.

26. Spitzel, *History After Hitler*, 49–81.

27. Hans Rothfels to Friedrich Meinecke, 12 October 1946, in Ritter, *German Refugee Historians*, 159–60; Helene Wieruszoswki to Friedrich Meinecke, 11 August 1946, in Ritter, *German Refugee Historians*, 325–26.

28. Rosenberg, 'Rückblick auf ein Historikerleben', 13.

29. Gilbert, 'German Historiography', 57.

30. Gilbert, 'Germany Revisited', 429, 431.

31. Felix Gilbert to Friedrich Meinecke, 14 June 1947, in Ritter, *German Refugee Historians*, 277.

32. Maier, 'Comment: Theodor Schieder', 393. For the roles played by German émigré historians in translating and reviewing Burckhardt's work, see Lionel Gossman, 'Jacob Burckhardt', 539–42.

33. A phrase that Rosenberg used as early as 13 February 1929 in a letter to his mother and siblings, in Ritter, *German Refugee Historians*, 340.

34. Hans Rosenberg to the Department of State, Division of Exchange of Persons, 11 November 1950, in Ritter, *German Refugee Historians*, 411.

35. Ritter, *German Refugee Historians*, 412.

36. Ritter, *German Refugee Historians*, 414, 409.

37. Schmeidler, 'Zur Psychologie des Historikers', 219–39, 304–27.

38. See, e.g., Weber, *Priester der Klio*.

39. Funding was generously provided by the Netherlands Organization for Scientific Research (NWO).

Bibliography

Ash, Mitchell G., and Alfons Söllner. 'Introduction: Forced Migration and Scientific Change after 1933', in Mitchell G. Ash and Alfons Söllner (eds), *Forced Migration and Scientific Change: Émigré German-Speaking Scientists and Scholars after 1933* (Cambridge: Cambridge University Press, 1996), 1–19.

Barkin, Kenneth D. 'German Émigré Historians in America: The Fifties, Sixties, and Seventies', in Hartmut Lehmann and James J. Sheehan (eds), *An Interrupted Past: German-Speaking Refugee Historians in the United States after 1933* (Cambridge: Cambridge University Press, 1991), 149–69.

Berger, Stefan. *The Search for Normality: National Identity and Historical Consciousness in Germany since 1800*. New York: Berghahn, 1997.

Daum, Andreas W. 'Refugees from Nazi Germany as Historians: Origins and Migrations, Interests and Identities', in Andreas W. Daum, Hartmut Lehmann, and James J. Sheehan (eds), *The Second Generation: Émigrés from Nazi Germany as Historians: With a Bibliographic Guide* (New York: Berghahn, 2016), 1–52.

Daum, Andreas W., Hartmut Lehmann, and James J. Sheehan (eds). *The Second Generation: Émigrés from Nazi Germany as Historians: With a Bibliographic Guide*. New York: Berghahn, 2016.

Eckel, Jan. *Hans Rothfels: Eine intellektuelle Biographie im 20. Jahrhundert*. Göttingen: Wallstein, 2005.

Gay, Peter. 'Reflections on Hitler's Refugees in the United States'. *The Leo Baeck Institute Year Book* 53(1) (2008), 117–26.

Gilbert, Felix. 'German Historiography during the Second World War: A Bibliographical Survey'. *The American Historical Review* 53(1) (1947), 50–58.

———. 'Germany Revisited: Some Impressions after Two Years'. *The World Today* 3(10) (1947), 424–31.

Gossman, Lionel. 'Jacob Burckhardt: Cold War Liberal?' *The Journal of Modern History* 74(3) (2002), 538–72.

Henz, Günter Johannes. *Leopold von Ranke in Geschichtsdenken und Forschung*, vol. 1. Berlin: Duncker & Humblot, 2014.

Kater, Michael H. 'Refugee Historians in America: Preemigration Germany to 1939', in Hartmut Lehmann and James J. Sheehan (eds), *An Interrupted Past: German-Speaking Refugee Historians in the United States after 1933* (Cambridge: Cambridge University Press, 1991), 73–93.

Katz, Barry M. 'German Historians in the Office of Strategic Services', in Hartmut Lehmann and James J. Sheehan (eds), *An Interrupted Past: German-Speaking Refugee Historians in the United States after 1933* (Cambridge: Cambridge University Press, 1991), 136–39.

Lehmann, Hartmut, and James J. Sheehan (eds). *An Interrupted Past: German-Speaking Refugee Historians in the United States after 1933*. Cambridge: Cambridge University Press, 1991.

Maier, Charles S. 'Comment: Theodor Schieder', in Hartmut Lehmann and James Van Horn Melton (eds), *Paths of Continuity: Central European Historiography from the 1930s to the 1950s* (Cambridge: Cambridge University Press, 1994), 389–96.

Masur, Gerhard. *Das ungewisse Herz: Berichte aus Berlin über die Suche nach dem Freien*. Holyoke, MA: Blenheim, 1978.

Mommsen, Wolfgang J. 'German Historiography during the Weimar Republic and the Émigré Historians', in Hartmut Lehmann and James J. Sheehan (eds), *An Interrupted Past: German-Speaking Refugee Historians in the United States after 1933* (Cambridge: Cambridge University Press, 1991), 32–66.

Park, Robert E. 'Human Migration and the Marginal Man', *The American Journal of Sociology* 33(6) (1928), 881–93.

Paul, Herman. 'The Virtues and Vices of Albert Naudé: Toward a History of Scholarly Personae'. *History of Humanities* 1(2) (2016), 327–38.

———. 'The Virtues of a Good Historian in Early Imperial Germany: The Case of Georg Waitz'. *Modern Intellectual History* 15(3) (2018), 681–709.

———. 'Scholarly Personae: What They Are and Why They Matter', in Herman Paul (ed.), *How to Be a Historian: Scholarly Personae in Historical Studies, 1800–2000* (Manchester: Manchester University Press, 2019), 1–14.

———. 'A Missing Link in the History of Historiography: Scholarly Personae in the World of Alfred Dove'. *History of European Ideas* 45(7) (2019), 1011–28.

Ritter, Gerhard A., and Alex Skinner. *German Refugee Historians and Friedrich Meinecke: Letters and Documents, 1910–1977*. Leiden: Brill, 2010.

Rosenberg, Hans. 'Rückblick auf ein Historikerleben zwischen zwei Kulturen', in Hans Rosenberg (ed.), *Machteliten und Wirtschaftskonjunkturen: Studien zur neueren deutschen Sozial- und Wirtschaftsgeschichte* (Göttingen: Vandenhoeck & Ruprecht, 1978), 11–23.

Schmeidler, Bernhard. 'Zur Psychologie des Historikers und zur Lage der Historie in der Gegenwart'. *Preußische Jahrbücher* 202 (1925), 219–39, 304–27.
Schorske, Carl E. 'The Refugee Scholar as Intellectual Educator: A Student's Recollections', in Hartmut Lehmann and James J. Sheehan (eds), *An Interrupted Past: German-Speaking Refugee Historians in the United States after 1933* (Cambridge: Cambridge University Press, 1991), 140–45.
Stelzel, Philipp. *History After Hitler: A Transatlantic Enterprise*. Philadelphia, PA: University of Pennsylvania Press, 2019.
Weber, Wolfgang. *Priester der Klio: Historisch-sozialwissenschaftliche Studien zur Herkunft und Karriere deutscher Historiker und zur Geschichte der Geschichtswissenschaft 1800–1970*. Frankfurt am Main: Peter Lang, 1984.

CHAPTER 3

The Long Arm of the Dictator

Cross-Border Persecution of Exiled Historians

Antoon De Baets

> From my own experience I know that exiles feed on hope.
> —— Aeschylus, *Agamemnon*, line 1668, 458 BCE

Introduction

In February 2019, Freedom House published a report to document and discuss the trend of a worldwide retrogression of democracy since 2005. The evidence mustered to prove such a trend included the following:

> [A] growing number of governments are reaching beyond their borders to target expatriates, exiles and diasporas. Freedom House found 24 countries around the world – including heavyweights like Russia, China, Turkey, Iran and Saudi Arabia – that have recently targeted political dissidents abroad with practices such as harassment, extradition requests, kidnapping and even assassination.[1]

Mapping this phenomenon of cross-border persecution in the historical field is the purpose of this chapter.

Historians leaving their countries because they are persecuted or threatened with persecution, and therefore unable or unwilling to return, are refugee historians or exiled historians.[2] The common assumption is that by fleeing these historians improved their overall situation despite the hardships

---

Notes for this section begin on page 71.

of exile, as they found themselves at last beyond the reach of the dictator's long arm. But this was not always the case. Pre-exile persecution could mutate into post-exile persecution. This is an often overlooked dimension when studying the pressures on exile scholarship.

A state can influence versions of its history abroad in many ways. In its simplest form, intervention of state A in state B for purposes of creating favourable versions of its past there can be structured as a typology with a scale from friendly to hostile:

Typology of Cross-Border, History-Related State Intervention
- State A's *cooperation* with state B influencing versions of A's history in B.
- State A's *appropriate interference* in state B influencing versions of A's history in B.
- State A's *polemics* with state B influencing versions of A's history in B.
- State A's *inappropriate interference* in state B to influence versions of A's history in B.
- State A's *dominance* over state B imposing versions of A's history in B.[3]

Post-exile persecution is an extreme form of the penultimate type, inappropriate cross-border interference with history. My focus is on state action, not on initiatives by private parties (for example, foundations pressuring history textbook content abroad, leagues suing for defamation abroad, anonymous death threats issued against historians living abroad), unless they are supported by the state. The emphasis, moreover, is on dictatorial states. Certainly, democratic states also attempt to influence versions of their pasts abroad, but as a rule they use the friendlier variants of the typology. Occasionally, historians experience persecution in democracies. The anti-communist McCarthyist campaign in the United States between 1948 and 1955, for example, hit historians specialised in the history of the Soviet Union and China, among others, and led to their dismissal and, for some,[4] to temporary or permanent semi-enforced emigration. However, this was domestic persecution with cross-border ramifications, not cross-border persecution. As populist and nationalist regimes are on the rise in democratic states, it cannot be excluded that we will soon spot the phenomenon of 'democratic cross-border retaliation'.[5] In any case, until now this has been extremely rare. It cannot be otherwise because democracies that persecute are deeply flawed and in danger of losing their democratic status. In limiting myself to dictatorships, I shall not cover all forms of intimidation they deploy abroad but only those that aim to influence the behaviour of exiled historians. I will also discuss how these historians react to these threats. I want to challenge the view that exiles were immune from the dictator's long arm.

Prevention Strategies

In counteracting and rectifying unwelcome versions of their state's history produced abroad, dictators apply two strategies. The first – prevention in the domestic context – may sound paradoxical, but it is most effective. It means that the circulation within country borders of unwelcome histories produced abroad is obstructed by censorship. Domestic historians can be seen as being involved in the creation of these unwelcome histories in many ways; for example, when they accepted foreign funding, imported books from abroad, talked to foreign journalists, delivered papers at conferences abroad, published on foreign websites, reviewed foreign work, or co-authored and edited international collections – exactly the kind of activities for which historians in democracies are praised. Depending on the case and the regime, these historians can have their passports confiscated and exit visas denied. Further down the road, they may become the subject of spurious legal charges such as 'enemy of the state', 'collaboration with the enemy', 'enemy propaganda', 'espionage' or 'treason', leading to their dismissal, imprisonment or exile.[6] Increasingly, countries resort to prolonged shutdowns of the internet, or they block access to specific websites.[7] Another domestic measure consists in stopping unwelcome foreign historians from crossing the border through the denial of entry visas. Visa blacklists can be backed up by other devices ranging from permanent bans on research or conference attendance to deportation and the ascription of persona non grata status. This does not exclude measures against critical foreign historians who entered the country legally: surveillance, harassment or worse.

How do attacks against exiled historians fit into these prevention strategies? The default retaliation measure is censorship here as well: works and activities of exiles are declared taboo at home. Less common is copyright infringement. Some exiles see their works published in their home countries without their authorisation, without their name or under another name. This occurred to Spanish historian Ramón Iglesia. His critical edition of the famous sixteenth-century chronicle *True History of the Conquest of New Spain*, which he had prepared for four or five years before the civil war and remained unpublished because of it, appeared in Spain in 1940 without any mention of his name, a treatment that would weigh on his shoulders his whole life.[8] Other historians are spied upon when they temporarily return to the home country, a privilege usually not extended to exiled historians. Shula Marks, an émigré from apartheid South Africa, was permitted to return there to do research. She was subjected to constant scrutiny in the archives, however, especially after the 1976 Soweto uprising, when archivists were warned to watch her research.[9] A colleague of hers commented: 'One feature of her career was her courage. She travelled to and from South

Africa, braving the inquisitions of a state increasingly managed by its police force and guided by its army chiefs.'[10]

The return of exiled historians can be blocked by arranging their civil death (the loss of their civil rights). Revocation measures prove very effective in this regard: exiles then have their right to teach withdrawn or are stripped of their academic titles. More drastically, their citizenship can be repealed, making temporary or definitive return impossible. Alternatively, extradition requests can be lodged in order to convince the host country to send back the exiled historian.

Another strategy, usually taking place under the radar, is intimidating the exiles' families that still live in the home country. Attempts to avoid this blackmail may lead to a permanent breakdown of communication between the exiles and their families. It can also have a chilling effect on their ability to publicly criticise their home countries and, eventually, on their other activities. Alternatively, exiled historians can also be lured back in with promises (either true or false).

Persecution Strategies

Whatever success prevention strategies bring, it stops at the border unless the host countries are willing to cooperate. Lobbying strategies designed to intervene beyond the border are more complicated. Depending on their operation and purpose, they can be appropriate or inappropriate. The most common appropriate strategy consists in lodging public diplomatic protests, often at international forums. Such protests target official historical statements delivered in other countries, or the adoption of memory laws or resolutions about historical atrocity crimes in their parliaments.[11] Alternatively, specific sources, works, films, exhibitions or statues can be singled out as sources of embarrassment.[12] If anything, diplomatic protests are strong indicators of topics that possess a taboo character in the protesting country.

Other, more daring lobbying strategies – often inappropriate but not always – apply soft power under the guise of propaganda or pressure. As part of cross-border propaganda campaigns, states fund and establish chairs, journals, foundations, research centres, educational and cultural institutes and travel to foreign congresses – everything to disseminate their official views under the cloak of independent scholarship. Many of these programmes are run discreetly.[13] Pressure can be diplomatic and financial. Whether this pressure is covert, corrupt and coercive – hence inappropriate – depends on the case. Government ministers can covertly contact colleagues or summon ambassadors to express their dissatisfaction with critical initiatives, especially if they enjoy official support in the targeted state. In the case of open controversy, the pressure to correct unwelcome versions of a state's past may include withdrawal of investment in the 'offending' state or economic sanctions against the latter's interests in the 'offended' state.

Retaliatory measures such as these can affect exiles in several ways. Sometimes, dictatorial regimes try to export their police and censorship techniques and prevent the publication of historical work. Franco's Spain, for example, tried to convince France to take steps against the left-wing exiled publisher Ruedo Ibérico (Iberian Wheel), based in Paris. Founded by historian José Martínez Guerricabeitia in 1961, it was an active publisher until 1982. Franco's secret service carefully watched it and in 1971 discovered the identity of Luís Ramírez, the pseudonymous author of the 1964 book *Franco: Historia de un mesianismo* (Franco: History of a messianism): Basque writer Luciano Rincón Vega. As he still lived in Spain, he was sentenced to four years' imprisonment.[14] Likewise, China watched dissident writers abroad. One of them was Gao Wenqian, before his exile a senior researcher in the Central Committee's Research Center on Party Literature. After the 1989 Tiananmen massacre, Gao began copying documents relating to Zhou Enlai, China's premier until his death in 1976, onto cards while memorising others. He did this for four years. When permitted to go to the United States in 1993, he left his enormous collection of notes with friends, who smuggled it out of the country. Although the Chinese government intimidated Gao and pressured his employer, Harvard University, in order to prevent any publication based on these archives, Gao's *Zhou Enlai's Later Years* was published in Chinese in Hong Kong in 2003 and in English in 2007.[15]

Elimination operations abroad were complicated, but the boldest led to disappearance or assassination. Below I identify eighteen exile history producers murdered for political reasons.[16] History producers should not be confused with historians: it is a broader category. To assume that historians are the only ones who deal with the past is too narrow a view. Everywhere, many different groups are involved in the production or practice of history. I therefore prefer to speak of history producers rather than historians to designate all those involved, professionally or otherwise, in the collection, creation or transmission of history. History producers include, for example, journalists who write works of contemporary history, directors of historical films or historical novelists. This broader pool of recruitment has the disadvantage that I had to decide whom to include and whom to exclude from the pool in more borderline cases than otherwise would probably have been the case. But excluding all those who were not officially historians and yet dealt systematically with the past was not an option. Almost all of the following exiled history producers killed for political reasons were national or international *causes célèbres*.

Dominican Republic under Rafael Leónidas Trujillo
- *Jesús de Galíndez Suárez* (1915–56), Basque historian, double exile from Spain (1939) and Dominican Republic (1946), abducted in New York with American help, transported to the Dominican Republic and assassinated on Trujillo's orders, body never found.

Germany, Nazi
- *Theodor Lessing* (1872–1933), German philosopher of history, critic of Nazism, exiled 1933, assassinated by Sudeten German Nazi sympathisers in Czechoslovakia, six months after leaving.
- *Rudolf Hilferding* (1877–1941), Austrian-German-Jewish historian, leading Weimar politician and political theorist, exiled 1933, arrested by the Gestapo as a socialist and anti-fascist, died in prison in Paris after torture, either suicide or murdered on orders of Adolf Hitler.
- *Simon Dubnow* (1860–1941), Russian-Jewish historian, exiled from Russia (1922) and Germany (1933), killed by the Nazis in the ghetto of Riga, Latvia.
- *Grigol Peradze* (1899–1942), Georgian priest, theologian, historian, exiled 1922 after the Soviet occupation of Georgia, arrested by the Gestapo in Germany in 1942, died in Auschwitz.
- *Isaac Osipovich Levin* (1876–1944), Russian-Jewish historian, publicist, exiled from Russia (year unknown) and Germany (1931 or 1932), arrested in early 1943, held in a camp near Paris but deported to a Nazi concentration camp where he died.

Iran under the Shah and under the Ayatollahs
- *Ali Shariati* (1933–77), Iranian historian and opposition politician, called 'the Ideologue of the Iranian Revolution', exiled 1977, either heart attack or murdered by secret police SAVAK in London, three weeks after leaving.
- *Kourosh Aryamanesh* (aka *Reza Mazluman*) (1934–96), Iranian historian and political opponent, exiled 1982, shot dead near Paris.

Italy, Fascist
- *Piero Gobetti* (1901–26), Italian journalist, historian, radical liberal, assaulted by fascist thugs and beaten up in 1925, exiled 1926, died of a cardiac depression (a likely consequence of the assault) thirteen days after leaving.
- *Carlo Rosselli* (1899–1937), Italian historian, brother of Nello Rosselli, anti-fascist, exiled 1929, murdered in France by cagoulards (French fascists), probably authorised by Benito Mussolini.
- *Nello Rosselli* (1900–1937), Italian historian, brother of Carlo Rosselli, anti-fascist, exiled 1929, murdered in France by cagoulards (French fascists), probably authorised by Benito Mussolini.

Japan, Imperialist
- *Sin Chae-ho* (1880–1936), Korean historian, anarchist, nationalist, exiled 1910, arrested by Japanese Military Police in Taiwan in 1928 for smuggling for anarchists, sentenced to ten years' imprisonment in China, died in solitary confinement in Port Arthur/Dalian.

Lebanon, Palestinian diaspora in
- *Abdul-Wahhab Kayyali* (1939–81), Palestinian historian, publisher, politician, exiled as a child 1949, shot dead by unidentified gunmen (possibly by Israeli intelligence agency Mossad, a Lebanese militia or a rival Palestinian faction) in Beirut.

Romania under and after Nicolae Ceaușescu
- *Vlad Georgescu* (1937–88), Romanian historian, exiled 1979, died of brain tumour, possibly after having been irradiated by the state security agency Securitate in Munich after broadcasting fragments from the memoirs of a Securitate general.
- *Ioan Culianu* (1950–91), Romanian historian of religion and magic, exiled 1972, shot dead in the Divinity School, Chicago, probably by a former Securitate agent or a Romanian neo-fascist.

Sri Lanka during the armed conflict (1983–2009)
- *Sabaratnam Sabalingham* (1952–94), Tamil writer and guerrilla, exiled 1981, documented the history of rival Tamil militant movements (including their assassinations); when it was to be published, he was shot dead in Paris by two Tamil Tigers on orders of Tamil Tiger leader Velupillai Prabhakaran.

Taiwan under Chiang Ching-kuo
- *Henry Liu* (1932–84), Taiwanese historian, journalist, exiled 1967, shot dead in Daly, California, by two Bamboo Union members on orders of Taiwan's Military Intelligence Bureau for critical work about Taiwan, including a biography of Chiang (son of Chiang Kai-shek).

USSR, Stalinist
- *Leon Trotsky* (pseudonym of Lev Bronstein) (1879–1940), Russian-Jewish writer, People's Commissar, historian of the recent period, exiled 1929, survived two murder attempts, stabbed in the head with an ice pick by a Stalinist agent in Mexico.[17]

The cases are part of a worldwide database of 428 history producers who were killed for political reasons throughout the centuries. Killed as far apart as 1926 and 1996, the eighteen were targeted by eleven regimes. The Nazi German regime took five lives, the Italian Fascist regime three, Communist Romania two and the Shah and Ayatollah regimes in Iran two as well. The regime with the highest incidence of history producers killed for political reasons, the Stalinist Soviet Union, is represented here by only one case because almost all the victims were killed inside the vast borders of this country.[18] The overview reveals that, given the regime variety, dictatorships of all kinds have tried, often more than once, to eliminate exiled historians.

Twelve history producers were assassinated for their political activities or ethnic origins, not for their historical work. But the murders of the remaining six – Trotsky, Galíndez, Liu, Georgescu, Culianu and Sabalingham – were connected, in whole or in part, to their historical scholarship. In all probability, the secret police had a hand in five of these six murders.[19] In sum, about one third of the victims had sharply criticised the recent history of their countries – the incumbent regimes and their immediate predecessors – and this had constituted a potent motive to kill them.

Elsewhere, I have performed two tests on the population of 428 killed history producers that can be compared with this finding of one third. The first test regarded a sample of 132 history producers, all killed after 1945, and showed that the deaths of almost one out of four murders (30 of 132 cases or 23%) had some substantial relationship to their historical output.[20] The second test was performed on all the archivists in the population of 418, nineteen in total. Four were killed for reasons partly related to their archival work: 25% of the sixteen cases (out of nineteen) for which enough specifics were known to identify or reject an archival component in the motive for the killing.[21] Both tests showed a pattern: roughly one fourth of the history producers killed for political reasons were so for reasons related to their historical scholarship. The list of political murders among exiles, however, reveals a stronger proportion, namely one third. This 'anomaly' can simply reflect the fact that the samples in the three tests are too small for meaningful generalisation. Another possibility is that the higher incidence of exiled history producers killed for reasons related to their historical work reflects reality. The finding would then suggest that history is weaponised *and* neutralised with higher frequency in exile contexts than in domestic contexts.

Survival Strategies

Exiled historians followed two strategies to counter attacks from outside: survival and destruction strategies. Obviously, the prime survival strategy consisted in continuing exile life as well as possible, if not walking, then stumbling. Additional survival strategies were aimed at maximising the margins of working life in the host countries. Many exiles engaged in low-profile activities such as smuggling sources and works from abroad back home (or vice versa) or staying discreetly in contact with those left behind via networks of messengers.[22] Some activities were undertaken with the explicit purpose of supplementing and refreshing the sources of knowledge as historical writing in the home country was utterly corrupt. A significant minority of exiled historians established publication outlets and historical institutions, including study centres and universities-in-exile.[23] Although some of this work took place anonymously or pseudonymously, much of it was public and sometimes highly visible. The same could be said about displays of moral, symbolic or material solidarity with those living under repression at home, such as signing petitions, resigning from academy memberships and returning honours.[24] These solidarity actions were meant to outbrave the dictator or boost the morale of those left behind. Some exiles took radical steps to become active in human rights work and politics, including by writing commentaries on the situation in the home country. In this regard, it is striking that several historians served as members of governments-in-exile.[25] Exiled historians who were active in the public arena and therefore possibly watched by the dictator's henchmen or by colleagues and students very likely developed special routines of caution. As we saw, this could not prevent some of them from being intimidated, harassed or murdered.

Destruction Strategies

The destruction strategies of exiled historians could follow three paths: abandoning the profession, destroying personal papers follow committing suicide. Not surprisingly, some exiles decided to abandon historical scholarship altogether. Taking a sample of 544 refugee historians (out of a database of 764), I calculated that 33.3% (181 persons) experienced fundamental career change during exile: 14% (76 persons) left the profession and 19.3% (105 persons) joined it during exile.[26] At first sight, gains trump losses. Also, many of those who dropped out of the profession found new employment elsewhere, which may have signified personal progress. And yet I call this a destruction strategy because the figures hide an asymmetry: there were relatively more experienced historians among the leavers and relatively more beginners among the newcomers. In addition, many of those who did not switch careers became unemployed or worked in worse conditions than before exile.

I found five examples of exiled historians who destroyed their personal papers.[27] Reasons for such a step are speculative but include safety, especially if the destruction took place before exile; fear that the contents of the papers would be abused or misunderstood; inward-directed rage; and a growing disappointment that historical research was futile, especially if the destruction occurred as part of a last will. As most historians are professional source collectors *par excellence*, I suspect that the decision to destroy biographical and working records, if taken voluntarily, is often an indicator of an unhappy life.

A step further than the destruction of one's personal papers is the destruction of one's own life. Here is an overview of nine cases of suicides characterised by an exile-related aspect:

Suicide on impending refoulement during the Second World War
- *Carl Einstein* (1885–1940), German-Jewish art historian and anarchist, exiled 1928, committed suicide by jumping from a bridge in a river when stuck in France and fearing arrival of Nazis.
- *Walter Benjamin* (1892–1940), German philosopher of history and cultural critic, suicide plans since 1931, exiled 1933, committed suicide with a morphine overdose when, fleeing deportation from France to Germany, he was arrested in Spain while crossing the border.
- *Aenne Liebreich* (1899–1940), German art historian of the Middle Ages, exiled 1933, committed suicide when the Nazis invaded Paris.
- *Rudolf Hilferding* (1877–1941), Austrian-German-Jewish historian, leading Weimar politician and political theorist, exiled 1933, arrested by the Gestapo as a socialist and anti-fascist, died in prison in Paris after torture, either by murder on orders of Adolf Hitler or by suicide.

- *Hedwig Hintze* (née *Guggenheimer*) (1884–1942), German-Jewish historian of the French Revolution, exiled 1939, died either by suicide or from heart failure as a refugee in the Netherlands after failed attempt to go to USA, then Switzerland, fearing deportation to Auschwitz.

Suicide after exile
- *Edgar Zilsel* (1891–1944), Austrian-Jewish philosopher of science and historian, exiled 1938, suicide in Oakland, California, with an overdose of sleeping pills.
- *Ramón Iglesia y Parga* (1905–48), Spanish historian of the conquest of Mexico, exiled 1939, first in Mexico, later in the USA, threw himself from his apartment window in Madison, Wisconsin.
- *Theodor Ernst Mommsen* (1905–58), German historian of the German and Italian Middle Ages, émigré or exiled 1936, worked, inter alia, at Cornell University, Ithaca, NY, committed suicide with an overdose of sleeping pills, his papers were destroyed after his death.
- *Jorge Cedrón* (1942–80), Argentinian director of historical films (Por los senderos del Libertador; Operación Masacre; Resistir), his name circulated on death lists, exiled 1977, died by suicide – stabbed himself several times in the heart while on a toilet in a police station in Paris, where he was reporting the abduction of his father-in-law.[28]

The nine cases were selected from the overlap in two databases mentioned above: the database of 428 killed history producers, which also includes cases of suicide as a result of severe political pressure, and the database of 764 exiled historians.[29] It is likely that the suicides in the face of refoulement (forced repatriation) were acts of impulsive despair directly connected to the failed exile attempt and the prospect of further persecution after refoulement.[30] In contrast, the suicides after settlement in exile were probably premeditated. Diaries, last letters, last words and suicide notes, if they exist, could shed light on the specifics of each case.

For individual history producers, additional predictors sometimes exist; not exactly for suicide as such but for a special sensitivity to painful existential experiences. Ramón Iglesia, for one, was deeply influenced by his participation in the Republican army during the Spanish Civil War and his exile in Mexico: both experiences led him to reconsider his earlier views of his subject of research, the 1521 conquest of Mexico. He also suffered the humiliation of having his work published in Spain without any mention of his name (about eight years before his suicide). But he also had a history of psychiatry. For the Germany émigré Theodore Ernst Mommsen, other factors than moving abroad help explain his suicide: intermittent psychological crises and depression, a broken relationship, the death of a friend, illness, even acute awareness of the boundaries of his – and anyone's – imperfect knowledge of the Middle Ages, and, importantly, the weight of having to live up to a famous family (he was a grandson of historian and 1902 Nobel laureate in literature Theodor Mommsen and a nephew of Max Weber).[31]

Comparisons between exile suicide and domestic suicide remain to be explored. There is evidence that at least forty history producers committed suicide after persecution in their home country (for example, in prison).[32] A list of eleven historians who committed suicide during the Cultural Revolution in China would be the most promising to serve as a control group.[33]

With only anecdotal evidence found in interviews and testimonies, important questions remain unanswered: Which part of the suicide decision of exiled historians is triggered by the exile experience as such? Hypothetically, would exiled historians who committed suicide have done so anyway? Perhaps even sooner? Is suicide more frequent in isolated exiles, not surrounded by a supportive diaspora? Are suicide rates of exiled historians different from those of other 'intellectual' exiles? Of other exiles in general? Is suicide more frequent earlier or later in exile? Do late-life effects, such as a resurgence of trauma, play a significant role?[34]

Eyewitnesses, and psychologists after them, have estimated suicide rates in politically extreme circumstances such as those in camps in Nazi Germany, in camps of the Soviet Gulag, during the Armenian genocide, during the Partition of British India and during the Cultural Revolution in China. It has led to contradictory theories. Recent research, including this one, invariably finds high suicide rates in politically extreme circumstances, but surviving eyewitnesses of the calibre of Primo Levi and Aleksandr Solzhenitsyn adhered to low-rate theories. How is this possible? The solution to this puzzle is probably that these eyewitnesses committed a reporting error: when they maintained that suicide was relatively rare in concentration and labour camps, they probably did not mean 'rare' in any absolute sense but 'rare' compared to the unusually high suicide expectations in extreme circumstances.[35]

If we define exile as a politically extreme context – albeit less harsh than a concentration camp, an ethnic cleansing or a genocide – the rates of exile suicides are very probably well above global average rates, given a stronger tendency to underreport suicides in politically extreme contexts. However, the rates of exile suicides are not necessarily higher than the rates of domestic suicides in dictatorships because living under a dictatorship constitutes a politically extreme context as much as exile.[36]

The literature on suicide in politically extreme circumstances suggests several reasons for suicide that are applicable to an exile context with relative ease. The sheer list of reasons for suicide illustrates the complexity of the phenomenon:

- *Past-related trauma*: stress of persecution and expulsion; rupture in family life, relationships, career, income level; pre-persecution nostalgia.
- *Present-related depression*: concentration problems; health problems; permanent homesickness; prolonged uncertainty about legal status;

extreme dependency on others; social isolation and loneliness; feeling of generalised failure; poor assimilation in the host country; xenophobia in the host country; imprisonment as enemy in the host country; fear of spies among exiles; fear of secret police of the home country; fear of refoulement or deportation.
- *Future-related meaninglessness*: inward-directed anger and blame; survivor guilt; inability to help those who stayed behind; perceived lack of recognition; perceived lack of solidarity; perceived meaninglessness of survival strategies; fear of falling into oblivion in the home country; fear of permanently blocked return; fear of returning after many years.
- *Suicide-related views*: earlier suicide attempts; thoughts and images of suicide; perception of suicide as an act of free will.

This overview reveals that reasons directly related to the fear for the dictator's long arm (expressed in such reasons as fear of spies among exiles; fear of secret police of the home country; fear of refoulement or deportation; fear of permanently blocked return), although very real, constitute but one series in a range of potentially explanatory factors for suicide in exile.

On Balance

The impact of exile on the knowledge production of refugee historians has an often-overlooked dimension: persecution by the dictatorship that drove them away. A first, perhaps surprising, finding revealed rather effective *prevention strategies*: dictators had an impressive array of measures at their disposal to prevent unwelcome versions of history produced abroad from spreading domestically: the censorship of works of exiled historians, the infringement of their copyright, the revocation of their right to teach and of their titles and citizenship, and the intimidation of any family members they left behind.

Persecution strategies, directly interfering with the lives of exiles abroad, were harder to prove. One state unmasked the pseudonymous author of a history published abroad and imprisoned him, another tried actively to prevent a publication abroad, a third ordered to spy on an émigré historian who returned home for archival work. Meddling could also end in murder. Eighteen cases of exiled history producers killed for political reasons were examined. Six of them were murdered partly or entirely because their acid historical criticism formed an unbearable indictment of the dictator and his predecessors.

The exiled historians steered away from such threats by applying diverging coping strategies. Most used multiple *survival strategies*: they continued their lives as well as possible, engaged in low-profile activities (such as smuggling sources or maintaining contact with home via discreet networks), took public initiatives such as establishing publication outlets and historical institutions, showed discrete or vocal solidarity with those living under repression in their home countries or participated in political and human rights activities.

Destruction strategies deserved particular attention in our context. One third of a sample of 544 refugee historians experienced a fundamental career change during exile. Of these career switchers, 14% left the historical profession and 19% joined it during exile. This would be a positive result for the profession if there was not a hidden asymmetry: the leavers were relatively more experienced and the newcomers relatively less. On the whole, a career switch meant loss of potential, and this was destructive for the profession. Other strategies were destructive not only for the profession but also for the individuals involved. They included the removal of personal papers (illustrated with five cases) and suicide (illustrated with nine cases). We are seduced into thinking that what was lost by snatching away the historians from their domestic intellectual biotopes was won in wisdom gained from the exile experience trickling into new insights, but this is a fallacy.

The domestic strategies of dictators were more effective than their strategies abroad. Most measures deployed abroad were typically cases of overstretch. The exception was the killing strategy: it made a real difference when vocal critics like a Trotsky or a Galíndez were eliminated. But even here there was a double backlash: the posthumous fame of those killed created ardent followers determined to continue in their footsteps; and in uncovering their brutal faces, dictatorships lost their last bit of respectability. Arguably, some of the dictators' other lobbying activities abroad were more successful, but their interventions into the history versions produced by exiles were rarely of any long-term consequence.

From the perspective of exiles, the main question is whether the exiles' coping strategies were directly attributable to the dictator's far-reaching influence. For a very tangible minority of exiles, this was the case, and it was awkward. If the dictator feared the power of their words, it could end in cold-blooded murder; if they feared the dictator, it could end in suicide. This was most clearly seen in cases of impending refoulement.

The majority of exiled historians was not directly hit by the dictatorial regime. They attained more or less stable lives, even if their professional lives were fragile, though this was often after years of upheaval. Their fate would almost certainly have been worse if they had stayed home. But even for this majority that survived and coped with the situation as well as it could, the dictator was the subject of daily conversation and endless speculation. And if most were not targeted directly, the *fear* that they were a target without knowing it – or that they could be targeted one day – took its toll among many. In this sense, most exiles were mildly but permanently terrorised by this vague threat, and it affected their work. In short, post-exile persecution played a big role for few and a small but real one for all. In terms of survival as well as scholarship, the refugee experience was, on the whole, bleak until the very end.

Notes

1. Freedom House, *Democracy in Retreat*, 6. All links to websites were last checked on 1 May 2022. I am grateful to all participants in the workshop 'Dynamics of Emigration, Epistemic Repercussions', held at the University of Bochum in 2019, for their comments, in particular Henning Trüper.
2. I follow the definition of the United Nations, *Convention Relating to the Status of Refugees*, Article 1A(2). The convention includes arrangements made since 1926: see Article 1A(1).
3. Examples of type 3: the controversy between Japan, South Korea and China about the history of the Pacific War; the controversy between Turkey and Armenia plus several Western countries about the recognition of the Armenian massacres as genocide. Comment on type 4: This type can be called *export of censorship*. Sometimes it spills over into *international censorship*, directed at international book series, international conferences or international history organisations. Comment on type 5: 'Dominance' includes colonisation, occupation and imperialism. Superpowers in particular invested much energy in imposing acceptable versions of their history abroad. For example, the USSR tried to equalise historical writing in the countries within its zones of influence after 1944; the Allied Powers imposed a set of history-related measures after occupying the Axis powers in Europe and the Far East in 1945.
4. Including Owen Lattimore, Stuart Schram, Moses Finley, Natalie Zemon Davis and W.E.B. DuBois.
5. For example, in Poland a controversial 2018 memory law to criminalise 'defamation of the Polish Nation' was dubbed 'Lex Gross' after Jan Tomasz Gross. A Polish-Jewish émigré historian working at Princeton University, Gross claimed that many Poles had been complicit in Nazi war crimes. This claim was officially described as 'historically untrue, harmful and insulting to Poland' in 2015. In 2016, Gross was interrogated for five hours in Katowice and almost stripped of an award. The American Historical Association, among others, expressed concern about this intimidation.
6. For a global overview of spurious accusations and charges directed at historians, see De Baets, *Crimes against History*, 82–84.
7. The conflict between Estonia and Russia about a Soviet monument in Tallinn even spilled over into what could have been, in 2007, the first cyberattack ever.
8. Ortega y Medina, 'Historia', 242–49; Matute, 'Ramón Iglesia', 70; Bernabéu Albert, 'La pasión de Ramón Iglesia Parga', 764; Thomas, *Biographical Dictionary*, 213–14.
9. Shula Marks, e-mail, 2 February 2001.
10. Birmingham, 'Shula', 401.
11. Memory laws: As did Israel in response to the adoption by Poland of its 2018 memory law. Resolutions: As did Turkey in response to the adoption by the French National Assembly of a proposal criminalising the denial of genocides, including the Armenian genocide.
12. See, for example, De Baets, 'Censuur van buitenlandse geschiedenis'.
13. Two examples are especially noteworthy in this respect: the Turkish government's lobby to promote its denialist views of the 1915 genocide of Armenians in European countries, Israel, the United States and the United Nations, especially since the mid-1970s; and the interference of Hindu nationalist associations with United States history textbooks to adapt them to their views, especially since 2002.

14. Juaristi, 'Fallece el escritor Luciano Rincón'.
15. Gao, 'The June Fourth that I Saw', 10–18; De Baets, *Crimes against History*, 130.
16. Excluded were political murders of history producers who were either internally displaced, exiled history students or expatriate historians. Among the history students were Brazilian Jorge Alberto Basso (?–1976), killed in Argentina, and Kamal Bamadhaj (1970–91), a New Zealander of Malaysian origin, killed in Indonesia. Among the expatriate historians were American Malcolm Kerr (1931–84) and French Michel Seurat (1947–86), both killed in Lebanon; the American Albert Glock (1925–92), killed in the Israeli-Occupied Territories, and possibly Canadian Steve Gordon (?–1992), killed in Colombia.
17. Source: author's own database. For database interpretation, see De Baets, *Crimes against History*, 9–40, 155–64.
18. De Baets, *Crimes against History*, 16–19.
19. The Sri Lankan case was the result of rivalry among Tamil groups.
20. De Baets, *Crimes against History*, 16–17.
21. De Baets, *Crimes against History*, 37.
22. De Baets, *Crimes against History*, 140.
23. De Baets, *Crimes against History*, 139; De Baets, 'Plutarch's Thesis', 33–36; De Baets, 'Exile and Acculturation', 344–48.
24. De Baets, *Crimes against History*, 140.
25. De Baets, 'Exile and Acculturation', 332–34.
26. De Baets, 'Plutarch's Thesis', 36–37; De Baets, 'Exile and Acculturation', 335–37.
27. For the cases (Elias Bickerman, Aron Freimann, Theodor Ernst Mommsen, Otto Neugebauer and Helene Wieruszowski), see Epstein, *A Past Renewed*, 38, 75, 224, 226, 345. The fact that all of them fled Nazi Germany probably merely reflects the fact that the exile wave from Nazi Germany is the best studied.
28. Source: author's own database. Suicide *attempts* were excluded.
29. See De Baets, 'Exile and Acculturation', 322–27, for an overview of the database.
30. See also Lester, *Suicide and the Holocaust*, chapters 4–6. I am grateful to David Lester for sending me his book.
31. Gilbert, *Lehrjahre*, 111–20.
32. They are listed in the provisional memorial for history producers in De Baets, *Crimes against History*, 155–64 (although their cause of death is not mentioned there).
33. These eleven Chinese historians are Zeng Zhaoyu (?–1964 or 1966), an anonymous historian (?–[1966]), Chen Mengjia (1911–66), Deng Tuo (1911/12–66), Li Pingxin (1907–66), Ma Bo-an (?–[1966]), Tian Jiaying (?–1966), Wang Deyi ([1937]–67), Li Jigu (?–1968), Jian Bozan (1898–1968) and Liu Shousong (1912–[69]). See also the remarks on China in De Baets, *Crimes against History*, 17, 26 and Lester, 'Suicide and the Cultural Revolution', 99–104. Domestic suicides in politically extreme circumstances in the Stalinist USSR included Usevalod Ignatovski (1881–1931), Mikola Skrypnyk (1872–1933), Sergei Teploukhov (1888–1934), Geidar Guseinov (1908–50) and, possibly, Paul Rykov (1884–1942).
34. Surprisingly, suicides on impending refoulement were 53 years on average, while suicides after settlement in exile 47 years. Also, I did not find examples of suicide among exiled historians after they returned home.
35. For a discussion of suicide rates, see Lester, *Suicide and the Holocaust*, preface and chapter 12. For a summary of suicide theories in politically extreme circumstances, see Lester and Krysinska, 'Suicide in the Soviet Gulag Camps', 175–76. For a thesis on the reporting mistakes of eyewitnesses, see Lester, 'The Suicide Rate in the Concentration Camps Was Extraordinarily High', 201. See also Lester, 'Suicide and the Cultural Revolution'; Lester, 'Bias in the Reporting of Suicide and Genocide'; Van der Veer, 'The Risk of Suicide among Refugees Seeking Asylum', in Van der Veer, *Counselling and Therapy with Refugees*, 189–98; López-Muñoz and Cuerda-Galindo, 'Suicide in Inmates in Nazi and Soviet Concentration Camps', 1–6.

36. For global figures: World Health Organization, *Suicide in the World*, 15 ('Changes in suicide rates over time'). For underreporting: Suicides are sometimes covered up as accidents; the database of killed history producers reveals, however, that murders are sometimes covered up as suicides.

Bibliography

Bernabéu Albert, Salvador. 'La pasión de Ramón Iglesia Parga (1905–1948)'. *Revista de Indias* 65(235) (2005), 755–72.
Birmingham, David. 'Shula: A Personal Tribute'. *Journal of Southern African Studies* 27(3) (2001), 399–404.
Cantor, Norman. *Inventing the Middle Ages: The Lives, Works and Ideas of the Great Medievalists of the Twentieth Century*. New York: Morrow, 1991.
De Baets, Antoon. 'Exile and Acculturation: Refugee Historians since the Second World War'. *International History Review* 28(2) (2006), 316–49.
———. 'Plutarch's Thesis: The Contribution of Refugee Historians to Historical Writing (1945–2015).' *Storia della Storiografia* 69(1) (2016), 27–38.
———. 'Censuur van buitenlandse geschiedenis in Nederland (1945–2018)'. [Censorship of the history of other countries in the Netherlands (1945–2018)] *Historici.nl* (2018).
———. *Crimes against History*. London: Routledge, 2019.
Epstein, Catherine. *A Past Renewed: A Catalog of German-Speaking Refugee Historians in the United States after 1933*. Cambridge: Cambridge University Press, 1993.
Freedom House. *Democracy in Retreat: Freedom in the World 2019*. Washington: Freedom House, 2019.
Gao, Wenqian. 'The June Fourth that I Saw'. *Human Rights in China (China Rights Forum)* 2 (2009), 10–18.
Gilbert, Felix. *Lehrjahre im alten Europa*. Berlin: Siedler, 1989.
Juaristi, Jon. 'Fallece el escritor Luciano Rincón'. *El País*, 5 September 1993.
Lester, David. 'The Suicide Rate in the Concentration Camps Was Extraordinarily High: A Comment on Bronisch and Lester'. *Archives of Suicide Research* 8(2) (2004), 199–201.
———. *Suicide and the Holocaust*. Hauppauge, NY: Nova Science Publishers, 2005.
———. 'Suicide and the Cultural Revolution'. *Archives of Suicide Research* 9(1) (2005), 99–104.
———. 'Bias in the Reporting of Suicide and Genocide'. *Suicide Studies* 1(2) (2020), 25–29.
Lester, David, and Karolina Krysinska. 'Suicide in the Soviet Gulag Camps'. *Archives of Suicide Research* 12(2) (2008), 170–79.
López-Muñoz, Francisco, and Esther Cuerda-Galindo. 'Suicide in Inmates in Nazi and Soviet Concentration Camps: Historical Overview and Critique'. *Frontiers in Psychiatry* 7(8) (2016), 1–6.
Matute, Álvaro. 'Ramón Iglesia: Del historiador como héroe trágico'. *Revista de la Universidad de México* 501–502 (2000), 67–70.
Ortega y Medina, Juan Antonio. 'Historia', in Fondo de Cultura Económica (ed.), *El exilio español en México 1939–1982* (México: Salvat, 1982), 242–49, 273–94.
Thomas, Jack. *Biographical Dictionary of Latin American Historians and Historiography*. Westport CT and London: Greenwood, 1984.
United Nations. *Convention Relating to the Status of Refugees*. Geneva: UNHCR, 1951.
Veer, Guus van der. *Counselling and Therapy with Refugees: Psychological Problems of Victims of War, Torture and Repression*. Chichester: Wiley & Sons, 1992.
World Health Organization. *Suicide in the World*. Geneva: WHO, 2019 (UN Doc. WHO/MSD/MER/19.3).

CHAPTER 4

Nativism and the Spectre of Antisemitism in the Placement of German Refugee Scholars, 1933–1945

Joseph Malherek

In the fall of 1933, only months after the Nazi Reich had enacted its radical law to 'restore' the professional civil service on April 7th, Stephen Duggan, an American leading an emergency effort to find positions for university professors displaced by the law, expressed his astonishment in response to the report of a colleague surveying the situation in Germany that many 'Aryan' professors there were 'glad' that they would no longer face competition from Jewish scholars. 'I cannot avoid expressing my amazement', Duggan wrote, 'that German intellectuals are willing that so many of the most distinguished figures in the field of scholarship should be driven out and that they should be willing to suffer the loss of German scholarship and prestige'.[1] Duggan's immediate concern was the preservation not of scholars themselves but of scholarship as such, a feeling he seemed to think would be pervasive among academicians in the United States. However, it would become increasingly clear to Duggan over the course of the next several years that petty professional jealousies and resentments could very easily morph into feelings of provincialism, nativism and even antisemitism. Despite the high-mindedness of the pursuit of scholarship and the desire of aid officers like Duggan to 'rescue' a tradition of science and learning from the destructive illiberalism of the Nazis, the very basic desire among American university teachers for professional status and job security would seriously complicate the efforts to

Notes for this section begin on page 86.

place the refugee scholars, especially in the economically precarious context of the Great Depression. In fact, as the records of correspondence and placement among the officers of the various international placement agencies demonstrate, the determination to avoid creating conditions that might stoke feelings of nativism and antisemitism in the United States would become a concern even more urgent than the very preservation of scholarship. The aid officers' frequently expressed worry pointed to a latent feeling that, among university professors and administrators, the commitment to liberal internationalism was ultimately very fragile and quite vulnerable to being superseded by parochial concerns, professional anxieties and deeper prejudices.

A Crisis of Refugee Scholars and Latent Fears of 'Anti-Foreignism'

A year and a half after Duggan's anxious but revealing letter, a short report entitled 'A Crisis in the University World' was prepared and distributed by the League of Nations' Office of the High Commissioner for Refugees (Jewish and Other) Coming from Germany. The pamphlet documented the work of the various national and international emergency committees that had come together under the Commission's 'Experts Committee' to coordinate their efforts to place the roughly 1,200 German university professors and teachers from all fields who had been summarily dismissed from their positions simply for being, in the view of the new regime, either 'unreliable' in their political ideology or insufficiently 'Aryan' in their racial constitution. By the time of the Commission's report in March 1935, about 650 academics had left Germany. Many of these émigrés were among the most esteemed representatives of their field, and most of the initial cohort had found either temporary or permanent positions – often with the help of the emergency committees – although some of the most prominent scholars had been offered positions straight away. With the Nuremberg Laws of September 1935 and further purges, the number of dismissed scholars would grow to as many as 2,000 by the end of the 1930s, about a third of all faculty members in Germany. With Germany's annexation of Austria in 1938, hundreds more scholars would be forcibly removed from their professional posts. Moreover, thousands of other professionals in law and medicine, as well as journalists and artists, would be forced from their livelihoods over the remaining years of Hitler's rule, a relatively small but culturally significant part of the roughly half-million refugees created by the Nazi regime.[2]

Quantifying the dismissals indicates the scope of the crisis, but the shock to the university world was so profound because of the central role that German universities, with their tradition of '*Lern- und Lehrfreiheit*', had played in the international community of science and learning.³ More than the individual fates of the displaced scholars, the very principle of academic freedom and the liberalising role of universities in modern societies seemed to be at stake. At the same time, however, it was a crisis of opportunity because suddenly hundreds of scholars of international renown had become available. One beneficiary of this global dispersion of intellectual might was Alvin Johnson, director of the New School for Social Research in New York, who quickly established a separate faculty for the refugee scholars only months after the initial wave of emigration; he would later refer to these émigrés as Hitler's 'gift' to American culture.⁴ But the 'University in Exile' (officially, the Graduate Faculty of Political and Social Science) was a special case, and Johnson, who was well aware of antisemitism at American universities, deliberately downplayed the Jewishness of his émigré faculty, instead promoting the institution as a bastion of intellectual freedom and cosmopolitan internationalism.⁵ More typically, the refugee scholars were spread across the world's universities on the presumption that to concentrate them in any one place would lead to alienation, resentment and antisemitism. From the perspective of their sponsors, it was a delicate task to place these refugee scholars in the context of a global economic depression in which many young academics themselves were facing daunting professional prospects.

When the refugee crisis hit, there already existed an international network that was prepared to take the initiative in placing the scholars. The New School itself was partly premised on the idea of the '*Volkshochschulen*', the German schools for adult higher education, and Johnson had also familiarised himself with the European academic system as an editor of the *Encyclopaedia of the Social Sciences*, a massive, international project sponsored by the Rockefeller and Carnegie foundations, which themselves had sponsored social scientists in Europe and would become key sponsors of the refugee scholars.⁶ The New York-based Institute of International Education (IIE), directed by Duggan and funded by the Carnegie Endowment for International Peace, had been established in 1919 to coordinate educational exchanges of students and professors.⁷ The International Student Service (ISS) in Geneva, the legacy of a wartime Christian relief organisation, organised international academic conferences and other activities under the direction of its general secretary, Walter Kotschnig.⁸ Duggan would lead the central American placement agency alluded to above, the Emergency Committee in Aid of Displaced German Scholars, formed in May of 1933, while Kotschnig would direct the High Commission's efforts to place refugee university teachers and members of the 'free professions'. Simultaneously, the Director of the London School of Economics (LSE), Sir William Beveridge, initiated the founding of Britain's Academic Assistance Council (AAC), which would be directed by its general secretary, Walter Adams. Shortly thereafter, a group of refugee scholars coalesced in Zurich to found the Notgemeinschaft deutscher Wissenschaftler im Ausland, led first by Philipp Schwartz and for most of its existence by Fritz Demuth.

When the committees first formed, the displacement of the German scholars appeared to be a temporary problem that demanded an immediate solution in the form of grants for temporary placements that might eventually become permanent positions. There was a fear among the leaders of the academic committees that some of the world's most accomplished scholars would fall out of academic life completely, becoming objects of relief rather than subjects of scholarship. For this reason, they viewed their efforts as part of a rescue mission to save a tradition of science and liberal scholarship from an illiberal, reactionary and racist attack. But as the Nazi regime became entrenched in Germany and the purges continued, these ad hoc organisations became increasingly established institutions for the placement and long-term maintenance of scholars. They coordinated through the Experts Committee and shared information on the refugee scholars, including detailed lists that categorised the scholars by discipline, employment status, age and country of origin, and graded them on their scholarly qualifications and the likelihood that they could be integrated into universities in the United States, the United Kingdom, or other countries able to accept them. The lists were shared with department chairs, deans and university presidents, who would themselves extend invitations to individual scholars for temporary posts entirely funded by the committees. In this way, about a third of the scholars who sought help from the committees were able to find positions within three years of the initial wave of terminations. Typically, they were placed in stand-alone positions at universities around the world, but there were special cases of concentrations, like at the New School, and Hebrew University in Palestine would appoint more than a dozen of the refugee scholars, most of whom were Jewish. The Notgemeinschaft achieved extraordinary success through an arrangement with the University of Istanbul, which, due to a major institutional reorganisation initiated by the Turkish government in 1933, was able to place 56 displaced German scholars in temporary positions.[9]

The story of the émigré scholars and their contributions to their host countries is of course well established in the secondary literature, beginning with early works often done with the participation of the émigrés themselves.[10] There have been encyclopaedic efforts to document the cultural impact of émigré intellectuals and artists around the world.[11] Later, edited collections often examined trends in the social sciences and other fields, as well as the extent to which the émigrés served as vessels for the transfer – or reimportation, in some cases – of Central European scholarly traditions to their host countries, often with the support of American foundations.[12] The intellectual communities of scholars abroad have attracted particular attention, particularly the University in Exile at the New School and Max Horkheimer's Institute of Social Research, better known as the 'Frankfurt School', which was hosted by Columbia University.[13] Another, more recent trend in scholarship considers the implications of the émigrés in terms of their impact on American economic and foreign policies.[14]

Much of the scholarly attention has been directed to the émigrés themselves and their own intellectual contributions, but a subset of the scholarship has looked into the network of aid organisations and directors, their relationships with each other and with the foundation officers who supported them, and their respective policies for evaluating and placing scholars. Notably, Christian Fleck has documented the role played by American foundations in supporting the work of European social scientists, who were the beneficiaries of fellowships and exchanges that nurtured a truly transatlantic academic community during the post-First World War era that quite naturally became the network through which exiled scholars sought refuge when the crisis hit in 1933. Politics then became an immediate concern, and foundation officers were forced to awkwardly adjust their grant-making policies to account for the new situation.[15] Both in Europe and the US, it was not exactly a pleasant position for dedicated liberal internationalists to find themselves in, and the historian Marjorie Lamberti has pointed out that Duggan's Emergency Committee 'eschewed publicity' and at least initially acted with extreme caution, 'inhibited by the fear of rising antisemitic feeling'.[16]

At times, there was an ironic, almost Kafkaesque quality to their efforts. The officers of the Emergency Committee were so fearful of stoking antisemitism and nativism in the US that they insisted that their grants to refugee scholars were for temporary appointments. At the same time, however, they demanded assurance from the university presidents with whom they corresponded that there was at least a 'fair chance' that the scholar would eventually be absorbed into the permanent faculty, thus providing a 'reasonable possibility of arriving at a final solution of the problem confronting the German scholar concerned', as Duggan once put it in private correspondence.[17] In the case that the scholar did not appear likely to be permanently absorbed in the faculty of the host university, the Committee was less inclined to renew the grant. In a sense, this appeared to be another kind of 'final solution' to the problem, as it were, because the scholar ceased to be the concern of the Emergency Committee and instead became merely a pitiable object of relief. This ostensibly cavalier attitude may be partly explained by the fact that the Emergency Committee was originally envisioned as a temporary organisation, and its officers felt compelled to have their work 'completed' in one way or another, but the fundamental contradiction remains.

In their relationships with other aid directors, foundation officers, and university presidents, the officers of the Emergency Committee felt it necessary to fiercely defend their policies. Both Duggan and his assistant, Edward R. Murrow (who later became famous as a broadcast news reporter on radio and television), had felt that Johnson's highly publicised scheme for the University in Exile, as a concentrated faculty of refugee scholars, was unwise and, in Murrow's words, 'an unfortunate move'.[18] But it proved to be successful, and Johnson defended his 'separate group' arrangement, which preserved the cohort of émigré scholars and their methods. He pointed out in an interview published in the 'New York Times' that a foreign professor who spent two years in a stand-alone position at an American university would be in line for a promotion that would otherwise 'naturally go to an American member of the faculty'. This statement made Murrow furious, and it 'disturbed the equilibrium' of the other members of the Committee, who demanded an apology from Johnson, who finally acquiesced.[19] Murrow and the other members of the Emergency Committee also objected to the Academic Assistance Council's general public appeals for financial support, because they viewed their job as finding permanent posts for the refugees in the US and considered it 'unwise in view of the existence of anti-foreignism, to publicize too widely our activities on behalf of the displaced Germans'.[20] For both the AAC and the Emergency Committee, concerns related to institutional reputation and public relations often took precedence over the actual well-being of the refugee scholars. Only the officers of the Notgemeinschaft, an organisation actually composed of and directed by refugee scholars themselves, seemed to be more concerned with the welfare of the scholars than with its own public reputation or its rate of success in 'rescuing' the German tradition of science and learning.

The peculiar preoccupations of the aid directors and foundation officers did not occur in a vacuum, of course; they were refracted expressions of latent cultural anxieties in the host countries, filtered through the specific interests and constraints of the institutions to which they belonged. These officers had an urgent mission of world-historical importance – nothing less than rescuing a great, liberal university tradition from the backward, reactionary forces of fascism – but that did not preclude a petty short-sightedness that often characterised their decision-making. The cultural values of the host societies, here mainly the United States and the United Kingdom, as well as the system of prestige that governed university appointments, may be starkly revealed through an examination of the strategies, conflicts, preferences and prejudices that governed the grant-making activities in the early years of the refugee crisis. The personal circumstances of the refugee intellectuals were, in the minds of the aid officers, meant to be of secondary importance to the quality and import of their scholarship, but a central irony of this historical episode is that those very personal circumstances of the émigré scholars often conspired to make the quality of the émigrés' scholarship irrelevant insofar as their success in receiving a placement was concerned. The émigrés who managed to make it through this gauntlet were able to continue their work, and the legacy of their scholarship is ultimately the product of the conditions of their emigration.

The Working Relationships within and between the International Aid Organisations

The origins of the relationships between the refugee aid committees came through the sharing of lists of displaced scholars. By early May 1933, Murrow and Kotschnig, in their capacities at the IIE and the ISS, respectively, were already receiving dozens of requests from dismissed German professors who were desperately looking for teaching positions outside Germany. Alfred E. Cohn, a scientist at the Rockefeller Institute for Medical Research, heard about the IIE lists and contacted Duggan, an old acquaintance of his, about acquiring them. Simultaneously, concern for the fate of the dismissed German scholars and scientists had spread in the New York philanthropic community, and two prominent philanthropists, Bernard Flexner and Fred M. Stein, were directed to the IIE by Alan Gregg, the director of Medical Sciences at the Rockefeller Foundation. Shortly thereafter, Cohn, Duggan, Flexner and Stein formed an organising committee, which they called the 'Emergency Committee in Aid of Displaced German Scholars'. In a letter to university presidents on 27 May 1933, Duggan explained the crisis facing the German refugee scholars and announced the intentions of the Emergency Committee to assist them. Duggan assured the university presidents that, given the difficult financial conditions facing universities at that time, all funds to assist the displaced scholars would come from outside sources, mainly foundations and wealthy individuals. The Emergency Committee would distribute lists of displaced scholars to university presidents, who would then extend invitations to individual scholars to fill 'honorary' chairs for a limited term, typically two years, an arrangement designed to avoid arousing the resentment of native American scholars. The salaries of the displaced scholars would be paid for by the Committee, which would be chaired by Livingston Farrand, president of Cornell University. A General Committee of university representatives was assembled, but the real work was done by the Executive Committee, with Duggan serving officially as secretary (essentially, director) and Murrow as his chief assistant. Gregg became the 'unofficial representative' of the Rockefeller Foundation on the Committee.[21]

At the same time, Beveridge was spearheading the formation of the Academic Assistance Council in London, which was conceived as a fundraising entity, information centre and placement agency for the displaced professors and lecturers. The motivations and funding scheme were quite different from the beginning. Already in May, the Professorial Council of the LSE elected to start a fund for the displaced scholars by voluntarily cutting their own salaries by three percent. It was hoped that professors would follow suit at other universities in England and, indeed, in the US, where some prominent German-Jewish professors had already established a foothold, notably Albert Einstein at the recently founded Institute for Advanced Study in Princeton, which would become another centre for émigré scholars.[22] The AAC went public for funding right from the beginning with an appeal published in the press on 23 May. Fearful of arousing 'anti-Jewish propaganda', the AAC in its public statements was adamant that the crisis it was addressing was not simply a Jewish problem but rather a more general concern with the defence of 'learning and science' as a matter of principle. Moreover, it committed itself to assisting all scholars displaced for political or racial reasons, whatever their nationality.

The Royal Society offered to accommodate the AAC in its offices in London. At its first meeting on 1 June, Lord Rutherford of Nelson was elected president, while Beveridge would serve as secretary and Walter Adams was appointed general secretary. A panel of referees was formed to judge the qualifications of the refugee scholars, and all British universities were sent inquiries about possible openings for any of the roughly 750 dispossessed German scholars it was aware of at that time. The AAC considered placements not only in the UK but also in Palestine and in the greater British Empire, as well as in South America, Turkey and Russia. Upon approval by the specialist referees, an 'Allocation Committee' would make decisions on the recipients of year-long grants, while a 'Campaign Committee' would run a propaganda campaign to promote subscriptions. By the middle of June, representatives of the AAC had established regular correspondence with their counterparts on the Emergency Committee and had begun to arrange meetings. By August, the AAC had shared its detailed lists of displaced scholars and their academic qualifications with the Emergency Committee.[23]

Switzerland was an early destination for many of the refugee scholars. In Zurich, a group of exiled German professors coalesced in June under the leadership of Philipp Schwartz to form a 'self-help' organisation, which called itself the Notgemeinschaft deutscher Wissenschaftler im Ausland. The Notgemeinschaft immediately reached out for assistance to many groups, including the AAC, the American Jewish Physicians' Committee, and the Emergency Committee, with whom they had established a regular correspondence by July.[24] Another committee for the placement of the refugee scholars formed in May in Geneva, the Comité International pour le Placement des Intellectuels Émigrés, with correspondents in Paris, London and

Madrid. By September, the Comité had gathered a thousand dossiers of displaced scholars but was desperately seeking funds to maintain its activities. Notably, France was excluded as a potential destination for the émigré scholars because French law forbade foreigners from teaching regularly in French schools or institutions of higher learning.[25]

By August of 1933, the various committees had established working relationships, and the Emergency Committee had even appointed a Columbia University professor, E.W. Bagster-Collins, as its European representative, headquartered at the American University Union in London. It was Kotschnig, however, who would become the more important liaison for the Emergency Committee in Europe, when the following spring the Committee recommended him for a new position on the staff of the League of Nations' High Commission, which was concerned specifically with the placement of German refugees in the 'free' professions, including university teachers but also other professionals, civil servants and students. The Committee also pledged to support half of the budget for the activities of this new position, which Kotschnig would assume in April 1934. The following month, representing the High Commissioner, Kotschnig proposed the 'Committee of Experts', which would be the official body of coordination for the various national and international committees aiding the refugee scholars.[26]

The first three years of the refugee scholar crisis was the period of the most intense work and collaboration between the various committees. But by July 1936, the AAC would morph into a permanent organisation, the Society for the Protection of Science and Learning, and though its task became less urgent after the initial wave of refugee scholars, it continued its placement work much as it had done before. Around the same time, the High Commission shifted its focus from placement to legal problems, and Kotschnig resigned, emigrating to the US for an appointment as a professor of comparative education at Smith and Mount Holyoke colleges. The work of the Notgemeinschaft would diminish somewhat in the late 1930s, but it continued to play an important role in the creation and distribution of lists of displaced scholars. The activity of the Emergency Committee waxed and waned with successive waves of émigrés, but it remained in existence through to the end of the Second World War, by which time it could claim to have placed 288 refugee scholars. Altogether, Walter Adams later estimated that, by the end of the war, 624 refugee scholars had found either permanent or temporary appointments in the US; 612 in Britain; 74 in Commonwealth Countries; 80 in Central and South America; 66 in Palestine and 62 in other parts of the Middle East and smaller European countries. This was the remarkable and lasting contribution of the work of the placement committees, which they could point to with pride, as Duggan did in his 1948 book on the work of the Emergency Committee, *The Rescue of Science and Learning: The Story of the Emergency Committee in Aid of Displaced Foreign Scholars* ('German' was dropped for the more inclusive 'Foreign' after the '*Anschluss*' of 1938), which he wrote with his assistant Betty Drury, who had assumed Murrow's role in 1937 after the brief tenure of John Whyte. Among the scholars to receive grants or appointments through the Emergency Committee were major figures such as Paul Tillich, Kurt Lewin, Thomas Mann and several scholars of the Institute of Social Research, including Franz Neumann and Herbert Marcuse.[27]

The Grant and Placement Policies of the Aid Organisations

While the grant-making policies and placement efforts of the refugee scholar committees may fairly be measured by these ultimate success stories, the procedures by which the grants were made, and the decisions and exclusions that were necessarily a part of the process, given the limitations on funds and available positions, reveal a hierarchy of values and a complex of anxieties that was often at odds with the public pronouncements of the officers of the emergency committees. Perhaps most importantly, the deep and perhaps justified fear that the officers had in stoking an antisemitic or anti-foreign backlash produced a regime of decision-making that was foundationally contradictory: the insistence that the grants were for temporary appointments did not square with the demand for assurance from university presidents and deans that the placed scholars would ultimately be absorbed into a permanent position on the faculty. This policy confused and irritated many of the Emergency Committee's allies in the effort to place the refugee scholars, such as the Carnegie Corporation and the Rockefeller Foundation, and even some members of the Emergency Committee, who were sometimes compelled to violate the policy.[28] The officers of the committees had noble goals, but their occasionally neurotic policies of grant-making and sometimes contradictory justification for their decisions underscore that legitimate fears of an antisemitic, nativist backlash were always very near the surface.

The main financial supporter of the Emergency Committee was the Rockefeller Foundation, which, in addition to providing a great portion of the financing for the administrative operations of the Committee, matched many of its grants to refugees (usually $2,000 of a total annual grant of $4,000) and had, by the end of 1945, expended nearly 1.5 million dollars for the purpose of aiding some three hundred scholars. Another major funder of the Committee over the years was the Oberlaender Trust, which was founded to promote the contributions to American society by German immigrants and Americans of German descent. But essential to supporting the work of the Emergency Committee, particularly in its early years, were foundations with ties to the Jewish community, especially the New York Foundation, the Nathan Hofheimer Foundation, the American Jewish Joint Distribution Committee, and the Rosenwald Family Association. 'Because of the early exhibition of Nazi hatred of Jews, the first refugee scholars were of that race', Duggan explained in the Committee's 1941 annual report. 'Their coreligionists in the United States rallied to their assistance and the financial support of the Committee came at first exclusively from Jewish foundations and individuals.' This fact, however, had 'no effect' upon the Committee's decisions, according to Duggan, a point on which the Jewish members of the Executive Committee of the Emergency Committee were 'particularly insistent'. The fact that Jewish members were a minority on the Committee was also 'not without meaning', according to a memorandum from the Committee to the New York Foundation.[29]

There is no reason whatsoever to doubt Duggan's statement. At the same time, however, the grant-making policies of the Emergency Committee, as well as its public pronouncements and, to a lesser extent, those of the AAC, indicate that a fear of provoking a nativist or antisemitic backlash was a central motivating factor for the members of the Emergency Committee, whether or not it consciously figured into their decisions. In a letter to a rabbi, Committee member Fred Stein pointed out that the placement of 'eminent Jewish scholars' could be an inspiration and promote the ideal of academic freedom while fighting antisemitism but that it had to be done 'very tactfully' so as not to arouse resentment among unemployed or precariously employed academics, and that this was the logic behind the limited, two-year appointments.[30] The Committee acknowledged the deleterious effect that the depression had had on the budgets of universities, which had already resulted in salary cuts and even dismissals, particularly of younger scholars. For this reason, it was especially important that 'foreigners' were not put in the 'invidious position' of appearing to compete with native scholars. The Committee preferred middle-aged scholars who had already 'made their mark' and to whom few would object to because of their 'eminence' in their field. The Committee members typically declined to place younger scholars in the US, and encouraged them to seek positions in other countries, partly because they had not proven themselves as scholars but also because they would be more likely to arouse nativist resentment in the competition for scarce university positions.[31]

The Emergency Committee's policy of insisting on invitations to individuals from university presidents and deans on the basis of distributed lists of available scholars – a procedure not strictly followed by the AAC – was also an indication of its nervousness about its own role in placing the scholars. While the Notgemeinschaft, for example, had been successful in negotiating the placement of dozens of scholars at the University of Istanbul, this was a course of action that the Emergency Committee would have refused. Such concentrations, moreover, would violate the Committee's desire to spread the refugee scholars around geographically to avoid the resentment that might arise from a large group of Jewish émigré scholars, particularly in places were antisemitism was thought to be prevalent, such as the South. The Emergency Committee was so strict on its policy of avoiding the direct orchestration of appointments, even of individuals, that it only 'occasionally' came into contact with a German professor himself. When the AAC successor organisation and the Oberlaender Trust organised tours of refugee scholars in the US, the members of the Emergency Committee strongly objected, again fearful about provoking resentment.[32]

When, in January of 1935, the Emergency Committee elected to continue its existence for another two years, until at least 30 June 1937, it simultaneously voted to make its first obligation the *renewal* of grants to those institutions who desired to retain their German scholars, and for this to take precedence over any new applications. The Rockefeller Foundation followed a similar course. Despite the fact that the Committee had insisted that its grants were for *temporary* positions, it wanted to continue to support its grantees until they could be permanently absorbed, which it considered to be a measure of its success. As for those scholars whose host institutions no longer wanted to maintain them, there was no possibility of insuring their 'academic usefulness', and their cases, while pitiable, no longer fell within the province of the Emergency Committee. Cohn, in particular, could be quite blunt in private correspondence; in a letter to Adams, he noted that the need for 'sifting' was urgent, and that only the most 'prominent and gifted' would be selected. 'About the rest and their fate', he concluded, 'we have no plan, as yet'.[33] By the spring of 1939, Duggan had observed a growing resentment at the employment of foreigners, and he reported that many professors felt that the 'saturation point' had been reached.[34]

Conclusion

Despite the loftiness of the international aid officers' mission to preserve a tradition of science and learning, the decisions they made in the successful placement of hundreds of scholars forced from their positions by the Nazi regime were often coloured by persistent fears of stoking feelings of nativism and antisemitism among native university professors and teachers in the receiving countries. The latent fears expressed themselves in contradictory and confusing placement policies, such as the insistence that placements were temporary coupled with a request of assurance from university presidents that there was a reasonable chance that the positions of the exiled scholars would eventually be made permanent. At the same time, the Emergency Committee preferred to 'maintain' its existing grantees rather than take on new cases. Although the Emergency Committee received substantial support from Jewish foundations, it insisted that its project was not about assisting Jewish scholars but rather about salvaging the learning accumulated in the minds of all persecuted scholars, regardless of race or religion. The members of the Emergency Committee also objected to reasonable initiatives of their allies among the international aid organisations, such as the AAC's public appeals for subscriptions. Despite the AAC's publicised insistence that its efforts were about saving scholarship and not specifically about the 'Jewish problem', members of the Emergency Committee objected to the practice based on the idea that such publicity could provoke antisemitism and 'anti-foreignism'. In the fall of 1933, Duggan had expressed astonishment at the baseness of some non-Jewish German scholars' undisguised pleasure upon being relieved from competition with their dismissed Jewish colleagues, but his disbelief would belie an unsavoury analogue in the American academic context.

The aid officers' often-expressed anxieties indicated a latent sense that an extremely delicate approach was required so that academicians' high-minded commitment to liberal values would not come into open conflict with a more basic desire to maintain their professional status and job security. One strategy pursued by the international aid agencies was the geographical dispersion of refugee scholars, facilitated by the sharing and maintenance of lists of displaced scholars and coordinated through the Committee of Experts. The Emergency Committee also insisted on invitations to specific scholars from the various universities themselves, which is why the maintenance and distribution of the lists was such a central project. An alternative to the dispersion paradigm was presented in Alvin Johnson's model of concentrating the émigrés in a single faculty at the New School. Although there was no reason the two models could not exist side by side, the competing visions became a source of conflict between Johnson and the officers of the Emergency Committee, who ought to have been allies. Only the refugee scholars' own self-help organisation, the Notgemeinschaft, sought to serve all its members, young and old, as a humanitarian endeavour relatively untroubled by the problem of disturbing the professional equilibrium of the host nations.

Notes

1. Stephen Duggan to Prof. Bagster-Collins, 19 October 1933.
2. 'An International Appeal on behalf of Displaced German Scholars', statement of the Office of the High Commissioner for Refugees (Jewish and Other) Coming from Germany, Geneva, 2 April, 1935; Krohn, *Intellectuals in Exile*, 11–12; Ash and Söllner, 'Introduction', 1–19.
3. Duggan and Drury, *The Rescue of Science and Learning*, 3.

4. Quoted in Ash and Söllner, 'Introduction', 3.
5. See Bessner, 'Rather More than One-Third Had No Jewish Blood'.
6. Krohn, *Intellectuals*, 60–61.
7. Fleck, *Transatlantic History*, 42.
8. Kotschnig, *Slaves Need No Leaders*, 165–66.
9. 'A Crisis in the Western Universities', 26 February 1936.
10. See, for example, Fermi, *Illustrious Immigrants*; Fleming and Bailyn, *The Intellectual Migration*; Hughes, *The Sea Change*.
11. See Palmier, *Weimar in Exile*.
12. See, for example, Ash and Söllner, *Forced Migration*; Kettler and Lauer, *Exile, Science, and Bildung*; Krohn et al., *Handbuch der deutschsprachigen Emigration*; Fleck, *Transatlantic History*. On the role of foundations in supporting the émigrés, see Gemelli, *The 'Unacceptables'*.
13. The major works on the Institute of Social Research include Jay, *The Dialectical Imagination*; Wiggershaus, *The Frankfurt School*; and Wheatland, *The Frankfurt School in Exile*. On the New School, see Krohn, *Intellectuals* and Friedlander, *A Light in Dark Times*.
14. See, for example, Burgin, *The Great Persuasion*; Greenberg, *The Weimar Century*; and Bessner, *Democracy in Exile*.
15. Fleck, *Transatlantic History*, 89–92.
16. Lamberti, 'The Reception of Refugee Scholars', 166, 183.
17. Stephen Duggan to Wesley C. Mitchell, 16 May 1935.
18. Stephen Duggan to Gilbert Murray, 6 June 1933.
19. Diana Rice, 'Exiles Aid Study Here'; E.R. Murrow to Alfred E. Cohn, 28 May 1934; Alfred E. Cohn to Alvin Johnson, 12 June 1934; Alvin Johnson, letter to the Editor of the *New York Times* [MS], 14 June 1934.
20. Edward R. Murrow to Walter Adams, 18 May 1935.
21. Edward R. Murrow to Walter Kotschnig, 9 May 1933; Alfred E. Cohn to Stephen Duggan, 19 May 1933; Duggan and Drury, *Rescue*, 6–7; 174–78; Edward R. Murrow to Max Mason, 30 June 1933.
22. Palmier, *Weimar in Exile*, 553.
23. Leo Szilard to Professor G. Breit, n.d., ca. 1933; 'Report of Special Meeting of Professorial Council Held on 17th May, 1933, The London School of Economics and Political Science (University of London)'; R.A. Lambert to Alan Gregg, 20 May 1933; 'Academic Assistance Council' [pamphlet], 22 May 1933; 'British to Aid German Teachers'; J. McKeen Cattell to Stephen Duggan, 6 June 1933; E.R. Murrow to Dr. J.M. Cattell, 19 June 1933; William Beveridge to Stephen Duggan, 19 June 1933; Walter Adams, 'Report on Progress', 1 August 1933; '(To be communicated to the press after the meeting of the Executive, August 1st, 1933)', folder 1, box 159; Walter Adams to Stephen Duggan, 4 August 1933.
24. Edgar Meyer to Herrn Professor Dr. Jones, 16 June 1933; Philipp Schwartz, R. Goldstein, and Max Born to American Jewish Physicians' Committee, 22 June 1933; Philipp Schwartz to Stephen Duggan, 2 July 1933; Edward R. Murrow to Monroe C. Deutsch, 9 September 1933.
25. 'International Committee for Securing Employment to Refugee Professional Workers', 23 May 1933; Marie Ginsberg to Mary L. Waite, 16 August 1933; 'Rapport sur l'activité du Comité international pour le Placement des Intellectuels Emigrés pendant les mois de juin, juillet et août 1933', 1 September 1933; Horation S. Krans to Stephen Duggan, 9 December 1933.
26. E.R. Murrow to Professor Max Born, 16 August 1933; E.R. Murrow to Walter Adams, 16 August 1933; E.R. Murrow to Professor E.W. Bagster-Collins, 12 April 1934; Walter Kotschnig to Edward R. Murrow, 19 April 1934; Walter Kotschnig to Emergency Committee for Displaced German Scholars, 16 May 1934.
27. Walter Adams to John Whyte, 26 February 1936; Walter Kotschnig to George Johnson, 16 June 1936; Walter Kotschnig to W.P. Shofstall, 22 June 1936; Walter Kotschnig to

Alfred Cohn, 14 July 1936; 'Walter M. Kotschnig: Biographical Notes', n.d., ca. 1937; Duggan and Drury, *Rescue*, 76; Walter Adams, 'The Refugee Scholars of the 1930s', 10; Duggan and Drury, 178.

28. Edward R. Murrow to Walter Adams, 20 April 1935; John Whyte, 'Minutes of the Meeting of the Executive Committee of the Emergency Committee in Aid of Displaced German Scholars', 4 February 1936; John Whyte to Walter Kotschnig, 19 May 1936; John Whyte to Stephen Duggan, 10 June 1936.

29. Edward R. Murrow to Alfred E. Cohen, 16 October 1934; Stephan Duggan, 'Annual Report: The Emergency Committee in aid of Displaced Foreign Scholars', 1 June 1941; Duggan and Drury, *Rescue*, 78–79, 86; 'Memorandum on the Emergency Committee in Aid of Displaced German Scholars for The New York Foundation', n.d.

30. Fred Stein to Rabbi William G. Braude, 5 October 1933.

31. 'Memorandum on the Emergency Committee in Aid of Displaced German Scholars for The New York Foundation', n.d.; Stephen Duggan to Gilbert Murray, 6 June 1933; Stephen Duggan, letter to Frederick P. Keppel, 15 April 1939.

32. Edward R. Murrow to Dr. Demuth, 10 November 1933; Alfred Cohn to Stephen Duggan, 20 February 1934; E.R. Murrow to A.J. Farsky, 24 October 1934; Betty Drury 'Informal Minutes of Luncheon Conference of Representatives of the Oberlaender Trust, The Rockefeller Foundation, The Carnegie Corporation, The John Simon Guggenheim Memorial Foundation, and the Emergency Committee in Aid of Displaced Foreign Scholars', 28 April 1939; Betty Drury, 'Minutes of the Luncheon Meeting of the Executive Committee of the Emergency Committee in Aid of Displaced Foreign Scholars', 9 May 1939; Betty Drury, 'Minutes of the Meeting of the Executive Committee of the Emergency Committee in Aid of Displaced Foreign Scholars', 9 October 1939.

33. 'Minutes of the Meeting of the Executive Committee of the Emergency Committee in Aid of Displaced German Scholars', 23 January 1935; Alfred E. Cohn to Walter Adams, 25 January 1935; Alfred E. Cohn to Walter Adams, 8 March 1935; John Whyte, 'Report of the Emergency Committee in Aid of Displaced German Scholars', [pamphlet] 1 March 1936; John Whyte 'Minutes of the Meeting of the Executive Committee of the Emergency Committee in Aid of Displaced German Scholars', 26 March 1936.

34. Stephen Duggan to Frederick P. Keppel, 15 April 1939.

Bibliography

Adams, Walter. 'The Refugee Scholars of the 1930s'. *The Political Quarterly* 39(1) (1968), 7–14.
Ash, Mitchell G., and Alfons Söllner. 'Introduction: Forced Migration and Scientific Change after 1933', in Mitchell G. Ash and Alfons Söllner (eds), *Forced Migration and Scientific Change: Emigré German-Speaking Scientists and Scholars after 1933* (Washington, D.C.: German Historical Institute; Cambridge, England: Cambridge University Press, 1996), 1–19.
Bessner, Daniel. *Democracy in Exile: Hans Speier and the Rise of the Defense Intellectual*. Ithaca: Cornell University Press, 2018.
———. '"Rather More than One-Third Had No Jewish Blood": American Progressivism and German-Jewish Cosmopolitanism at the New School for Social Research, 1933–1939'. *Religions* 3 (2012), 99–129.
'British to Aid German Teachers'. *New York Times*, 24 May 1933.
Burgin, Angus. *The Great Persuasion: Reinventing Free Markets since the Depression*. Cambridge: Harvard University Press, 2012.
Duggan, Stephen, and Betty Drury. *The Rescue of Science and Learning: The Story of the Emergency Committee in Aid of Displaced Foreign Scholars*. New York: The Macmillan Company, 1948.

Fermi, Laura. *Illustrious Immigrants: The Intellectual Migration from Europe, 1930–41*. Chicago: University of Chicago Press, 1968.
Fleck, Christian. *A Transatlantic History of the Social Sciences: Robber Barons, the Third Reich and the Invention of Empirical Social Research*, trans. Hella Beister. London: Bloomsbury Academic, 2011.
Fleming, Donald, and Bernard Bailyn (eds). *The Intellectual Migration: Europe and America, 1930–1960*. Cambridge, MA: Harvard University Press, 1969.
Friedlander, Judith. *A Light in Dark Times: The New School for Social Research and Its University in Exile*. New York: Columbia University Press, 2019.
Gemelli, Giuliana (ed.). *The 'Unacceptables': American Foundations and Refugee Scholars between the Two Wars and after*. Brussels: P.I.E.-Peter Lang, 2000.
Greenberg, Udi. *The Weimar Century: German Émigrés and the Ideological Foundations of the Cold War*. Princeton: Princeton University Press, 2014.
Hughes, H. Stuart. *The Sea Change: The Migration of Social Thought, 1930–1965*. New York: Harper & Row, 1975.
Jay, Martin. *The Dialectical Imagination: A History of the Frankfurt School and the Institute of Social Research*. Boston: Little, Brown and Company, 1973.
Kettler, David, and Gerhard Lauer (eds). *Exile, Science, and Bildung: The Contested Legacies of German Emigre Intellectuals*. New York: Palgrave Macmillan, 2005.
Kotschnig, Walter M. *Slaves Need No Leaders: An Answer to the Fascist Challenge to Education*. New York: Oxford University Press, 1943.
Krohn, Claus-Dieter. *Intellectuals in Exile: Refugee Scholars and the New School for Social Research*, trans. Rita and Robert Kimber. Amherst: University of Massachusetts Press, 1993.
Krohn, Claus-Dieter et al. (eds). *Handbuch der deutschsprachigen Emigration, 1933–1945*. Darmstadt: Primus, 1998.
Lamberti, Marjorie. 'The Reception of Refugee Scholars from Nazi Germany in America: Philanthropy and Social Change in Higher Education'. *Jewish Social Studies* 12 (Spring 2006), 157–92.
Palmier, Jean-Michel. *Weimar in Exile: The Antifascist Emigration in Europe and America*, trans. David Fernbach. New York: Verso, 2006 [original 1987].
Rice, Diana. 'Exiles Aid Study Here; German Scholars Placed on American Campuses Through Two Plans'. *New York Times*, 27 May 1934.
Wheatland, Thomas. *The Frankfurt School in Exile*. Minneapolis: University of Minnesota Press, 2009.
Wiggershaus, Rolf. *The Frankfurt School: Its History, Theories, and Political Significance*, trans. Michael Robertson. Cambridge, MA: Polity Press, 1994.

Archival Sources

'A Crisis in the Western Universities', 26 February 1936, folder 9, box 159, Emergency Committee in Aid of Displaced Foreign Scholars Records, Manuscripts and Archives Division, New York Public Library.
'Academic Assistance Council' [pamphlet], 22 May 1933, folder 1, box 159, Emergency Committee in Aid of Displaced Foreign Scholars Records, Manuscripts and Archives Division, New York Public Library.
'An International Appeal on behalf of Displaced German Scholars', statement of the Office of the High Commissioner for Refugees (Jewish and Other) Coming from Germany, Geneva, 2 April 1935, folder 8, box 4, Alfred E. Cohn Papers, Rockefeller Archive Center, Sleepy Hollow, New York.
'International Committee for Securing Employment to Refugee Professional Workers', 23 May 1933, folder 17, box 163, Emergency Committee in Aid of Displaced Foreign Scholars Records, Manuscripts and Archives Division, New York Public Library.

'Memorandum on the Emergency Committee in Aid of Displaced German Scholars for The New York Foundation', n.d., folder 2, box 172, Emergency Committee in Aid of Displaced Foreign Scholars Records, Manuscripts and Archives Division, New York Public Library.

'Minutes of the Meeting of the Executive Committee of the Emergency Committee in Aid of Displaced German Scholars', 23 January 1935, folder 19, box 6, Alfred E. Cohn Papers.

'Rapport sur l'activité du Comité international pour le Placement des Intellectuels Emigrés pendant les mois de juin, juillet et août 1933', 1 September 1933, folder 17, box 163, Emergency Committee in Aid of Displaced Foreign Scholars Records, Manuscripts and Archives Division, New York Public Library.

'Report of Special Meeting of Professorial Council Held on 17th May 1933, The London School of Economics and Political Science (University of London)', folder 1, box 159, Emergency Committee in Aid of Displaced Foreign Scholars Records, Manuscripts and Archives Division, New York Public Library.

'(To be communicated to the press after the meeting of the Executive, August 1st 1933)', folder 1, box 159, Emergency Committee in Aid of Displaced Foreign Scholars Records, Manuscripts and Archives Division, New York Public Library.

'Walter M. Kotschnig: Biographical Notes', n.d., ca. 1937, folder 9, box 180, Emergency Committee in Aid of Displaced Foreign Scholars Records, Manuscripts and Archives Division, New York Public Library.

Alfred E. Cohn to Alvin Johnson, 12 June 1934, folder 2, box 148, Emergency Committee in Aid of Displaced Foreign Scholars Records, Manuscripts and Archives Division, New York Public Library.

Alfred E. Cohn to Stephen Duggan, 19 May 1933, folder 21, box 4, Alfred E. Cohn Papers.

Alfred Cohn to Stephen Duggan, 20 February 1934, folder 2, box 159, Emergency Committee in Aid of Displaced Foreign Scholars Records, Manuscripts and Archives Division, New York Public Library.

Alfred E. Cohn to Walter Adams, 25 January 1935, folder 5, box 159, Emergency Committee in Aid of Displaced Foreign Scholars Records, Manuscripts and Archives Division, New York Public Library.

Alfred E. Cohn to Walter Adams, 8 March 1935, folder 6, box 159, Emergency Committee in Aid of Displaced Foreign Scholars Records, Manuscripts and Archives Division, New York Public Library.

Alvin Johnson, letter to the Editor of the New York Times, 14 June 1934, folder 3, box 4, Alfred E. Cohn Papers.

Betty Drury, 'Informal Minutes of Luncheon Conference of Representatives of the Oberlaender Trust, The Rockefeller Foundation, The Carnegie Corporation, The John Simon Guggenheim Memorial Foundation, and the Emergency Committee in Aid of Displaced Foreign Scholars', 28 April 1939, folder 22, box 6, Alfred E. Cohn Papers.

Betty Drury, 'Minutes of the Luncheon Meeting of the Executive Committee of the Emergency Committee in Aid of Displaced Foreign Scholars', 9 May 1939, folder 22, box 6, Alfred E. Cohn Papers.

Betty Drury, 'Minutes of the Meeting of the Executive Committee of the Emergency Committee in Aid of Displaced Foreign Scholars', 9 October 1939, folder 23, box 6, Alfred E. Cohn Papers.

E.R. Murrow to Alfred E. Cohn, 28 May 1934, folder 3, box 4, Alfred E. Cohn Papers.

E.R. Murrow to A.J. Farsky, 24 October 1934, folder 2, box 148, Emergency Committee in Aid of Displaced Foreign Scholars Records, Manuscripts and Archives Division, New York Public Library.

E.R. Murrow to Dr. J.M. Cattell, 19 June 1933, folder 1, box 159, Emergency Committee in Aid of Displaced Foreign Scholars Records, Manuscripts and Archives Division, New York Public Library.

E.R. Murrow to Professor E.W. Bagster-Collins, 12 April 1934, folder 6, box 169, Emergency Committee in Aid of Displaced Foreign Scholars Records, Manuscripts and Archives Division, New York Public Library.

E.R. Murrow to Professor Max Born, 16 August 1933, folder 5, box 169, Emergency Committee in Aid of Displaced Foreign Scholars Records, Manuscripts and Archives Division, New York Public Library.

E.R. Murrow to Walter Adams, 16 August 1933, folder 1, box 159, Emergency Committee in Aid of Displaced Foreign Scholars Records, Manuscripts and Archives Division, New York Public Library.

Edgar Meyer to Herrn Professor Dr. Jones, 16 June 1933, folder 5, box 169, Emergency Committee in Aid of Displaced Foreign Scholars Records, Manuscripts and Archives Division, New York Public Library.

Edward R. Murrow to Dr. Demuth, 10 November 1933, folder 5, box 169, Emergency Committee in Aid of Displaced Foreign Scholars Records, Manuscripts and Archives Division, New York Public Library.

Edward R. Murrow to Karl Vogt, 15 February 1934, folder 2, box 148, Emergency Committee in Aid of Displaced Foreign Scholars Records, Manuscripts and Archives Division, New York Public Library.

Edward R. Murrow, letter to Max Mason, 30 June 1933, folder 4, box 172, Emergency Committee in Aid of Displaced Foreign Scholars Records, Manuscripts and Archives Division, New York Public Library.

Edward R. Murrow, memorandum to Alfred E. Cohen, 16 October 1934, folder 4, box 4, Alfred E. Cohn Papers.

Edward R. Murrow to Monroe C. Deutsch, 9 September 1933, folder 5, box 169, Emergency Committee in Aid of Displaced Foreign Scholars Records, Manuscripts and Archives Division, New York Public Library.

Edward R. Murrow to Walter Adams, 20 April 1935, folder 6, box 159, Emergency Committee in Aid of Displaced Foreign Scholars Records, Manuscripts and Archives Division, New York Public Library.

Edward R. Murrow to Walter Adams, 18 May 1935, folder 7, box 159, Emergency Committee in Aid of Displaced Foreign Scholars Records, Manuscripts and Archives Division, New York Public Library.

Edward R. Murrow to Walter Kotschnig, 9 May 1933, Reel 9-HF, Series 3, Institute of International Education Records, Rockefeller Archive Center, Sleepy Hollow, New York.

Fred Stein, letter to Rabbi William G. Braude, 5 October 1933, folder 23, box 138, Emergency Committee in Aid of Displaced Foreign Scholars Records, Manuscripts and Archives Division, New York Public Library.

Horation S. Krans to Stephen Duggan, 9 December 1933, folder 17, box 163, Emergency Committee in Aid of Displaced Foreign Scholars Records, Manuscripts and Archives Division, New York Public Library.

J. McKeen Cattell to Stephen Duggan, 6 June 1933, folder 1, box 159, Emergency Committee in Aid of Displaced Foreign Scholars Records, Manuscripts and Archives Division, New York Public Library.

John Whyte, 'Minutes of the Meeting of the Executive Committee of the Emergency Committee in Aid of Displaced German Scholars', 4 February 1936, folder 20, box 6, Alfred E. Cohn Papers

John Whyte, 'Minutes of the Meeting of the Executive Committee of the Emergency Committee in Aid of Displaced German Scholars', 26 March 1936, folder 20, box 6, Alfred E. Cohn Papers.

John Whyte, 'Report of the Emergency Committee in Aid of Displaced German Scholars', [pamphlet] 1 March 1936, folder 13, box 5, Alfred E. Cohn Papers.

John Whyte to Stephen Duggan, 10 June 1936, folder 2, box 173, Emergency Committee in Aid of Displaced Foreign Scholars Records, Manuscripts and Archives Division, New York Public Library.
John Whyte to Walter Kotschnig, 19 May 1936, folder 7, box 180, Emergency Committee in Aid of Displaced Foreign Scholars Records, Manuscripts and Archives Division, New York Public Library.
Leo Szilard to Professor G. Breit, n.d., ca. 1933, folder 1, box 159, Emergency Committee in Aid of Displaced Foreign Scholars Records, Manuscripts and Archives Division, New York Public Library.
Marie Ginsberg to Mary L. Waite, 16 August 1933, folder 17, box 163, Emergency Committee in Aid of Displaced Foreign Scholars Records, Manuscripts and Archives Division, New York Public Library.
Philipp Schwartz, R. Goldstein, and Max Born to American Jewish Physicians' Committee, 22 June 1933, folder 5, box 169, Emergency Committee in Aid of Displaced Foreign Scholars Records, Manuscripts and Archives Division, New York Public Library.
Philipp Schwartz to Stephen Duggan, 2 July 1933, folder 5, box 169, Emergency Committee in Aid of Displaced Foreign Scholars Records, Manuscripts and Archives Division, New York Public Library.
R.A. Lambert to Alan Gregg, 20 May 1933, folder 1, box 159, Emergency Committee in Aid of Displaced Foreign Scholars Records, Manuscripts and Archives Division, New York Public Library.
Stephan Duggan, 'Annual Report: The Emergency Committee in aid of Displaced Foreign Scholars', 1 June 1941, folder 11, box 4, Alfred E. Cohn Papers.
Stephen Duggan, letter to Frederick P. Keppel, 15 April 1939, folder 29, box 4, Alfred E. Cohn Papers.
Stephen Duggan to Gilbert Murray, 6 June 1933, folder 1, box 159, Emergency Committee in Aid of Displaced Foreign Scholars Records, Manuscripts and Archives Division, New York Public Library.
Stephen Duggan to Prof. Bagster-Collins, 19 October 1933, folder 23, box 138, Emergency Committee in Aid of Displaced Foreign Scholars Records, Manuscripts and Archives Division, New York Public Library.
Stephen Duggan to Wesley C. Mitchell, 16 May 1935, folder 1, box 173, Emergency Committee in Aid of Displaced Foreign Scholars Records, Manuscripts and Archives Division, New York Public Library.
Walter Adams, 'Report on Progress', 1 August 1933, folder 1, box 159, Emergency Committee in Aid of Displaced Foreign Scholars Records, Manuscripts and Archives Division, New York Public Library.
Walter Adams to John Whyte, 26 February 1936, folder 9, box 159, Emergency Committee in Aid of Displaced Foreign Scholars Records, Manuscripts and Archives Division, New York Public Library.
Walter Adams to Stephen Duggan, 4 August 1933, folder 1, box 159, Emergency Committee in Aid of Displaced Foreign Scholars Records, Manuscripts and Archives Division, New York Public Library.
Walter Kotschnig to Alfred Cohn, 14 July 1936, folder 8, box 180, Emergency Committee in Aid of Displaced Foreign Scholars Records, Manuscripts and Archives Division, New York Public Library.
Walter Kotschnig to Edward R. Murrow, 19 April 1934, folder 2, box 159, Emergency Committee in Aid of Displaced Foreign Scholars Records, Manuscripts and Archives Division, New York Public Library.
Walter Kotschnig to Emergency Committee for Displaced German Scholars, 16 May 1934, folder 6, box 169, Emergency Committee in Aid of Displaced Foreign Scholars Records, Manuscripts and Archives Division, New York Public Library.

Walter Kotschnig to George Johnson, 16 June 1936, folder 8, box 180, Emergency Committee in Aid of Displaced Foreign Scholars Records, Manuscripts and Archives Division, New York Public Library.

Walter Kotschnig to W.P. Shofstall, 22 June 1936, folder 8, box 180, Emergency Committee in Aid of Displaced Foreign Scholars Records, Manuscripts and Archives Division, New York Public Library.

William Beveridge to Stephen Duggan, 19 June 1933, folder 1, box 159, Emergency Committee in Aid of Displaced Foreign Scholars Records, Manuscripts and Archives Division, New York Public Library.

CHAPTER 5

Defending Objectivity

Paul Oskar Kristeller and the Controversy over Historical Knowledge in the United States

Iryna Mykhailova

Introduction

Paul Oskar Kristeller was one of the most important scholars of the Renaissance in the twentieth century. His numerous contributions to the study of Italian humanism and philosophy substantially changed the landscape of Renaissance studies in Europe and North America.[1] Kristeller belonged to the generation of German-Jewish exiled intellectuals who escaped Germany due to the Nazi persecution in the 1930s. In the United States, where he immigrated in February 1939, Kristeller built an outstanding academic career and, along with Hans Baron, Felix Gilbert, Erwin Panofsky, and other German émigré scholars, significantly promoted the image of Renaissance as an independent historical epoch in the American scholarly circles. Besides extraordinary erudition and excellent university training, Kristeller possessed impressive productivity that altogether resulted in his professional success.[2] A question of whether Kristeller's traumatic exile experience influenced his scholarship can hardly be answered unambiguously. As a philosopher and practising historian, Kristeller argued for minimising the element of subjectivity in historical scholarship and strictly followed this rule. He was sceptical about the desire of his contemporaries, particularly political historians, to formulate 'psychological explanations' of historical phenomena unless such explanations were based on verified biographical documents.[3] Kristeller him-

---

Notes for this section begin on page 104.

self has left rich autobiographical material, which includes notes of different periods, an extensive oral history memoir and numerous correspondences. These sources reconstruct in detail all the challenges the promising German scholar encountered while relocating to another continent and adapting to the alien American academic culture. One of these challenges was uncongenial to Kristeller: the American intellectual climate, which manifested itself, particularly, in the domination of analytic philosophy and dissemination of historical relativism.[4] Kristeller, whose philosophical 'universe focused on Plato and Kant',[5] cultivated an approach to philosophy and history that he developed in Germany in the 1920s while studying with prominent philosophers of his time, among whom were Martin Heidegger, Karl Jaspers and Heinrich Rickert. In a brief autobiographical note written for the Leo Baeck Institute in New York in 1998, shortly before his death, Kristeller recollected Heidegger's seminar[6] at Marburg, which he attended in 1926: 'He [Heidegger] had . . . praised me for having formulated my own original theory of history which was superior to the conventional one (and which I practised ever since in my work in America).'[7] Not only did Kristeller not abandon his 'original theory of history' after the emigration, but from the 1940s onwards, he also became a relentless critic of any attempts of analytic philosophers to interfere in the matters of history, and he fought mercilessly against all forms of historical relativism. I argue that emigration to the United States did not cause a methodological shift in Kristeller's approach to philosophy and history but rather strengthened his belief in the correctness of his methods of historical research. Through the debates on historical knowledge with American philosophers and historians, Kristeller continued to advocate and transmit the ideals of German philosophical and historical scholarship, viewing the 'German method' as a reliable instrument to attain historical truth. I shall start from a brief outline of Kristeller's emigration as well as his general perception of American academic culture and the philosophical trends then prevailing in the country. I shall then proceed to Kristeller's critique of the American analytic philosophy of history from the Neo-Kantian positions and simultaneously expound his view on historical objectivity and the actual method of historical research. Finally, I will briefly refer to Kristeller's judgment on historical relativism as well as the relationship between scholarship and politics.

Kristeller's Emigration and American Philosophical Community in the 1940s

Paul Oskar Kristeller was born in Berlin in 1905 to a middle class non-orthodox Jewish family. From 1923 to 1928, he studied philosophy,[8] history and classical philology at the universities of Heidelberg, Marburg, Freiburg and Berlin. In 1928, Kristeller obtained a doctorate in philosophy, with the dissertation on Plotinus, under supervision of a scholar of Platonism, Ernst Hoffmann at Heidelberg. In 1931, Kristeller started the 'Habilitationsschrift' on Renaissance Neo-Platonist philosopher Marsilio Ficino for Martin Heidegger at Freiburg University, but due to the Nazi rise to power, he had to interrupt this project and leave Germany. In 1934, Kristeller moved to Italy, where he developed essential skills of manuscript research and established numerous professional contacts with Italian intellectuals, who actively supported his study of Renaissance humanism. Unfortunately, even Kristeller's most powerful patron, Giovanni Gentile, was unable to secure his position in Italy when racial laws were adopted in 1938. In February 1939, Kristeller had to go into exile for a second time and settle in the United States, where he lived and worked for the rest of his life.

Recollecting his first years in America, Kristeller remarked: 'when people came to this country they had to have either a bankbook or an address book. I didn't have a bankbook but I had an address book.'[9] As someone who experienced double exile and went through years of uncertainty, Kristeller knew the real price of the 'address book', which twice turned out to be instrumental in his rescue. He was invited to the United States by Roland H. Bainton, an American church historian, to teach a seminar on Plotinus at Yale for one semester. Despite Kristeller having not yet gained proficiency in English, he quickly resumed scholarly activities and expanded his network of professional and personal contacts. Besides the obligatory seminar, Kristeller intensively worked on publications[10] and travelled across the country to give lectures, including at Harvard, Princeton and Columbia, as 'the whole academic system [in the United States] was different . . . your career depended very much on personal contacts and on local decisions, there was nothing like the corporate procedure in Germany or the national competition in Italy.'[11] Herbert Schneider, a chairman in the Columbia Department of Philosophy, attended Kristeller's lecture at the meeting of the American Society for Church History and later offered Kristeller a position in the Department as an Associate in Philosophy. The offer was accepted, but it took nine years before Kristeller was tenured, in 1948. His institutional affiliation with Columbia lasted for almost sixty years.

Kristeller first encountered the 'cool' attitude of the American philosophers to his field of research, history of Renaissance philosophy, at Yale. Wilmon Henry Sheldon (1875–1981), a major exponent of the process philosophy school, once indifferently told Kristeller: 'Well, we are not interested here in the kind of things you are doing.'[12] Not only did Renaissance philosophy not occupy a significant place in the curricula of the American universities at that time, but the history of philosophy itself was also viewed by the majority of philosophers as an old-fashioned practice. Kristeller, however, was lucky enough to restart his career specifically at Columbia, which, at least in the 1940s, was still 'a bastion of the history of philosophy'.[13] Unwillingness to leave this 'bastion' was the main reason why Kristeller declined a financially attractive offer from the History Department at Harvard in 1964. For him, it was 'a matter of principle', since Harvard

> for years had turned its back on the history of philosophy, and in a sense I would have felt that I betrayed the ranks of the historians of philosophy by turning to a history department and thus even seeming to approve the idea that the history of philosophy is the business of historians rather than of philosophers, which is against my basic convictions.[14]

At the Columbia Department of Philosophy, Kristeller's work was generally well accepted, but it was especially welcomed by historians of philosophy, who constituted the apparent minority there. Such a misbalance between the history of philosophy and analytic philosophy was a consequence of the Department's consistent policy directed toward the strengthening of the analytic philosophy segment. Kristeller disappointedly admitted that such a policy blocked the appointments of scholars with specialisations other than those in fashionable philosophical trends. Moreover, analytic philosophers viewed the history of philosophy as an outdated metaphysics or even a 'collection of errors'.[15] It resulted in the history of philosophy having a lower disciplinary status within the structure of philosophical knowledge in the United States than it had in Europe. Kristeller, on the contrary, argued for the educational and heuristic value of his discipline and, though he supported friendly relationships with many of his colleagues-analytic philosophers, he openly characterised their approach as one-sided and dogmatic.[16] Analytic philosophy also prevailed in the American Philosophical Association, which Kristeller joined soon after emigration. He was never active in this organisation; as he explained it, its philosophical agenda was not interesting to him, and eventually he started to feel 'alienated' from it.[17] After 1968, his detachment from the Association significantly strengthened, as it started to pass political resolutions, which he did not support.[18]

Historian of Philosophy against Philosopher of History: Kristeller's Critique of Carl Hempel

In the 1930s, analytic philosophy occupied the leading positions in the United States and was mainly represented by the schools of logical positivism (logical empiricism) and linguistic philosophy.[19] Pragmatism was another extremely influential philosophical school, which Kristeller, though he was introduced to John Dewey at Columbia, did not accept. What these schools had in common is that they were, in Kristeller's words, 'antihistorical'.[20] From the 1940s onward, logical positivists attempted to construct an analytic philosophy of history, which, unlike a metaphysical speculative one, should deal 'not with overall interpretive schemes, but with the immanent logic of historical inquiry'.[21] Based on the principle of the methodological unity of science and guided by the scientific ideals of natural sciences, logical positivists attempted to formulate principles of historical explanation. One of the main exponents of this movement was Carl Hempel (1904–1997), who published the article 'The Function of General Laws in History' (1942) in *The Journal of Philosophy*. Kristeller responded to this significant event in the philosophical community as follows:

> With my somewhat different background I was disturbed by the way philosophers in this country treated historical research, and there was an article by the Vienna circle man Carl Hempel whom by the way I respect as a person and a scholar published in *The Journal of Philosophy*. It was an article on history which I found upsetting.[22]

Carl Hempel was a German émigré scientist and philosopher, one of the leading philosophers of logical positivism in the United States. He studied in Göttingen, Berlin, and Vienna, but he had to escape Europe in 1937, as his wife was Jewish. In the 1942 article, Hempel aimed to refute 'the widely held opinion that history . . . is concerned with the description of particular events of the past rather than with the search for general laws which might govern those events'.[23] The 'widely held opinion' apparently belonged to the Baden School of Neo-Kantians, whose major representatives, Wilhelm Windelband and Heinrich Rickert, viewed the historian as someone who understands and interprets individual unique events of the past, rather than someone who formulates universal historical laws. Hempel, on the contrary, insisted that general laws 'have quite analogous functions in history and natural sciences'[24] – that is, explanation and prediction. Hempel's argument was based on the deductive-nomological model of scientific explanation, which was also formulated by Karl Popper in his 'Logik der Forschung' (1935).[25] Hempel, however, applied this model to the domain of history. It supposes that if we know singular historical events and one or several general laws of history that altogether constitute the premise, we can infer the future events – that is, predict future historical developments. Neither Kristeller nor Popper shared Hempel's idea that future historical events can be anticipated based on this model. Popper famously refuted such claims in his book *The Poverty of Historicism* (1957),[26] in which he argued against the possibility of any sort of historical predictions and chose Marxism as the main target of his critique. Hempel, in turn, insisted on the total methodological unity of science, viewing history as part of this and, consequently, justifying the application of universal hypotheses to historical knowledge.

Kristeller described himself as someone who is 'usually diplomatic' but who blows up 'when principles are involved'.[27] He immediately reacted to Hempel's article by publishing a vast contribution 'Some Remarks on the Method of History' also in *The Journal of Philosophy*. Statements, which he articulated in this vast paper, were reformulated in his later publications on the same subject in the 1960s and 1980s. The paper, which was written jointly with a younger scholar of philosophy, Lincoln Reis,[28] contained a sharp critique of Hempel's statements and simultaneously introduced what Kristeller regarded as an actual method of historical research. From 1943 onwards, Kristeller's critique was directed against three main positivist statements: 1) there is no difference between historical and scientific methods; 2) history should produce general laws, which govern individual events; 3) history belongs to the social sciences.

Kristeller viewed the positivist problem of historical explanation itself as 'marginal, if not irrelevant, to the enterprise of the historian'.[29] Most of the logical positivists received scientific training and had vague notions of what a historian actually does. As a practising historian, he noticed an apparent discrepancy between Hempel's idea of historical method and the real process of historical investigation. Historians and scientists, he argued, though they use similar logical principles in their work, like rules of inference or burden of proof, have different goals. The goal of a historian is 'to ascertain, describe, and interpret the specific events, developments, and situations of the human past'.[30] Kristeller embraced this Neo-Kantian idea through his Heidelberg teacher Heinrich Rickert, though he 'did not endorse all his [Rickert's] positions without criticism'.[31] Kristeller read Rickert's *Die Grenzen der naturwissenschaftlichen Begriffsbildung* during his student years and found 'some insights that contemporary American philosophy with its exclusive emphasis on the natural sciences fails to appreciate'.[32] Like Rickert, Kristeller took as a starting point of his critique of positivism a real practice of writing history.

Kristeller makes a clear distinction between general laws in natural sciences and historical generalisations (inductive method), which historians use to reconstruct singular events of the past as a certain unity. However, historical generalisations and natural laws possess different epistemological status: natural laws are valid for any historical time and number of events, while historical generalisations have no universality. Kristeller argues that universal laws 'have no place in the actual work of the historian',[33] but they can be formulated before or after the actual process of historical research by philosophers of history or sociologists, though not historians. Consequently, if no laws of history exist, a demand for historians to anticipate future events and improve social conditions is meaningless, while the desire of people to know the future is 'purely emotional'.[34] Kristeller was generally sceptical about any philosophy of history, either analytic or Hegelian, but he admitted that any historian is a philosopher of history in a certain way, and the only requirement he set upon such philosophy of history was that it should be critical in Kantian sense.

In refuting a positivist model of historical explanation, Kristeller introduced two self-sufficient and complimentary procedures of historical research: fact-finding and interpretation.[35] Neither was clearly understood by the positivists. As a scholar whose work was based on thorough analysis of the original Renaissance manuscripts, Kristeller was amused by his positivist opponents, who seemed to believe that

> the basic facts of history are well known so that all the historian has to do is to draw general inferences from those facts and to form historical laws, and the like. If we ask how the historical facts are known and where they are to be found, the likely answer will be that they are available in any textbook of history.[36]

Kristeller viewed such an approach to the facts as superficial and misleading. If the errors take place early on, during the stage of fact-finding, they might bring a historian to invalid results during the stage of interpretation. Inference of general laws relying on 'basic facts' leads to the neglect of details (*minutae*), which constitute the core of historical scholarship and represent an effective instrument against historical relativism. Kristeller believed in historical objectivity, even if too many details make the historical picture 'obscure'. He put forward the truly Platonic rhetorical question: 'Do we really wish to reject the truth because it is not simple?'[37] Positivists, he continued, do not take into account the complexity of existing procedures of fact-finding (collection, selection, evaluation and reconstruction), and he recommends books of European historians in which these classical procedures are fully described.[38] Among these books are Bernheim's 'Lehrbuch der historischen Methode und der Geschichtsphilosophie' (1914)[39], Langlois and C. Seignobos's 'Introduction aux études historiques' (1898)[40] and, finally, Droysen's 'Grundriss der Historik' (1925).[41]

Finding and describing facts is not the ultimate end of a historian, Kristeller continues; there is the task of interpretation, which 'positivistic historiography ... tended to disregard'.[42] It should be a historian's responsibility to understand the facts but not mechanically generalise raw historical material. Kristeller opposed the model of causal explanation in history, as historical events are never determined by one universal cause as, for instance, Marx argued: 'The social scientist thinks that the main task of the historian is to understand causes, by which he means general cause and one particular type of it at that, such as the economic or the social'.[43] Historians, Kristeller insists, never deal with sufficient causes. Following Rickert, he argues that we can interpret only the number of specific causes of individual historical events. Disregard of Marxism and a lack of interest in politics and sociology were among the reasons why Kristeller never established friendly relationships with the Max Horkheimer circle and the New School for Social Research.[44] He emphasised that he was connected to people, above all, though 'the common intellectual background and interest',[45] rather than through the common religion, nationality or political views.

Kristeller's 1943 article against Hempel was addressed not to the historians, most of whom would find nothing new in it, but, first of all, to the philosophers leaving the room for discussion. However, no discussion followed after the publication: Kristeller's critique was totally ignored by Hempel and other 'advocates of the "scientific" method', among whom Kristeller listed Maurice Mandelbaum, Philip Paul Wiener, Frederick John Teggart, and Morris Raphael Cohen.[46] The only brief reply he received came from Morton White, Hempel's supporter.[47] What is remarkable about the debate on historical explanation is that analytical philosophers continued to perform their 'exercises' in the philosophy of history even though historians evaluated them as useless for their work.[48] Due to his negative characterisation of contemporary philosophy, Kristeller experienced unpleasant episodes in submitting articles to the respected journals. For instance, his paper 'History of Philosophy and History of Ideas' (1964) was supposed to be published by Australian philosopher John Passmore in the journal *History and Theory*. After Passmore has read the article, he refused to publish it, since it contained 'some sarcastic remarks about linguistic analysis . . .', and Passmore felt he 'could not afford to offer that to his audience'.[49]

Kristeller never aimed to please certain audiences. In his imagination, a historian is 'a seeker after truth', not 'a bad journalist' who chooses a research subject depending on its relevance to the current political situation, rather than on his inner scholarly preferences.[50] Kristeller blamed the 'hunt for actuality' on frankly biased studies that did much harm to the objectivity of historical research and to the image of the historical profession. The historian 'is most actual in being true, and this is an actuality which does not fade so quickly',[51] but Kristeller recognised that objectivity is more an ideal to strive for, rather than an achievable goal. Relativists, in his opinion, confused criticism and interpretation of the facts at each step of historical investigation, starting from choosing a topic of research and ending with a public presentation of its results. However, he admitted that it is impossible to fully reduce subjectivity in historical research, since values are constantly present in historical interpretations. For Rickert, values were inseparable from the individualising historical method, as a historian always connects values with events he studies.[52] However, Kristeller argued that only general human values can affect the historical research, while personal values should be reduced.

Kristeller viewed the roots of contemporary methodological problems of historical knowledge in the United States in grouping history with the social sciences.⁵³ Social and political problems, which humanity faced especially tangibly in the twentieth century, gave social sciences an exceptional significance. The rapid development of social sciences, in turn, affected historical methodology in the way that historians started to apply methods of social sciences in their work. It negatively affected, stated Kristeller, historical discipline and historians' understanding of their own methods. The label of social science applied to history though it 'promises the historian a share in the high prestige which the natural sciences enjoy today, the historian cannot forget that this inclusion among the 'social sciences' is after all but a kind of slogan'.⁵⁴ History, insisted Kristeller, has more in common with the humanities, which it has belonged to since classical Antiquity. The historian does not need methods of natural sciences to produce a valid historical knowledge, since history, having its own inner logic, also possesses 'valid and more or less rigorous methods that lead in some, if not in all, instances to solid conclusions'.⁵⁵ In Germany, history and philology acquired the prestige of being 'genuine' sciences without adopting methods of natural sciences, while in the United States, Kristeller admitted, they occupied a lower position.⁵⁶ This lower status of the humanities, he believed, caused the flourishing of relativism in American academic culture. Kristeller's concerns especially strengthened after the student protests at Columbia in 1968, 'a period which brought our whole political and cultural world out of joint'.⁵⁷ Kristeller did not approve of the protests, but it was not a consequence of his conservatism and inability to accept the rules and adapt to American society. He simply believed that scholarship should be strictly separated from ideology and politics and was disappointed that politics started to infiltrate campus life.

Kristeller was never politically active, but after 1968, he even stopped labelling himself as liberal.⁵⁸ He constantly articulated that liberal education does not equal political liberalism, since liberal arts existed long before the concept of political liberalism was born: 'Education and culture are autonomous, have their own traditions, and are not merely the products of political and social forces that happen to prevail at a given time.'⁵⁹ Kristeller proudly called himself 'a product of *Humanistisches Gymnasium*'⁶⁰ and regarded as particularly valuable his school education, which he obtained at Mommsen Gymnasium in Berlin. He warmly recollected how pupils engaged in challenging tasks, such as translating Greek poems and solving mathematical problems. These exercises developed his skills in working scrupulously with texts and nurtured the idea that any opinion should be well substantiated:

> I found it very educational in my life that I was brought up with the idea that there was a difference between what was correct and what was incorrect, and that we should aim at being correct in most instances, as far as possible, whereas now they get out of it thinking everything is private opinion.⁶¹

Conclusion

The bitter irony of Kristeller's position is the fact that although he was among those scholars who played a substantial role in breaking the isolation of American historical scholarship and promoting American Renaissance Studies, he felt himself isolated. In a 1988 autobiographical sketch, Kristeller wrote with sadness:

> I feel that my philosophical ideas and sympathies are rejected and disregarded as wrong and old fashioned by most of my professional colleagues, and I must be satisfied with the modest claim that I have tried to contribute to a better understanding of many past thinkers and currents whose merits may perhaps be better understood and appreciated at some future time than they are right now.[62]

Kristeller's approach to the history of philosophy was based on a combination of solid philosophical knowledge and rigorous methods of historical and philological research.[63] Historical methods should be applied for the accurate reconstruction of the life and career of a philosopher from the available sources, while philological instruments should serve the correct understanding of the original philosophical texts and their critical comprehension. He mastered several European languages[64] and constantly emphasised the importance of language proficiency for the historian and philosopher: 'philology is a tool and *Geistesgeschichte* is a goal, and they should not be separated from each other. *Geistesgeschichte* if not based on philology is empty.'[65]

Kristeller's success in the United States paradoxically coexisted with his unwillingness to change neither the field nor the methods of his research despite the fact a scholarly reorientation to the prevailing American philosophical and historical trends could possibly have brought him more professional opportunities. Being 'more stubborn than courageous',[66] as he described himself, Kristeller was never afraid to belong to the unpopular minority and defended his principles, 'basically Platonic and Kantian, which have guided my life, my thought and my work'.[67] While perfectly adapting to American reality and being grateful to the United States for becoming his second home, Kristeller managed to preserve his German 'persona' and intellectual independence in the environment and under circumstances where losing it would have been simple. In dynamic and crowded New York, Kristeller continued to lead a '19th-century style of life',[68] attending concerts of Bach and Mozart and teaching his Columbia students using the 'German method, where much of the academic work is voluntary . . . It's an elitist system, and contrary to most journalists and many colleagues of the present day for me the word elitist is a laudatory and not a derogatory term.'[69] He was attached to German culture but did not resume scholarly contacts with Germany till after the war, when he did not associate it with Nazis anymore. Kristeller certainly experienced episodes of nostalgia, but, unlike Theodor Adorno or

Kristeller's friend Karl Löwith, he never considered leaving the United States for Germany.

Kristeller's 'German method' of historical research was formed in the 1920s under the influence of Plato and Kant, Ranke and Burckhardt, Rickert and Dilthey, but it crystallised and took its final shape in the United Stated through the endless debates with his opponents, 'advocates of the "scientific" method' in history and historical relativists. He believed in the Republic of Letters and defended it as the most precious legacy that remained of his forever lost Homeland.

This chapter contains the results of the research carried out at the Lichtenberg-Kolleg – The Göttingen Institute for Advanced Study in the Humanities and Social Sciences, where I was lucky to work as an Early Career Fellow (2017–2019). I greatly thank John Monfasani and anonymous reviewers for their precious comments on the first version of the chapter. I am also grateful to Stefan Berger and Philipp Müller for giving me an opportunity to contribute to this volume.

Notes

1. On the impact of German émigré scholars on the development of the Renaissance studies in the United States see, for instance, Muir, 'The Italian Renaissance in America', 1095–118; Molho, 'The Italian Renaissance, Made in the USA', 263–94.
2. On Kristeller's biography and contribution to the Renaissance studies, see Monfasani, *Kristeller Reconsidered*. For the complete list of Kristeller's published works, see Gilbhard, *Bibliographia Kristelleriana*. Most of Kristeller's works were published first in the United States in English, except for the dissertation on Plotinus, 'Der Begriff der Seele in der Ethik des Plotins', which appeared in German in 1929.
3. Kristeller, 'Some Problems of Historical Knowledge', 93.
4. Kristeller, 'The Reminiscences of Paul Oskar Kristeller', 952: 'My emigration first to Italy and then to America discourage any further work along these lines, since I encountered a philosophical climate, especially in America, that was quite uncongenial to my philosophical outlook.'
5. 'The Reminiscences of Paul Oskar Kristeller', 952.
6. The course title was 'Übungen über Geschichte und historische Erkenntnis im Anschluss an J.B. Droysen. Grundriß an J.B. Droysen, Grundriß der Historik'.
7. Kristeller, Letter to Leo Baeck Institute in New York from 13 January 1998, 2.
8. On Kristeller's philosophical background, among others, see Monfasani, 'Paul Oskar Kristeller and Philosophy', 383–413; Blum, 'The Young Paul Oskar Kristeller as a Philosopher', 19–38; Hankins, 'Kristeller and Ancient Philosophy', 131–38.
9. 'The Reminiscences of Paul Oskar Kristeller', 375.
10. Among Kristeller's important articles published in the first years in the United States was 'The Study of the Philosophies of the Renaissance', 449–96, jointly written with John Herman Randall, Jr. It outlined a clear working plan for the historians of Renaissance philosophy to make original humanist texts available for scholars along with critical interpretation.
11. 'The Reminiscences of Paul Oskar Kristeller', 375.
12. 'The Reminiscences of Paul Oskar Kristeller', 369.
13. 'The Reminiscences of Paul Oskar Kristeller', 655.

14. 'The Reminiscences of Paul Oskar Kristeller', 655.
Small typographical errors have been corrected in this quote.
15. Kristeller, Paul Oskar. 'History of Philosophy and History of Ideas', 2.
16. 'The Reminiscences of Paul Oskar Kristeller', 416; see also Kristeller, 'Some Remarks on the Method of History', 244.
17. 'The Reminiscences of Paul Oskar Kristeller', 494–95: 'But my alienation from the American Philosophical Association is not only due to this politicizing aspect but also to the fashions in philosophy, where fields like logic, the philosophy of science and analytical philosophy of language have become predominant schools, and they dominate program committees and for years there have been no decent talks in the areas of the history of philosophy that I am interested in, so that is one more reason why I have not been active.'
18. 'The Reminiscences of Paul Oskar Kristeller', 493: 'A professional organization should not make and pass political resolutions that are not approved by all its members, because you do not join them to make political statements – you join them for professional reasons.'
19. 'The Reminiscences of Paul Oskar Kristeller', 402: 'I had a very friendly reception, although in his case I had certain specific reservations about his philosophy of pragmatism. I mean my background was more Kantian if not Platonist, and I saw certain weaknesses in pragmatism, but I respected him.'
20. Kristeller, 'Autobiographical Sketch of 1988'.
21. Novick, *That Noble Dream*, 392.
22. 'The Reminiscences of Paul Oskar Kristeller', 517.
23. Hempel, 'The Function of General Laws in History', 35. For more on Kristeller's critique of analytic philosophy of history, see Dewulf, 'Revisiting Hempel's 1942 Contribution to Philosophy of History', 385–406.
24. Hempel, 'The Function of General Laws in History', 35.
25. In 'Logik der Forschung', Karl Popper refers to the problem of causation, scientific explanation and prediction in subsection 12 'Kausalität, Erklärung, Prognosendeduktion'. See Popper, *Logik der Forschung: Zur Erkenntnistheorie der Modernen Naturwissenschaft*, 26-28.
26. Popper, *The Poverty of Historicism*.
27. 'The Reminiscences of Paul Oskar Kristeller', 490.
28. In 'The Reminiscences', 447, Kristeller recollects: 'During the first period at Columbia I had numerous discussions with him also about problems of historiography, and the result of that is that we jointly published an article in *The Journal of Philosophy* on some problems of historical knowledge, in which although I think most of the ideas were mine, they jelled in the conversations I had with him, and so I felt it was proper to publish them with both names.'
29. Kristeller, 'History of Philosophy and History of Ideas', 3.
30. Kristeller, 'Some Problems of Historical Knowledge', 86.
31. 'The Reminiscences of Paul Oskar Kristeller', 100–1; when comprehending the process of historical generalisation, Kristeller specifies what was lacking in Rickert's theory: 'It is this type of inductive generalization which H. Rickert does not seem to have sufficiently taken into consideration.' Kristeller, 'Some Remarks on the Method of History', 229.
32. Kristeller, 'Some Remarks on the Method of History', 229.
33. Kristeller, 'The Reminiscences of Paul Oskar Kristeller', 101.
34. Kristeller, 'Some Remarks on the Method of History', 232.
35. Kristeller, 'Some Remarks on the Method of History', 235.
36. Kristeller, 'Some Remarks on the Method of History', 226.
37. Kristeller, 'Some Remarks on the Method of History', 230.
38. Kristeller, 'Some Remarks on the Method of History', 235.
39. Bernheim, *Lehrbuch der historischen Methode und der Geschichtsphilosophie: Mit Nachweis der wichtigsten Quellen und Hilfsmittel zum Studium der Geschichte*.
40. Langlois, Seignobos, *Introduction aux études historiques*.

41. Droysen, *Grundriss der Historik*.
42. Kristeller, 'Some Remarks on the Method of History', 239.
43. Kristeller, 'Some Remarks on the Method of History', 241.
44. 'The Reminiscences of Paul Oskar Kristeller', 465.
45. 'The Reminiscences of Paul Oskar Kristeller', 476.
46. Kristeller refers to the following works: Wiener, 'On Methodology in the Philosophy of History', 309–24; Teggart, 'Causation in Historical Events', 3–11; Cohen, 'Causation and its Application to History', 12–29; Mandelbaum, 'Causal Analysis in History', 30–50.
47. See White, 'A Note on the Method of History', 319. For Kristeller's reply to White, see Reis and Kristeller, 'A Reply to Dr. White', 319–20.
48. See, for instance, Novick, *That Noble Dream*, 398: 'Bernard Bailyn was surely speaking for many of his colleagues when he said that however interesting these issues were to philosophers, neither he nor any historian he knew found them at all helpful to their professional work.'
49. It contained, among other things, attacks against the statement that was shared by many of linguistic philosophers that 'the key to truth is an analysis of ordinary English. My article, subsequently published elsewhere, contains the phrase "ordinary English as far as philosophical terminology is concerned is the sediment of over 2000 years of extraordinary thinking, most of it done in languages other than English, such as Greek, Latin, French and German". This was an unforgivable statement which I intentionally made and succeeded in printing'. 'The Reminiscences of Paul Oskar Kristeller', 691.
50. Kristeller, 'Some Remarks on the Method of History', 231.
51. Kristeller, 'Some Remarks on the Method of History', 231.
52. See Rickert, *Die Grenzen der naturwissenschaftlichen Begriffsbildung*; Rickert, *Die Philosophie des Lebens*.
53. Kristeller, 'Some Remarks on the Method of History', 233–34.
54. Kristeller, 'Some Remarks on the Method of History', 225.
55. Kristeller, 'Some Problems of Historical Knowledge', 92.
56. Kristeller, 'Some Problems of Historical Knowledge', 87.
57. 'The Reminiscences of Paul Oskar Kristeller', 773.
58. 'The Reminiscences of Paul Oskar Kristeller', 812.
59. Kristeller, 'Humanistic Education and Its Lessons'.
60. Kristeller, 'Humanistic Education and Its Lessons'.
61. 'The Reminiscences of Paul Oskar Kristeller', 38–39.
62. Kristeller, 'Autobiographical Sketch of 1988'.
63. 'The Reminiscences of Paul Oskar Kristeller', 952: 'My universe focused on Plato and Kant, not on Feudalism and the Reformation or on Dante and Shakespeare. The paradox of my method and outlook, both philosophical and historical, is probably resolved if it is understood that I am an empiricist in historical research, not a positivist, but a transcendental realist attentive to detail, a Platonic and Kantian idealist when it comes to the realm of pure thought and of basic principles, and an existentialist when it comes to personal and spiritual, if you wish, religious or mystical experience, which is above reason, in the Kantian and not in the positivist sense of the word, but never opposed to reason.'
64. See, for instance, Kristeller, 'Philosophy and Its Historiography', 623: 'I have never written, and shall never write, about philosophers whom I am unable to read in their original language, whether it be Chinese or Sanskrit, Arabic or Hebrew, Russian or Danish.'
65. 'The Reminiscences of Paul Oskar Kristeller', 454.
66. 'The Reminiscences of Paul Oskar Kristeller', 806.
67. 'The Reminiscences of Paul Oskar Kristeller', 946.
68. 'The Reminiscences of Paul Oskar Kristeller', 653
69. 'The Reminiscences of Paul Oskar Kristeller', 872–73.

Bibliography

Bernheim, Ernst. *Lehrbuch der historischen Methode und der Geschichtsphilosophie: Mit Nachweis der wichtigsten Quellen und Hilfsmittel zum Studium der Geschichte*. München Leipzig: Duncker & Humblot, 1914.
Blum, Paul Richard. 'The Young Paul Oskar Kristeller as a Philosopher', in John Monfasani (ed.), *Kristeller Reconsidered: Essays on His Life and Scholarship* (New York: Italica Press, 2006), 19–38.
Cohen, Morris R. 'Causation and its Application to History'. *Journal of the History of Ideas* 3(1) (1942), 12–29.
Dewulf, Fons. 'Revisiting Hempel's 1942 Contribution to Philosophy of History'. *Journal of the History of Ideas* 79(3) (2018), 385–406.
Droysen, Johann G. *Grundriss der Historik*. Halle/Saale: Max Niemeyer, 1925.
Gilbhard, Thomas. *Bibliographia Kristelleriana: A Bibliography of the Publications of Paul Oskar Kristeller 1929–1999*. Roma: Edizioni di Storia e Letteratura, 2006.
Hankins, James. 'Kristeller and Ancient Philosophy', in John Monfasani (ed.), *Kristeller Reconsidered: Essays on His Life and Scholarship* (New York: Italica Press, 2006), 131–38.
Hempel, Carl G. 'The Function of General Laws in History'. *The Journal of Philosophy* 39(2) (1942), 35–48.
Kristeller, Paul Oskar. *Der Begriff der Seele in der Ethik des Plotins*. Tübingen: Mohr, 1929.
———. 'Some Remarks on the Method of History'. *Journal of Philosophy* 40(9) (1943), 225–45.
———. 'Some Problems of Historical Knowledge'. *The Journal of Philosophy* 58(4) (1961), 85–110.
———. 'History of Philosophy and History of Ideas'. *Journal of the History of Philosophy* 2(1) (1964), 1–14.
———. 'Philosophy and Its Historiography'. *The Journal of Philosophy* 82(11) (1985), 618–25.
Kristeller, Paul Oskar, and John Herman Randall, Jr. 'The Study of the Philosophies of the Renaissance'. *The Journal of the History of Ideas* 2(4) (1941), 449–96.
Langlois, Charles-Victor; Seignobos, Charles. *Introduction aux études historiques*. Paris: Hachette, 1898.
Mandelbaum, Maurice. 'Causal Analysis in History'. *Journal of the History of Ideas* 3(1) (1942), 30–50.
Molho, Anthony. 'The Italian Renaissance, Made in the USA', in Anthony Molho and Gordon S. Wood (eds), *Imagined Histories: Historians Interpret the Past* (Princeton, New Jersey: Princeton University Press, 1998), 263–94.
Monfasani, John. 'Paul Oskar Kristeller and Philosophy'. *Bulletin De Philosophie Médiévale* 57 (2015), 383–413.
Monfasani, John (ed.). *Kristeller Reconsidered: Essays on His Life and Scholarship*. New York: Italica Press, 2006.
Muir, Edward. 'The Italian Renaissance in America'. *The American Historical Review* 100(4) (1995), 1095–118.
Novick, Peter. *That Noble Dream: The 'Objectivity Question' and the American Historical Profession*. Cambridge: Cambridge University Press, 1998.
Popper, Karl R. *Logik der Forschung: Zur Erkenntnistheorie der Modernen Naturwissenschaft*. Wien: J. Springer, 1935.
Popper, Karl R. *The Poverty of Historicism*. London: Routledge and Kegan Paul, 1957.
Reis, Lincoln, and Paul Oskar Kristeller. 'A Reply to Dr. White'. *The Journal of Philosophy* 40(12) (1943), 319–20.
Rickert, Heinrich. *Die Grenzen der naturwissenschaftlichen Begriffsbildung: Eine logische Einleitung in die historischen Wissenschaften*. Freiburg und Leipzig: Verlag von J.C.B. Mohr, 1896.

———. *Die Philosophie des Lebens: Darstellung und Kritik der philosophischen Modeströmungen unserer Zeit*. Tübingen: Verlag Von J.K.B. Mohr, 1920.

Teggart, Frederick J. 'Causation in Historical Events'. *Journal of the History of Ideas* 3(1) (1942), 3–11.

White, Morton G. 'A Note on the Method of History'. *The Journal of Philosophy* 40(12) (1943), 317–19.

Wiener, Philip P. 'On Methodology in the Philosophy of History'. *The Journal of Philosophy* 38(12) (1941), 309–24.

Archival Sources

Kristeller, Paul Oskar. 'Autobiographical Sketch of 1988'. Box 119, folder 15, in the Paul Oskar Kristeller Papers of Columbia University's Rare Book and Manuscript Library.

Kristeller, Paul Oskar. 'Humanistic Education and Its Lessons'. Box 119 in the Paul Oskar Kristeller Papers of Columbia University's Rare Book and Manuscript Library.

Kristeller, Paul Oskar. 'The Reminiscences of Paul Oskar Kristeller'. Typescript, Oral History Collection of Columbia University, 1983.

Kristeller, Paul Oskar. Letter to Leo Baeck Institute in New York from 13 January 1998, p. 2; Retrieved 21 March 2022 from https://archive.org/details/pauloskarkristellerf001/page/n7.

CHAPTER 6

Émigré Historians and the Postwar Transatlantic Dialogue

PHILIPP STELZEL

When the German historian Hans Rothfels celebrated his 65th birthday in 1956, he received an effusive congratulatory letter from a younger colleague. After delivering his birthday wishes, Walther Peter Fuchs, a professor at the University of Erlangen, concluded:

> German historians discredited themselves around the world with their behavior during the Third Reich. Therefore we are extremely indebted to you for your decision years ago to return into our midst. You have done us all a tremendous service. Please forgive an insignificant historian like myself for expressing this sentiment to you.[1]

One could add many more examples of German historians displaying gratitude toward émigré (or, in Rothfels' case, remigré) historians. Hans Rosenberg's number of admirers among West German historians likely matched that of Rothfels. As a visiting professor at Free University of Berlin in 1949/50, Rosenberg quickly became a formative influence for young scholars such as Karl Dietrich Bracher, Gerhard A. Ritter, Gerhard Schulz, Helga Grebing and Gilbert Ziebura. On a more personal level, Hans-Ulrich Wehler's decades-long correspondence reveals that Rosenberg was somewhat of a father figure for the younger German, whose own father had died in the Second World War.[2]

On the other side of the Atlantic, the émigré Hajo Holborn, now teaching at Yale, trained dozens of graduate students who later assumed influential

---

Notes for this section begin on page 119.

positions in the field themselves, including Leonard Krieger, Otto Pflanze, Theodore Hamerow and Arno Mayer. Younger émigrés such as Peter Gay, Fritz Stern and George Mosse became leading scholars of European and German intellectual and cultural history in the 1960s and 1970s, likewise with a large number of students. Stern even developed a public presence in West Germany: in 1987 he was the first foreigner to deliver the commemorative speech in the German Bundestag on June 17, then the Day of German Unity. A few years later, he served as adviser to the US Ambassador to Germany, Richard Holbrooke.[3]

These examples illustrate the significance of émigré historians for their discipline on both sides of the Atlantic. Émigrés of the first and the second generation – that is, those who had been historians prior to their emigration and those who fled Germany as children or teenagers and were educated in their adopted home country – became and remained important voices in the emerging and intensifying transatlantic conversation on German history. In many respects, émigré contributions to the transatlantic intellectual community after 1945 amount to a success story.[4]

This assessment of émigré historians, now widely accepted, contrasts significantly with that of earlier decades. In this chapter I will therefore discuss the place of émigrés in the postwar transatlantic scholarly community. A closer examination of émigré scholars in West Germany and the United States reveals their methodological and political diversity, as well as their substantial and varied impact on both sides of the Atlantic. The chapter then turns to postwar German attitudes toward émigrés, which were often marked by significant suspicion. Finally, the analysis considers the ways in which a younger cohort of German historians, born in the 1930s and 1940, engaged with the émigrés' work. Since the transatlantic dialogue under consideration here was until the 1980s almost exclusively a West German-American one, this chapter does not include the exiled historians who returned to the future East Germany.

Émigrés in West Germany

Considering the conservative and nationalist tradition of the German historical profession, it should not come as a surprise that those émigré historians who returned soon after the war and remained permanently were the most conservative ones, namely Hans-Joachim Schoeps and Hans Rothfels. In many respects, Rothfels was the perfect émigré to assume an influential role in postwar West Germany, serving as chair at the University of Tübingen, editor of *Vierteljahrshefte für Zeitgeschichte*, and as chairman of the German Historical Association, among many other functions in the discipline. A staunch German nationalist prior to his emigration, Rothfels had in many respects welcomed the advent of the Nazi regime and in a letter to a colleague in 1933 even admitted to sharing Nazi antisemitism to a certain degree.[5]

Rothfels undoubtedly modified his positions while teaching in the United States, yet his postwar views remained within the mainstream conservatism of the West German historical profession. While still a professor at the University of Chicago (he moved to Tübingen in 1951), Rothfels delivered the keynote speech at the first postwar convention of the German Historical Association in 1949. This was a highly symbolic appearance, as he had also given the closing speech at the Association's last convention prior to the establishment of the Nazi dictatorship. Rothfels had initially been hesitant, as he feared that his colleagues would perceive him as a re-educator, but Gerhard Ritter and Hermann Aubin ultimately persuaded him to appear at the convention. In his keynote 'Bismarck and the Nineteenth Century', Rothfels cast the Iron Chancellor as both a German and a European statesman, whose ultimate goal for the German Empire had not been hegemony.[6] By emphasising the Empire's moderation, Rothfels and many of his colleagues at the time also implied that Nazi Germany had been a distinct break with the course of German history.

Additionally, in his short book *The German Opposition to Hitler*, Rothfels portrayed the anti-Nazi resistance as anchored in all segments of German society, in an attempt to counter wartime publications in Great Britain and the United States that many Germans perceived as accusations of 'collective guilt'. Against a view prevalent among German society at the time, which dismissed the resisters as traitors, Rothfels insisted on the moral legitimacy of resistance to National Socialism. In contrast to Gerhard Ritter, who scorned the communist resisters as having been 'in the service of the enemy', Rothfels also gave credit to Arvid Harnack's 'Rote Kapelle'.[7] Yet, more problematically, he included artists and intellectuals who had chosen the so-called 'inner emigration' in the anti-Nazi resistance.[8]

While Rothfels became a towering figure in the West German historical discipline, the liberal historian Hans Rosenberg declined the offer of a professorship at the University of Cologne in 1947, citing both personal and political reasons (the latter included the uncertain future of the Western occupation zones), though he later regretted this decision.[9] Rosenberg did, however, spend several semesters in West Germany as a visiting professor, most notably at the Free University Berlin in 1949/50. In a nine-page report Rosenberg sent to the US State Department's Division of Exchange of Persons after his return to the United States, he voiced cautious optimism about the democratic potential of the students he had encountered. By contrast, his take on his German colleagues was decidedly critical:

> The professional historians of western Germany today, except for a bare handful of men, do not think it proper to pay serious attention to the scientific study and teaching of contemporary history, broadly conceived. This negative attitude which in its practical consequences entails a rather irresponsible and complacent escape from the present is, no doubt, in line with the allegedly 'nonpolitical' tradition of the German university.[10]

Regardless of Rosenberg's dismissive take on his colleagues, many of the younger historians with whom Rosenberg interacted as a visiting professor emphasised how much they benefited from his guidance. Decades later, Gerhard A. Ritter recalled Rosenberg's teaching as an 'unforgettable experience', as the émigré confronted students with 'new questions and methods and developed an interpretation of German history which diverged considerably from traditional opinions'.[11] Conversely, Rosenberg regarded the year in Berlin as a highlight of his teaching career and almost two decades later dedicated *Grosse Depression und Bismarckzeit* to his 'old students at the Free University Berlin'.[12]

Dietrich Gerhard – like Rothfels and Rosenberg a student of Friedrich Meinecke's – was another émigré who after the Second World War spent considerable time in Germany. Gerhard had obtained a professorship for European history at Washington University in St. Louis in 1936, soon after his arrival in the United States. After the Second World War, he worked out an arrangement with his university that allowed him to divide his time between St. Louis and Cologne, where he became a professor of American history in 1955. In 1961, he assumed a position at the relatively new Max Planck Institute for History in Göttingen, which he helped develop a more international profile. Gerhard turned out to be a 'stroke of luck' for the institute, as he embodied the tradition of German academia and at the same time had become 'a real American who could give the institute new impulses'; for example, by adopting a comparative, transatlantic perspective.[13]

Émigrés in the United States

On the other side of the Atlantic, émigré historians helped shape the field of German history. While this was certainly a result of their talents, the expansion of higher education in the United States after the Second World War also offered them excellent conditions: between 1940 and 1970, the overall number of professorships in history increased fivefold.[14] Secondly, since the rise of National Socialism demanded explanation, German history assumed greater relevance, and history departments of many major universities hired historians specialising in modern Germany.[15]

As mentioned above, Hajo Holborn at Yale directed more than fifty dissertations, and many of his students later assumed influential positions in the discipline.[16] Hans Rosenberg began advising graduate students later in his career, after UC Berkeley offered him a chair in 1959. He also left a mark teaching undergraduates at Brooklyn College for twenty years, including Holocaust history pioneer Raul Hilberg, who wrote in his memoirs of the 'deep and lasting influence' Rosenberg had on him. The historian of slavery, Eugene Genovese, who also took Rosenberg's classes, recalled that he 'taught history with a combination of cold objectivity and hot passion' and was 'everything a college professor must be'.[17]

After sixteen years of teaching at Bryn Mawr College, Felix Gilbert joined the Institute for Advanced Study in Princeton in 1962, where he became an important link in the transatlantic intellectual community by mentoring younger German historians who received fellowships at the Institute, including Karl Dietrich Bracher, Hans and Wolfgang J. Mommsen and Thomas Nipperdey.[18] As Fritz Stern emphasised in his obituary, Gilbert 'supported especially younger German scholars; he contributed significantly to the intellectual relations between Germany and the United States'.[19]

Second-generation émigrés likewise became important figures in the American discipline, as scholars, teachers and mentors.[20] First at Columbia University and then at Yale, Peter Gay was an exceptionally prolific historian, who published on reform socialism, the Enlightenment, nineteenth-century cultural history, Weimar culture, modernism and historiography.[21] Among the many memoirs by émigré historians, Peter Gay's moving reflections on growing up in Nazi Berlin stand out for their insights, perhaps a result of his immersion in psychoanalysis.[22]

An extraordinarily charismatic teacher, George Mosse had a cult following among undergraduates at the University of Wisconsin, where he taught for more than thirty years. Of even greater significance for the discipline was Mosse's advising of many graduate students, including Steven Aschheim, Anson Rabinbach and David Sabean. In addition, Mosse was an extremely generous mentor to dozens of other historians, as their voluminous correspondence collected in his personal papers illustrates. At least as importantly, Mosse was one of the pioneers of the study of fascism, and later the history of sexuality.[23] Finally, in 1966 Mosse and his fellow émigré Walter Laqueur co-founded the *Journal of Contemporary History*.

'Empathy and Understanding'

In light of these examples from both West Germany and the United States, the significance of émigrés as scholars and teachers of German history and as mentors of subsequent cohorts of historians seems impossible to dispute. Yet soon after the end of the war, Germans often revealed scepticism about their émigré colleagues. In 1949, Gerhard Ritter published a positive review of Hans Rothfels' *The German Opposition to Hitler*, in which he did not mince words:

> Writings on the German problem by German émigrés in England and the United States have often been confusing rather than enlightening. Where it rules without restraint, resentment is not a fertile soil for sober and objective history, and long-term alienation from Germany easily leads to a distorted view or reality.[24]

To Ritter, Rothfels was a rare exception among the émigrés, who otherwise could not be trusted to arrive at 'enlightened' conclusions. In a similar fashion, Ritter rejected émigré sociologist Helmuth Plessner's 'Verspätete Nation', considering it 'not real history, but the product of an émigré's imagination'.[25] For Ritter, Plessner's geographical distance from Germany (he spent most of the Nazi years in the Netherlands) had led to a lack of empathy, without which objective history could not be written.

Ritter might have been more blunt than most of his colleagues, but he was not alone in his belief about the likely deficiency of émigré perspectives. Many German historians in the first two postwar decades also assumed that foreign interpretations of the German past were likely to be flawed for the same reason. In a review of the American historian Koppel Pinson's widely read survey *Modern Germany*, Hans Herzfeld acknowledged that Pinson had provided 'one of the most serious foreign attempts to grapple with the difficult problems of nineteenth and twentieth century German history', but he 'inevitably' – as Herzfeld put it – fell short in some respects as well.[26]

Remarkably, even some émigré historians, such as Klaus Epstein himself, were not above advancing such a claim about foreign perspectives. In a review essay on three American studies of German socialism in the early twentieth century, Epstein contended that American scholars sympathising with the Social Democrat's left wing had, because of their nationality, difficulties understanding the no-win situation in which the moderate Social Democrats had found themselves. In Epstein's apodictic words,

> American historians are handicapped when dealing with German developments by the deep-rooted American faith that all problems can be solved by intelligence and good will . . . American historians have underestimated the impersonal forces and conditions which have made German socialists act the way they did, and they have engaged in the futile search for villains.[27]

Ironically, one of the scholars accused of such a handicap was Epstein's fellow émigré Peter Gay, who in contrast to his reviewer (who had left Germany in 1934 at the age of eight) had spent most of his teenage years in Germany, escaping with his family at the last minute in 1939.[28]

At times, the widespread German prejudice manifested itself in backhanded compliments: when Hajo Holborn, who had emigrated to the

United States in 1934, published the first of his three-volume *A History of Modern Germany* in 1959, Gerhard Ritter sent him a letter in which he congratulated Holborn on this achievement. The German historian expressed relief that Holborn had emphasised the 'tragic character' of German political history and added:

> One has to compliment you on having maintained a true and warm understanding (*'ein echtes und warmes Verständnis'*) of the history of your German fatherland, which you have managed to preserve despite your Americanism (*'trotz Ihres Amerikanismus'*), and despite the distance from Germany in which you have been lived since the 1930s.[29]

Ritter clearly assumed such a *warmes Verständnis* to be an essential precondition to write properly about German history, and it seemed equally self-evident to him that one could not expect this of an émigré historian now teaching in the United States.

Such sceptical or outright dismissive German comments tell us more about those historians than about the émigrés, who held diverse and nuanced views on modern German history. What is more, it was the émigré Fritz T. Epstein who did his best to help Ritter with the publication of a book in the United States. In a letter to publisher Henry Regnery, Epstein wrote:

> I am very glad to learn of your interest in Prof. Ritter's book *Europa und die deutsche Frage*. I think I am not mistaken to regard this book as a work of outstanding importance for the evaluation of German historiography; it strives for restoring the high standards of historical research of the pre-Hitler era and goes far in suggesting certain revisions in dealing with problems of modern German history. In the words of Professor Sidney B. Fay of Harvard University, this book would correct here many false notions still very prevalent about pre-war Germany and the past. What is equally important: Professor Ritter more than any other German historian can be regarded as the spokesman for his profession in Germany. This book represents what the best German historians now think.[30]

A revealing example of the diversity of émigré opinions was the Fischer-Kontroverse during the 1960s. While Fritz Stern's appearance at the 1964 Historikertag and his support of Fischer's arguments are better known, another émigré historian emerged as one of Fischer's main critics in the United States. Joachim Remak, born in Berlin in 1920 and now a professor at UC Santa Barbara, took aim at the Hamburg historian's arguments in a series of publications in the 1960s and early 1970s and in 1971 asserted that 'Fritz Fischers's decade has ended.'[31] And Hans Rosenberg wrote in no uncertain terms to Hans Herzfeld about his disappointment with Fischer's talk at UC Berkeley in 1964, which also reflected more fundamental concerns:

> Fischer's appearance here, as I indicated already, turned out to be a great intellectual and scholarly disappointment [*eine große geistig-wissenschaftliche Enttäuschung*]. Had the German Foreign Office not tried to silence him, he would have encountered strong criticism over here. But given the political background

we all turned a blind eye on his assumptions and at times sloppy methods, even though we by no means endorse them'.³²

If there was one issue on which émigrés (as well as American historians) could agree, it was their opposition to the attempts by German historians and politicians to keep Fischer from travelling to the United States, but that did not translate into endorsing Fischer's views.

Another example of the diverse views among émigrés was the reception of Fritz Stern's and George Mosse's studies on the intellectual origins of National Socialism. Two other émigrés, Klaus Epstein and Klemens von Klemperer, reviewed Stern's *Politics of Cultural Despair* and Mosse's *Crisis of the German Ideology*. While both seemed convinced by Stern's analysis, Klemperer castigated Mosse for his 'vastly exaggerated' conclusions and found that his 'picture of Wilhelmian Germany [was] distorted and forced into a "Volkish" strait jacket'.³³ He also took issue with Mosse's methodology, disputed his emphasis on the importance of early nineteenth-century romanticism for the genesis of Nazi ideology and even compared the book to the 'From Luther to Hitler' studies of the war and immediate postwar years. Klemperer concluded: 'Just because it is understandable and indeed inevitable that in these days German history should be written with the catastrophe in mind, it is up to the historian to exercise the necessary restraint.'³⁴

In personal letters, émigrés expressed their disagreements even more openly. Asked for his opinion about potential candidates for a chair at the University of Toronto, Hans Rosenberg did not mince words:

> I do have a low opinion of Mosse's scholarship which I find shallow, unoriginal, pretentious and awfully repetitious. As for Stern, he writes a fine style and may be an excellent teacher. However, the scholarly value of his publications, few as they are, are, I submit, greatly overrated on this side of the Atlantic.³⁵

Unfortunately, these diverse views of émigrés were generally lost on especially those West German historians who dominated the discipline between the end of the Second World War and the 1960s. For them, an 'acceptable' émigré displayed what by their standards amounted to the required empathy and understanding vis-à-vis German history. Historians such as Fritz Stern and George Mosse, with their interpretations of National Socialism's ideological roots, certainly did not pass the test. Stern's appearance at the 1964 Historikertag in particular did not sit well with Gerhard Ritter and Karl Dietrich Erdmann. Ritter complained in a letter to Erdmann about 'Mr. Stern's babble', which had deeply annoyed him, while Erdmann as the editor of the journal *Geschichte in Wissenschaft und Unterricht* vetoed the publication of Stern's Historikertag paper. Erdmann dismissed it as 'merely emotional in nature' and containing 'not a single factual argument'.³⁶

There were, however, exceptions: the second-generation émigré Klaus Epstein was an acceptable historian in the eyes of some Germans, and his name frequently appeared in the context of available professorships in West Germany. In the early 1960s, Theodor Schieder, who was at the time arguably the most influential person in the discipline and was often asked to suggest or rank potential candidates, recommended Epstein for a number of appointments, including at the Universities of Bonn and Frankfurt. In one of his letters, Schieder explained that Epstein was 'an extraordinarily astute thinker, perhaps at times a bit pretentious in his judgments, but of an impressive ability to empathize with the German conditions, from which his biographical trajectory has removed him, after all' – a curiously euphemistic way to refer to Epstein's emigration. He concluded: 'should a German university succeed in alluring him, this would constitute an important enrichment for the discipline.'[37] That Schieder found it necessary to emphasise Epstein's 'ability to empathize with the German conditions' illustrates that this could not be expected from someone writing German history abroad.

The responses to William Shirer's simplistic yet immensely successful *The Rise and Fall of the Third Reich* illustrate that German and émigré historians could also be in absolute interpretive agreement with one another. While the reactions of German and American media as well as the general public differed dramatically, historians on both sides of the Atlantic offered similarly devastating evaluations.[38] Klaus Epstein's comprehensive assessment in the *Review of Politics* was as negative as Martin Broszat's in *Historische Zeitschrift*, and its tone was even more blunt. Epstein argued that Shirer's 'one-sided misjudgments on Germany's political history appear[ed] relatively insignificant when compared with his systematic prejudice when dealing with Germany's cultural heritage', and he accused Shirer of the 'rewarming of the wartime tale that German history is a one-way road leading from Luther to Hitler'.[39] George Mosse's review of Shirer's study in *The Progressive* was more moderate in tone but also quite critical.[40]

Finally, the evaluations of the German resistance to Hitler are yet another example of why the distinction between German and émigré perspectives is misleading.[41] The respective historian's politics mattered more in this respect. Conservative émigrés such as Hans Rothfels and Klemens von Klemperer arrived at sympathetic characterisations of the military resistance, while among the more liberal ones, Hajo Holborn placed greater emphasis on Social Democratic circles, and George Mosse adopted a dismissive attitude toward the conservative resistance.[42] The fault lines between the émigrés' perspectives on the resistance resemble those of the non-émigré German historians: whereas Peter Hoffmann offered a fairly sympathetic interpretation of the conservative resistance, left-leaning scholars such as Hans

Mommsen focused more on the anti-democratic nature of their plans for a postwar Germany.[43]

A Transatlantic Conversation

The defensive attitudes among German historians receded after the mid-1960s, owing much to the generational change within the discipline. A younger cohort of German scholars, born between the late 1920s and early 1940s, was much less likely to distinguish between 'German' and 'foreign' perspectives on German history, and to dismiss the latter as unreliable. Several of them had met émigré historians either already in Germany or during student exchange years in the United States and subsequently maintained ties to them and to the American historical profession more generally.[44] When Hans-Ulrich Wehler received the American Historical Association's honorary foreign membership in 2000, he emphasised that 'the generations of Carl Schorske, Leonard Krieger, Hajo Holborn, Arno Mayer, Jim Sheehan, Henry Turner, Gerald Feldman, Charles Maier, and others, have influenced in a lasting way the political generation in Germany to which I belong' – a list including American-born as well as first- and second-generation émigré scholars.[45]

Such a claim of intellectual proximity or at least influence coexisted with – perhaps surprising – instances of non-reception: Fritz Stern's and George Mosse's studies on ideological roots of National Socialism hardly found an echo on the German side, where historians pursuing a critical re-evaluation of the German Empire focused on social and economic rather than cultural questions. As a result, the ideological and cultural special path sketched by the émigrés remained untravelled by the younger Germans.[46] Criticising this non-reception, Steven Aschheim has termed Wehler's and others' brand of social history 'at once *skeptical* and *protective*' and 'a navigation exercise: formulating a necessarily critical narrative of the past while at the same time leaving questions of personal complicity and ideological and intellectual convictions relatively untouched'.[47]

My interpretation is a different one: younger German social historians disregarded intellectual history because they associated it with an older German historiographical tradition; namely, Friedrich Meinecke's, which they considered potentially apologetic or heuristically of limited value.[48] Within the German historiographical context of the 1950s and early 1960s, this assessment carried a certain plausibility. The historians' respective biographies offer a second explanation of their methodological and theoretical orientation. Unlike the German-Jewish émigrés, these younger German social historians had of course not been personally affected by Nazi antisemitism in the 1930s, and therefore might have been less drawn to the study of its origins. For the same generation's historiography on National Socialism, one could posit a similar argument in explaining the relative neglect of its victims by non-Jewish German historians. For those growing up in the society of perpetrators, a focus on those rather than on the victims of National Socialism was not surprising. Finally, one has to consider the age difference of ten to twenty years between intellectual and cultural historians (born in the late 1910s to mid-1920s) and social historians (born between ca. 1930 and 1940). As students, the latter encountered a discipline that had begun to open itself to the social sciences.

Yet this particular instance of non-reception does little to change the overall picture: during the postwar decades, and particularly since the 1960s, a continuous transatlantic conversation developed, significantly shaped by first- and second-generation émigrés as intermediaries. Perhaps as a result of their methodological, interpretive and political diversity, the émigrés supported the pluralisation of the German historical profession (most notably during the Fischer-Kontroverse). Without ever becoming partisan to any of the West German historiographical 'camps' engaged in often acrimonious debates, they contributed and reinforced critical perspectives on the recent German past.

Notes

1. Walther Peter Fuchs to Hans Rothfels, 14 May 1956.
2. Hans-Ulrich Wehler to Hans Rosenberg, 30 May 1963, where Wehler mentions the loss of his father explicitly.
3. Fritz Stern, *Five Germanys I Have Known*, 443–48 and 481–500.
4. Several books evaluating the impact of émigré historians as individuals or as a group testify to that view. They include Lehmann and Sheehan, *An Interrupted Past*; Daum, Lehmann and Sheehan, *The Second Generation*; Payne, Sorkin and Tortorice, *What History Tells*. For the postwar transatlantic intellectual community as a whole, see Stelzel, *History after Hitler*.
5. Hans Rothfels to Siegfried A. Kaehler, 23 April 1933, 147.
6. The keynote was later published as Rothfels, 'Bismarck und das 19. Jahrhundert', 233–48.
7. Ritter, *Carl Goerdeler*, 103; Rothfels, *The German Opposition to Hitler*, 12.
8. Rothfels, *The German Opposition to Hitler*, 14.
9. Hans Rosenberg to Friedrich Meinecke, 6 October 1948.
10. Hans Rosenberg to Department of State, Division of Exchange of Persons, 11 November 1950.
11. Ritter, 'Hans Rosenberg', 297.
12. Rosenberg, *Grosse Depression und Bismarckzeit*, vii.
13. Schöttler, *Das Max-Planck-Institut*, 40–43, quote on 41; Gerhard, *Alte und neue Welt in vergleichender Geschichtsbetrachtung*.
14. Novick, *That Noble Dream*, 362–67.

15. Epstein, 'German Historians at the Back of the Pack', 599–639, provides evidence that despite increasing interest in German history, the field remained less well-represented in US history departments than British, French and Russian history.

16. In 1970, Holborn's students taught at many of the major American history departments: Dartmouth College (Henry L. Roberts), UCLA (Andrew Lossky), Columbia University (Leonard Krieger, who also taught at Yale and Chicago), University of Minnesota (Otto Pflanze), University of Wisconsin (Theodore Hamerow), Catholic University of America (John K. Zeender), University of Massachusetts (Harold J. Gordon, Miriam Usher Chrisman), Duke University (William E. Scott), Princeton University (Arno J. Mayer), University of Pittsburgh (Richard N. Hunt), Emory University (Douglas A. Unfug), Pennsylvania State University (Dan Paul Silverman), Yale University (Nicholas X. Rizopoulos), New York University (Stewart A. Staehlin), University of Chicago (F. Gregory Campbell), Middlebury College (Marjorie Lamberti), University of Pennsylvania (Charles McClelland).

17. Hilberg, *The Politics of Memory*, 57; Genovese, 'Hans Rosenberg at Brooklyn College', 57.

18. When Gilbert received the prestigious medal Pour le Mérite in 1981, the honorific speech mentioned this explicitly. BAK NL Theodor Schieder, Box 19, no author or date given.

19. Fritz Stern, 'Nachruf auf Felix Gilbert', 135. See also Stern, *Five Germanys I Have Known*, 282.

20. Daum, Lehmann and Sheehan, *The Second Generation*.

21. Smith, 'Reluctant Return', 210–28.

22. Gay, *My German Question*.

23. George L. Mosse, *Toward the Final Solution: A History of European Racism* (New York, 1978); Id., *The Fascist Revolution: Toward a General Theory of Fascism* (New York, 1999); Id., *Nationalism and Sexuality: Respectability and Abnormal Sexuality in Modern Europe* (New York, 1985).

24. Ritter, 'Review of Hans Rothfels, *The German Opposition to Hitler*', 402.

25. Gerhard Ritter to Theodor Schieder, [undated, ca. 1961]. The sociologist Helmuth Plessner (1892–1985) in *Verspätete Nation* (1959, first published under a different title in 1935) analysed what he considered the belated and defective form of the modernisation of the German economy and society (in particular of the *Bürgertum*). See Dietze, *Nachgeholtes Leben: Helmuth Plessner, 1892–1985*.

26. Herzfeld, 'Modern Germany', 402–5, quotes on 402.

27. Epstein, 'Three Studies of German Socialism', 650–51. The studies under review were Gay, *The Dilemma of Democratic Socialism*; Schorske, *German Social Democracy, 1905–1917*; and Berlau, *German Social Democracy, 1914–1924*.

28. Gay, *My German Question*, 138–54.

29. Gerhard Ritter to Hajo Holborn, 13 October 1960. The German original read 'Ihnen . . . muss man nachrühmen, dass Sie trotz Ihres Amerikanismus und trotz der großen Distanz, in die Sie seit den dreißiger Jahren Deutschland gegenüber geraten sind, sich ein echtes und warmes Verständnis für die Geschichte Ihres deutschen Vaterlandes bewahrt haben'. Holborn's books were published as *A History of Modern Germany. Vol. I: The Reformation; Vol. II: 1648–1840; Vol. III: 1840–1945*.

30. Fritz T. Epstein to Henry Regnery, 17 March 1949.

31. Joachim Remak, '1914 – The Third Balkan War', 353; Remak, *The Origins of World War I, 1871–1914*; Remak, *The First World War*.

32. Hans Rosenberg to Hans Herzfeld, 24 May 1964.

33. Klemperer, 'Review of George Mosse, *The Crisis of German Ideology*', 609.

34. Klemperer, 'Review of George Mosse, *The Crisis of German Ideology*', 609.

35. Hans Rosenberg to John C. Cairns (University of Toronto, Dept. Of History), 8 February 1971.

36. Gerhard Ritter to Karl Dietrich Erdmann, 14 October 1964; Karl Dietrich Erdmann to Friedrich Dieckmann and Felix Messerschmid, 1 November 1964.
37. Theodor Schieder to Dean H. Moser, University of Bonn, 5 February 1964. Schieder argued along the same lines in a letter to his colleague Dietrich Geyer (University of Frankfurt), 30 January 30, 1963.
38. For the public reception, see Rosenfeld, 'The Reception of Williams Shirer's *The Rise and Fall of the Third Reich*', 95–128.
39. Epstein, 'Shirer's History of Nazi Germany', 232 and 245.
40. Mosse, 'Review of Shirer, *The Rise and Fall of Nazi Germany*', 40–42.
41. For a discussion of émigré interpretations of the resistance, see Lamberti, 'The Search for the "Other Germany"', 402–29.
42. Klemperer, *German Resistance against Hitler*; Holborn, 'The German Opposition to Hitler', 239–40.
43. Hoffmann, *Widerstand*; Mommsen, *Alternative zu Hitler*.
44. See Stelzel, *History after Hitler*, chapter 3.
45. Daum, 'German Historiography', 121
46. For a critique of this non-reception, see Aschheim, 'The Tensions of Historical Wissenschaft', 45–80.
47. Aschheim, 'The Tensions of Historical Wissenschaft', 52.
48. Nolte, 'Die Historiker der Bundesrepublik', 413–32; for Wehler's views on intellectual history, see his 'Geschichtswissenschaft heute', 13–41.

Bibliography

Aschheim, Steven. 'The Tensions of Historical Wissenschaft: The Émigré Historians and the Making of German Cultural History', in Steven Aschheim (ed.), *Beyond the Border: The German-Jewish Legacy Abroad* (Princeton, NJ: Princeton University Press, 2007), 45–80.
Berlau, Joseph. *German Social Democracy, 1914–1924*. New York: Columbia University Press, 1949.
Daum, Andreas. 'German Historiography in a Transatlantic Perspective: Interview with Hans-Ulrich Wehler'. *Bulletin of the German Historical Institute, Washington, D.C.* 26 (2000).
Daum, Andreas, Hartmut Lehmann and James J. Sheehan (eds). *The Second Generation: Émigrés from Nazi Germany as Historians*. New York: Berghahn Books, 2016.
———. *The Second Generation: Émigrés from Nazi Germany as Historians*. New York: Berghahn Books, 2016.
Dietze, Carola. *Nachgeholtes Leben: Helmuth Plessner, 1892–1985*. Göttingen: Wallstein Verlag, 2006.
Epstein, Catherine. 'German Historians at the Back of the Pack: Hiring Patterns in Modern European History, 1945–2010'. *Central European History* 46(3) (2013), 599–639.
Epstein, Klaus. 'Three Studies of German Socialism'. *World Politics* 11(4) (1959), 629–51.
———. 'Shirer's History of Nazi Germany'. *Review of Politics* 23(2) (1961), 230–45.
Gay, Peter. *The Dilemma of Democratic Socialism: Eduard Bernstein's Challenge to Marx*. New York: Columbia University Press, 1952.
———. *My German Question: Growing Up in Nazi Berlin*. New Haven: Yale University Press, 1998.
Genovese, Eugene. 'Hans Rosenberg at Brooklyn College: A Communist Student's Recollections of the Classroom as War Zone'. *Central European History* 24(1) (1991), 51–57.
Hans Rosenberg to Friedrich Meinecke, 6 October 1948, in Gerhard A. Ritter (ed.), *Friedrich Meinecke: Akademischer Lehrer und emigrierte Schüler: Briefe und Aufzeichnungen 1910–1977* (Munich: Oldenbourg Verlag, 2006), 372–73.

Hans Rothfels to Siegfried A. Kaehler, 23 April 1933, in Gerhard A. Ritter (ed.), Friedrich Meinecke: *Akademischer Lehrer und emigrierte Schüler. Briefe und Aufzeichnungen 1910–1977* (Munich: Oldenbourg Verlag, 2006), 147.

Herzfeld, Hans. 'Modern Germany: Its History and Civilization by Koppel S. Pinson'. *Historische Zeitschrift* 182(2) (1956), 402–5.

Hilberg, Raul. *The Politics of Memory: The Journey of a Holocaust Historian*. Chicago, IL: Ivan R. Dee Publisher.

Hoffmann, Peter. *Widerstand, Staatsstreich, Attentat: Der Kampf der Opposition gegen Hitler*. Munich: Piper, 1969.

Holborn, Hajo. *A History of Modern Germany* (Vol. I: The Reformation; Vol. II: 1648–1840; Vol. III: 1840–1945). New York: Princeton University Press, 1959–1969.

———. 'The German Opposition to Hitler', in Hajo Holborn (ed.), *Germany and Europe: Historical Essays* (Garden City, NJ: Doubleday, 1970), 239–40.

Klemperer, Klemens von. 'Review of George Mosse, *The Crisis of German Ideology: Intellectual Origins of the Third Reich*'. *American Historical Review* 71(2) (1966), 608–10.

———. *German Resistance against Hitler: The Search for Allies Abroad*. Oxford: Clarendon Press, 1992.

Lamberti, Majorie. 'The Search for the "Other Germany": Refugee Historians from Nazi Germany and the Contested Historical Legacy of the Resistance to Hitler'. *Central European History* 47(2) (2014), 402–29.

Lehmann, Hartmut, and James J. Sheehan (eds). *An Interrupted Past: German-Speaking Refugee Historians in the United States after 1933*. Cambridge: Cambridge University Press, 1991.

Mommsen, Hans. *Alternative zu Hitler: Studien zur Geschichte des deutschen Widerstandes*. Munich: C.H. Beck, 2000.

Mosse, George. 'Review of Shirer, The Rise and Fall of Nazi Germany'. *The Progressive* (December 1960), 40–42.

Nolte, Paul. 'Die Historiker der Bundesrepublik: Rückblick auf eine "lange Generation"', *Merkur* 53 (1999), 413–32.

Novick, Peter. *That Noble Dream: The 'Objectivity Question' and the American Historical Profession*. Cambridge: Cambridge University Press, 1988.

Payne, Stanley G., David Jan Sorkin, and John S. Tortorice (eds). *What History Tells: George L. Mosse and the Culture of Modern Europe*. Madison: Wisconsin University Press, 2004.

Plessner, Helmuth. *Die verspätete Nation: Über die politische Verführbarkeit bürgerlichen Geistes*. Stuttgart: W. Kohlhammer Verlag, 1959.

Remak, Joachim. *The Origins of World War I, 1871–1914*. New York: Putman, 1967.

———. '1914 – The Third Balkan War: Origins Reconsidered'. *Journal of Modern History* 43(3) (1971), 353–66.

———. *The First World War: Causes, Conduct, Consequences*. New York: Wiley, 1971.

Ritter, Gerhard. 'Review of Hans Rothfels, *The German Opposition to Hitler*'. *Historische Zeitschrift* 169 (1949), 402–5.

———. *Carl Goerdeler und die deutsche Widerstandsbewegung*. Stuttgart: DVA, 1954.

Ritter, Gerhard A. 'Hans Rosenberg, 1904–1988'. *Geschichte und Gesellschaft* 15(2) (1989), 282–302.

Rosenberg, Hans. *Grosse Depression und Bismarckzeit: Wirtschaftsablauf, Gesellschaft und Politik in Mitteleuropa*. Berlin: De Gruyter, 1967.

Rosenfeld, Gavriel. 'The Reception of Williams Shirer's *The Rise and Fall of the Third Reich* in the United States and West Germany, 1960–62'. *Journal of Contemporary History* 29(1) (1994), 95–128.

Rothfels, Hans. *The German Opposition to Hitler: An Appraisal*. Hinsdale, IL: Henry Regnery Company, 1948.

———. 'Bismarck und das 19. Jahrhundert', in Walther Hubatsch (ed.), *Schicksalwege deutscher Vergangenheit: Beiträge zur geschichtlichen Deutung der letzten hundertfünfzig Jahre* (Düsseldorf: Droste, 1950), 233–48.

Schorske, Carl. *German Social Democracy, 1905–1917: The Development of the Great Schism.* Cambridge, MA: Harvard University Press, 1955.

Schöttler, Peter. *Das Max-Planck-Institut für Geschichte im historischen Kontext: Die Ära Heimpel.* Berlin: Forschungsprogramm Geschichte der Max-Planck-Gesellschaft, 2017.

Smith, Helmut Walser. 'Reluctant Return: Peter Gay and the Cosmopolitan Work of a Historian', in Andreas Daum, Hartmut Lehmann, and James J. Sheehan (eds), *The Second Generation: Émigrés from Nazi Germany as Historians* (New York: Berghahn Books, 2016), 210–28.

Stelzel, Philipp. *History after Hitler: A Transatlantic Enterprise.* Philadelphia: University of Pennsylvania Press, 2019.

Stern, Fritz. 'Nachruf auf Felix Gilbert'. *Geschichte und Gesellschaft* 18(1) (1992), 133–35.

———. *Five Germanys I Have Known.* New York: Farrar, Straus & Giroux, 2006.

Wehler, Hans Ulrich. 'Geschichtswissenschaft heute', in Hans-Ulrich Wehler (Ed.), *Historische Sozialwissenschaft und Geschichtsschreibung: Studien zu Aufgaben und Traditionen deutscher Geschichtswissenschaft* (Göttingen: Vandenhoeck & Ruprecht, 1980), 13–41.

Archival Sources

Fritz T. Epstein to Henry Regnery, 17 March 1949, Bundesarchiv Koblenz, Nachlass Fritz T. Epstein, Box 4.

Gerhard Ritter to Hajo Holborn, 13 October 1960, Bundesarchiv Koblenz, Nachlass Gerhard Ritter, NL 1166, Box 350.

Gerhard Ritter to Karl Dietrich Erdmann, 14 October 14, 1964, Bundesarchiv Koblenz, Nachlass Ritter, Box 270.

Gerhard Ritter to Theodor Schieder, [undated, ca. 1961], Bundesarchiv Koblenz, Nachlass Schieder, Box 506.

Hans Rosenberg to Department of State, Division of Exchange of Persons, 11 November 1950, Bundesarchiv Koblenz, Nachlass Hans Rosenberg, Box 42.

Hans Rosenberg to Hans Herzfeld, 24 May 1964, Bundesarchiv Koblenz, Nachlass Herzfeld, Box 12.

Hans Rosenberg to John C. Cairns (University of Toronto, Dept. Of History), 8 February 1971, Bundesarchiv Koblenz, Nachlass Hans Rosenberg, Box 46.

Hans-Ulrich Wehler to Hans Rosenberg, 30 May 1963, Bundesarchiv Koblenz, Nachlass Hans Rosenberg, Box 38.

Karl Dietrich Erdmann to Friedrich Dieckmann and Felix Messerschmid, 1 November 1964, Bundesarchiv Koblenz, Nachlass Erdmann, Box 21.

Bundesarchiv Koblenz, Nachlass Theodor Schieder, Box 19, no author or date given.

Theodor Schieder to Dean H. Moser, University of Bonn, 5 February 1964. Koblenz, Nachlass Schieder, Box 115.

Walther Peter Fuchs to Hans Rothfels, 14 May 1956. Bundesarchiv Koblenz, Nachlass Hans Rothfels, Box 1.

CHAPTER 7

Between Integration and Institutional Self-Organisation

Polish Émigré Scholarship in the United States, 1939–1989

KAI JOHANN WILLMS

The displacement of scholars resulting from the wars and dictatorships of the twentieth century was for many of those affected a personal tragedy, a biographical rupture that was difficult to cope with. Nonetheless, involuntary migration could also create new opportunities for the circulation of knowledge and ideas, for encounters of intellectual traditions. The cultural historian Peter Burke has described these possible epistemic effects as a 'double deprovincialization'. By confronting their environment with knowledge and styles of thought from their native culture, émigré scholars thus deprovincialised their hosts; and by adopting new ideas from their host society, they deprovincialised themselves and possibly, if their works found their way back into the discourse of their native societies, also their compatriots at home.[1] Such a double deprovincialisation, however, had its preconditions. In the host society, there had to be a demand for knowledge that émigré scholars could satisfy, and the latter had to regard their situation not only as a tragical fate but also as an opportunity to disseminate their knowledge and to broaden their horizons by getting acquainted with a foreign culture. Already in 1984, Edward Said noted that the alienation that émigrés experience in their new environment can indeed produce both effects: the nostalgia for

Notes for this section begin on page 134.

the lost homeland can enforce traditional notions of group identity and increase the émigrés' 'self-assertion'; at the same time, émigrés can also learn to perceive both their native culture and that of their hosts with the eyes of a foreigner, which may increase their 'self-awareness'.[2]

Which of these effects occur is not only a matter of individual choices or predispositions. Institutional arrangements have a significant impact on the way émigré scholars might become actors of 'deprovincialisation'. Finding employment at scholarly institutions of the host society gives them the opportunity to become familiar with a new academic culture, while establishing institutions of their own helps to sustain networks with their fellow émigrés and to preserve their native scholarly traditions. Therefore, a historiography of twentieth-century émigré scholarship that aims to transcend the framework of individual biographies has to take account of institutional dynamics – as national communities of émigrés differed considerably in this regard. In his history of the Russian emigration during the interwar period, Marc Raeff demonstrated that émigrés from Soviet Russia, instead of assimilating to their new environment, had created a distinct Russian society in exile with a cultural and scholarly life of its own, which they understood as perhaps even more authentically 'Russian' than the Russian society under the Bolshevik regime.[3] Historians of the intellectual emigration from Nazi Germany, on the other hand, have emphasised the rapid integration of the émigrés into the American elite.[4] The present chapter takes a closer look at Polish émigré scholarship in the United States during the Cold War period as an example of how these tendencies, integration and institutional self-organisation can coexist in an émigré community.

Setting up Polish Scholarship in Exile

When Poland was occupied by Germany and the Soviet Union at the outbreak of the Second World War, the Polish government and numerous members of the interwar Polish intelligentsia escaped from their native country, in many cases with the intention of continuing the tradition of Polish statehood and scholarship in exile until it would be possible to return to a liberated Poland. In Paris, where the government-in-exile initially established itself, a Polish university in exile was organised.[5] After the German invasion of France in 1940, it had to be closed again, and a large group of Polish émigré scholars escaped together with the government-in-exile to London; another group arrived in the United States. In New York, the latter established in 1942 the Polish Institute of Arts and Sciences in America (PIASA) as 'an autonomous research center of the Polish Academy of Arts and Sciences'[6]

(Polska Akademia Umiejętności, PAU), an institution in Kraków that had been liquidated by the German occupants. The PIASA was to take the Academy's place until Poland regained its independence.

From the outset, the institute pursued two divergent agendas. Firstly, its prescribed aim was 'to establish permanent collaboration between Polish and American scholars, to spread knowledge of Poland and her culture in the United States, and to assist Polish scholars in becoming acquainted with America and her culture'.[7] To this end, the founders of the PIASA invited American experts on Central and East European affairs to become members of the institute and chose Bronisław Malinowski, the Polish-born social anthropologist who had already firmly established himself in the Anglophone academic world during the interwar period, as their president. Secondly, the institute aimed to ensure 'the continuity of Polish research work, at present rendered impossible at home'.[8] This line was especially enforced by the government-in-exile in London, which sponsored the PIASA during the war. When Malinowski unexpectedly died only one day after the institute's inauguration, the government-in-exile backed Jan Kucharzewski, an expert on Russian history who was loyal to its political line but who reportedly did not speak English and was little known in the American academic world, as the institute's new president.[9]

Among some Polish scholars in the United States, the orientation of the PIASA as a substitute for the closed PAU met with scepticism from the very beginning. Most prominently, the economist Oskar Lange and the literary critic Manfred Kridl argued that a Polish academic institution in the United States should not grant privileged membership to members of the PAU but treat all Polish researchers in America equally, and that it should engage with the political and intellectual heritage of the Second Polish Republic in a critical way. In particular, they criticised the appointment of chemist Wojciech Świętosławski to serve on the board of the new institute because he had been responsible for discriminatory measures against Jewish students at Polish universities during his tenure as Minister of Religious Affairs and Public Education.[10] In Lange's and Kridl's eyes, the fact that a former member of Poland's authoritarian government belonged to the institute's inner circle posed a threat to its reputation in the American academic milieu – as Kridl put it in a letter to Kucharzewski, 'most American scholars are liberal, progressive, democratic people', and 'Polish scholars should be especially careful not to contribute to the fairly widespread view that a Polish professor is a synonym for a reactionist and fascist'.[11] Most of the émigrés involved in the founding of the PIASA, however, did not align with this standpoint; for instance, the first executive director of the institute, the historian Oskar Halecki, argued that it was inappropriate to critically reassess the development of the Polish humanities at a time when many of their leading representatives were being tortured and killed in German concentration camps.[12] In consequence, Lange, Kridl and a few like-minded scholars resigned their PIASA membership and distanced themselves from the milieu of the institute's founders. After the war, Lange returned to Poland and entered the diplomatic service of the Polish People's Republic; Kridl stayed in the United States but accepted a chair of Polish literature at Columbia University in 1948 that was sponsored by the Communist government.

In the postwar era, the PIASA thus started out as an institution of émigrés who strongly disapproved of the Communist takeover in Poland and, while identifying with different political camps, largely shared an affirmative perspective on the heritage of the Second Polish Republic. Opposing the Sovietisation of the humanities and social sciences in Poland, its leadership considered the institute an independent research centre enabling the continuation and free expression of a perhaps even more authentically 'Polish' scholarly tradition, which found itself under political pressure from the Communist regime.[13] As will be shown below, this agenda of defending a seemingly threatened intellectual tradition initially hampered the exchange of ideas with the American host society. In the course of decades, however, several external factors as well as internal dynamics of the émigré community facilitated a gradual 'Americanisation' of Polish émigré scholarship. First and foremost, the rapid expansion of East European studies in the United States during the early Cold War created job opportunities for émigré scholars and enabled their integration into American society.[14] Furthermore, even among those émigrés with strong anti-communist convictions, a growing group came to realise that in order to win the intellectual Cold War, it was necessary to abandon a nostalgic perspective on the past and to modernise Polish intellectual life. This line was mainly represented by the journal *Kultura*, which appeared from 1948 in a suburb of Paris and created a transnational network of Polish émigrés who were willing to bring Polish traditions into dialogue with intellectual trends in the West and in Communist Poland.[15] Finally, Polish émigré scholarship in the United States changed its character when the generation who had already been active scholars in interwar Poland and who had founded the émigré institutions were gradually replaced over the course of the 1970s by a younger cohort of émigrés, who had received their academic training at Western universities.

Nonetheless, this gradual integration of the Polish émigré community did not lead to the dissolution of the institutions that had been created during the 1940s. On the contrary, most of the latter survived until the end of the Cold War, adapting their agenda to new historical circumstances; the PIASA exists until the present day, defining itself now as 'a liaison between American and Polish academic circles'.[16] In the following, I will trace this process and its implications for the development of Polish émigré scholarship by focusing on three scholars who were closely involved in the activities of the PIASA and at the same time illustrate the political and generational diversity of the émigré community: the aforementioned historian Oskar Halecki (1891–1973), the sociologist Feliks Gross (1906–2006), and the political scientist Zbigniew Brzeziński (1928–2017).

The First Generation of Polish Émigré Scholars

Oskar Halecki and Feliks Gross both spent their childhood in the late Habsburg Empire and started their academic careers as students at the Jagiellonian University in Kraków. But apart from that, their backgrounds were very different: Halecki was born the son of a noble Catholic family in Vienna; one of his remote ancestors, Dymitr Chalecki, had acted as envoy to the Polish king at the Union of Brest, where the Ruthenian Orthodox bishops in the early modern Polish-Lithuanian Commonwealth acknowledged the authority of the Pope, and his father served as an officer in the Austro-Hungarian army.[17] Gross, by contrast, came from a prominent bourgeois family of assimilated Jews in Kraków; his father was a lawyer and a liberal deputy in the lower house of the Austrian Imperial Council. These backgrounds had an impact on Halecki's and Gross's early research interests and political commitments. In the Second Polish Republic, Halecki, after being appointed professor of East European history at the University of Warsaw in 1918, soon rose to be a leading figure of Polish historiography and was well connected in government circles; he advised the Polish delegation at the Paris Peace Conference, providing it with historical arguments in favour of claiming disputed territories in the East for the reborn Polish state,[18] and he served as secretary of the International Committee on Intellectual Cooperation, an organisation affiliated with the League of Nations.[19] In his scholarly work, Halecki advocated an affirmative perspective on Polish history, particularly on the history of the Polish-Lithuanian Commonwealth, which he depicted as the ideal of Polish statehood and as a bulwark of Western civilisation against aggressors from the East.[20] By means of extensive lecture tours to Western Europe and, in 1938, to North America, Halecki also tried to popularise the idea of Poland as an integral part of Western civilization on the international level.

For various reasons, Gross did not achieve a comparable status in interwar Poland. Fifteen years Halecki's junior, he earned a doctorate in law in 1930; six years later, he completed his habilitation. His research interests drew him towards the social sciences, which were still a nascent field in interwar Poland.[21] An active member of the Polish Socialist Party, Gross turned his scholarly attention to the situation of underprivileged groups in Poland. For instance, he wrote about the cultural life of the proletariat and co-edited a volume of autobiographical writings by Polish workers.²² After a visit to the London School of Economics (LSE), where he attended Bronisław Malinowski's seminar and became familiar with the latter's anthropological method, Gross also began to conduct fieldwork in Kraków's Jewish district, Kazimierz.²³ In the political climate of the 1930s, both his Jewish descent and his political views were impediments to an academic career. He was not assigned an academic position in Poland; an appointment as lecturer at the LSE, which Malinowski had organised for him, did not materialise due to the outbreak of the war.²⁴

Halecki's and Gross's ways into exile were as different as their early careers. When Nazi Germany invaded Poland, Halecki was on a trip in Switzerland; he decided not to return to Poland and moved to Paris, where he initiated the short-lived Polish University in Exile and served as its rector.²⁵ After the German attack on France, he escaped via Spain and Portugal to New York. Thanks to his series of lectures two years before, his name was not unknown in the United States, and he was appointed lecturer at Vassar College in Poughkeepsie, New York; in 1944, he became professor at Fordham University. Over the following decades, he taught as visiting professor at several other American institutions, including Columbia University. At the same time, it was a major concern for him to create an institution that would allow Polish émigré scholars to stay in touch with each other and to continue their scholarly traditions; he was among the founders of the PIASA and stayed until the mid-1960s as the *spiritus movens* of the institute, acting as its executive director from 1942 to 1952 and its president from 1952 to 1964.²⁶

Gross, on the other hand, fled at the outbreak of war from his native Kraków, which was occupied by Nazi Germany, to Lwów in the Soviet zone of occupation and further to Vilnius. When rumours occurred that Germany planned an attack on the Soviet Union, he took a train to Vladivostok and then a boat to Japan, where he tried to obtain an American visa. At that time, he was in touch with his mentor Malinowski, now a professor at Yale University, who tried to find an academic position for him. In his correspondence with the Emergency Committee in Aid of Displaced Foreign Scholars, Malinowski stressed that from his earlier contact with Gross he could testify to 'what I would define as a great likelihood of rapid and effective adaptation to American ways of life and academic work in this country'.²⁷ But given the large number of émigré scholars that had already come to the United States by 1941, Malinowski's efforts turned out unsuccessful; Gross had to wait until 1946 until he could join the faculty of Brooklyn College of the City University of New York.²⁸ Upon his arrival in the US, he therefore started out working as a journalist for the émigré monthly *New Europe* and served as secretary general for the Central and Eastern European

Planning Board, an organisation set up by representatives of the exiled governments of Poland, Czechoslovakia, Yugoslavia and Greece in order to prepare for the region's postwar reconstruction. In this context, he cooperated with Halecki; in contrast to other left-wing oriented scholars, Gross had no reservations towards members of the pro-government intellectual elite. Halecki and Gross shared the conviction that in postwar Europe the countries between Germany and the Soviet Union should build a federation that would foster their defensive capabilities and would help to overcome national rivalries. As a potential label for such a federation, they brought up the term 'East Central Europe'.[29] In 1944, Gross was invited to become a member of the PIASA.[30]

The idea of 'East Central Europe' as a region with an identity of its own, which formed the basis for the wartime federalist plans, became a cornerstone of Halecki's postwar scholarly activities. Joining in the American debate on the historical foundations of the emerging 'Atlantic community', he elaborated a concept of 'East Central Europe' as a historical region that had always had close ties to the West and was fundamentally different from Russia.[31] In doing so, he remained faithful to the basic elements of his affirmative approach to Polish history and emphasised Christian values as the foundation of the West – in his eyes, it was America's duty in the context of the new 'Atlantic community' to preserve a European spiritual heritage that was threatened by totalitarianism.[32] While this perspective was not entirely foreign to the contemporary American discourse,[33] it still placed Halecki on the sidelines of new trends in Western historiography. He explicitly rejected the turn towards social history as it was represented by the *Annales* school, as 'materialist',[34] and urged that both Europeans and Americans should 'revitalize the spiritual elements of their heritage, if they want it to survive and not to be submerged by the machine age'.[35] Also within the Polish émigré community, Halecki persistently opposed attempts to revise Polish intellectual traditions; he did not cooperate with the journal *Kultura*[36] and strove against plans of some members of the PIASA staff to intensify cooperation with institutions in the People's Republic of Poland.[37]

Gross was generally sympathetic to Halecki's efforts to introduce an East Central European perspective into the American discourse of the 'Atlantic community'. Referring to Halecki's history of East Central Europe, he once stated that 'had not Professor Halecki written this book, I might have been compelled to do so, though my efforts would have been far inferior to his.'[38] Over the course of his postwar career as a sociologist, Gross sometimes also expressed doubts as to whether American social science was developing in the right direction. In his correspondence with other European émigré scholars, he criticised what he perceived as a tendency towards moral relativism.[39] Nonetheless, his perspective on the changes in American society and academia after 1945 was less sceptical than Halecki's. In particular, he became interested in the emancipation of ethnic minorities in the United States and wrote articles for *Kultura* in which he reflected on these developments.[40] The problem of multiethnicity became a leitmotif of Gross's oeuvre; drawing on his research and personal experiences in interwar Poland as well as on the discussion of this problem in postwar American sociology, he tried to develop a theory of how multiethnic societies can be organised in a way that facilitates peaceful coexistence.[41] During the early Cold War period, these interests were not typical for the leadership of the PIASA, but over the decades that followed the situation was supposed to change.

The Second Generation of Polish Émigré Scholars

In 1970, the leadership of the PIASA conducted a survey among the institute's members – at that time already several hundred scholars, scientists and artists. The respondents filled in a questionnaire and answered questions such as what they considered the institute's greatest achievements and weaknesses, what kind of reputation the institute had in the American academic world and what could be done to increase its impact on East European studies in the United States. The results of this survey could hardly have been more divergent. On the one hand, the founders of Polish émigré scholarship in America, who had been socialised in the academic world of interwar Poland, were mostly satisfied with what they had achieved. The 79-year-old Halecki stated in Polish that 'on the whole, the institute enjoys a good opinion in American scholarly circles'. In the future, it should 'remain faithful to the ideational principles on which it was based from the beginning'. The most effective way to promote Polish studies in the United States was thus to demonstrate 'the imperishable values of Polish culture'.[42]

On the other hand, younger Polish-born scholars who had started their careers at Western universities were more sceptical about the path that the institute had taken so far. For instance, Zbigniew Brzeziński, at that time already an eminent political scientist who had advised the presidential campaigns of John F. Kennedy and Hubert Humphrey, pointed out that 'the Polish Institute is reasonably well respected as a small scale source of bibliographic information and cultural activity, but it is certainly not viewed as a major intellectual force'.[43] In order to promote Polish studies effectively, the institute should stop pretending to be an academic body in itself; instead, it should try to initiate chairs of Polish language and culture 'at a few, highly selected and leading universities'[44] and develop into a cultural centre of the Polish-American community, which comprised not only wartime émigrés from Poland but also Americans of Polish descent. Indeed, some of the latter had so far felt excluded from the institute's inner circle of émigré scholars, and in the survey it was they who expressed the sharpest criticism. Walter Jajko, for example, a military expert and brigadier general who was born the son of Polish immigrants in the United States, claimed that the institute had the reputation of being a 'coterie of geriatric exiles who live in an unlamented past that is gone forever and who have produced little work of academic distinction'.[45] He complained about 'the unreality and fantasy of continuing to live in a world that died forever in 1939 – *thirty years ago!*' and the 'inability of the staff to make the Institute prosper in a modern, American milieu'.[46]

As this clash of opinions indicates, the early 1970s became a turning point in the history of the PIASA and of Polish émigré scholarship in the United States. The émigré scholars of the founding generation were losing their dominant position in the institutions they had created, and a younger generation of scholars who had left Poland as children or teenagers – in many cases because their parents had decided to emigrate – were less inclined to preserve their native traditions than to integrate into the American academic community. However, they did not consider those institutions dispensable; instead of its dissolution, the second-generation émigrés advocated a reform that would make the PIASA more capable of connecting with the American academic milieu. In 1974, for the first time an American by birth was elected president of the institute: the former government official and diplomat John A. Gronouski. One year later, Feliks Gross was elected executive director of the PIASA.[47] Gross might have appeared as the best candidate to integrate the heterogeneous émigré community; biographically, he belonged to the older generation rooted in the academic world of the Second Polish Republic, but his divergent political views and his interest in the situation of ethnic minorities, both in Poland and in the United States, made him a representative of younger scholars willing to integrate into American society as well. Shortly after his election, Gross stated in the institute's journal that a

> Polish born American has the right to chose [sic] freely his identification and association. One may chose [sic] freely integral assimilation, while another may prefer to consider himself a political exile and nothing more beyond his political affiliation as an American citizen. . . . The Polish Institutes of Arts and Sciences in the USA and Canada is, in turn, a pluralistic association.[48]

In 1977 Brzeziński, at that time National Security Advisor of President Jimmy Carter, congratulated Gross on the new course the PIASA had taken: 'Under your leadership, the Institute is undergoing a renaissance!'[49]

While many of the younger Polish émigré scholars rose to high academic positions, Brzeziński stands out. The son of a Polish diplomat, who had decided to stay in Canada after the Communist takeover in Poland, he was one of the very few descendants of the wartime Polish emigration who did not only have an impact on the development of East European studies in Cold War America but also a significant influence on American foreign policy. Over the course of his career, which led him from the Russian Research Center at Harvard to a professorship at Columbia University and finally into the White House, Brzeziński became so integrated into the American academic and political elites that he did not consider himself an 'émigré' at all.[50] Nonetheless, he never lost contact with the institutions that maintained the networks of Polish émigré scholars. His father had already been actively involved in the affairs of the PIASA, in particular in those of the institute's Canadian branch, and had been in touch with Jerzy Giedroyc, the editor of *Kultura*.[51] Brzeziński himself remained from his time at Harvard University until the 1990s a frequent correspondent of Giedroyc[52] and served for several years on the board of the PIASA. To an American colleague, he stressed in 1971 that one should not 'have any doubts about my feelings concerning exiles: I think they have played an honorable and historic role and they remain still an important political force. I have great respect for them in a historical sense and real admiration for some of them individually'.[53]

Both in the American public and in the Polish émigré community, Brzeziński's ambivalent status as a highly assimilated migrant raised the question of his loyalty. Advocates of détente surmised that his 'hawkish' stance on American foreign policy was due to the anti-Russian sentiment of a Polish nationalist.[54] Polish émigrés, on the other hand, were not always sure whether he was still 'one of them'. When Brzeziński was referred to in a *Kultura* article as 'our former compatriot',[55] readers complained that it was illegitimate to call his Polishness into question.[56] In retrospect, Brzeziński himself stressed that during his time as National Security Advisor he had acted as an American politician; the fact that Poland played a special role in his geostrategic thinking was thus only due to the objective convergence of American and Polish interests. Nevertheless, he confessed a strong attachment to his country of origin, without being fully able to determine to what extent it shaped his political actions.[57]

Conclusion

This chapter asked about the significance of institutional settings in the history of twentieth-century émigré scholarship. It focused on Polish émigré scholarship in Cold War America as an example of how two conflicting aims could coexist – the intention to preserve a scholarly tradition, which was perceived as threatened in the native country, and to bring it into dialogue with the intellectual environment of the host society. The example shows that when émigré scholars established institutions of their own, which provided a platform for the continuation of their native culture of knowledge, this could pose an obstacle to the 'deprovincialising' effects of the exile situation. But still, such an institutional setting could not prevent, in the course of decades, significant parts of the émigré community – in this case, primarily émigrés of a younger generation – from becoming integrated into the academic milieu of their host society. While maintaining a sense of loyalty towards the intentions that had led to the founding of the émigré institutions, the latter did acquire what Said described as an 'awareness of simultaneous dimensions':[58] the ability to perceive both their native culture and that of their hosts with the eyes of foreigners.

Notes

1. Burke, *Exiles and Expatriates*, 187.
2. Said, 'Reflections on Exile', 184.
3. Raeff, *Russia Abroad*.
4. Greenberg, *Weimar Century*, 19.
5. Stobiecki, 'Oskar Halecki jako organizator'.
6. Statute of the Polish Institute of Arts and Sciences in America, 1942.
7. Statute of the Polish Institute of Arts and Sciences in America, 1942.
8. Statute of the Polish Institute of Arts and Sciences in America, 1942.
9. Dorosz, *Nowojorski pasjans*, 75–80.
10. Letter to the board of the Polish Institute of Arts and Sciences in America, signed by Ludwig Anigstein, Gustaw Bychowski, Manfred Kridl, Oskar Lange, Aleksander Wundheiler, Bohdan Zawadzki, and Antoni Zygmund, December 1942.
11. Letter from Manfred Kridl to Jan Kucharzewski, 1 February 1943.
12. Cf. letter from Oskar Halecki to Manfred Kridl, 11 January 1943.
13. In 1946, the PIASA described its mission as a 'contribution to Polish culture, freely and faithfully expressing its great tradition which has so much in common with the American heritage'. PIASA, 'Introduction', 8.
14. On how American institutions at that time actively tried to mobilise the knowledge of émigrés, see Faure, 'Guerre froide et mobilisations'.
15. On this journal and its network of contributors, see, most recently, Wiaderny, *Schule des politischen Denkens*; Labov, 'Re-reading *Kultura*'.
16. Gromada, 'About PIASA'.
17. On Halecki's family background, Stobiecki, *Klio za wielką wodą*, 139.
18. Bömelburg, 'Zwischen imperialer Geschichte und Ostmitteleuropa', 107.
19. On this point of Halecki's biography, in detail Brzeziński, *Oskar Halecki a Liga Narodów*.
20. His programmatic essays: Halecki, 'Granica z r. 1772'; Halecki, 'Idea jagiellońska'.
21. On the formation and institutionalisation of sociology in the Second Polish Republic: Markiewicz-Lagneau, *La formation d'une pensée*; Kraśko, *Instytucjonalizacja socjologii*.
22. Gross, *Proletariat i kultura*; Mysłakowski and Gross, *Robotnicy piszą*.
23. Kubica, 'The Survey of the Ghetto'.
24. Lebow, 'The Polish Peasant', 188.
25. Stobiecki, 'Oskar Halecki jako organizator'.
26. Gromada, 'About PIASA'.
27. Letter from Bronisław Malinowski to Laurens Seelye, 14 January 1941.

28. Krase, 'Feliks Gross', 175.

29. Halecki, 'East Central Europe in Postwar Organization'; Gross, *Crossroads of Two Continents*. On the federalist plans of Polish émigrés in the United States, see in detail Łukasiewicz, *Trzecia Europa*.

30. Invitation to the annual General Assembly of the Polish Institute of Arts and Sciences in America, 8 May 1944.

31. Halecki, *Limits and Divisions*; Halecki, *Borderlands of Western Civilization*.

32. Halecki, *Limits and Divisions*, 58.

33. On the role of religious ideas in early American conceptualisations of an 'Atlantic community', see Alessandri, 'Atlantic Community as Christendom'.

34. Halecki, 'Kongres Historyczny', 140; also Stobiecki, 'Historycy polscy na uchodźstwie', 78.

35. Halecki, *Millennium of Europe*, 382.

36. Kornat, 'Profesor Oskar Halecki', 269–70.

37. Stobiecki, *Klio za wielką wodą*, 81–82.

38. Letter from Feliks Gross to William H. Foster, 23 April 1952.

39. Letter from Feliks Gross to Pitirim Sorokin, 2 January 1956: 'The whole field of sociology – which in fact is the field of social sciences, is lost today in some kind of secondary search for trivia. . . . The great moral issues of our times, have been entirely relegated – the relativists have convinced most of our students . . . that moral values are relative to a point, that they do not exist'. On the differences between Gross's approach to sociology and the postwar development of American social science, see also Lebow, 'The Polish Peasant', 203–4.

40. Gross, 'Demokracja i kolor'; Gross, 'Rewolucja etniczna'.

41. Towards the end of his life, Gross provided a synthesis of his thinking on this subject in the books: Gross, *The Civic and the Tribal State*; Gross, *Citizenship and Ethnicity*.

42. The Sendzimir Questionnaire, completed by Oskar Halecki.

43. The Sendzimir Questionnaire, completed by Zbigniew Brzeziński.

44. The Sendzimir Questionnaire, completed by Zbigniew Brzeziński.

45. The Sendzimir Questionnaire, completed by Walter Jajko.

46. The Sendzimir Questionnaire, completed by Walter Jajko.

47. Gromada, 'About PIASA'.

48. Gross, 'Notes on the Ethnic Revolution', 168.

49. Letter from Zbigniew Brzeziński to Feliks Gross, 22 March 1977.

50. Vaïsse, *Zbigniew Brzezinski*, 243.

51. The Sendzimir Questionnaire, completed by Tadeusz Brzeziński; Correspondence of Tadeusz Brzeziński with Jerzy Giedroyc.

52. The correspondence of Zbigniew Brzeziński with Jerzy Giedroyc.

53. Letter from Zbigniew Brzeziński to Christopher Emmet, 2 December 1971.

54. Vaïsse, *Zbigniew Brzezinski*, 243.

55. Brukselczyk, 'Widziane z Brukseli', 66.

56. Letter from Witold S. Sworakowski to Jerzy Giedroyc, 17 July 1977.

57. Brzeziński, 'Czy amerykański polityk może służyć Polsce?'.

58. Said, 'Reflections on Exile', 186.

Bibliography

Alessandri, Emiliano. 'The Atlantic Community as Christendom: Some Reflections on Christian Atlanticism in America, circa 1900–1950', in Marco Mariano (ed.), *Defining the Atlantic Community: Culture, Intellectuals, and Policies in the Mid-Twentieth Century* (New York and London: Routledge, 2010), 47–70.

Bömelburg, Hans-Jürgen. 'Zwischen imperialer Geschichte und Ostmitteleuropa als Geschichtsregion: Oskar Halecki und die polnische "jagiellonische Idee"', in Frank Hadler and Mathias Mesenhöller (eds), *Vergangene Größe und Ohnmacht in Ostmitteleuropa: Repräsentationen imperialer Erfahrung in der Historiographie seit 1918* (Leipzig: Akademische Verlagsanstalt, 2007), 99–129.

Brzeziński, Andrzej Maciej. *Oskar Halecki a Liga Narodów: Poglądy i działalność*. Łódź: Wydawnictwo Uniwersytetu Łódzkiego, 2016.

Burke, Peter. *Exiles and Expatriates in the History of Knowledge, 1500–2000*. Waltham, MA: Brandeis University Press, 2017.

Dorosz, Beata. *Nowojorski pasjans: Polski Instytut Naukowy w Ameryce, Jan Lechoń, Kazimierz Wierzyński*. Warsaw: Biblioteka 'Więzi', 2013.

Faure, Justine. 'Guerre froide et mobilisations des savoirs exilés sur l'Europe de l'Est: L'exemple des Etats-Unis', in Matthieu Gillabert and Tiphaine Robert (eds), *Zuflucht suchen: Phasen des Exils aus Osteuropa im Kalten Krieg – Chercher refuge: Les phases d'exil d'Europe centrale pendant la Guerre froide* (Basel: Schwabe Verlag, 2017), 97–114.

Greenberg, Udi. *The Weimar Century: German Émigrés and the Ideological Foundations of the Cold War*. Princeton, NJ and Oxford: Princeton University Press, 2014.

Gromada, Thaddeus V. 'About PIASA'. Retrieved 29 March 2022 from http://piasa.org/about-piasa.html.

Kornat, Marek. 'Profesor Oskar Halecki w życiu politycznym Polski i na forum międzynarodowym', in Małgorzata Dąbrowska (ed.), *Oskar Halecki i jego wizja Europy*, Vol. 3 (Warsaw: Instytut Pamięci Narodowej, 2015), 232–88.

Krase, Jerome. 'Feliks Gross: Between Assimilation and Multiculturalism'. *The Polish Review* 52(2) (2007), 171–87.

Kraśko, Nina. *Instytucjonalizacja socjologii w Polsce 1920–1970*. Warsaw: Wydawnictwo Naukowe PWN, 1996.

Kubica, Grażyna. '"The Survey of the Ghetto" in the Time of Anti-Semitism: Feliks Gross and His Unfinished Fieldwork on the Jewish Quarters of Krakow and Vilna, 1938–1940'. *East European Politics and Societies* 28(2) (2014), 318–40.

Labov, Jessie. 'Re-reading *Kultura* from a Distance', in Irene Kacandes and Yuliya Komska (eds), *Eastern Europe Unmapped: Beyond Borders and Peripheries* (New York and Oxford: Berghahn Books, 2018), 104–30.

Lebow, Katherine. 'The Polish Peasant on the Sugar Plantation: Bronisław Malinowski, Feliks Gross and Józef Obrębski in the New World'. *Contemporary European History* 28(2) (2019), 188–204.

Łukasiewicz, Sławomir. *Trzecia Europa: Polska myśl federalistyczna w Stanach Zjednoczonych 1940–1971*. Warsaw: Instytut Pamięci Narodowej, 2010.

Markiewicz-Lagneau, Janina. *La formation d'une pensée sociologique: La société polonaise de l'entre-deux-guerres*. Paris: Édition de la maison des sciences de l'homme, 1982.

Raeff, Marc. *Russia Abroad: A Cultural History of the Russian Emigration, 1919–1939*. New York and Oxford: Oxford University Press, 1990.

Said, Edward W. 'Reflections on Exile' [1984], in Edward W. Said, *Reflections on Exile and Other Essays*. Second edition (Cambridge, MA: Harvard University Press, 2001), 173–86.

Stobiecki, Rafał. 'Historycy polscy na uchodźstwie na Międzynarodowych Kongresach Nauk Historycznych'. *Dzieje Najnowsze* 34(3) (2002), 75–93.

———. 'Oskar Halecki jako organizator Uniwersytetu Polskiego Zagranicą', in Małgorzata Dąbrowska (ed.), *Oskar Halecki a jego wizja Europy*. Vol. 3 (Warsaw: Instytut Pamięci Narodowej, 2015), 172–86.

———. *Klio za wielką wodą: Polscy historycy w Stanach Zjednoczonych po 1945 roku*. Warsaw: Instytut Pamięci Narodowej, 2017.

Vaïsse, Justin. *Zbigniew Brzezinski: America's Grand Strategist*. Cambridge, MA: Harvard University Press, 2018.

Wiaderny, Bernard. *'Schule des politischen Denkens': Die Exilzeitschrift 'Kultura' im Kampf um die Unabhängigkeit Polens 1947–1991*. Paderborn: Ferdinand Schöningh, 2018.

Archival Sources

Archives of the Instytut Literacki 'Kultura' (ILK), Le Mesnil-le-Roi

Correspondence of Tadeusz Brzeziński with Jerzy Giedroyc. Archives of the Instytut Literacki "Kultura" (ILK), Le Mesnil-le-Roi: KOR RED Brzeziński T.

Correspondence of Zbigniew Brzeziński with Jerzy Giedroyc. ILK Archives, Le Mesnil-le-Roi KOR RED Brzeziński Z.

Letter from Witold S. Sworakowski to Jerzy Giedroyc, 17 July 1977. ILK Archives, Le Mesnil-le-Roi KOR RED Sworakowski.

Archiwum Akt Nowych [Polish Central Archive of Modern Records], Warsaw

Letter from Zbigniew Brzeziński to Christopher Emmet, 2 December 1971. Archiwum Akt Nowych [Polish Central Archive of Modern Records], Stefan and Zofia Korboński Papers (2/2500), folder 351.

Columbia University, Rare Book & Manuscript Library, New York: Manfred Kridl Papers

Letter to the board of the Polish Institute of Arts and Sciences in America, signed by Ludwig Anigstein, Gustaw Bychowski, Manfred Kridl, Oskar Lange, Aleksander Wundheiler, Bohdan Zawadzki, and Antoni Zygmund, December 1942. Columbia University, Rare Book & Manuscript Library, New York: Manfred Kridl Papers, Series II, box 4.

Letter from Oskar Halecki to Manfred Kridl, 11 January 1943. Columbia University, Rare Book & Manuscript Library, New York: Manfred Kridl Papers, Series II, box 4.

Letter from Manfred Kridl to Jan Kucharzewski, 1 February 1943. Columbia University, Rare Book & Manuscript Library, New York: Manfred Kridl Papers, Series II, box 4.

Emergency Committee in Aid of Displaced Foreign Scholars Records. Manuscripts and Archives Division. The New York Public Library. Astor, Lenox, and Tilden Foundations, New York

Letter from Bronisław Malinowski to Laurens Seelye, 14 January 1941. Emergency Committee in Aid of Displaced Foreign Scholars Records. Manuscripts and Archives Division. The New York Public Library. Astor, Lenox, and Tilden Foundations, New York, box 65, older 35.

Polish Institute of Arts and Sciences of America Archives (PIASA Archives), New York

Statute of the Polish Institute of Arts and Sciences in America, 1942. PIASA Archives, 17/144.

Invitation to the annual General Assembly of the Polish Institute of Arts and Sciences in America, 8 May 1944. PIASA Archives, 17/57.

Letter from Feliks Gross to William H. Foster, 23 April 1952. PIASA Archives, 50/76, 166.

Letter from Feliks Gross to Pitirim Sorokin, 2 January 1956. PIASA Archives, 4/230.

The Sendzimir Questionnaire, completed by Oskar Halecki. PIASA Archives, 17/86.

The Sendzimir Questionnaire, completed by Zbigniew Brzeziński. PIASA Archives, 17/85.

The Sendzimir Questionnaire, completed by Walter Jajko. PIASA Archives, 17/85.

Letter from Zbigniew Brzeziński to Feliks Gross, 22 March 1977. PIASA Archives, 17/806.

The Sendzimir Questionnaire, completed by Tadeusz Brzeziński. PIASA Archives, 17/86.

Published Sources

Brukselczyk [Leopold Unger]. 'Widziane z Brukseli'. *Kultura* 4 (1977), 58–72.
Brzeziński, Zbigniew. 'Czy amerykański polityk może służyć Polsce?'. *Dziennik Polski*, 18 August 1988, 3.
Gross, Feliks. *Proletariat i kultura: Warunki społeczne i gospodarcze kultury proletariatu*. Warsaw: Związek Zawodowy Pracowników Kolejowych, 1938.
———. *Crossroads of Two Continents: A Democratic Federation of East-Central Europe*. New York: Columbia University Press, 1945.
———. 'Demokracja i kolor'. *Kultura* 11 (1961), 67–83.
———. 'Rewolucja etniczna'. *Kultura* 7–8 (1975), 89–95.
———. 'Notes on the Ethnic Revolution and the Polish Immigration in the U.S.A'. *The Polish Review* 21(3) (1976), 149–76.
———. *The Civic and the Tribal State: The State, Ethnicity, and the Multiethnic State*. Westport, CT and London: Greenwood Press, 1998.
———. *Citizenship and Ethnicity: The Growth and Development of a Democratic Multiethnic Institution*. Westport, CT and London: Greenwood Press, 1999.
Halecki, Oskar. 'Granica z r. 1772 a nasz program obecny'. *Wschód Polski* 1(4) (1920), 1–11.
———. 'Idea jagiellońska'. *Kwartalnik Historyczny* 51 (1937), 486–510.
———. 'East Central Europe in Postwar Organization'. *Annals of the American Academy of Political and Social Sciences* 228 (1943), 52–59.
———. 'Kongres Historyczny w Paryżu'. *Teki Historyczne* 4 (1950), 137–40.
———. *The Limits and Divisions of European History*. New York: Sheed & Ward, 1950.
———. *Borderlands of Western Civilization: A History of East Central Europe*. New York: Ronald Press, 1952.
———. *The Millennium of Europe*. Notre Dame, IN: University of Notre Dame Press, 1963.
Mysłakowski, Zygmunt, and Feliks Gross (eds). *Robotnicy piszą: Pamiętniki robotników*. Kraków: Księgarnia Powszechna, 1938.
PIASA. 'Introduction', *Bulletin of the Polish Institute of Arts and Sciences in America* 4 (1945–46), 7–8.

CHAPTER 8

The Unlikely Careers of Laura Polanyi (1882–1959) as a Historian

The Intersections of Exile, Gender, Class and Age

Judith Szapor

Introduction

In 1957, two years before her death at the age of seventy-seven, the Hungarian émigré historian Laura Polanyi Stricker (1882–1959) submitted an account of her professional life in response to the query of an American historian.[1] A single page, the document is the shortest of professional autobiographies – but it helps to shed light on the gendered aspect of the Central European intellectual émigré experience.

Polanyi was one of the first Hungarian women to earn a doctorate in History – she received her degree in 1909 – but afterwards took a long detour before finding her way back to academia. It was only in the United States during the 1950s, the last decade of her life, that she became, once more, a professional historian – or, rather, what we would call an independent scholar today. The brief professional autobiography shows Polanyi as a consummate historian, able to turn an unconventional and fractured trajectory into a cohesive narrative; and as such, deserves to be quoted in full:

> When in 1900 the Hungarian universities admitted women students, I was with the first group of girls which invaded the holy halls. I received there my Ph.D. in History and English Literature as subsidiary subject.

Notes for this section begin on page 152.

I had to register my main occupations since for the Virginia Historical Society publicity and am sending you a copy. You will find that the 'occupations' seem very erratic. This is due to the fact that they were influenced by the possibilities, trends, and impossibilities of this semi-century. For example when my habilitation thesis would have been recognized as valid for an assistant professorship (Dozentur), my university decided never to admit women to the faculty. I turned my main interest from history to pedagogics. This was also motivated by my son and daughter reaching the age when I would have had to send them to schools I trusted less if I did not organize a school of our own. We started it trying out most of the ideas and methods the first decennium of this century brought forth.

War and Peace, defeat and occupation, revolutions and inflation supplied us with problems 1914–1924.

With the approach of Fascism and Communism my historical interest revived. The planned economy of 18th century mercantilism and the trends in economics and politics of the time tempted to historical research and comparative studies. Maria Theresia [*sic*].

Since October 1951 when Bradford Smith was led to me as to a Hungarian historian who could look into the question of truthfulness of Captain John Smith's report on his alleged Hungarian adventures and thus help him with his biography of Captain John Smith, I am exclusively interested in this problem. I regard it as a great gift and privilege that I was given this opportunity to serve as a Hungarian historian to vindicate the honor and valor of America's most enthusiastic champion.[2]

I will return to the details of Laura Polanyi's account for a closer look, to examine the historical and personal context behind the seemingly flawless arc of its narrative. For now, I will consider the brief text as a singular ego-document that offers important insights into the fate of intellectual émigré women. Polanyi's case is distinguished by the expansive geographical range she had travelled (both literally and figuratively) and the unwillingness to completely abandon her ambitions as a historian. Acutely aware of her extended family's intellectual accomplishments, Polanyi became the family's unofficial historian. The resulting, extensive family archive is rare among the intellectual refugees, most of whom escaped in haste and with few possessions; and it provides an exceptionally rich documentation of the family's escape from Hitler's Europe but also of Polanyi's intellectual pursuits.

Her case defies easy categorisation in other ways, transcending political eras and movements, national histories, and major trends of women's emancipation. Polanyi was born in Vienna and raised in Budapest; she became a member of the first cohort of mainly middle-class women educated at the first academic high school for women and at the Faculty of Arts and Medicine (opened by ministerial decree in 1896). Her self-identity was further complicated by her lifelong ties to her native Vienna and her secular but firmly Jewish identity at a time when similarly assimilated Jews in Hungary converted *en masse*.

Her political loyalties and ties to leading political figures had ranged, over time, from the liberal Hungarian intellectual and political establishment to the bourgeois feminist movement and included electoral campaigning on behalf of the liberal socialist Bourgeois Radical Party during the postwar liberal revolution in Hungary. In the 1920s and early 1930s, she withdrew into a quiet bourgeois life but still participated in her children's lives – including their left-wing politics. In emigration, she kept up ties with other political émigrés, although staying in the background, never again engaging publicly in their debates.[3] These multiple attachments, as well as her frequent moves first between Vienna and Budapest, then to Berlin, the Soviet Union, England and the United States make her a veritable transnational subject, well suited for an individual biographical treatment – but also an uneasy fit for existing bodies of scholarship. Similarly, while she was among the first Hungarian women earning a doctorate and destined for academic trailblazing, she would abandon academic pursuits for four decades, only taking them up much later in the US. Thus, she would not be a natural subject for a study on pioneering academic women, a field of scholarship organised by academic discipline and national historical context.[4]

By the same token, Polanyi's early life – enrolment in the first academic high school for girls in Hungary and then being among the first Hungarian women to go to university alongside employment as a researcher and bibliographer – identifies her as one of the first female academic historians in Hungary, a subject covered, albeit in other European contexts, by recent scholarship.[5] Her subsequent life choices, including early and financially advantageous marriage and decades of family life in upper-middle-class comfort without sustained scholarly activities, would seem to exclude her from academia. The sudden shifts between bourgeois family life and academic interests influenced by both external conditions and autonomous decisions continued throughout her life. For instance, after abruptly abandoning her studies in 1904 and in between giving birth to her three children, in 1909 she completed a doctorate in economic history. Shortly after, she abandoned academic pursuits once more but for highly legitimate reasons, cited in her short biography as 'War and Peace, defeat and occupation, revolutions and inflation . . .'.[6]

Lastly, her late professional success in exile took place on the margins of American academia, leaving her out of the accounts of émigré historians in general, even the handful of recent studies dedicated to female émigré historians.[7] This omission may also be explained by the small numbers of Hungarian émigré historians; after all, they failed to make the grade even in recent accounts, which are strong on German scholars and include Poles and Czechoslovaks but not a single Hungarian.[8] As for the relatively recent branch of the history of science that focuses on women and gender in academia, it has covered mainly the natural and life sciences, not the humanities.⁹

These difficulties of categorisation notwithstanding, Polanyi's case should not be dismissed, because it is despite or, rather, because of her differences from the majority of émigré historians in age, previous education and ambitions that we can address the interplay and respective roles of gender and age in the success (or lack thereof) of a female intellectual émigré. To what degree did Polanyi's age and gender determine her unique professional trajectory? Can we locate her in any of the cohorts or generations of émigré historians? Or should she be filed away as an outlier, both in terms of gender and age?

Furthermore, what changes if we add class to the interplay of gender and age? We should note here that the dynamic or respective weight of these factors was far from stable during Polanyi's life course, a point that should be acknowledged by any analysis. The following examples should help clarify this point: Laura Polanyi's age facilitated her membership in – and offered the solidarity of – the small cohort of university-bound Hungarian women born around the last decade of the nineteenth-century. In contrast, when settling in the United States, her age placed her at a disadvantage: not only did she lack the support of a group of peers but faced the stigma of an older woman trying to (re-)enter academia. Similarly, her upper-middle-class upbringing and Hungarian-Jewish ethnic and cultural background were perceived as either a relative advantage or a handicap depending on the specific sociopolitical setting, whether fin-de-siècle Budapest, interwar Vienna or postwar New York City.

Her case can also contribute to a discussion of émigré strategies vis-à-vis the academic cultures they found in their new environment compared to the academic environment of their origin. Few European refugees were better prepared to take the measure of American academia than Laura Polanyi. She had participated in the struggle for women's emancipation in higher education in pre-war Hungary and Austria and experienced the ebb and flow of academia's resistance to women's admittance. As a parent supervising her children's education and who founded an experimental kindergarten herself, she was well placed to observe the drastic changes in postwar Hungarian, Austrian and German academia. And as her brothers, Michael and Karl Polanyi, émigré academics themselves, carved a path in the Austrian, German and English intellectual elite in the 1920s and 1930s, she gained an understanding, if for the time indirectly, of the intellectual émigré condition.

Well before her own arrival in the United States in 1939, through members of her academically and intellectually gifted extended family, Laura Polanyi had been connected to multiple academic and intellectual networks in Europe. After the rise of Nazism in Germany and its march across Europe, many of these networks would be partly transplanted to Great Britain and the United States – such as the physicists' network Polanyi was connected to through family and friends.[10] Her life trajectory thus offers a privileged vantage point from which to observe the workings of these networks in the process of emigration as well as in shaping scholarly employment opportunities. As we will see, her own and her family's place in the transnational networks of émigré intellectuals, physicists and social scientists may have supplied the initial entry for Polanyi into American academia. And the advantages of an upper-middle-class upbringing, including early exposure to several languages, among them English, should not be underestimated.[11]

One could legitimately raise all these and quite possibly more questions – and I had considered some of them in my monograph on the women of the Polanyi family.[12] But I welcome the opportunity provided here to consider Polanyi in the context of émigré historians; and after a brief historiographical overview, I will focus on three aspects that can benefit from a discussion of her trajectory and contribute to this already substantial literature. The first concerns the 'catching up' of women's and gender history with the broader history of the intellectual migration: I ask whether this convergence had in fact happened or remains a largely unexplored, potential research direction. Secondly, I will consider whether the case of Laura Polanyi, despite or with all its specifics, can help us reconsider the émigré historians from the perspective of gender and, to a lesser degree, age and class. Lastly, I aim to broaden the persistent German focus of inquiry and challenge the practice of treating Hungarians, if at all, within a 'German-speaking' category.[13]

Historiographical Context

A brief look at the scholarly literature on émigré historians offers few, if any, references to the women in their ranks. With the exception of the short study of Catherine Epstein on a small group of German-speaking historians[14] and another, more recent article by Marjorie Lamberti on Gerda Lerner's contribution to American women's history,[15] we will find no literature on women, let alone any female Hungarian historians. The very consideration of émigré historians as a distinct cohort within the larger population of émigré scholars/the intellectual migration/the Hitler emigration is relatively recent, as it only began in the early 1990s.[16] It emerged in parallel with another development that turned the focus from the outstanding figures of the Hitler emigration to their study as cohorts or groups and their specific impact on American intellectual and academic life.

It should also be noted that history was a relatively late addition to studies of émigrés in other scholarly fields, such as sociology, law, psychology, psychoanalysis, political science and anthropology, to mention just a few. It is perhaps understandable that history was not included in the first, flagship volume on 'The Intellectual Migration'[17] that almost singlehandedly established the field as the subject of historical inquiry – perhaps it would have been considered too self-indulgent. (This despite the fact that historians were very much present in the volume; even those, such as Peter Gay, considered a prime representative of the so-called second-generation émigré German historians.[18])

The other pioneering study on the subject was the almost simultaneously published *Illustrious Immigrants: The Intellectual Migration from Europe, 1930–41*, compiled by Laura Fermi,[19] wife of the Nobel-laureate physicist Enrico Fermi. Laura Fermi, in contrast to the Fleming–Bailyn volume, did include historians and, in a separate but similarly short section, Orientalists. (Fermi was also a bone fide historian, the author of one of the first biographies of Mussolini,[20] and despite her modesty she included herself in the chapter on historians.) For *Illustrious Immigrants*, she used her extensive social networks among Italian anti-fascist émigrés and physicists. She collected the material for her book by sending out questionnaires and corresponding with a vast number of her protagonists. The book's organisation may leave much to be desired, yet it should be appreciated for its inclusivity and insights, far ahead of her time. Instead of the recognition it so richly deserved from fellow historians, it received a condescending acknowledgement from the editors of the Fleming–Bailyn volume. In a footnote of their Introduction, they referred their readers to Fermi's book: 'For the numbers involved, and for a charming [*sic*] and valuable personal portrayal of leading intellectuals among the refugees' – praise today we would justifiably consider sexist – while also thanking her 'for her kindness in allowing us to see a portion of her book in manuscript, and for discussing the movement as a whole with us'.[21]

Not long after the pioneering works on the so-called first generation of émigré historians (without a single exception, men who received their training in Germany) published in the early 1990s, a wave of memoirs by members of the second generation followed. The most prominent members of this cohort, defined as historians who emigrated to the US or elsewhere as children or adolescents – Fritz Stern, Peter Gay and George Mosse – all published autobiographies around 2000.[22] But it was only in 2016 that they became the subject of a scholarly volume – one that was still not entirely scholarly but mixed scholarly essays with first-person memoirs by the protagonists and their students.[23] As with the 1991 Lehmann and Sheehan volume, it contained the proceedings of a conference organised by the German Historical Institute in D.C.– thus highlighting the role of the institution that from its inaugural conference in 1988 singlehandedly laid the foundations of this field. (That these research and publishing activities also resulted in an overwhelmingly German focus should go without saying.)

The two flagship volumes issued by the German Historical Institute established the by now widely accepted periodisation, a categorisation not entirely unproblematic: when it comes to the distinction between the first and second generations, it is far from clear and neither is it unanimously accepted by the subjects themselves. Walter Laqueur, slotted into the second generation, used a slightly different definition in his own book, *Generation Exodus*. Members of his 'generation Exodus' were born between 1914 and 1928 and were 'old enough to appreciate the loss of their homeland and the experience of flight but often young and flexible enough to survive and even flourish in new environments. Many would go on to make great contributions to their new countries and the world'.[24]

These debatable points aside, there can be no question that the focus on German historians is justified not simply by their intellectual influence but by their numerical presence: they numbered 98 in the first generation, 107 in the second. But what about non-German, and more relevant to my subject, Hungarian émigré historians? The scholarly literature is silent on them. One has to conclude, reluctantly, that the silence is justified, for Hungarian émigré historians could be counted on one hand. Jewish and leftist Hungarian intellectuals and artists may have gotten a head start in 1919 when they escaped a right-wing dictatorship,[25] yet very few of them had been or had become historians.[26]

German-Speaking Women Émigré Historians in the United States

Catherine Epstein, one of the first scholars working on the émigré German historians, came to this task honestly as the daughter and granddaughter of eminent German émigré historians.[27] She is also the author of the only study to date on women émigré historians. Her short study was coincidentally produced by the method pioneered by Laura Fermi many decades earlier: based on a questionnaire sent out to German-born women historians, all living at the time in the US, with the single exception of Rita Thälmann, a professor at the Sorbonne.

The answers of sixteen women were then moulded into a sort of inventory that in turn served as the basis for a few conclusions. Out of the possible demographic and educational factors, Epstein considered age, gender and the émigré experience itself as almost equally significant, with gender ending up the most significant when it came to the success – or, in most cases, lack thereof – of the sixteen women historians' professional career.

Epstein's position is less clear-cut when it comes to comparing the educational and professional opportunities of women, and in particular Jewish women, in Weimar Germany vs. 1930s America. She seems to come down on both sides of the fence when trying to explain the lack of academic success of her subjects, pointing to academic antisemitism and entrenched patriarchal bias in American academia combined with the refugees' lack of English and familiarity with the American system of education on the one hand, and the Prussian rigidity and strict hierarchy of Weimar academia (at their point of departure) on the other. She mentions the over-representation of Jewish women among university students in Weimar Germany but not women's relatively high representation in the professions (among others, in public health, social work, law, sociology, or psychology). She ends by raising a question based on counterfactuals: What would have happened to German women in academia without a Nazi takeover ? Her overall conclusion reflects the dearth of data, the small number of German women historians who 'made it' in the United States and, as she readily admits, the difficulty of establishing patterns of success or, more often, lack thereof on such a limited database.

Bridging Two Eras and Continents: The Unlikely First and Second Careers of Laura Polanyi as a Historian

A member of a distinguished family of academics, intellectuals and artists, Laura Polanyi was born the eldest of five siblings in Vienna in 1882.[28] Her parents met and raised a family in the Austro-Hungarian Monarchy, with their respective lines combining two paths of Jewish assimilation; the mother, Cecile Wohl, was the daughter of an assimilationist professor of the Vilna Rabbinical Seminary. She became a celebrated wit and salonist, a unique fixture on the Budapest intellectual and modernist scene of the early twentieth-century. Laura Polanyi's father hailed from Northern Hungary and became a railway-building engineer and entrepreneur first in Vienna, then in Budapest. Two of Laura's younger brothers, Karl and Michael, both became émigrés in the wake of the failed revolutions in Hungary in 1919 and went on to have illustrious academic careers, in economics and political science and in science and philosophy, respectively. With countless cousins and members of the extended family born or married into it, the Polanyi clan became intellectual and artistic royalty, first in Budapest and Vienna, then in Weimar Berlin. After Hitler's rise to power, the extended family found its way onto three continents.

Back at the turn of the century in Hungary, the assimilating Jewish upper-middle class of which the Polanyis were a part was instrumental in economic modernisation, as well as in the era's progressive intellectual, political and artistic movements. Daughters of these families were the pioneers of higher education, entering the faculties of art and medicine that opened in Hungary in 1896. (There is a small, somewhat self-serving inconsistency in Laura Polanyi's short bio cited above, where she conflates the date of the opening of university faculties with her own entry in 1900.)

The following decades of Polanyi's life can be divided into roughly three periods: her beginnings in Hungary put her squarely at the centre of this political avant-garde, with a university degree in History and English awarded in 1904, membership in the Association of Feminists, and a doctorate – certainly one of the first among women – in History in 1909. Her dissertation was written under the supervision of the leading Hungarian historian of the early modern period, Henrik Marczali, on a topic that would have been considered quite masculine, the economic policies of Charles VI, the father of Maria Theresa.

Between the two degrees, however, Polanyi took a detour: she married a wealthy industrialist fourteen years her senior, went on to have three children and commanded an upper-class household – and founded an experimental kindergarten based on 'Freudian principles', attended by her own children and, among others, the 5-year-old Arthur Koestler. During and after the 1918–1919 revolutions, Laura's three siblings left Hungary while she remained and abandoned all professional or academic plans; in the two decades between the wars, Laura Polanyi travelled to wherever her adult children moved, from Vienna to Weimar Germany to the Soviet Union, giving up her ambitions as a historian.

In my monograph dedicated to the Polanyi women, an entire chapter titled 'The Odyssey of the Polanyis' describes the overwhelmingly successful escape of the extended family from Hitler' Europe, but this is not the place to describe the details of this process even in the most general way. A few points, however, should be briefly highlighted: Laura Polanyi (along with younger brother Michael Polanyi, who had settled in England) was the family member who came to commandeer the rescue operations, putting her research and language skills to practical use. Polanyi's heroic and at times frantic activities in this extended rescue operation could be interpreted as a relapse from her previous academic and political activities to roles gendered as quintessentially female: that of the immigrant matriarch, emotional centre, and record keeper of an extended family.

But the story did not end with Polanyi's resignation to the conventional, grandmotherly role befitting her age and social status. In the early 1950s, she had a sudden burst of professional engagement and a relative measure of success. To make a long and serendipitous story short, Karl Polanyi, then a visiting professor at Columbia University, was asked by an American author of popular historical biographies for a recommendation for a research assistant who could read Latin and German and was familiar with the history of the Habsburg Empire in the early seventeenth-century. Bradford Smith was writing a new biography of Captain Smith, the founder of the colony of Virginia and needed to check the veracity of the Captain's 'Travels in Hungary and Transylvania'. Karl Polanyi referred Bradford Smith to her older sister – and the rest became the story of her last years.

This seems to be an opportune point to consider the impact of age on Laura Polanyi's chances to re-enter academia. It would seem logical to assume that her age – she was already in her late fifties when she escaped from Austria to England in 1938, and, in August 1939, reached the US – would have put her at a distinct disadvantage in professional terms. After all, she was a product of Central European education, not expected to be familiar with the ways of American academia. But this assumption may be deceptive, for Polanyi also enjoyed a number of advantages over most of the rank-and-file émigrés. She was a member of the large, talented and successful Polanyi 'clan', with the family's multiple, professional and familial networks supplying some of the preconditions for her own success. Moreover, her three children, who had all reached the US before her, were adults and successful in their own right; thus Polanyi was exempt of the often insurmountable obstacles faced by younger professional women, whose professional career was thwarted by childrearing responsibilities or the need to support their husband's career and financial survival. For their part, the Polanyis, in contrast to Jewish citizens of the Reich, did not have to surrender their assets to the Hungarian state, and so Laura Polanyi was relatively comfortable in financial terms – and a research assistant position did not represent to her a financial lifeline on which her family depended.

Instead, it served as her entry – or re-entry – into the historical trade: for Laura Polanyi spent these years in feverish research in American, English, Austrian and Hungarian archives, translating, writing and publishing, and ultimately restoring the Captain's previous, dubious reputation. In the process, she turned the research assistantship into a project, limited in its scope but nevertheless independent. It became the obsession, 'my *Besessenheit*',[29] as she put it to Karl Polanyi, of the last years of her life.

Between 1951 and 1958 this work resulted in a range of publications. Laura Polanyi's article, 'Captain John Smith's Hungary and Transylvania' was appended to Bradford Smith's biography of Captain Smith, published in 1953 by Lippincott, a respected trade publisher.[30] Bradford Smith graciously introduced his erstwhile research assistant's essay as 'a masterpiece of history patiently reconstructed'[31] and dedicated the book to 'Laura Polanyi, collaborator and friend'.[32]

She also published an article, 'The Hungarian Historian, Lewis L. Kropf, on Captain John Smith's True Travels: A Reappraisal', in the scholarly *Virginia Magazine of History and Biography*. It supplied the last word on the veracity of Smith's 'True Travels', along with a devastating revision of the prevailing wisdom, established by the nineteenth-century historian Kropf, himself an émigré of a previous generation.[33] Lastly, Polanyi translated from Latin into English a late seventeenth-century English source on Smith and published it with a scholarly introduction.[34] This time, the publisher was the Virginia Historical Society via the University of North Carolina Press. Her research revised the previously reigning wisdom that the Captain was a braggard and a liar, and she confirmed the veracity of every detail of his 'Travels'. It also earned Polanyi, courtesy of the author of a review article, the moniker the 'Hungarian Pocahontas', who saved not the Captain's life but, perhaps equally importantly from a historian's perspective, his reputation.[35]

What to make of this output? What does it say about Polanyi's accomplishment as a historian and her acceptance by the American historical profession? Her success should not be underestimated: Polanyi started out as the research assistant of a writer of popular biographies (a genre on the margins of American academia) and ended up as the author of bona fide scholarly publications and the acknowledged expert on Smith's Eastern European period. Despite her admirable energy and promotional skills, it was a topic limited in scope and of limited interest to the profession but one that made perfect use of the unique combination of the languages and research skills Polanyi had acquired half a century earlier. And it was, crucially, meaningful to both American historians and a popular readership, attested to by the favourable reviews of Bradford Smith's biography in high-profile, mainstream newspapers – but, alas, not in scholarly journals, which took note of Polanyi's contribution.[36]

Her declining health and mobility did not deter Polanyi from trips to Europe, combining family visits with archival research. She took pride in – and was amused by the high irony of – the fact that it took an émigré to restore the reputation of a true American hero. There was a good measure of personal validation in this late twist of fate, and Polanyi clearly enjoyed the professional activities this work brought to her: the hunt in Hungarian and Austrian archives in person or by proxy, and the correspondence and meetings with leading historians in Hungary and Austria.[37] But the correspondence of her last years also reveals instances when leading historians she had approached with suggestions for research collaboration would be baffled by her offer and mistook her for a prospective research assistant. Such was the case with Marshall Fishwick, perhaps the leading historian of Virginia at the time, whom Polanyi approached offering collaboration on an article: Fishwick declined her offer quite gruffly.[38]

It is to Fishwick's credit that he subsequently went on to acknowledge Polanyi's contribution to scholarship – but only in a popular magazine.[39] Clearly, the family name, the close connection to intellectual and academic networks on two continents, the best European manners and a perfect command of English only went so far with the American historical profession.

Perhaps the most unexpected benefit of this late outburst of professional success, as she confessed, tongue firmly in cheek, to her oldest friend, the wife of Oscar Jászi, was purely intellectual. The children, all successful, the grandchildren, charming and promising, gave her much joy. But

> '[t]he friend of my seventies has, of course, made my seventies as exciting and, I must concede, happy as nothing else could have done. I mean, of course, Captain John Smith. . . . I, of course, overrate the importance of my mission, but for me it is enough. It really was my main concern, even much excitement, during the last years'.[40]

And as much as it was a moderate success, it was still exceptional for an outsider, and a woman of her age.

Conclusions

Can we expect to learn more about women émigré historians, and, if so, where should we look for sources? And how can the case of Laura Polanyi contribute to this history? Catherine Epstein, whose study is the most comprehensive to date, admitted that her sample was statistically too small to lead to meaningful conclusions. One should also note the discrepancy between the veritable industry of autobiographies by highly established émigré male historians compared with the autobiography of a single but perhaps professionally the most successful woman historian in Epstein's sample, Gerda Lerner.[41] This brings me to the first of my concluding points. We may be able to find more material if we include women who did not 'make it', as well as women outside of the 'German-speaking' category. We should also look for unpublished autobiographies written by émigré women in any field – Polanyi's short overview of her professional life is an example of the potential hiding in even the shortest of ego-documents.

Such short biographies, making the connection and comparing life before and after emigration (to paraphrase the famed collection of Columbia University), could also bring into sharper focus the differences of academic systems pre- and post-emigration, from a perspective of women's opportunities and limitations. This is one area where an exclusively German perspective shows its limits: Weimar Germany's academic system did have commonalities with other European countries – but also important differences, especially when it came to attitudes towards women and Jewish women in higher education and the professions. To widen the previous, almost exclusively German scope and include Hungary, with its 1920 introduction of the numerus clausus law, the Italian and Czechoslovak cases, where many Hungarian Jewish women ended up studying, as well as the Polish and Romanian antisemitic practices, might prove to be illuminating.

What about the more general question, the impact of gender on academic success? We should note that émigré Jewish women were burdened by multiple handicaps as the obstacles for women were heightened by the antisemitism prevalent at leading American universities. The dimension of class further complicates this picture. While in Weimar Germany it had become acceptable for middle-class professional women to keep an academic or professional career going after marriage, a decade or more later in the United States the same was still unacceptable: academic wives' behaviour was subject to an unwritten social code that was breached only in exceptional cases. What happened to the women pioneers of European countries in North America? Epstein proposes the likely hypothesis that as a cohort they became trailblazers of women's emancipation in American academia.[42] But if we broaden the sample of women academics to include not only German but Italian, Hungarian and Russian women professionals and scientists who had received their training in their home country, we may venture a slightly different conclusion. These women were pioneers in their fields in their homeland where they had already achieved considerable success. They then brought their perception of more egalitarian gender roles with them and confronted the American gender norms and found them lagging behind – and some of them succeeded, while most of them had given up altogether. But whether they succeeded in their original field, in another field, or failed to make it, in every case, through different channels, they advanced the values of women's emancipation. (The example of Gerda Lerner, who became a pioneer of women's history in the US, underscores this point.) The case of Laura Polanyi, a pioneer of higher education, suffragist and historian, is exceptional in many respects but could still bring new perspectives to the study of émigré women scholars or, failing that, point to the need for further research. Her case highlights the extraordinary obstacles refugee intellectual and professional women faced. It also allows us to compare women's educational and professional opportunities in the US in the 1930s vis-à-vis those in Central Europe in the previous decade; and in turn address the contradiction between the popular, triumphalist narrative of the Hitler emigration and the reality of the antisemitic and patriarchal academic world the émigrés encountered in the United States.

Lastly, if we look beyond the statistics of age and the variables of familial connections and previous life experiences, we could argue that the case of Laura Polanyi, with its interruptions, unfulfilled promises and partial successes, was, after all, representative of the European female intellectual émigré experience. Her life, with its planned or forced directions, changes of occupations and migrations – in other words, a transnational life of an intellectual woman pioneer – illustrates the claim of feminists of a much later generation: you can have it all, just not at the same time.

Notes

1. Laura Polanyi to Marshall W. Fishwick, 13 April 1957.
2. Laura Polanyi to Marshall W. Fishwick, 13 April 1957.
3. For more details, see Szapor, *The Hungarian Pocahontas*.
4. The excellent study of Freidenreich, *Female, Jewish, and Educated* exemplifies the attempt to broaden the national and disciplinary approach but uses the 'German-speaking' category that excludes Hungarians. Our own edited collection, Szapor, Pető, Calloni, and Hametz, *Jewish Intellectual Women in Central Europe, 1860–2000* sidestepped this problem by using a definition of Central Europe beyond the German-speaking areas, to include the non-German former Habsburg lands.
5. O'Dowd, 'Popular Writers', 351–71.
6. Laura Polanyi to Marshall W. Fischwick, 13 April 1957.
7. Epstein, 'Fashioning Fortuna's Whim', 301–24; Mandelickova and Goddeeris, 'Living in the Past', 399–414.
8. Mandelickova and Goddeeris, 'Living in the Past', 399–414.
9. Among others, Creager, Lunbeck, and Schiebinger, *Feminism in Twentieth-Century Science, Technology and Medicine*; Etzkowitz, Kemelgor and Uzzi, *Athena Unbound*.
10. Weiner, 'A New Site for the Seminar', 190–234. Szapor, 'Private Archives and Public Lives', 93–110 details the Polanyi family's connection to the physicists' network.
11. Members of the legendary cohort of Hungarian physicists, instrumental in the Manhattan Project (popularly called the 'Martians'), all came from an upper-middle-class milieu similar to that of the Polanyis, but this social historical aspect is rarely discussed in the substantial, scholarly and popular literature on the subject.
12. Szapor, *The Hungarian Pocahontas*.
13. As I will point out in the following, this has become accepted practice in studies on the intellectual migration.
14. Epstein, 'Fashioning Fortuna's Whim', 301–24.
15. Lamberti, 'Blazing New Paths in Historiography', 244–58. In the same volume figures the single, eminent exception of a woman, Hanna Holborn Gray, professor emerita and former president of The University of Chicago.
16. Epstein, *A Past Renewed*; Lehmann and Sheehan, *An Interrupted Past*.
17. Fleming and Bailyn, *The Intellectual Migration*. This pioneering volume also established the 'German-speaking' category of refugee studies, but for the time being it included refugees 'not only from Germany and Austria but also from elsewhere in Central Europe – Hungary in particular – where German was the usual language of high culture.' Fleming and Bailyn, *The Intellectual Migration*, 6.
18. Gay, *Weimar Culture*, first published in the volume above, went on to become a classic.
19. Fermi, *Illustrious Immigrants*.
20. Fermi, *Mussolini*.
21. Fleming and Bailyn, *The Intellectual Migration*, 3.
22. Gay, *My German Question*; Mosse, *Confronting History*; Stern, *Five Germanys I Have Known*; Laqueur, *Generation Exodus* should be added, even if it represents a slightly different, 'hybrid', part personal, part scholarly genre. And we should add Hobsbawm, whose name is usually missing from the overviews, and his memoir *Interesting Times*.
23. Daum, Lehmann, and Sheehan, *The Second Generation*.

24. Laqueur *Generation Exodus*, cover.
25. Congdon, *Exile and Social Thought* is still the best overview of this early wave of emigration.
26. One of the few exceptions is Oscar Jászi, who would go on to a professorship at Oberlin and who by virtue of his classic *The Dissolution of the Habsburg Monarchy* could be regarded as a historian – and yet he was a reluctant academic whose field was sociology or political science and his calling, politics. The two most prominent historians who originally came from or had been trained in Hungary are John Lukacs and István Deák and by age belong to the second generation.
27. Epstein, 'Fashioning Fortuna's Whim'.
28. For a detailed account of the family's history, see Szapor, *The Hungarian Pocahontas*.
29. Laura Polanyi to Karl Polanyi, no date.
30. Smith, *Captain John Smith*.
31. Smith, *Captain John Smith*, 9.
32. Smith, *Captain John Smith*, 5.
33. Smith, *Captain John Smith*. Polanyi's article, 'Captain John Smith's Hungary and Transylvania' was appended to Bradford Smith's biography. Polanyi, 'The Hungarian Historian'.
34. Wharton, *The Life of John Smith English Soldier*.
35. Fishwick, 'Was John Smith a Liar?', 28–33 and 110–11, 132.
36. Meager, 'Acclaiming an American Hero', 11; Smith, 'The Many Lives of Captain John Smith', 4.
37. She developed a professional partnership with an Austrian archivist, Franz Pichler, and the leading Hungarian historian of the early modern period, Kálmán Benda.
38. Marshall Fishwick to Laura Polanyi, 29 June 1957.
39. Fishwick, 'Was John Smith a Liar?'.
40. Laura Polanyi to Recha Jászi, 16 March 1958.
41. Gerda Lerner, *Fireweed*.
42. Epstein, 'Fashioning Fortuna's Whim', 323.

Bibliography

Congdon, Lee. *Exile and Social Thought: Hungarian Intellectuals in Germany and Austria, 1919–1933*. Princeton, NJ: Princeton University Press, 1991.

Creager, Angela N.H., Elizabeth Lunbeck, and Londa Schiebinger (eds). *Feminism in Twentieth-Century Science, Technology and Medicine*. Chicago and London: Chicago University Press, 2001.

Daum Andreas W., Hartmut Lehmann, James J. Sheehan (eds). *The Second Generation: Émigrés from Nazi Germany as Historians, With a Bibliographical Guide*. New York: Berghahn, 2016.

Epstein, Catharine. *A Past Renewed: A Catalog of German-Speaking Refugee Historians in the United States after 1933*. Cambridge: Cambridge University Press, 1993.

———. 'Fashioning Fortuna's Whim: German-Speaking Women Emigrant Historians in the United States', in Sibylle Quack (ed.), *Between Sorrow and Strength; Women Refugees of the Nazi Period* (German Historical Institute, Washington D.C. and Cambridge, MA: Cambridge University Press, 1995, first paperback edition, 2002), 301–24.

Etzkowitz, Henry, Carol Kemelgor and Brian Uzzi (eds). *Athena Unbound; The Advancement of Women in Science and Technology*. Cambridge: Cambridge University Press, 2000.

Fermi, Laura. *Mussolini*. Chicago: The University of Chicago Press, 1961.

———. *Illustrious Immigrants; The Intellectual Migration from Europe, 1930–41*. Chicago: The University of Chicago Press, 1968.

Fishwick, Marshall W. 'Was John Smith a Liar?' *American Heritage* 9(6) (1958), 28–33; 110–11.

Fleming, Donald, and Bernard Bailyn (eds). *The Intellectual Migration; Europe and America, 1930–1960*. Cambridge: MA: The Belknap Press of Harvard University Press, 1969.

Freidenreich, Harriet P. *Female, Jewish, and Educated: The Lives of Central European University Women*. Bloomington, IN: Indiana University Press, 2002.

Gay, Peter. *Weimar Culture: The Outsider as Insider*. New York: Harper & Row, 1968.

———. *My German Question: Growing up in Nazi Berlin*. New Haven, CT: Yale University Press, 1998.

Hobsbawm, Eric. *Interesting Times; A Twentieth-Century Life*. London: Allen Lane, 2002.

Jászi, Oscar. *The Dissolution of the Habsburg Monarchy*. Chicago: Chicago University Press, 1929.

Lamberti, Marjorie. 'Blazing New Paths in Historiography: "Refugee Effect" and American Experience in the Professional Trajectory of Gerda Lerner', in Andreas W. Daum, Hartmut Lehmann, James J. Sheehan (eds), *The Second Generation: Émigrés from Nazi Germany as Historians, With a Bibliographical Guide* (New York: Berghahn, 2016), 244–58.

Laqueur, Walter. *Generation Exodus*. Hanover, NH: Brandeis University Press, 2001.

Lehmann, Hartmut, and James J. Sheehan (eds). *An Interrupted Past: German-Speaking Refugee Historians in the United States after 1933*. Washington, D.C.: German Historical Institute, 1991.

Lerner, Gerda. *Fireweed: A Political Autobiography*. Philadelphia: Temple University Press, 2003.

Mandelickova, Monika, and Idesbald Goddeeris. 'Living in the Past: Historians in Exile', in Ilaria Prociani and Jo Tollebeek (eds), *Setting the Standards; Institutions, Networks and Communities of National Historiography* (London: Palgrave Macmillan, 2012), 399–414.

Meager, William. 'Acclaiming an American Hero'. *Christian Science Monitor*, 1 October 1953, 11.

Mosse, George L. *Confronting History: A Memoir*. Madison, WI: The University of Wisconsin Press, 2000).

O'Dowd, Mary. 'Popular Writers: Women Historians, the Academic Community and National History Writing', in Ilaria Porciani and Jo Tollebeek (eds), *Setting the Standards; Institutions, Networks and Communities of National Historiography* (New York: Palgrave Macmillan, 2012), 351–71.

Polanyi, Stricker Laura. 'The Hungarian historian, Lewis L. Kropf, on Captain John Smith's True Travels: A Reappraisal', *Virginia Magazine of History and Biography* 66(1) (1958), 22–43.

Smith, Ellen Hart. 'The Many Lives of Captain John Smith'. *New York Herald Tribune Book Review*, 4 October 1953, 4.

Stern, Fritz R. *Five Germanys I Have Known*. New York: Farrar, Straus and Giroux, 2006.

Szapor, Judith. *The Hungarian Pocahontas; The Life and Times of Laura Polanyi Stricker, 1882–1959*. Boulder, CO: East European Monographs, distributed by Columbia University Press, 2005.

———. 'Private Archives and Public Lives; The Migrations of Alexander Weissberg and the Polanyi Archives', in James Jordan, Lisa Leff and Joachim Schlör (eds), *Jewish Migration and the Archive* (London and New York: Routledge, 2016), 93–110.

Szapor, Judith et al. (eds). *Jewish Intellectual Women in Central Europe, 1860–2000; Twelve Biographical Essays*. New York: Edwin Mellen Press, 2012.

Weiner, Charles. 'A New Site for the Seminar: The Refugees and American Physics in the Thirties', in Donald Fleming and Bernard Bailyn (eds), *The Intellectual Migration: Europe and America, 1930–1960* (Cambridge, MA: The Belknap Press of Harvard University Press, 1969), 190–234.

Wharton, Henry. *The Life of John Smith English Soldier*. Chapel Hill: Virginia Historical Society by the University of North Carolina Press, 1957.

Archival Sources

Laura Polanyi to Karl Polanyi, no date. Polányi Collection, Hungarian National Library Manuscript Division, font 212.

Laura Polanyi to Marshall W. Fishwick, 13 April 1957. Polányi Collection, Hungarian National Library, Manuscript Division, font 212.

Laura Polanyi to Recha Jászi, 16 March 1958. Polányi Collection, Hungarian National Library.

Marshall Fishwick to Laura Polanyi, 29 June 1957. Polányi Collection, Hungarian National Library.

CHAPTER 9

'From *Geistesgeschichte* to Public History'

The Years of Emigration of the Hungarian Historian Béla Iványi-Grünwald, Jr.

Vilmos Erős

Three basic waves of Hungarian emigration can be distinguished in the development of its historiography until 1956: the first one took place after the revolution and war of independence in 1848/49, and its most relevant figures were Mihály Horváth, László Szalay, Ferenc Pulszky and Jácint Rónai. Their works were imbued with national-liberal ideas, which had a deep influence on the domestic historical-political strivings. At the same time, they contributed significantly to the professionalisation of Hungarian historical writing, as they familiarised themselves with this new method in their emigration.[1]

The next wave encompassed the emigration between the two World Wars. Here we can point out such names as Oszkár Jászi, Lajos Hatvany, György Lukács, Arnold Hauser, Karl Mannheim, Elek Bolgár, Erzsébet Andics and József Révai. Their impact was especially significant from a theoretical point of view, with new innovations in social and spiritual history accomplished by domestic efforts instead.[2]

After the Second World War, there were two other waves: between 1945–48 we can mention the so-called extreme right-wing 'historians' (with some of them even being members of the Arrow Cross Party), such as Ödön Málnási, Tibor Baráth, Ida Bobula, János Weidlein, Tibor Badiny Joós, Viktor Padányi. They maintained (or formulated) their views about the Turanist, racist character of Hungarian ancient history.³

In opposition to them, another stream can be discerned, such as Béla Iványi-Grünwald, Jr., Károly Kerényi, József Deér, András Alföldi, Gyula Miskolczy and Tamás Bogyay. They represented the so-called '*Geistesgeschichte*'⁴ tradition of Hungarian historical writing, deeply rooted in rather conservative and, at the same time, anti-fascist ideology. They pursued a sort of 'intellectual' or 'cultural' history and highlighted the close relationship of Hungarian history with Western European developments.⁵

The following study scrutinises one of the representatives of this latter school, Béla Iványi-Grünwald, Jr., who was a highly promising student of Gyula Szekfű and Bálint Hóman, both of them being the 'godfathers' of Hungarian Geistesgeschichte,⁶ in the first period of his career, which changed fundamentally during his self-imposed emigration throughout and, mainly after, the Second World War.

In Hungary: 'Geistesgeschichte'

The career of historian Béla Iványi-Grünwald, Jr. began in the period between the two World Wars, in the second half of the 1920s.⁷ He wrote his thesis about a topic in economic history, analysing Count István Széchenyi's views on the subject.⁸

As a result, he was trusted with an important task in the 'Fontes' series, well-known at the time in Hungary;⁹ and within the framework of the series in 1930 he published one of the main works of the Count, the book titled *Credit*, accompanied by a voluminous introduction, which bore explicit features of 'Geistesgeschichte'.¹⁰ If we survey historical works from the 1930s, we can furthermore point out some other studies by him, such as studies about Ranke, Bentham, Széchenyi (again),¹¹ and his theoretical debate with Sándor Gyömrei in the first half of the 1930s.¹² The debate concerned the application of the approaches of 'Geistesgeschichte' in the history of economics, and Béla Iványi-Grünwald, Jr. vehemently championed 'Geistesgeschichte' while heavily criticising the positivist, materialist, one-sided liberal views of his opponent, which were heavily rooted in sociology.¹³

The most important achievement of Béla Iványi-Grünwald, Jr. can be considered as from this period- the fourth volume of the 'Universal History' series, edited by Bálint Hóman, Gyula Szekfű, and Károly Kerényi.¹⁴ This volume outspokenly and very consciously summarises the main trends, processes and events of European history in the nineteenth and, to a lesser extent, twentieth century, with the means of 'Geistesgeschichte' thoroughly digested by Iványi-Grünwald, Jr.¹⁵

It is essential to emphasise the striking influence of a special stream of 'Geistesgeschichte' on his work - and, at the same time, on his whole career - that of 'Christian personalism'.[16] The main representatives of this direction were, in this period, Max Scheler, Jacques Maritain, Karl Jaspers, Nikolai Berdiaieff and Emmanuel Mounier.[17] According to the end notes of Iványi-Grünwald, Jr.'s book, Max Scheler and Karl Mannheim[18] had a particular influence on him. Proceeding in the footsteps of this German philosopher and thinker, Iványi-Grünwald, Jr. constructed the category of the so-called 'intellectual' and more specifically 'spiritual individual', which played a pivotal role - as we will see later on - in his further writings as well, so it can be evaluated as a certain 'leitmotif'.[19]

For the historian in question, the aforementioned Count István Széchenyi[20] can be most probably regarded an archetype of this 'spiritual individual' or 'intellectual' – a main, great personality that can be seen as having fundamentally shaped the course of world history. Other such persons and 'intellectuals' include, for instance, Napoleon, of course, and Bismarck, but basically they were not only politicians, as they were epitomised by the aforementioned Széchenyi and by Kossuth, as well as representatives of the big spiritual, cultural, ideological movements of the nineteenth-century, such as liberalism, romanticism, nationalism, and, to a lesser extent, positivism, socialism and imperialism, from Jeremy Bentham, Thomas Jefferson, Charles Forbes René de Montalembert, Ernst Moritz Arndt, Joseph Görres to Wilhelm Dilthey, Henri Bergson, August Comte, Karl Marx and Ludwig Gumplowicz.[21]

One of the most important messages of Iványi-Grünwald, Jr.'s – perfectly in tune with the world view or '*Weltanschauung*' of 'Geistesgeschichte' – is decline theory:[22] the most important feature of the Modern Age – that is, the nineteenth and twentieth centuries – which was the pushing into the background the 'intellectual'/'spiritual individual'. Furthermore, there is the disappearance, or even oppression, of the 'person' / 'personality', the coming to the fore and even the victory of the crowd and the mob, and parallel with it, that of economy, materialism, the egotistical interest, money and business, and so in the last quarter of the century, that of imperialism, extreme materialism and biologism.[23]

Iványi-Grünwald, Jr.'s synthesis indulges in general in the other characteristics of 'Geistesgeschichte'. This had been epitomised by the constant striving for synthesis, the predominance of the inner motifs of the spiritual-moral; basically, by the overwhelming presence of literature, referring very often to literary works, ideas, streams, figures of literature and respectively analysing them. Furthermore – as it already appeared in the debate with Sándor Gyömrei – there is the almost total omission of a sociological approach.[24]

In Emigration

The emigration of Béla Iványi-Grünwald, Jr. began in 1938, although at that time there was no word about emigration, especially not about a definite one.[25] That year, he was charged by the minister of cultural and religious affairs, Bálint Hóman[26] (one of the spiritual mentors of the aforementioned 'Universal History'), to travel to London and collect a wide range of source materials about the relationship between Lajos Kossuth and the English working classes for the previously mentioned 'Fontes' series.[27]

In London, Iványi-Grünwald, Jr. set to his research zealously, but because of the war and other political events (he was Jewish, and at the end of the 1930s the anti-Jewish laws had been promulgated in Hungary as a gesture towards Hitler for the newly regained territories in Slovakia and Romania[28]), he decided not to return to Hungary and to remain indefinitely in England. During the war, he assumed an active political role (for the BBC as well) and took part in the activities of the Hungarian immigrant community. Among the two anti-Hitler organisations that undertook such activities, he attached himself to the rather conservative, bourgeois organisation of Free Hungarians, in opposition to the leftist group led and represented by Count Mihály Károlyi, which was finding a path to the Soviet Union.[29]

After the war, his circumstances became unstable, as he managed to gain merely temporary positions at the Hungarian Department of the University of London. Later, mainly in the second half of the 1950s, he held radio lectures for the Hungarian department of the BBC.[30] He did not give up his career as a historian in this period either, though the possibilities available to him before the war in Hungary did not manifest themselves again. Already in 1945 he published a significant book, in collaboration with Alan Bell, about the Allies' peace preparation attempts, during the war, which finally led to the Potsdam Agreement.[31] He published significant articles in this time in various Western European journals about the relationship between Church and State in Eastern European countries.[32] He even edited part of his voluminous source collection about the Kossuth emigration[33], and he returned time and again to the topic of Széchenyi, who played such an important role in his pre-war research. He set up a large-scale collection of different published materials (manuscripts, prints, pamphlets, maps, carvings, etc.) about Hungary, found or rather discovered by him in England.[34] He wrote more or less regularly about different issues, mainly historical and political topics for the Hungarian journals of the emigration, for *Irodalmi Újság* (Literary Paper) in Paris, *Új Látóhatár* (New Horizon) in Munich, and the journal of the Imre Nagy Institute, *Szemle* (Review) in Brussels.[35]

We can evaluate his already mentioned lecture series for the BBC as perhaps his most significant achievement during his emigration, from the year 1955 onwards, the texts of which have been preserved at his bequest in Budapest, in the Manuscript Collection of the Hungarian Academy of Sciences. He held these lectures in Hungarian and in English till 1964; the series included about 80–90 pieces, about 350–400 pages altogether, which touched upon numerous topics and figures of the history, literature, politics and culture of Hungary, such as Oszkár Jászi, Count István Széchenyi and Lajos Kossuth; as well as problems of the revolution and fight for independence in 1848–49 and its parallels with the revolution in 1956. The lectures also dealt with personalities like Béla Kun, József Mindszenty, Gyula Szekfű, László Mátrai, Béla Illés, György Bölöni, József Darvas, István Bibó, Saint Stephen, Franz Liszt, Ernő Dohnányi,[36] as well as with the British William Blake, Charles Morgan, Daniel Defoe and many others.[37] All of these lectures conveyed – without exception – current political messages. A harsh and bitter critique of the reigning Hungarian administration played the central role in them, and Iványi-Grünwald, Jr. carried it out through spiritual rather than journalistic tools, inasmuch as they reflected the main chronology of the period in question as well.[38] According to this, in 1955 and 1956 he provided fundamental accounts about the programmes of the Petőfi Circle, about the Revolt of Writers, etc., and all of these were meant as preparation for the oncoming Revolution.[39]

In 1956, of course, the events of the revolution came to the fore, such as the echo of the October/November events, which were perceptible among the university-youth in England, particularly in Oxford.[40] Then came the reprisal and the revenge of Khrushchev, highlighting the parallels between 1849 and 1956, pointing out the similarities and, at the same time, the little bit more human character of the Habsburgs' actions.[41] In his lectures, he remembered Imre Nagy several times, including his execution, and criticised harshly - sometimes with bitter irony - the first steps of the Kádár consolidation as well.[42] An important point in his lectures is that he kept comparing totalitarian Eastern European dictatorships to the English democracy, with arguments based on the inalienable rights of individual freedom.

'Geistesgeschichte' in Emigration

In the following, I would like to scrutinise this question: is there any continuity in the views and activities of Béla Iványi-Grünwald, Jr. before and after the war – that is, in his emigration, and if there has been a change, what is the extent of it? This question is particularly pivotal, if the historian can, in this period, still be characterised as a spiritual historian,[43]

As indicated earlier, the most significant idea of Iványi-Grünwald, Jr. that he conceived explicitly within the arsenal of 'Geistegeschichte' was the so-called 'intellectual/spiritual individual', which can be assessed in the framework of 'Christian personalism'.[44] Iványi-Grünwald, Jr. maintained this notion even during the years of his emigration. He referred to it several times, including in analysing Khrushchev's speech at the Hungarian Academy of Sciences at the end of the 1950s, as well as in the cases of Szekfű, Széchenyi, Kossuth and Charles Morgan, and so it can be regarded as a fundamental pillar of his historical views during the entirety of his career.[45] This statement implies that he regarded 'spiritual intellectuals' as the impetus of history; they represent the moral forces, the 'personality' in the sense of Christian personalism[46] – they epitomise and represent its main idea. This stays in constant opposition with the masses and in consequence with multitudinous, quantifiable phenomena, which can be described with the tools of sociology.[47]

There is a new feature, however, in the thinking of Iványi-Grünwald, Jr., which is perfectly in tune with his earlier views regarding what he called a 'spiritual intellectual': Hungarian intellectuals opposing or even revolting against Rákosi's government (they were writers, scholars, scientists, journalists, etc.). That is why he paid so much attention to the debates in the Petőfi Circle, and to the so-called mutiny of writers: Tibor Déry, Gyula Háy, László Benjámin, Tibor Méray, Tamás Aczél, Lajos Kassák, Gyula Illyés.[48] All in all, he considers this opposition the main factor in the preparation and breaking out of the revolution in 1956 as well. As referred to previously, this idea of the 'intellectual' was interconnected with 'Christian personalism', and there was no change in the application of this view during his emigration years, either. Even after the war, he considered Christian religiosity very relevant, the main repository of individual freedom and autonomy. Therefore, he harshly criticised Eastern European communist administrations in the 1950s, as they strove for the amalgamation or even '*Gleichschaltung*' of the churches.[49] In scrutinising Hungarian circumstances, Iványi-Grünwald, Jr. acknowledges with great joy that, despite huge pressure from the government, religious and national sentiments were not extinguished in the Hungarian youth. There were many young people who were not willing to yield to this pressure from the government and did not regard their Christian fellow-beings as 'class enemies'.[50]

A very significant component of the Christian-Catholic continuity in question is, according to the views of Iványi-Grünwald, Jr., the nearly constant references to Saint Stephen, particularly the state of Saint Stephen, which in the 1930s became a central idea for him but also for the official policy and for the historical craft as well.[51] In one of his lectures for the BBC in the 1950s, he evoked at length Hungarian historians before the war (first of all Gyula Szekfű, but also Bálint Hóman, Gyula Kornis, József Deér and Győző Ember) who depicted thoroughly – and, for their age, also relevantly – the main moments of the almost 1000 years of worship of Saint Stephen in Hungary.[52] It should be added that in the 1930s as well as in the 1950s, Saint Stephen was considered a symbol of Hungarians belonging to the Western World – similarly for Béla Iványi-Grünwald, Jr. as well.[53]

Many further features can be cited to prove the continuity of the arsenal of 'Geistesgeschichte' in the thoughts and activities of Iványi-Grünwald, Jr. as a historian, such as the vigorous affection for literature and philology (and for the means of expression of literature),[54] which ran parallel to his distrust towards the approaches of sociology, whereas in 1960, in one of his studies concerning the genesis of Széchenyi's views, he significantly took into consideration the conclusions of the new Hungarian economic and social history.[55] This ardent interest in literature manifested itself in many forms, such as in his genuine 'bookinist' inclinations,[56] in the constant references to significant figures of literature (e.g. Gyula Illyés), the so-called Populists, while, at the same time, the condemnation of József Darvas, Béla Illés and György Bölöni. Furthermore, English literature was important for him as well, including William Blake and Daniel Defoe,[57] and we can also refer to his collection of English publications about Hungarian affairs mentioned earlier.[58]

Another basic tenet that underlies a continuity in the views of Iványi-Grünwald, Jr. between the values and views before the war and his emigration period is his interpretation of the idea of the nation.[59] As mentioned earlier, he established with some satisfaction that the Communist government did not manage to eradicate national feeling in the Hungarian youth, and, referring to 1848/49, he refuted the Marxist historiography as well, according to which 'class struggle' dominated the revolution much more than the fight for national independence. We should note, though, that this national consciousness cannot be brought into connection with, and fundamentally differs from, the efforts of another branch of the historiography in Western European Hungarian emigration, which put Hungarian ancient history at the fore in denying the Finno-Ugric origins of Hungarians and instead glorifying their Turkish and even Japanese ancestry, while trying to prove bitterly the Sumeric-Hungarian kinship on a racial basis, and, all in all, pursued history as a glorification of a great national past, as in the works of Tibor Baráth, László Götz, Ferenc Badiny Joós, Viktor Padányi, Ida Bobula and János Drábik.[60] In contrast with this Asia-oriented, basically Turanist ideology (that is very popular and even widespread in present day Hungary), Iványi-Grünwald, Jr. – in the spirit of Széchenyi – championed the Western orientation of Hungarians and the Western European embedding of Hungarian history and culture.[61] His ideal – as mentioned before – was, until the very end of his life, English democracy, deeming individual freedom pivotal.⁶²

From 'Geistesgeschichte' to Public History

It should be added to the above that significant changes, even breaks can be detected in the activities and thinking of Iványi-Grünwald, Jr. during his emigration. One of these changes meant placing a greater emphasis on the tradition of liberal independence in Hungarian history; see, for example, the role of Kossuth, which obviously came to the fore in connection with the events of 1956.⁶³ Another factor of a certain change in his views is his pushing into the background the decline idea, so characteristic of 'Geistesgeschichte', which was even directed against Western European values but never with the claim of a dictatorship, which according to previous statements had lost its validity with the harsh critique of the Soviet Union and of Eastern European communist dictatorships.

One of the perhaps most striking breaks constituted the fact that he was forced to renounce the construction of a large-scale historical synthesis, which can be assessed also as a core question for 'Geistesgeschichte', and which played such an important role in his activities before the War.⁶⁴ The cause of this can be sought in his living conditions, as he had not managed to secure a university position, which would have been essential for such an undertaking. In this respect, he differed significantly from others, also in terms of historians operating with 'Geistesgeschichte', respectively art historians, such as: József Deér, András Alföldi, Károly Kerényi, Károly Tolnai, Gyula Miskolczy.⁶⁵ These scholars did not simply continue with their work but in many cases fulfilled their oeuvres, sometimes even making their careers in emigration, creating great syntheses, almost all of them in the spirit of 'Geistesgeschichte'.⁶⁶ For Iványi-Grünwald, Jr., however, what remained was partial studies, partial results, source publications, bibliographies, collections, journalism and a certain kind of history politics, through which he got into an immediate connection with current politics.⁶⁷

This is not entirely new in the history of the Hungarian 'Geistesgeschichte' either.⁶⁸ One of the masters of Iványi-Grünwald, Jr., Gyula Szekfű,⁶⁹ who never strayed far from journalism, at the end of the 1930s and in the first half of the 1940s threw himself into politics with full force, during the fight against the extreme right and against the Nazis.⁷⁰ He wrote in one of his articles in *Magyar Nemzet* (Hungarian Nation): in contrast with Jacob Burckhardt's aestheticism, in his age it is no longer possible to delight in life 'from the other riverbank', twiddling one's thumbs as empires collapse and the world bursts into flames, but – though taking the risk of getting dirty –

the historian should take an active – even militant – role in the fight against the forces he considered evil.[71] Obviously the same, or at least similar motives operated in the most significant activities of Iványi-Grünwald, Jr. in his emigration – that is in his BBC lectures: with bitter criticism of the Rákosi government and the Kádár system,[72] which he regarded as evil, and with the faithful chronicles of 1956, he acted in the framework of the – by him probably not much appreciated – spirit of György Lukács's 'existential thinking'.[73] That is, he acted for the refashioning of his age according to his 'Christian humanist' values. It should be noted that this last feature is also a basic idea of 'Geistesgeschichte'. It is enough to revoke the ideas of Benedetto Croce, who was also a favourite of Gyula Szekfű,[74] about history as idea and action, in Italian: 'La storia come pensiero e azione.'[75]

Conclusions

According to German philosopher and aesthete Siegfried Kracauer,[76] the emigrant position offers a possibility for the historian to get rid of his one-sided, narrow points of view. Having been untied from the bindings of his native environment, and at the same time still not being assimilated to the circumstances of his new country, he is positioned in the marginal role of the 'outsider'. This offers him a possibility to conceive his ideas from different, polyphonic and reflected aspects, and for many great historians, from Thucydides to Lewis Namier, this served as a great advantage and stimulated them to create their great accomplishments.[77]

For the Hungarian historian Béla Iványi-Grünwald, this statement holds true in many respects. He commenced his career as an outstanding representative of the so-called 'Geistesgeschichte' between the two World Wars in Hungary. In his self-imposed emigration during and after the Second World War, while sticking to the main ideas and values of 'Christian personalism', which was a branch within 'Geistesgeschichte', he had been forced – because of existential concerns – to turn to journalism – instead of great syntheses – to pursue a certain 'public history' in a positive sense,[78] mainly through holding lectures for the BBC.[79] The essential message of this activity was of protest against the dictatorships in his homeland and in Eastern Europe. To the regimes he opposed, the idea of individual freedom was epitomised by the English democracy, which had been regarded as such even by his first main protagonist, Count István Széchenyi. Béla Iványi-Grünwald, Jr. accomplished this via spiritual tools, by transmitting the national culture of his earlier motherland. That means that his adherence to this national culture and to its specific values is also consistent in his thinking, while he fiercely attacked the political system of the so-called Horthy era as well, which compelled him to his first emigration and epitomised, as such, an authoritarian regime too.

Notes

1. Vardy, *Modern Hungarian Historiography*.
2. About Hungarian (mainly Jewish) emigration between the two World Wars in general, see Frank, *Double Exile*. About emigration after 1945, Borbándi, *A magyar emigráció*.
3. Baráth, *L'histoire en Hongrie*.
4. 'Geistesgeschichte' is a special term, difficult to translate into English, which roughly equates to 'spiritual history' and is certainly not the same as 'intellectual history' (which is rather a subdiscipline of history). The author of the present study disagrees with the view according to which the American *Journal of the Histoy of Ideas* (founded in 1940) can be regarded as having established Geistesgeschichte in Anglo-Saxon historical discipline and culture (for many protagonists of Geistesgeschichte, the important idea of the decline of modern culture and cultural pessimism, let alone an original concept about the epistemology of history, is basically missing from the discourse of intellectual history). Therefore, in the following, I will adhere to its original German form. To the relevant literature, see still note 10.
5. After 1956, many historians left the country as well, such as Miklós Molnár, Béla Várdy, Péter Gosztonyi, Péter Kende, István Deák, but the analysis of them is outside the scope of the present study.
6. Vardy, *Modern Hungarian Historiography*, 79–94.
7. For literature about him, see Mcdonald, *Béla Iványi-Grünwald*; Czigány, 'Emigráns sorsok'; Nagy, 'Ifj. Iványi Grünwald Béla életpályája'. Béla Iványi-Grünwlad Jr. was one of the most talented young historians in Hungary between the two World Wars, and as a student and follower of the leading historians of Hungarian Geistesgeschichte – Gyula Szekfű and Bálint Hóman – the analysis of his entire career offers an opportunity to investigate the problem of a possible fate/destiny of Geistesgeschichte under entirely different political and cultural circumstances. In addition, a significant part of his bequest (as shall be seen) can be found in Budapest, which is a rare case with regards to Hungarian emigrant historians, and this can further the research of his oeuvre to a great extent.
8. Iványi-Grünwald, *Széchenyi magánhitelügyi koncepciójának*.
9. Glatz, *Történetíró és politika*.
10. About 'Geistesgeschichte', see Joó, *Bevezetés a szellemtörténetbe*; Iggers, *The German Conception of History*; Beiser, *The German Historicist Tradition*; Vardy, *Modern Hungarian Historiography*, 62–101. In other historiographies of Eastern Europe, Čtvrtník, *Geschichte der Geschichtswissenschaft*.
11. Iványi-Grünwald, 'Széchenyi István vallásosságának a kérdése'; Iványi-Grünwald, *Der Trug vom unabänderlichen Gesetz*; Iványi-Grünwald, *Ranke a világtörténetíró és nemzetnevelő*.
12. Kövér, 'A gazdaságtörténet-írás újabb', 283; Gyömrei, 'A magyar gazdaságtörténetírás'.
13. Iványi-Grünwald, *Vita*.
14. Iványi-Grünwald, *A legújabb kor története*.
15. Istványi, 'A legújabb kor'.
16. Erős, 'Erkölcs és államrezon'.
17. Frenyó and Turgonyi, *Jacques Maritain*. In an interview, Iványi-Grünwald claimed Maritain a representative of modern Catholicism, and he translated some of his articles in the Catholic journal *Korunk Szava* in the 1930s as well. See *Harc*, 1944. 08. 05. 3. About *Korunk Szava*, see Vásárhelyi, 'Korunk Szava'.
18. Ferretti, *Max Scheler*; Deininger-Meyn, 'Philosophische Grundlagen'. See endnote 14. Gyömrei highlighted in his review the influence of Heinrich Rickert as well. About Rickert, see, e.g., Beiser, *The German Historicist Tradition*.

19. Iványi-Grünwald, *A legújabb kor története*; Gyömrei, Iványi-Grünwald Béla: A legújabb kor története.
20. Iványi-Grünwald, *Hitel*.
21. Iványi-Grünwald, *A legújabb kor története*.
22. Erős, 'In the Lure of "Geistesgeschichte"'.
23. Iványi-Grünwald, *A legújabb kor története*.
24. See earlier.
25. Nagy,'Ifj. Iványi Grünwald Béla életpályája'.
26. About Hóman, see Ujváry, Történeti átértékelés.
27. Iványi-Grünwald, 'The Working Classes in Britain and the East European Revolutions'.
28. About Hungarian history in general, see e.g. Kontler, *History of Hungary*.
29. Varga, 'Az angliai magyar tanács története (1944–45)'; Varga, 'Károlyi és az antifasiszta emigráció egységfrontja'; *Harc*, 1944. 08. 05. 3; About his relationship with Károlyi, see Iványi-Grünwald, 'Hungarian Memories'.
30. Basically, Iványi-Grünwald, Jr. was one of the three initiators of the Hungarian broadcasting programme for the BBC, with George Mikes and György Tarján already in 1939. See Pál, 'Jó estét kívánok, itt Macartney Elemér beszél', 343. The British historian Macartney supported rather the conservative wing of the Hungarian emigration in England, to which belonged Iványi-Grünwald, Jr. as well. See Beretzky, *Scotus Viator és Macartney*. As for the lecture by the Hungarian historian in which he highlighted the importance of the independence struggles in Hungarian history, see Iványi-Grünwald, 'The Significance of October 6th'.
31. Iványi-Grünwald-Bell, *Route to Potsdam*.
32. Iványi-Grünwald, 'Church and State'.
33. Iványi-Grünwald, 'The Working Classes in Britain'.
34. See *Hungarica*.
35. E.g. Iványi-Grünwald, 'Széchenyi'; Iványi-Grünwald, 'A két világháború közötti ellenforradalom problematikája'; Iványi-Grünwald, 'Szent István napján'.
36. Iványi-Grünwald, *Mindszenty and the Counter-revolution*; Iványi-Grünwald, *Szekfű Obituary*; Iványi-Grünwald, *Mr. Darvas's Confession*.
37. E.g. Iványi-Grünwald, *Blake*.
38. Iványi-Grünwald, *Hungarian Youth and Nationalism*. For more about the revolution in BBC in detail, see Pallai, *A szabadság hullámhosszán*. About the Communist takeover in the BBC in 1948/49, see Pallai, *Némi demokráciától a népi demokráciáig*.
39. Iványi-Grünwald, *Eastern European Writers in Revolt*.
40. Iványi-Grünwald, *Oxford and Hungary*.
41. Iványi-Grünwald, *Khruschchov's Address*.
42. E.g. Iványi-Grünwald, *Anniversary of the Constitution*; Iványi-Grünwald, *6th October*. Here he draws parallels between the executions in 1849 and 1956–1958.
43. Iványi-Grünwald, *The Credit*.
44. See earlier.
45. Iványi-Grünwald, *Charles Morgan*.
46. Even in the 1960s, in one of his lectures, Iványi-Grünwald maintains that in the whole pedagogic and political culture there should be more emphasis on 'personality'. Iványi-Grünwald, *Trends & Events in Hungary*.
47. Miskolczy, *Szellem és nemzet*.
48. Iványi-Grünwald, *Hungarian Writers*.
49. Iványi-Grünwald, 'Church and State'.
50. Iványi-Grünwald, *University Youth*.
51. Hóman, *Szent István*.
52. About the cult of St. Stephen, see Klimó, *Nation, Konfession, Geschichte*; Berger, *The Past as History*, 114.
53. Iványi-Grünwald, *St. Stephen*; Iványi-Grünwald, *St. Stephen's Day*.

54. Iványi-Grünwald, *New Trends in Hungarian Literature*; Iványi-Grünwald, *Hungarian Books Published in Great Britain*.
55. Iványi-Grünwald, 'From Feudalism to Capitalism'.
56. Czigány, 'Emigráns sorsok'.
57. He discovered and identified Defoe as the author of a previously unknown pamphlet from the eighteenth century. See Iványi-Grünwald, 'Defoe's Prelude to The Family Instructor'.
58. See *Hungarica*; Iványi-Grünwald, *Antiquarian Book Trade*. In one of his lectures, Iványi-Grünwald deals with a monography about the Dualist-Hungary by Macartney, and his criticism is that the image of a spiritual life is missing from it. See Iványi-Grünwald, *Macartney's Book*. Anyway, as mentioned earlier, his political views were close to Macartney, who opposed in many respects the wing of emigration during the War led by Mihály Károlyi. About Macartney, see still Lojkó, 'Macartney and Central Europe'.
59. See Czigány, 'Emigráns sorsok'.
60. Komoróczy, *Sumer és magyar?*; Ablonczy, *Keletre, magyar*.
61. See the role of Saint Stephen.
62. Iványi-Grünwald, *Széchenyi*; Iványi-Grünwald, *Széchenyi-Exhibition*; Iványi-Grünwald, *Széchenyi in England*.
63. Iványi-Grünwald, *Lajos Kossuth*; Grünwald-Iványi, *Louis Kossuth*.
64. See earlier.
65. Lackó, 'Sziget és külvilág'. Some parallels can be detected with that of Iványi-Grünwald, Jr. in the career of the historians Ferenc Fejtő and Thomas von Bogyay as far as they also pursued journalism in their emigration (mainly Fejtő, who was originally and fundamentally a journalist). Meanwhile, they also managed to create large-scale syntheses as well (even if not in the sense of '*Geistesgeschichte*'); see, e.g., the magnificent book by Fejtő about the Eastern European 'people-democracies' in the 1940s and 1950s. See Lengyel, *Der gelehrsame Exilant*; Fejtő, *Où va le Temps Qui passe?*; Fejtő, *Histoire des democraties populaires*.
66. See, e.g., *Deér József emlékezete*.
67. About 'public history', see Bösch and Goschler, *Public History*; Noiret, 'La Public History?' About its capacities in a positive sense, see Lücke and Zündorf, *Einführung in die Public History*.
68. See most recently, Miskolczy, *Szellem és nemzet*.
69. As mentioned earlier, he wrote his obituary in 1955. See Iványi-Grünwald, *Szekfű Obituary*. About Szekfű, see Epstein, *Gyula Szekfű*; Dénes, *A történelmi Magyarország eszménye*; Monostori, *Szekfű Gyula a változó időkben*.
70. Erős, *A Szekfű-Mályusz vita*.
71. Szekfű, 'Aki a partról nézi'. In this respect, Szekfű can be considered an explicitly 'engaged historian' in whom many see a mere ideological message. See *The Engaged Historian*.
72. Regarding Iványi-Grünwald's attitude towards the so-called 'Kádár consolidation', see, e.g., Strassenreiter, 'Az 1962-63-as levelezés'.
73. About Lukács see Erős, 'In the Lure of "Geistesgeschichte"'.
74. See Szekfű, *Forradalom után*, 9.
75. Galasso, *Croce e lo spirito del suo tempo*.
76. Kracauer, *History*, 168–69.
77. Ibidem.
78. In contrast to the above-mentioned historical conception of emigration of the extreme right, which is also a genuine 'public history' but much more in a negative, anti-democratic, totalitarian sense.
79. It is important to note that in some of these articles he initiated and carried out primary-source publications about the Hungarian history. See, e.g., Iványi-Grünwald, 'Magyar Múzeum'.

Bibliography

Ablonczy, Balázs. *Keletre, magyar! A magyar turanizmus története.* [To the East, Hungarians! The History of Hungarian Turanism.] Budapest: Jaffa, 2016.
Baráth, Tibor. *L'histoire en Hongrie (1867–1935).* Paris: Librairie, 1936.
Beiser, Frederick Charles. *The German Historicist Tradition.* New York-Oxford: Oxford University Press, 2011.
Beretzky, Ágnes. *Scotus Viator és Macartney.* [Scotus Viator and Macartney.] Budapest: Akadémiai Kiadó, 2005.
Berger, Stefan (with Ch. Conrad). *The Past as History: National Identity and Historical Consciousness in Modern Europe.* Basingstoke: Palgrave-Macmillan, 2015.
Berger, Stefan (ed.). *The Engaged Historian.* Basingstoke: Palgrave-Macmillan, 2019.
Borbándi, Gyla. *A magyar emigráció életrajza: 1945–1985.* [The Biography of the Hungarian Emigration.] I–II. Budapest: Európa, 1989.
Bösch, Frank, and Constantin Goschler. *Public History: Öffentliche Darstellungen des Nationalsozialismus jenseits der Geschichtswissenschaft.* Göttingen: Vandenhoeck & Ruprecht, 2009.
Čtvrtník, Mikuláš. *Geschichte der Geschichtswissenschaft: der tschechische Historiker Zdeněk Kalista und die Tradition der deutschen Geistesgeschichte.* Hamburg: Diplomatica Verlag, 2010.
Czigány, Lóránt. 'Emigráns sorsok'. [Emigrant Fates.] *Kortárs* 46(2–3) (2002), 126–31.
Deininger-Meyn, Gisela. 'Philosophische Grundlagen der Wissenssoziologie Karl Mannheims und Max Schelers'. Dissertation. Heidelberg University, 1986.
Dénes, Iván Zoltán. *A történelmi Magyarország eszménye: Szekfű Gyula a történetíró és ideológus.* [The Ideal of the Historical Hungary: Gyula Szekfű the Historian and Ideologue.] Pozsony: Kalligram, 2015.
Epstein, Irene Raab. *Gyula Szekfű: A Study in the Political Basis of Hungarian Historiography.* New York: Garland Publishing Inc., 1987.
Erős, Vilmos. *A Szekfű-Mályusz vita.* [The Szekfű-Mályusz Debate.] Debrecen: Csokonai Kiadó, 2000.
———. 'A szellemtörténet'. [Geistesgeschichte.] *Valóság* 51(5) (2008), 20–35.
———. 'Erkölcs és államrezon: Szekfű Gyula és Jacques Maritain kapcsolata'. [Ethic and Raison d'État: The Connections between Gyula Szekfű and Jacques Maritain.] *Világosság* 49(9–10) (2008), 167–74.
———. 'In the Lure of "Geistesgeschichte"'. [The Theme of Decline in the Hungarian Historiography and Historical Thinking Between the Two World Wars.] *European Review of History / Revue européenne d'histoire* 22(3) (2015), 411–32.
Fejtő, François. *Histoire des democraties populaires.* Paris: Seuil, 1972.
———. *Où va le Temps Qui passe?* Paris: Ballard, 1991.
Ferretti, Giovanni. *Max Scheler. 1. Fenomenologia e antropologia personalsitica. 2. Filosofia delle religione.* Milano: Vita e pensiero, 1972.
Frank, Tibor. *Double Exile: Migrations of Jewish Hungarian Professionals through Germany to the United States.* Oxford: Peter Lang, 2009.
Frenyó, Zoltán, and Zoltán Turgonyi. *Jacques Maritain: Tanulmányok.* [Jacques Maritain: Studies.] Budapest: L'Harmattan, 2007.
Galasso, Guiseppe. *Croce e lo spirito del suo tempo.* Roma-Bari: Laterza, 2002.
Glatz, Ferenc. *Történetíró és politika.* [The Historian and Politics.] Budapest: Akadémiai, 1980.
Gyömrei, Sándor. 'A magyar gazdaságtörténetírás új útja'. [New Paths in Hungarian Economic-History Writing.] *Közgazdasági Szemle* 56(10) (1932), 661–79.
———. 'Iványi-Grünwald Béla: A legújabb kor története'. [Iványi-Grünwald Béla: The History of the Modern Age.] *Közgazdasági Szemle* 62 (1938), 157–60.
Hóman, Bálint. *Szent István.* [Saint Stephen.] Budapest: Királyi Magyar Egyetemi Nyomda, 1938.

Iggers, Georg G. *The German Conception of History: The National Tradition from Herder to the Present*. Middletown, CT: Wesleyan University Press, 1968.
Istványi, Géza. 'A legújabb kor'. [The Modern Age.] *Magyar Szemle* 10(31) (1937), 368–73.
Iványi-Grünwald, Béla Jr. *Széchenyi magánhitelügyi koncepciójának szellemi és gazdasági eredményei és következményei a rendi Magyarországon, 1790–1848*. [The Intellectual and Economic Results and Consequences of Széchenyi's Concept about Private-Credit in the Hungary of Estates, 1790–1848.] Pécs: Dunántúl, 1927.
———. *Hitel, a Taglalat és a Hitellel foglalkozó kisebb iratok*. [The Credit, the Analysis, and Smaller Papers concerning the Credit.] Budapest: Magyar Történelmi Társulat, 1930.
———. 'Vita a gazdaságtörténet módszeréről'. [Debate about the Method of Economic-History.] *Közgazdasági Szemle* 57 (1933), 360–68.
———. *Der Trug vom unabänderlichen Gesetz*. Pester Lloyd, 1934.
———. *Ranke a világtörténetíró és nemzetnevelő*. [Ranke as World-Historian and the Teacher of the Nation.] Pesti Napló, Pesti Hírlap, 1936. December [Originally a radio lecture].
———. 'Széchenyi István vallásosságának a kérdése'. [The Question of Széchenyi's Religiosity.] *Regnum* 2(11) (1937), 263–79.
———. *A legújabb kor története*. [The History of the Modern Age.] Budapest: Magyar Szemle Társaság, 1937.
———. The Significance of October 6th, 1849 [In Hungarian]. University Extension Lectures, arranged by the Association of Hungarians in Great Britain. 10th session, 3 October 1942. London.
———. 'The Working Classes in Britain and the East European Revolutions' (of 1848, with special reference to the Hungarian War of Independence). *The Slavonic and East European Review* 26 (1947), 107–25.
———. 'Church and State in Eastern Europe'. *The Yearbook of World Affairs* (6) (1952), 98–123.
———. 'Hungarian Memories'. [A review article of M. Horthy's and M. Károlyi's memoires.] *Tide and Tide*, 4 February 37 (1956) 02.04. 137–38. MTA KIK Kt., Ms 2565/11.
———. 'Széchenyi Akadémiája 1825–1960'. [Széchenyi's Academy 1825–1960]. *Irodalmi Újság* 11 (1960) 12. 15., 3.
———. 'From Feudalism to Capitalism: The Economic Background to Széchenyi's Reform in Hungary'. *Journal of Central European Affairs* 20(3) (1960) 270–88.
———. 'Széchenyi'. *Irodalmi Újság* 11 (1960) 04. 15., 1–12.
———. 'Szent István napján'. [On the Day of Saint Stephen.] *Irodalmi Újság* 11 (1960) 08. 15., 1–4.
———. 'Magyar Múzeum. I–III. Rész'. [Hungarian Museum. I–III.] *Irodalmi Újság* 12 (1961) 15 February, 9.
———. 'A két világháború közötti ellenforradalom problematikája'. [The Problematics of the Counter-Revolution between the Two World Wars.] *Szemle* 4(4) (1963), 69–73.
———. 'Defoe's Prelude to The Family Instructor'. *The Times Literary Supplement*, 7 April 1966, 312.
———. *Hungarica*. (English Books, Prints, Maps, Periodicals, etc. Relating to Hungary). Collected by Béla Iványi-Grünwald. Suffolk: Withins, Alphamstone, 1967.
Iványi-Grünwald, Béla Jr., and A. Bell. *Route to Potsdam: The Story of the Peace Aims*. London: A. Vintage, 1945.
Joó, Tibor. *Bevezetés a szellemtörténetbe*. [Introduction to Geistesgeschichte.] Budapest: Franklin, 1935.
Klimó, Árpád von. *Nation, Konfession, Geschichte: Zur nationalen Geschichtskultur Ungarns im europaeischen Ausland (1860–1948)*. München: Oldenburg, 2003.
Komoróczy, Géza. *Sumer és magyar?* [Sumerian and Hungarian?] Budapest: Magvető, 1976.
Kontler, Laszlo. *History of Hungary*. Budapest: Atlantisz, 2002.

Kövér, György. 'A gazdaságtörténet-írás újabb útjai' [The New Paths in Economic-History], in Bódy Zsombor-Ö and József Kovács (eds), *Bevezetés a társadalomtörténetbe*. [Introduction to Social-History.] (Budapest: Osiris, 2003), 281–301.

Kracauer, Siegfried. *History: The Last Things before the Last*. New York: Oxford University Press, 1969.

Lackó, Miklós. 'Sziget és külvilág: Kerényi Károly és a magyar szellemi élet'. [The Island and the Outside World: Károly Kerényi and the Hungarian Intellectual World.], in Miklós Lackó, *Sziget és külvilág: Válogatott tanulmányok*. [The Island and the Outside World: Selected Studies.] (Budapest: MTA Történettudományi Intézete, 1996), 305–34.

László, Koszta (ed.). *Deér József emlékezete, Tanulmányok Deér József (1905–1972) professzor születésének centenáriumára*. [The Memory of József Deér: Studies for the Centenary of the Birth of József Deér (1905–1972).] Szeged: JATE Press, 2006.

Lengyel, Zsolt K. *Der gelehrsame Exilant: Eine kleine Biographie des Historikers Thomas von Bogyay*. Regensburg: Verlag Friedrich Pustet, 2018.

Lojkó, Miklós. 'C.A. Macartney and Central Europe'. *European Review of History/Revue Européenne d'Histoire* 6(1) (1999), 37–57.

Lücke, Martin, and Irmgard Zündorf. *Einführung in die Public History*. Göttingen: Vandenhoeck & Ruprecht, 2018.

Mcdonald, Gregory. 'Béla Iványi-Grünwald 1902–1965', in Jocelyn Ivanyi (ed.), *Hungarica*. (English Books, Prints, Maps, Periodicals, etc. Relating to Hungary). (Collected by Béla Iványi-Günwald. Suffolk, 1967), 7–15.

Miskolczy, Ambrus. *Szellem és nemzet*. [Spirit and Nation.] Budapest: Napvilág, 2000.

Monostori, Imre. *Szekfű Gyula a változó időkben: Életmű-fogadtatás-utókor 1913–2016*. [Gyula Szekfű in Changing Times: Oeuvre-Reception-Posterity 1913–2016.] Pécs: Pannónia Könyvek, 2017.

Nagy, Brigitta. 'Ifj. Iványi Grünwald Béla életpályája és munkásságának állomásai'. [The Main Stages of the Career and Oeuvre of Béla Iványi-Grünwald Jr.] MA thesis. Debreceni Egyetem BtK, Történelmi Intézet, 2019.

Noiret, Serge. 'La Public History? Una disciplina fantasma?' *Memoria e Ricerca, Rivista di Storia Contemporanea* 37 (2011), 9–35.

Pál, Monika. 'Jó estét kívánok, itt Macartney Elemér beszél: C.A. Macartney és a BBC magyar adása'. [Good Evening, Elemér Macartney Speaking: C.A. Macartney and the Hungarian Program of BBC.] in Tibor Frank (ed.), *Angliától Nagy-Britanniáig: Magyar kutatók tanulmányai a brit történelemről*. [From England to Great Britain: Studies of Hungarian Scholars about British History.] (Budapest: Gondolat Kiadó, 2004), 340–56.

Pallai, Péter. *A szabadság hullámhosszán: az 1956-os forradalom története a BBC elmondásában*. [On the Wavelength of Freedom: The History of the Hungarian Revolution in 1956 in the Narrative of BBC.] Budapest: Helikon, 2006.

———. *Némi demokráciától a népi demokráciáig: a kommunista hatalomátvétel története a BBC adásai tükrében*. [From Some Democracy to the People's Democracy: The History of the Communist Taking-Power in the Mirror of the Programs of BBC.] Budapest: Helikon, 2008.

Strassenreiter, Erzsébet. 'Az 1962-63-as levelezés'. [The Correspondence in 1962–63.] *Kritika* 34(7–8) (2005), 38–43.

Szekfű, Gyla. 'Aki a partról nézi'. [Who is Watching from the Riverside.] *Magyar Nemzet* 3(109) (1940), 7.

———. *Forradalom után*. [After Revolution.] Budapest: Cserépfalvi, 1947.

Ujváry, Gábor (ed.). *Történeti átértékelés: Hóman Bálint, a történész és a politikus*. [Historical Re-evaluation: Bálint Hóman the Historian and Politician.] Budapest: Ráció Kiadó, 2011.

Vardy, Steven Béla. *Modern Hungarian Historiography*. New York: Columbia University Press, 1976.

Varga, F. János. 'Károlyi és az antifasiszta emigráció egységfrontja (1941–1944)'. [Károlyi and the Unity-Front of the Antifascist Emigration, 1941–1944.] *Történelmi Szemle* 18(2–3) (1975), 231–43.

———. 'Az angliai magyar tanács története (1944–45)'. [The History of the Hungarian Council in England (1944–45).] *Századok* 117 (1983), 152–75.

Vásárhelyi, Miklós. 'Korunk Szava (1931–1938)' [The Journal 'Korunk Szava.] in Murányi Gábor (ed.), *A bilincsbe vert beszéd: Vásárhelyi Miklós sajtótörténeti tanulmányai.* [The Handcuffed Speech: The Studies of Miklós Vásárhelyi about Press-History.] (Budapest: Élet és Irodalom, 2002), 125–41.

Archival Sources

MTA KIK Kt.: A Magyar Tudományos Akadémia Könyvtár *és* Információs Központ Kézirattára (Budapest) [The Manuscript Collection of the Library and Information Centre of the Hungarian Academy of Sciences in Budapest].

Harc, 1944. 08. 05. 03. Iványi Grünwald Béla nyilatkozik a Harc számára. [An interview with Endre Havas.] MTA KIK Kt., Ms 2565/5.

Grünwald Iványi, Béla., Jr. Louis Kossuth. [A letter to the centenary of Kossuth's arrival in England.] *Time and Tide*, Nov. 3. (1951) vol. 33. 1059. MTA KIK Kt., Ms 2565/8.

Iványi-Grünwald, Béla. Jr. *St. Stephen* (BBC lecture, in Hungarian, 1955. 08. 20.) MTA KIK Kt., Ms 2565/42.

Iványi-Grünwald, Béla. Jr. *Szekfű Obituary* (BBC lecture, in Hungarian, 1955. 09. 26.) MTA KIK Kt., Ms 2565/47.

Iványi-Grünwald, Béla. Jr. *Hungarian Youth and Nationalism* (BBC lecture, in Hungarian, 1955. 10. 27.) MTA KIK Kt., Ms 2565/49.

Iványi-Grünwald, Béla. Jr. *Hungarian Writers* (BBC lecture, in English, 1955. 12. 27.) MTA KIK Kt., Ms 2565/52.

Iványi-Grünwald, Béla. Jr. *University Youth* (BBC lecture, in Hungarian, 1955–1956 [sic!]) MTA KIK Kt., Ms 2565/54.

Iványi-Grünwald, Béla. Jr. *Mr. Darvas's Confession* (BBC lecture, in Hungarian, 1956 [sic!]) MTA KIK Kt., Ms 2565/71.

Iványi-Grünwald, Béla. Jr. *Oxford and Hungary* (BBC lecture, 1956. 02. 02.) MTA KIK Kt., Ms 2565/58.

Iványi-Grünwald, Béla. Jr. *Eastern European Writers in Revolt* (BBC lecture, 1956. 05. 08.) MTA, KIK, Kt., Ms 2565/63.

Iványi-Grünwald, Béla. Jr. *New Trends in Hungarian Literature* (BBC lecture, in English, 1956. 05. 20.) MTA KIK Kt., Ms 2565/64.

Iványi-Grünwald, Béla. Jr. *Mindszenty and the Counter-revolution* (BBC lecture, in English, 1956. 12. 06.) MTA KIK Kt., Ms 2565/70.

Iványi-Grünwald, Béla. Jr. *Blake* (BBC lecture, in English, 1957. 02. 28.) MTA KIK Kt., Ms 2565/73.

Iványi-Grünwald, Béla. Jr. *Khruschchov's Address to the Hungarian Academy* (BBC lecture, in Hungarian, 1958. 04. 17.) MTA KIK Kt., Ms 2565/90.

Iványi-Grünwald, Béla. Jr. *Charles Morgan* (BBC lecture, in English, 1958. 02. 07.) MTA KIK Kt., Ms 2565/86.

Iványi-Grünwald, Béla. Jr. *Antiquarian Book Trade* (BBC lecture, in English, 1959. 04. 23.) MTA KIK Kt., Ms 2565/104.

Iványi-Grünwald, Béla. Jr. *Lajos Kossuth* (BBC lecture, in English, 1959. 06. 06.) MTA KIK Kt., Ms 2565/106.

Iványi-Grünwald, Béla. Jr. *St. Stephen's Day* (BBC lecture, in English, 1959. 08. 20.) MTA KIK Kt., Ms 2565/109.
Iványi-Grünwald, Béla. Jr. *Anniversary of the Constitution* (BBC lecture, in English, 1959. 08. 20.) MTA KIK Kt., Ms 2565/108.
Iványi-Günwald, Béla. Jr. *The Credit* (BBC lecture, in English, 1960. 01. 26.) MTA KIK Kt., Ms 2565/115.
Iványi-Grünwald, Béla. Jr. *Széchenyi* (BBC lecture, 1960. 04. 08.) MTA KIK Kt., Ms 2565/119.
Iványi-Grünwald, Béla. Jr. *Széchenyi in England* (BBC lecture, in English, 1960. 04. 26.) MTA KIK Kt., Ms 2565/121.
Iványi-Grünwald, Béla. Jr. *Széchenyi-Exhibition in the British Museum* (BBC lecture, in English, 1960. 09. 04.) MTA KIK Kt., Ms 2565/120.
Iványi-Grünwald, Béla. Jr. *6th October* (BBC lecture, in English, 1960. 10. 04.) MTA KIK Kt., Ms 2565/125. The same in Hungarian MTA KIK Kt., Ms 2565/126.
Iványi-Grünwald, Béla. Jr. *Trends & Events in Hungary* (BBC lecture, in Hungarian, 1961. 04. 21.) MTA KIK Kt., Ms 2565/131.
Iványi-Grünwald, Béla. Jr. *Hungarian Books Published in Great Britain* (BBC lecture, in English, 1961. 07. 14.) MTA KIK Kt., Ms 2565/132.
Iványi-Grünwald, Béla Jr. *Macartney's Book* (BBC lecture, 1962. 09. 19.) MTA KIK Kt., Ms 2565/143.

CHAPTER 10

Building New Networks

Russian Émigré Scholars in Yugoslavia

Branimir Janković

Why Study the History of Russian Émigré Scholars in Yugoslavia?

A case study of twentieth-century Russian émigré scholars in Yugoslavia provides a stimulating option that shifts our focus from individual biographies to a larger group of scholars, thus freeing the research from a predominantly biographical narrative structure. The study of Russian émigré scholars in this way enables us to overcome biographical research by emphasising networks and the fragile political and socio-economic conditions of their work abroad. Russian scholars brought to Yugoslavia new history topics and sub-disciplines and reinvigorated the existing ones, which strengthened the local universities. They also founded new research institutes, and even convinced existing ones, such as the Kondakov Institute in Prague, to relocate to Belgrade. However, we should avoid a master narrative of success so typical of biographies of scholars. In this particular case, Russian scholars and their interests were often confronted by local scholars and by the changing political climate of the 'age of extremes' of the twentieth century, which made their position exceedingly vulnerable.

Therefore, it will be interesting to analyse the strategies that Russian émigré scholars adopted in Yugoslavia to establish themselves in a new political environment, to enter foreign academic institutions, and to maintain the positions they managed to achieve by using their transnational networks.

Notes for this section begin on page 185.

I will also analyse how Yugoslav institutions tried to appropriate or take advantage of Russian émigré scholars for their own national goals. Subsequent attempts in the post-Yugoslav countries to nationalise Russian émigré scholars will also be discussed. Finally, I will argue that is impossible to completely nationalise this group of transnational and internationally oriented émigré scholars.

Another reason why it is interesting to study this group is the recent European 'migrant crisis', which has given a strong impetus to the study of migration in the humanities and the social sciences. At the same time, new theoretical and methodological insights have emerged in the study of émigré scholars.[1] Although migration has been shown to be among the most important public issues, post-Yugoslav historians in the last few years have not dealt with this topic. For instance, Croatian historians have studied Croatian emigration throughout history (mostly regarding the so-called 'Croatian diaspora'). However, there are many immigrant groups in Croatia, and in the former Yugoslavia, that have been largely neglected.

One such group is the large number of Russian émigrés, in both Yugoslavia and Croatia, many of whom were scholars, which fits very well into migration studies from a historical perspective. Like the very well researched German intellectuals and scholars who migrated to the United States in the 1930s,[2] post-revolutionary Russian emigration to the West has also been a well-researched field.[3] But this emphasis on the Russian emigration to the West has mostly ignored – from the global picture of the Russian post-revolutionary emigration – Russian emigration to the Balkans, although there have been a few publications on such Russian emigration.[4] In addition, a case study of Russian emigration to Southeast Europe, the Balkans and Yugoslavia in the twentieth century can be compelling because of the region's position between East and West, Europe and Asia, and as an extremely interesting region in itself.[5]

Russian Emigration to Yugoslavia

Most refugees fleeing from the October Revolution of 1917 came to Southeast Europe, the Balkans and the newly established state of Yugoslavia (then officially known since its creation in 1918 as the Kingdom of Serbs, Croats and Slovenes, and later as the Kingdom of Yugoslavia) immediately after the defeat of the White forces in the Russian Civil War, in 1920. The largest number of these refugees went to Yugoslavia and Bulgaria (and in smaller numbers to Romania and Greece). In the years that followed, they also found refuge in Czechoslovakia, France and the United States. However, in the interwar period, Belgrade, as the capital of the new Yugoslav state, was one of the more important centres for Russian emigration after Paris, Berlin and Prague because it was relatively close to other European metropolises.

Russian emigration to Yugoslavia was initially very well received by the Yugoslav authorities.[6] They organised public welcome ceremonies for 'their brothers', or 'their Orthodox brothers'. For many Russian émigrés, Yugoslavia, especially Serbia, was an excellent choice because they shared the Orthodox religion, the Cyrillic alphabet, a Slavic background and a history of strong cultural and political ties; Russia and Serbia had been allies in the First World War. For these reasons, the Yugoslav authorities were more than willing to accept Russian refugees as 'our brothers who lost their homeland'.[7]

Apart from broader help to Russian emigrants, Yugoslavia also provided many employment opportunities for them throughout the 1920s as teachers in Yugoslav elementary and high schools and universities. A shortage of scientific elites in the less developed and predominantly agrarian Yugoslavia was one important reason for its openness to highly educated emigrants. The Yugoslav authorities also financed Russian schools, and émigrés could find employment as teachers, professors and scholars in all fields of education, from the natural and technical sciences to social sciences and the humanities. Overall, the response of Yugoslav higher education institutions to these émigré scholars was generally very positive. The problems came later, with internal conflict between local and foreign scholars and with the changing political situation, especially in the mid-twentieth century, all of which made the attitude toward Russian emigration quite ambivalent.

In general, Russian émigrés successfully integrated into interwar Yugoslav society. For instance, many of them enjoyed successful scientific and artistic careers. However, their everyday life was not as idyllic as it seemed, which was particularly noticed in later years with an increased number of complaints about the behaviour of some Russian teachers in primary and secondary schools. The list of complaints ranged from the stereotypical – drunkenness or giving bad marks to students – to the more politically sensitive issue of language. Archive material from the Ministry of Education of the Kingdom of Yugoslavia includes several letters from officials describing the sensitive linguistic situation in southern Yugoslavia (with its variety of languages and ethnic groups) as the reason why the government should insist that schools teachers not be of foreign origin but Serbian.[8] All of this reveals the constant local conflicts around Russian émigrés, the permanent insecurity of their material conditions and their gradually increasing political uncertainty within Yugoslavia. For this reason, they had to develop and continuously foster specific adaptation strategies in their new environment.

The Scientific Politics of Russian Émigré Scholars

Despite the initial openness of Yugoslav universities to Russian scholars, it was not easy for Russian émigré historians to obtain a position in the faculties of the humanities and social sciences. Employment in these faculties in Yugoslavia often provoked fierce conflicts with local scientists and their particular personnel or staff interests, which is why Russian historians often worked only part-time in these faculties while also working as teachers in local gymnasiums. It should be pointed out that most Russian émigré historians came to Yugoslavia as young historians and scholars who had received their university degrees (including a few doctoral degrees) in Russia in the wake of the October Revolution, but who in general had obtained their PhDs abroad as émigrés, for instance in Yugoslavia. Therefore, as young historians and scholars, they belonged to a certain extent to the so-called second emigrant generation, and they had to build new networks in a new environment.

There were four major Russian émigré historians in Yugoslavia who can be singled out, not in the form of an individual biography but as a kind of collective biography, to illustrate the broader network of Russian émigré scholars and their scientific strategies. These four scholars are Aleksandar Solovjev (1890–1971), Aleksije Jelačić (1892–1941), Vladimir Mošin (1894–1987), George Ostrogorsky (1902–1976). The most famous among them is Ostrogorsky, a world-renowned Byzantinist who found his way into the *Encyclopedia of Historians and Historical Writing*, which states that 'Russian-born George Ostrogorsky played a major role in overcoming the negative stigma that had been attached to Byzantine studies prior to the 1920s.'[9]

Having relocated to southeastern Europe, the Balkans and Yugoslavia, Russian émigrés formed in the 1920s a wide range of cultural and scientific associations, such as Russian archaeological societies and Russian scientific institutes (just as in Central and Western Europe). Yugoslavia already had a network of local and national historical associations and mostly acted separately from the newly established Russian associations, which had an international orientation and were also striving to foster a 'Slavic ideology'.[10] A first step for Russian émigré scholars was to connect with and inform Russian refugees by establishing associations and journals in the Russian language. But this strategy often somewhat disconnected them from their local communities. That is the reason why, in later years, Russian emigrants also launched journals in Serbo-Croatian.[11] Moreover, teachers and professors sought to obtain (and mostly acquired) Yugoslav citizenship as a way to obtain permanent positions at Yugoslav universities, better salaries and a generally higher status. They did not want to be constantly perceived as foreigners, so they needed to adapt fully to the local academic culture in their new Yugoslav environment while maintaining their transnational networks and scholarly interests.

To enter and establish scholarly circles in Yugoslavia, Russian historians sought specific fields of study that would be interesting both for themselves and for local scholars and universities. Eventually, they came to rely most on two major fields – Slavic studies and Byzantine studies, but especially the latter: '. . . the upsurge in Byzantine studies in Europe and in the region'[12] was a very attractive choice that provided Russian émigrés a better chance at university employment and to achieve social mobility. However, few of them managed to obtain positions in either existing higher education faculties and institutes or newly founded ones, and their status, due to the constantly changing political situation, always remained quite ambiguous.

Focusing on medieval and early modern history within the framework of Slavic and Byzantine studies, Russian émigré scholars could apply the scholarly tradition that had existed in Russian humanities and at universities since the nineteenth century. This was the knowledge that Russian émigré historians brought with them to their new countries. Moreover, Russian émigré scholars could benefit from contacts and networks of university professors from Russia, the Balkans and Europe that had already been established in the nineteenth century and at the beginning of the twentieth century in the field of Slavic studies. Relying on Slavic studies and Byzantine studies was a win-win situation for both sides because they were fields in which they could apply their specific knowledge of Russian and Slavic history, culture and languages.

For the Yugoslav humanities, Slavic studies and Byzantine were an interesting and important international framework to foster national history and culture. For instance, the search for the earliest or most important Byzantine or Slavic medieval manuscripts and documents as sources for Serbian or Croatian history and culture, and their subsequent publication as critical editions in multiple languages, contributed to the international affirmation of Yugoslav humanities within the field of Slavic and Byzantine studies and at the same time helped to build up or strengthen Yugoslav national philology and historiography, and Yugoslav national and cultural identity. This approach illustrates how international and transnational scholarly work can co-exist with nationally oriented projects, particularly during the nation-building process.[13] It should be noted that this point remains completely overlooked in the existing scholarship on Russian emigration to Yugoslavia.

With the help of Russian émigré scholars, Yugoslav universities and institutes became more international, but at the same time they served national goals to develop Yugoslav scholarship and to present it and integrate it into the international community. However, even internationally oriented scholarship is inevitably framed locally – that is, within national borders.

Publication projects were initially financed, for instance, by Croatian, Serbian or Macedonian national institutions. Thus, despite an implied Yugoslav supranational framework, they always served both supranational and specific national needs.

This point can be illustrated by the case of Russian émigré scholars, who always emphasised a Yugoslav supranational or international South Slavic and Slavic stand while they were publishing new editions of old manuscripts and documents written in Latin, Cyrillic or Greek. They constantly pointed out that their editions served the needs of Yugoslav science. Vladimir Mošin even expressed his gratitude to Yugoslav science and to the Yugoslav people for their hospitality.[14] However, thanks to the particular national institutions involved in publication of the specific national histories and cultures represented in these manuscripts and documents, they continued to be a subject of national use. This can clearly be seen after the dissolution of Yugoslavia in the 1990s, when these old manuscripts came to be observed only in a narrow and specific framework (e.g. Croatian, Serbian, Macedonian, etc.) of national identity. Along with the increasing nationalisation of transnational written and other heritages, post-Yugoslav historiographies have also started to nationalise Russian emigrants, which will be discussed later.

On the other hand, Slavic and Byzantine studies gave Russian émigré scholars space to develop and maintain their widespread international contacts and networks, forged through their constant cooperation with European Slavic and Byzantine studies journals and regular participation in the numerous European Slavic and Byzantine studies congresses, as well as through international congresses of the historical sciences. Although Yugoslav historians also participated in historical conferences abroad, Russian émigré scholars were much more active. Moreover, they were constantly publishing in Yugoslav journals reviews of the international congresses and conferences in which they had participated. In this way, the émigré scholars used these activities as a kind of symbolic capital vis-à-vis local historians as part of a strategy to enhance their position in the new Yugoslav state, for instance in the long struggle to obtain permanent positions at Yugoslav universities.

Last but not least, Russian émigré historians in Yugoslavia generally spent their summer vacations abroad – sometimes even for research – in France, Czechoslovakia and other European countries with strong Russian émigré networks and consequently programmes for Slavic and Byzantine studies.[15] Basically, they kept themselves moving more than local (native) historians. As teachers and university professors, they were constantly on the move, taking full advantage of their cross-border networks, ranging from the local scientific communities in Yugoslavia to international scholars, and Russian émigré scholarly circles throughout Europe.

The Scientific Politics of Yugoslav Institutions

However, this chapter is not just a story about the scientific politics practised by Russian émigré scholars. It is also about the politics within Yugoslav scientific institutions. Specifically, Yugoslav institutions were trying to attract some Russian émigré institutions in Europe to Yugoslavia. Archive documents from 1919 shed light on one such attempt by the Yugoslav historian Stanoje Stanojević, who appealed to the Yugoslav authorities to convince the Russian Archaeological Institute in Constantinople to move to Yugoslavia.[16] In 1933, Stanojević invited George Ostrogorsky to move from Germany to the University of Belgrade. Stanojević's first effort failed, but the second one succeeded. After the Second World War, Ostrogorsky became the leading Yugoslav Byzantinist, and he significantly improved Byzantine studies in Yugoslavia by establishing the Byzantine Institute in Belgrade in 1948. As a consequence, 'because of his efforts, the institute became one of the world's leading centers of Byzantine studies and provided Yugoslav historians with contacts in the global community of scholars'.[17]

Although several Russian émigré scholars in the interwar period relocated from Yugoslavia to other European countries and the United States, others migrated in the opposite direction. For example, Ostrogorsky settled in Yugoslavia in 1933, followed by others who fled after Hitler came to power in Germany and after the annexation and occupation of Czechoslovakia (1938–39). In 1938, Yugoslavia also managed to attract the famous Kondakov Institute, which focused on Slavic and Byzantine studies, from Prague to Belgrade (with Ostrogorsky as its director) and with financial assistance from the Yugoslav government.[18] These efforts were the result not only of the personal contacts with Russian émigré historians in Yugoslavia – primarily Ostrogorsky and Vladimir Mošin – but also of a gradual and successful affirmation of research in Slavic and Byzantine studies conducted by Russian historians in Yugoslavia in the 1920s and 1930s.

However, the interests of Yugoslav institutions and Russian émigrés were not always the same. In fact, they sometimes even collided with each other. For some Yugoslav institutions in Belgrade or Zagreb, Yugoslav supranational history, as well as Croatian or Serbian national history, was sometimes of greater importance than international Slavic or Byzantine history. At the same time, new research fields were opening. The Balkan Institute was established in Yugoslavia in 1934. It focused on the new field of Balkan studies (Balkanology),[19] which was firmly separate and distinct from Byzantine studies.[20] This new field was strongly supported by the Yugoslav authorities and even became a focus of national policy. In the same year that the Balkan Institute was established, Yugoslavia signed the Balkan Pact, an alliance between Yugoslavia, Greece, Turkey and Romania. At that point,

Balkan studies officially became more important than Slavic studies and instilled a sense of 'Balkan patriotism'.[21] With Yugoslavia's increasingly close relations with Hitler's Germany in the late 1930s (and its subsequent accession to the Tripartite Pact), Yugoslav institutions significantly increased their contacts with German institutes, whose activities centred on southeastern Europe as an instrument for spreading German influence in the region (comparable with the German Mitteleuropa project[22]), and which also opposed Slavic studies (as the mutual cooperation of Slavic peoples).

Running Away from Contemporary History

Russian émigré historians were oriented to Slavic and Byzantine studies – predominantly focused on the distant past, e.g. medieval and early modern history – because they were trying to escape from politically sensitive issues of recent history, especially recent Russian history. Avoiding ideologically sensitive issues was one of the important strategies adopted by Russian émigré historians operating in their new environment. Among my four selected Russian émigré historians in Yugoslavia, only one of them – Aleksije Jelačić – wrote about contemporary political and social history, including even the Russian Revolution, mainly in liberal and social-democratic journals, which exposed him to attacks from the pro-communist left.

Unlike most Russian historians in Yugoslavia, Jelačić did not shy away from the role of a public intellectual engaged in discussions on postrevolutionary Soviet Russia. Moreover, he organised his historical knowledge production into popular books for the broader Yugoslav public (written in Serbo-Croatian), for example *The History of Russia* (1929), *Czechoslovak History* (preface by Edvard Beneš, 1931) and *The History of Poland* (preface by Oskar Halecki, 1933).[23] Emigration had significantly transformed Jelačić as a historian and pushed him into the role of a major knowledge producer in Yugoslavia on Russian history. Although Jelačić wrote a paper in 1937 on the theory of historical science, which discussed idiographic vs. nomothetic approaches,[24] he did not reflect theoretically on how to research the contemporary history about which he was writing. However, it was common in the interwar period not to reflect on contemporary history ('history that is not yet history'). Only later, in the second half of the twentieth century, did European and American historians develop a theoretical basis for the specific nature of writing about recent history.[25] However, contemporary history (the October Revolution, Stalin's Soviet Union, Hitler's Germany, and the global conflict between fascism and communism, etc.) was not the only highly sensitive topic in the eyes of Russian émigré scholars. The same was true for Russian émigrés in Yugoslavia.

The Highly Sensitive Long-Term Position of Russian Émigré Scholars

Russian emigrants were welcomed by the Yugoslav government beginning in 1920, but what constantly made them especially vulnerable – in addition to their émigré background – were the political upheavals of the twentieth century. When they arrived in Yugoslavia, and throughout 1920s and the 1930s, Yugoslav authorities were fighting against communist sympathisers, communist propaganda and individuals who might be connected in some way with the Soviet Union. This is the reason why even the Russian émigré historian Aleksije Jelačić (who had been criticised by the pro-communist left for his liberal interpretation of the Russian Revolution) was fired from a gymnasium for holding a public lecture on the Russian Marxist thinker Georgi Plekhanov. Jelačić soon returned to his job because the subsequent investigation revealed that his lecture did not have a political purpose.[26]

On the other hand, Yugoslav communists and their supporters among the ranks of university professors and school teachers expressed hostility toward Russian émigré scholars as opponents of the October Revolution and even as counter-revolutionaries. In addition to political issues, there were a variety of personnel interests and employment conflicts between Russian émigré scholars and local university professors.[27] These are the reasons why in the interwar period Russian émigré historians who were appointed professors at Yugoslav faculties of humanities were later often held back, denied permanent employment and advancement, or faced a variety of other difficulties.

During the Second World War and German occupation of Yugoslavia and the establishment of the German-allied Independent State of Croatia, some Russian émigrés sided with the Germans, especially those who had sympathised with fascism before or who were counting on the overthrow of the Soviet regime with Hitler's help. Other émigrés joined Tito's Partisan forces and fought against fascism. However, many Russian teachers and professors generally remained silent during the Second World War, including the four selected historians.

After the Second World War, in the now communist Yugoslav state, the position of Russian émigré historians as post-revolutionary emigrants became even more vulnerable. The new regime in Yugoslavia was strongly oriented toward the Soviet Union, for which the anti-Bolshevik Russian émigrés remained a principal enemy. However, Russian scholars managed to maintain their institutional positions, primarily because of the status that they had achieved in the interwar period but also due to the direct personal intervention of prominent communist historians and politicians, as was the case with George Ostrogorsky at the University of Belgrade, who was protected by Vaso Čubrilović.[28] In 1948, Ostrogorsky became director of the new Byzantine Institute in Belgrade. Vladimir Mošin also maintained and even improved his position by becoming in 1947 a director of the Archive of the Yugoslav Academy of Sciences and Arts in Zagreb, although he later came into conflict with several communist scholars at the same institution.

It may seem that the story of Aleksandar Solovjev, a legal historian, was also a success when after the Second World War he became dean of the faculty of law in Sarajevo, where he moved from Belgrade. But a substantial political breakdown soon took place. In 1948, a major conflict erupted between two communist leaders, Tito and Stalin, which resulted in a major break between Yugoslavia and the Soviet Union that lasted until Stalin's death in 1953. Yugoslavia tried to develop its own path to socialism by fostering cooperation with the United States and seeking a balance between the East and the West. However, this policy led to ruthless clashes with pro-Soviet groups in Yugoslavia and other potentially 'suspect' individuals. One of them was Solovjev. He was arrested in 1949, imprisoned for almost two years, and then after his release, emigrated to Switzerland, where he taught Slavic studies at the University of Geneva. Aleksije Jelačić, the last of my four selected historians, died in 1941 soon after the beginning of the Second World War in Yugoslavia.

In general, Russian emigration consisted of groups with very different political orientations. For the most part, Russian émigré scholars did not comment on politics in public. However, they constantly tried to demonstrate loyalty to the Yugoslav government throughout the twentieth century. By supporting the dominant supranational master narratives in the first and second Yugoslavia, they avoided Croatian-Serbian national conflicts and supporting any other political opposition groups.

The Dynamics of Change in the Work of Russian Émigré Scholars

Although Russian émigré scholars after the Second World War continued to deal with Slavic and Byzantine studies, they now focused more on subdisciplines in which there was a lack of scholars in Yugoslavia, seeking areas of study that would give them the best opportunity to advance in comparison to local Yugoslav scholars. One such area was palaeography, where they kept in touch with recent developments and with trends in publishing manuscripts and documents originally written in Old Slavic or other languages. Filigranology was a new field within the auxiliary sciences of history that was first promoted in postwar Yugoslavia by Vladimir Mošin.[29] Social and economic history was promoted by George Ostrogorsky, who made a major contribution to Byzantine studies and to Yugoslav medieval studies in general. The émigré scholars also maintained contacts with distinguished historians abroad, again as symbolic capital vis-à-vis Yugoslav historians, trying to ensure a strong, almost irreplaceable position within Yugoslav academia.

Since the communist authorities expected complete loyalty from them, Russian émigré historians periodically participated in Yugoslav socialist patriotism. For instance, Mošin conducted a long-term project for publishing the oldest documents in the Macedonian Slavic language to emphasise the difference between it and the Bulgarian Slavic language and Bulgaria itself, with whom Yugoslavia had constant tensions over Macedonia. For the newly established Yugoslav republic of Macedonia, Mošin developed the notion of a small nation whose culture had been successfully preserved for centuries, regardless of foreign powers and their policies of assimilation within its territory.[30] What should also be discussed is whether this notion developed by Mošin was based on the experience of Russia and the Soviet Union as a federation of different nations similar to Yugoslavia.

However, Mošin's ideas were one more example of how the transnational figures among Russian émigré scholars served the nationalising purposes of the Yugoslav state in the nation-building or identity-forging process. Mošin carried out his work so that it was of particular use for supranational or national identities in Yugoslavia. The same is also true for other Russian émigré scholars in Yugoslavia in the twentieth century. Historical knowledge production and its design was used by émigré scholars as a strategy to strengthen their position in the field.

How to Write a History of Russian Émigré Scholars in Yugoslavia?

A history of Russian émigré scholars should be comprised of analyses of their work through the twentieth century. Twenty years after moving to their new country, Russian émigrés had historicised themselves through the perspective of pride and idealisation, unifying their different voices into an unique anti-Bolshevik orientation.[31] The actors themselves in their memoirs tried to behave apolitically and to emphasise only the positive aspects of both Yugoslavias,[32] avoiding ideological disputes and conflicts with other Russian émigrés in Yugoslavia (based on their quite different stances toward Soviet Russia in the 1920s and 1930s, and later with divisions between supporters and opponents of fascism).

After the break-up of the Yugoslavia in the 1990s, Serbian and Croatian historiography (now strongly divided and often confrontational) attempted to nationalise Russian émigré scholars who wrote about Serbian or Croatian history. One example is the case of Aleksije Jelačić. Croatian historiography emphasises his alleged Croatian family origins,[33] while Serbian historiography often calls him a Serbian historian.[34] In the 2000s and the 2010s, his books *The History of Russia*, *Russia and the Balkans* and *The Russian Revolution and Its Origins* were reprinted in Serbia because of the strong political and cultural influence of Russia in Serbia.

Even though Russian émigré historians were deeply integrated into Yugoslavia (including both Serbia and Croatia), it is almost impossible to nationalise such transnational and internationally oriented figures who lived and worked in several European countries and had successfully crossed the frontiers of national historiographies. Recent specialists in Russian emigration to Yugoslavia (for example, Miroslav Jovanović)[35] have tried to avoid such nationalisation by writing about Russian emigration to the Balkans in general and not only to Serbia, Croatia or Yugoslavia.

However, the topic of Russian émigré historians still raises many research questions, especially if we consider them as transnational figures, an issue that so far has not attracted any attention at all and that makes an exploration of how they used transnational networks to forge their positions in the scientific and social fields more important. This can be achieved thanks to the many books, articles, letters and personal accounts that they wrote, and to the vast archival material about them (because they were a social group that was closely monitored by the authorities). Contrary to the prevailing works, it is more illustrative not to focus only on the interwar period, which is considered the 'golden age' of Russian emigration to Yugoslavia and abroad, but on the entire twentieth century, and even its 'afterlife' in the twenty-first century.

In this respect, it can be concluded that despite their positive welcome at the beginning, the position of Russian émigré scholars in Yugoslavia in the twentieth century was very uncertain. They arrived during a period of rapid political change, which was permanent and dramatic in the Yugoslav 'age of extremes'. To overcome all challenges and to establish themselves in the new Yugoslav state, Russian émigré historians avoided current politics and contemporary history. Instead, they focused on Slavic and Byzantine studies, simultaneously employing various international networks. However, both fields served not only to reinforce the transnational scope of Russian émigré scholars but also specific Yugoslav scientific and national purposes.

This tension between transnational and national still plays an important role in the ongoing efforts of post-Yugoslav countries to nationalise the transnational figures of Russian émigré scholars. Nevertheless, as truly transnational and internationally oriented figures, these scholars successfully opposed such nationalisation. Moreover, they spoke out in favour of more transnational perspectives in today's symbolic struggles against nationally exclusive settings. At the same time, and in light of the current European migration crisis, a case study of Russian émigré scholars in Yugoslavia is more of a call for migration studies to adopt a broader historical perspective, at least back to the twentieth century.[36]

Notes

1. Burke, *Exiles and Expatriates*.
2. Iggers, *Refugee Historians from Nazi Germany*; Fair-Schulz and Kessler, *German Scholars in Exile*.
3. Raeff, *Russia Abroad*; Gorboff, *La Russie fantôme*; Glad, *Russia Abroad*; Andreyev and Savický, *Russia Abroad*.
4. Jovanović, *Ruska emigracija na Balkanu*. For the attempt to integrate Southeast Europe into the global history of migrations, see Brunnbauer, *Globalizing Southeastern Europe*.
5. Mishkova, Stråth, and Trencsényi, 'Regional History as a "Challenge"'; Mishkova, 'Balkans/Southeastern Europe'.
6. For a comparison with Czechoslovakia, see Mchitarjan, 'Prague as the Centre of Russian Educational Emigration'.
7. Puškadija-Ribkin, *Emigranti iz Rusije*, 64.
8. Arhiv Jugoslavije (AJ) [Archive of Yugoslavia], Fond 66 – Ministry of Education of the Kingdom of Yugoslavia, AJ-66-16-42, Dopis, Skoplje, 27.VIII.1935.
9. Forrest, 'Ostrogorsky, George', 890.
10. AJ-66-419-683, Ruski naučni institut Beograd, 15.V.1939.
11. Matović and Barać, Časopis *Ruski arhiv (1928–1937)*.
12. Mishkova, *Beyond Balkanism*, 77.
13. For 'the relationship between history writing and the construction of national identities in modern Europe', see Berger, *The Past as History*.
14. Mošin, *Ćirilski rukopisi Jugoslavenske akademije*, 19.
15. Mošin, *Pod teretom*.
16. AJ-66-140-413, Dopis, Stanoje Stanojević, 1921.
17. Forrest, 'Ostrogorsky, George', 890.
18. Lovino, 'Constructing the Past through the Present', 27; Mošin, *Pod teretom*, 117–21.
19. Mishkova, *Beyond Balkanism*, 74–78.
20. Subotić, 'Naša predratna balkanistika o tradiciji', 167–68.
21. Mishkova, Stråth and Trencsényi, 'Regional History as a "Challenge"', 279.
22. Mishkova, 'Balkans/Southeastern Europe'.
23. 'JELAČIĆ, Aleksije', Hrvatski biografski leksikon.
24. Jelačić, *Prilozi teoriji istoriske nauke*.
25. Rousso, *The Latest Catastrophe*.
26. AJ-66-873-1290, Izveštaj, Aleksije Jelačić, 1932.
27. Mošin, *Pod teretom*, 121–22.
28. Antonić, 'Vasa Čubrilović (1897–1990)', 148.
29. Mošin, *Pod teretom*, 149–52.
30. Mošin, *Pod teretom*, 201–2.
31. Fedorov, *Ruska emigracija*.
32. Mošin, *Pod teretom*.
33. 'JELAČIĆ, Aleksije', Hrvatski biografski leksikon.
34. https://sh.wikipedia.org/wiki/Aleksej_Jelačić; https://en.wikipedia.org/wiki/Aleksej_Jelačić

35. Jovanović, *Ruska emigracija na Balkanu*.

36. Both Brunnbauer, *Globalizing Southeastern Europe*, and Ivanović, 'Human Work Drain vs. Brain Drain', emphasise the importance of generations and the tradition of emigration for Yugoslav migration history.

Bibliography

Andreyev, Catherine, and Savický, Ivan. *Russia Abroad: Prague and the Russian Diaspora, 1918–1938*. New Haven: Yale University Press, 2004.
Antonić, Zdravko. 'Vasa Čubrilović (1897–1990)'. *Balcanica Annuaire de l'institut des études balkaniques* 30–31 (2000), 139–65.
Berger, Stefan. *The Past as History: National Identity and Historical Consciousness in Modern Europe*. Basingstoke: Palgrave Macmillan, 2015.
Brunnbauer, Ulf. *Globalizing Southeastern Europe: Emigrants, America, and the State since the Late Nineteenth Century*. London: Lexington Books, 2016.
Burke, Peter. *Exiles and Expatriates in the History of Knowledge, 1500–2000*. Waltham: Brandeis University Press, 2017.
Fair-Schulz, Axel, and Kessler, Mario (eds). *German Scholars in Exile: New Studies in Intellectual History*. Lanham, MD: Lexington Books, 2011.
Fedorov, Nikolaj. *Ruska emigracija: 1919–1939*. Zagreb, 1939.
Forrest, R.F. 'Ostrogorsky, George', in Kelly Boyd (ed.), *Encyclopedia of Historians and Historical Writing* (London and Chicago: Fitzroy Dearborn, 1999), 890–91.
Glad, John. *Russia Abroad: Writers, History, Politics*. Tenafly, NJ: Hermitage & Birchbark Press, 1999.
Gorboff, Marina. *La Russie fantôme: L'émigration russe de 1920 à 1950*. Lausanne: L'Âge d'homme, 1995.
Iggers, Georg. *Refugee Historians from Nazi Germany: Political Attitudes towards Democracy*. Washington, D.C: United States Holocaust Memorial Museum, 2006.
Ivanović, Vladimir. 'Human Work Drain vs. Brain Drain: Beitrag zur Geschichte der bosnischen Flüchtlinge in Österreich'. *Wissenschaftliches Jahrbuch der Tiroler Landesmuseen* 11 (2018), 147–60.
Jelačić, Aleksije. *Prilozi teoriji istoriske nauke*. Skoplje, 1937.
Jovanović, Miroslav. *Ruska emigracija na Balkanu 1920–1940*. Belgrade: Čigoja štampa, 2006.
Lovino, Francesco. 'Constructing the Past through the Present: The Eurasian View of Byzantium in the Pages of *Seminarium Kondakovianum*', in Matthew Kinloch and Alex MacFarlane (eds), *Trends and Turning Points: Constructing the Late Antique and Byzantine World* (Leiden: Brill, 2019), 14–28.
Matović, Vesna, and Barać, Stanislava (eds). *Časopis Ruski arhiv (1928–1937) i kultura ruske emigracije u Kraljevini SHS/Jugoslaviji*. Beograd: Institut za književnost i umetnost, 2015.
Mchitarjan, Irina. 'Prague as the Center of Russian Educational Emigration: Czechoslovakia's Educational Policy for Russian Emigrants (1918–1938)'. *Paedagogica Historica* 45(3) (2009), 369–402.
Mishkova, Diana. 'Balkans/Southeastern Europe', in Diana Mishkova and Balázs Trencsényi (eds), *European Regions and Boundaries: A Conceptual History* (New York/Oxford: Berghahn Books, 2017), 143–65.
———. *Beyond Balkanism: The Scholarly Politics of Region Making*. New York and London: Routledge, 2018.
Mishkova, Diana, Bo Stråth, and Balázs Trencsényi. 'Regional History as a "Challenge" to National Frameworks of Historiography: The Case of Central, Southeast, and Northern

Europe', in Matthias Middell and Lluis Roura (eds), *Transnational Challenges to National History Writing* (Palgrave Macmillan, 2013), 257–314.

Mošin, Vladimir. *Ćirilski rukopisi Jugoslavenske akademije*. Dio 1: Opis rukopisa. Zagreb: Jugoslavenska akademija znanosti i umjetnosti, 1955.

———. *Pod teretom: Autobiografija*. Belgrade and Pančevo: Narodna biblioteka Srbije; Gradska biblioteka, 2008.

Puškadija-Ribkin, Tatjana. *Emigranti iz Rusije u znanstvenom i kulturnom životu Zagreba*. Zagreb: Prosvjeta, 2006.

Raef, Marc. *Russia Abroad: A Cultural History of Russian Emigration, 1919–1939*. New York: Oxford University Press, 1990.

Rousso, Henry. *The Latest Catastrophe: History, the Present, the Contemporary*. Chicago: University of Chicago Press, 2016.

Subotić, D.S. 'Naša predratna balkanistika o tradiciji, religiji i nauci na Balkanu', *Teme* 20 (1997) 1–2, 163–85.

CHAPTER 11

Networking in Santa Barbara, Writing History

Dimitrije Đorđević and the Comparative History of Balkan Nations

Michael Antolović

In the obituary written on the occasion of Dimitrije Đorđević's death in Santa Barbara, California, his former student Bernd Jürgen Fischer appraised Đorđević as 'one of the most distinguished scholars of Serbian and Balkan history'.[1] As a historian with an extensive knowledge and diverse interests, Dimitrije Đorđević (1922–2009) did not only make an important contribution to the development of modern Balkan Studies but, during his long life, he was also witness to the paths and side roads of Serbian history in the 'age of extremes'. Putting Đorđević in the context of émigré historians of the twentieth century, the aim of this chapter is to discuss in which way Đorđević's experience of emigration influenced his approach to researching and writing history.

A descendant of the Serbian bourgeois elite, member of the royalist resistance movement during the Second World War, Mauthausen Concentration Camp inmate, and political prisoner in the first postwar years, Đorđević managed to graduate in history at the Faculty of Philosophy in Belgrade in 1954.[2] However, having in mind his bourgeois origin as well as his political views marked by strong anti-communism, the Yugoslav authorities perceived Đorđević as a 'subversive reactionary' totally unacceptable for the

---

Notes for this section begin on page 200.

newly established socialist society. This fact ruined his professors' intention to keep him in the History Department as a teaching assistant: 'the prospects of a former prisoner to enter the flows of the new society were poor except for Canossa, which he was refusing.'[3] Yet, in spite of the fact that as a member of the dispossessed bourgeoisie Đorđević was left without his family property in the process of the 'expropriation of the expropriators', it turned out that he had considerable social and cultural capital.[4] Primarily, the members of the pre-war Serbian *haute bourgeoisie* kept their social connections, helping one another in order to survive under the regime that proclaimed them 'class enemies'.[5] Moreover, with his general knowledge and command of languages, Đorđević had considerable advantages over his colleagues, whose intellectual horizons (as in the case of the so-called *obrazovanshchina* in the Soviet Union), in spite of their formal education, were often superficial and limited. Using his advantages, as a social outsider, Đorđević began his professional affirmation in Serbian and Yugoslav historiography.

Becoming a Historian in Socialist Yugoslavia

The establishment of the 'dictatorship of the proletariat' carried out by the Communist Party of Yugoslavia decisively influenced the physiognomy of Serbian historiography after the Second World War. After the stabilisation of the new political order, the authorities implemented a policy of inclusion of the intellectual elite, which, descending from the bourgeois social strata, predominantly did not share sympathies for the communist ideology.[6] At the same time, trying to transform Yugoslavia following the model of the Soviet Union, the revolutionary government began the 'sovietisation' of the entire Yugoslav society, economy and culture. Within this process, Yugoslav historiography[7] found itself under severe ideological surveillance. Following the ideas of the leading party ideologue Milovan Đilas about the necessity of refuting the 'bourgeois way of thinking' and establishing historical studies on the principles of dialectic materialism (as part of a broader 'battle of socialism against capitalism'), the production and dissemination of historical knowledge was put under ideological control. In the first place, this meant the political functionalising of historical scholarship and especially the history teaching in schools. Instead to provide the society with rational knowledge about the past, historiography was primarily expected to be a form of 'political pedagogy' that simultaneously ought to legitimise the revolutionary transformation and the newly established order.[8] Therefore, striving to clash with the so-called 'bourgeois interpretation of history', during the first postwar years, the revolutionary authorities imposed on historiography dogmatic

Marxism as the obligatory ideological model, expecting, at the same time, that historiography ought to begin with 'foreseeing historical directions, further historical developments'.⁹

In the circumstances of the striking ideologisation of historical studies, the most prominent Serbian historians (as well as Croatian and Slovenian), who had been educated before the war and revolution, resorted to a kind of intellectual escapism. Trying to integrate themselves into the new society, the 'old-school historians' nominally accepted the Marxist interpretation of history with some Marxist phraseology and mostly directed their research focus to Medieval and Modern History.¹⁰ The fact that the revolutionary authorities were primarily interested in the most recent past, perceiving the Second World War and the revolution as their founding myth, gave additional impetus for such a practice of Serbian historians.¹¹ It did not only leave research into twentieth-century history to the younger generation of party historians overwhelmingly interested in the history of the Communist Party, Labour Movement, People's Liberation War and revolution, but also had important theoretical and methodological repercussions. In the first place, it determined the conservation of the traditional historiography mostly focused on establishing individual historical facts in the field of politics and diplomatic relations.¹² This circumstance determined the decades in which Yugoslav historiographies fell behind regarding the global directions of historical thought regarding the second half of the twentieth century. It was dominated by three theoretical models until the end of the 1980s: on the one hand, there was the 'traditional political historiography', on the other hand, there was dogmatic Marxist historiography, whereas between these extremes was 'Marxist positivism' as a kind of 'middle way'.¹³

These characteristics of Yugoslav historiographies presented the intellectual context in which Đorđević began his historical work, with the support of Professor Vaso Čubrilović, Nestor of Serbian historiography and head of the History Department at the Faculty of Philosophy in Belgrade for several years. A former member of Young Bosnia and participant in the Assassination in Sarajevo in 1914, Čubrilović became part of the communist regime after the Second World War. This fact enabled him to influence the politics of 'historiographical discourse' in the community of Serbian historians over the following decades. Giving priority to profession over ideology, Čubrilović protected some of the most prominent 'bourgeois historians' (including the renowned Byzantinist George Ostrogorsky).¹⁴ Đorđević, as Čubrilović's protégé, was appointed to the Archive – and then to the Historical Institute of the Serbian Academy of Sciences and Arts (1958). The young scholar paid special attention to the history of Serbia at the beginning of the twentieth century (1903–1914), an issue that was not sufficiently researched at that time. This decade was perceived as the 'Golden Age' of modern Serbian history: the establishment of parliamentarism and liberal democracy was followed by a dynamic economic and cultural development and by the territorial expansion of Serbia after the Balkan Wars in 1912/13. Considering that this relatively short period of Serbian history was a clear antithesis to the reality of Serbia in the middle of twentieth century, Đorđević was especially interested in it: 'This Golden Age of the Serbian nation in the prime of life before the First World War offered, in a way, some consolation for the fate of Serbian nation in the communist period.'[15]

Although Đorđević used a positivistic methodology at the beginning of his historical research, already in his early writings he showed the innovative potential that was to become a permanent feature of his further work in the field of Serbian and then of Balkan history. Striving for an approach to history that would be as comprehensive as possible, he, as self-taught, accepted the method of the French 'Annales' (whose reception by Yugoslav historiographies then was only in its beginnings),[16] as well as the approach of oral history. Whereas the influence of the *Annalistes* was primarily visible in the inclusion of social and economic factors in historical explanation, the oral history method enabled Đorđević to broaden the concept of historical sources that were traditionally identified with archival documents. He already applied this approach to historical research in his first more detailed monograph 'Serbia's Outlet to the Adriatic Sea and the 1912 Ambassadors' Conference in London' (1956), published by himself as a *samizdat* book.[17] Drawing his conclusion on the basis of various historical sources (diplomatic, memoirs, oral) and historical literature, he analysed this question from the field of international relations in the broad context of the European and Balkan politics of that time. Two facts regarding Đorđević's methodology were especially important: he did not remain within the realm of traditional diplomatic history but rather included some intellectual, economic and social factors in his interpretations. In contrast to the professional mainstream, Đorđević did not use the Marxist vocabulary that was widespread at that time. This fact did not remain unnoticed in the historiographical circles abroad, which appraised the book as a 'final *mise au point*' in the research of this question.[18]

In 1962, at the Faculty of Philosophy in Belgrade, Đorđević defended his doctoral dissertation under the title 'Customs War between Austria-Hungary and Serbia, 1906–1911' and, in the same year, published it in the form of a voluminous scholarly monograph of more than 700 pages.[19] Đorđević analysed the subject of his research (the so-called 'Pig War') in a broader context, which, besides economic ones, included social, ideological and political factors. In that way, he showed how the independent Serbian Kingdom was exposed to the imperialist aspirations of the Dual Monarchy, which eventually led to the outbreak of the European War in 1914. Through its factographic richness as well as its methodological innovativeness, which by applying approaches of economic and social history, greatly transcended the limitations of the narrowly conceived political history, very soon Đorđević's monograph earned the reputation as 'one of the best works of Serbian historiography after the Second World War'.[20] The biography of the Serbian diplomat Milovan Milovanović, the chief creator of the Balkan League (in 1912), also belongs to the same field of research. Written simultaneously with his work on the dissertation, it indicated Đorđević's interest in outstanding personalities of modern Serbian history, the subject he remained wedded to during his entire subsequent career.[21]

Conducting Academic Diplomacy

With these works, Đorđević established his position in Serbian historiography, while his international contacts enabled him to enter Balkan and European historiographies. Besides his scholarly approved qualities, these activities were facilitated by the fact that socialist Yugoslavia, creating the Non-Aligned Movement, returned to the international stage.[22] Coinciding with the restored cultural exchange with Western Europe and the US, this circumstance favourably influenced the inclusion of Yugoslavian historiography in international professional organisations such as the International Committee of Historical Sciences (ICHS). This global change in Yugoslavian foreign policy enabled Đorđević to invest his intellectual capital into conducting the academic diplomacy of the Historical Institute in Belgrade. Due to his command of foreign languages, in the first place (which was a rare skill among the younger generation of historians devoted to the research of the history of the Communist Party and labour movement), and in spite of the fact that he was not a member of the Communist Party and that he was an opponent to the communist regime in Yugoslavia, he took part in almost all international projects of the Historical Institute under the leadership of Jorjo Tadić.[23] A specialist on the history of the Republic of Ragusa and a friend of Fernand Braudel, who shared similar views on history, Tadić gave his full support to Đorđević, who began to establish professional contacts with colleagues in Greece (including the prominent Hellenist and Byzantinist Basil Laourdas),[24] and subsequently, as a secretary of the Yugoslavic section of the ICHS, with many historians in Europe and the US. A study trip to the Institute for Balkan Studies in Thessaloniki (1963–1964) turned out to be especially important in a double sense. In Thessaloniki, which was one of the world's centres of Balkan Studies during the 1960s, Đorđević did not only meet the leading specialists of the Balkans, establishing friendly relationships with them, but he also broadened his professional interests, directed mostly to Serbian history and its international context, to include the 'common past of the Balkan peoples exposed if not to the same then to the similar conditions of social, economic and cultural development'.[25]

This methodological redirection is visible in several of Đorđević's works that originated in the 1960s, including the *History of Serbia, 1804–1918*, which was published in Greek by the Institute for Balkan Studies in Thessaloniki in 1970.[26] However, he applied the comparative approach to Balkan history consistently in the monograph *Révolutions nationales des peuples balkaniques, 1804–1914* (1965), presented at the XII Congress of ICHS in Vienna in 1965. In the shadow of Fischer's controversy, which stirred up fierce polemics,[27] Đorđević presented his innovative interpretation of the making of the Balkan nations in the nineteenth century. Understanding nations as phenomena resulting from the process of modernisation of European societies, he encompassed the emergence and development of Balkan nationalisms (in his terminology 'national revolutions' and 'national movements') from the time of the Serbian and Greek revolutions at the beginning of the nineteenth century, including then the emergence of Rumanian, Bulgarian and Albanian nationalism up to the outbreak of the First World War. Đorđević analysed the creation of modern Balkan nationalisms from the comparative perspective, trying to determine similarities between and differences in the development of each nation. What is especially important is the fact that searching for the roots of the 'national revolutions' of the Balkan nations he included social, economic and intellectual factors in his explanation that in the mutual interaction determined the dynamics of individual political phenomena. Keeping in mind this distinctiveness of Đorđević's approach, his interpretation was original in several ways. In regard to theory and methodology, he managed to analyse the Balkan 'national movements' during the 'long nineteenth-century' from a comparative perspective and to give one of the rare syntheses of Balkan history at that time.[28] The importance of this approach was even greater, since Đorđević overcame the ethnocentrism that heavily characterised the historical writing in the Balkans. The fact that also deserves attention is that although Đorđević worked within the nominally Marxist Serbian and Yugoslav historiographies, he completely avoided stereotypical interpretations of the so-called 'national question', which were among the characteristics of the Marxist historiographies in Eastern Europe.[29]

Đorđević's international contacts as well as still existing family ties paved the way to historiographical circles abroad. As a visiting scholar, he went to several universities in Western Europe and the US in the second half of the 1960s. In the autumn of 1965, he gave lectures about Serbian and Balkan history at the most prestigious universities in England – at Cambridge, at Oxford and at the School of Slavonic and East European Studies. As a result of these contacts, Đorđević was invited to the conference about the

'National problem in the Habsburg Monarchy in the nineteenth-century' organised in 1966 at Indiana University Bloomington, the leading centre for research of Central Europe and the Balkans in the US at that time.[30] During his visit to the US, he delivered a few lectures about modern Serbian history and contemporary Yugoslavian historiography in several cities (from Detroit via Santa Barbara and Minneapolis to New Haven), establishing close relations with the most notable American specialists in the history of the Balkans and Eastern Europe. During this 'American tour', Đorđević went to the University of Santa Barbara, California as a visiting professor. At the same time, as a research fellow of a newly founded Institute for Balkan Studies in Belgrade (1969), Đorđević continued to conduct academic diplomacy and to simultaneously develop an international network of professional and private contacts.

'In the Heaven of an Eternal Spring in Santa Barbara'

Considering Đorđević's point of departure (as a concentration camp inmate and political prisoner), he achieved an almost unbelievable success in the following two decades (1950–1970): he had important professional results; in the scholarly circles abroad he was respected as one of the most outstanding Yugoslav specialists in modern history of the Balkans; and with his international contacts he substantially contributed to the inclusion of Serbian and Yugoslav historiographies in the mainstream of international historiographical developments. It is not an unimportant fact that in Yugoslavia, in spite of ideological surveillance, he enjoyed a certain degree of academic autonomy: although he 'could not write anything he wanted to', he did not 'have to write what he did not want'.[31] On the other hand, during his visit to the US, Đorđević became acquainted with the scale of the civil unrest and student revolts against the Vietnam War, which spread across campuses of American universities in 1968. Although this experience, according to his own confession, 'heavily undermined his devotion to American democracy', after repeated invitations he decided to emigrate to the US.[32] The reasons for this far-reaching decision were probably related to his position as an outsider under the Yugoslavian regime to which he did not belong, neither intellectually nor socially. In spite of the political liberalisation of socialist Yugoslavia in the 1960s, Đorđević had a reputation as a 'subversive person', which could be abused at any time. Disregarding his professional results, the authorities made it impossible for him to be appointed Professor at the University of Belgrade. Feeling a 'cloud of suspicion from the authorities hanging over me', Đorđević was 48 when he swapped his native Belgrade for California.[33]

At the beginning of 1970, he signed a contract, becoming a tenured Professor at the University of California, Santa Barbara (UCSB). Apart from the respect that he enjoyed in the professional circles in Europe and the US, as well as many personal contacts that he had established in the previous decade, the crucial fact that enabled Đorđević to gain a permanent position at an American university was related to the specific economic and intellectual conditions during the 1960s and early 1970s. In the context of a growing competition between the US and USSR, the American government raised investments in higher education, which resulted in the expansion of universities and the arrival of numerous foreign scholars in the US. In that way, the pre-war emigration of intellectuals (also including historians) continued during the Cold War. Among prominent historians who left the Eastern Bloc and emigrated to the US were, *inter alia*, Hungarian historians Andreas Alföldi, Béla Király and István Deák (after the Revolution of 1956), the Polish historian Jan T. Gross (1969), as well as Russian historians Alexander Nekrich (1976) and Alexander Kazhdan (1979). Therefore, Đorđević's arrival in Santa Barbara (coinciding with the emigration of the illustrious Serbian Byzantinist Bariša Krekić, who also left Yugoslavia and came to the University of California, Los Angeles) was part of a wider process of *voluntary emigration* of intellectuals from Eastern Europe who found refuge in the US from the political repression they were exposed to in their native countries, although to different extents.[34]

As a Professor of European and Balkanic history, Đorđević entered the circles of American Slavic Studies and was especially driven by the need to research the USSR and countries in its sphere of interest. From the Russian and East European Studies existing at prestigious universities – such as Harvard, Stanford, Columbia and Indiana – gradually developed Byzantine, Ottoman and Habsburg Studies and, simultaneously, multidisciplinary Balkan studies. Considering the complexity of this discipline (which requires the knowledge of various languages), its pioneers in the US were often people of Balkanic and/or Central and East European origin, which was also the case with Russian and Austrian studies.[35] Balkan Studies were established in the US during the interwar years by Francis Dvornik and Harrison Thomson, specialists in Byzantine history and the history of Slavs in the Middle Ages, as well as Bernadotte E. Schmitt, a specialist in the causes of the First Word War. After the Second World War, the work of these pioneers of Slavic and Balkan Studies in the US was continued by historians of Balkan origin: besides Leften S. Stavrianos and Traian Stoianovich, who both adopted a comparative approach, Stephen Fischer-Galati, Keith Hitchins, Stavro Skëndi, Peter Sugar as well as the couple Barbara and Charles Jelavich (only to mention the most notable personalities). They researched the history of some Balkan nations. Within this circle of experts on the Balkans,

Wayne Vucinich, Michael B. Petrovich, Alex N. Dragnich, Gale Stokes, David MacKenzie and John R. Lampe devoted themselves especially to South Slavic/Yugoslav history.

Having established close cooperation with American specialists in Balkanic and Eastern European history during the following two decades, Đorđević adapted to the American traditions of historical writing in terms of his research subjects and his methodological approach. This 'historiographical acculturation', also noticeable in other émigré historians, was facilitated by their openness to different theoretical and methodological directions.[36] Having started his 'historian's craft' within the community of historians marked by positivism, he expanded his approach both in the methodological (social and comparative history) and thematic sense (history of the Balkans). Moreover, Đorđević's turn to social history, obvious already in his previous works, received additional impetus in the US, especially because the mainstream in American historiography during the 1960s and 1970s were characterised by the rise of social history.[37] Regarding his relation to Marxist historiography, Đorđević emphasised that he 'did not reject Marxism in principle'.[38] Accepting the most valuable achievements of Marxist historiography, he enriched his own interpretations of political phenomena, contextualising them in the framework of social and economic history. In that manner, the absence of dogmatic exclusiveness enabled him to achieve a fruitful synthesis of the mainstream of twentieth-century historical thought in his own work. Although he was not a Marxist, Đorđević was aware that under the 'ideological and cliché-ridden shell, the Russian i.e. Soviet historiography on Europe was on solid, fact-oriented grounds'.[39]

The main subjects of Đorđević's research during his time as a Professor in Santa Barbara exhibit the evolution of his methodological approach. Since he was no longer able to research Serbian and European archives, his papers written in the US were mainly founded on published sources, as well as historical literature. Although this fact imposed certain limitations on his work, it was stimulating, since it is by accepting new theoretical concepts that Đorđević demonstrated his innovativeness in the interpretation of historical phenomena. Trying to determine similarities and differences, he focused his research on the comparative history of the Balkan societies during the 'long nineteenth-century'. His monograph on the *National Revolutions of the Balkan Peoples* went through a revised English edition, with the addition of a chapter about social and political unrests in the Balkans in the seventeenth and eighteenth centuries written by Stephen Fischer-Galati.[40] Pointing to a comprehensive approach and to its clarity, the reviewers appraised the book as an 'excellent study', which 'clearly shows how and to what extent the well-accepted myths of the Balkan peoples differ from historical truth'.[41] Đorđević followed the comparative approach to the social history of the

Balkans presented in this book more clearly in several papers published in the 1970s and 1980s. These were devoted to the role of some key factors that determined the development of the Balkan societies in the nineteenth century: political (creation of national states),[42] socio-economic (the peasantry as a prevailing social stratum),[43] institutional (military)[44] and intellectual (ideas of the Enlightenment, nationalism and constitutionalism).[45] The common theme connecting the given papers was Đorđević's main idea that the modernisation of the Balkan societies, as well as the constituting of modern nations, was influenced by two main processes: common anti-Ottoman aspirations and the peasantry's continuous demands for their own land.[46]

In addition to these main subjects, Đorđević continued his work on the history of Serbs in the Habsburg Monarchy and the history of the Kingdom of Serbia at the turn of the century, as well as on some outstanding personalities in Serbian history. Considering the first subject, his most important work is the one he wrote for the great edition *Die Habsburger Monarchie 1848–1918*, devoted to the 'peoples of the Empire' and edited by Adam Wandruszka and Peter Urbanitsch.[47] Đorđević presented the demographic, socio-economic, cultural and political development of Serbs in the Monarchy from the Revolution of 1848 until the outbreak of the First World War. It deserves to be mentioned that Đorđević's contribution to this monumental achievement of postwar Austrian historiography was also a sign of special acknowledgement of the scholarly reputation he enjoyed in European academia – of the Serbian specialists in the history of Serbs in the Monarchy, the editors had chosen Đorđević. At the same time, Đorđević took part in the central project of Serbian historiography in the late 1970s and early 1980s – the multivolume *History of the Serbian People*. Relying on his previous research, Đorđević gave a synthetic account of the social, economic, intellectual and political history of the Kingdom of Serbia from the end of the 1880s until the beginning of the First World War. Just as he did in his works published in English, Đorđević paid special attention to the social and economic conditions, which were mostly neglected in earlier historiography.[48]

However, Đorđević's focus on social history was followed by his continuous interest in outstanding personalities of modern Serbian history. His main intention was not so much to discover new facts about some historical figures as it was to present them and to 'stress their significance' to Anglo-American historiography. In this sense, besides the article about Slobodan Jovanović, written at the invitation of Walter Laqueur for the special issue of the *Journal of Contemporary History* devoted to 'historians in politics',[49] his paper about the historian and diplomat Stojan Novaković should be mentioned,[50] then the paper on Radomir Putnik, Chief of the Serbian General Staff in the First World War,[51] and an article about the language reformer Vuk Karadžić as a historian of the Serbian Revolution.[52] Finally, Đorđević also contributed to the history of Serbian historiography. Despite the fact that it was neither the primary field of his scholarly interests nor his systematic concern, he contributed to the international dictionary *Great Historians from Antiquity to 1800* and *Great Historians of the Modern Age* edited by Lucian Boia. Having written several entries about the most prominent representatives of modern Serbian and Croatian historiography, he made them an integral part of the 'ecumene of historians'.[53]

Having entered the circles of American Balkanistics, Đorđević continued to foster relationships with his colleagues in Europe and Yugoslavia and to act as an intermediary between Serbian and Balkan historiographies on one side and American historiography on the other. In this sense, his cooperation with the project 'War and Society in East Central Europe', carried out by the historian Béla K. Király as part of the 'Brooklyn College Studies in Society in Change Program', was of special importance. Focused on the influences of wars on the modern Balkan societies, the project was highly multidisciplinary and brought together specialists in different fields. The results of seven conferences, organised between 1978 and 1984 and attended by dozens of historians from the US, Europe and the Balkans, were presented in seven voluminous monographs published in English.[54] Apart from that, Đorđević organised three scholarly conferences – on the Enlightenment in the Balkans and Europe (1973), on the creation of Yugoslavia (1978) and on migrations in Balkan history (1988). Published in three proceedings (of the conference) edited by Đorđević, the first one (devoted to the creation of Yugoslavia) mainly presented works from the field of political and diplomatic history.[55] The second one (on the influence of the Balkan Wars on the societies in East Central Europe)[56] and the third one (on migrations in the history of the Balkans) are characterised by very distinct approaches of social and comparative history.[57] At the same time, having integrated himself into the American *academia*, Đorđević started the Program of Balkan Studies in the History Department of the UCSB. In addition to the advancement of Balkanistics, Đorđević's main goal was 'to join together the best achievements of Balkan and American scholarship in Balkan Studies'.[58]

Legacy

In all the above-mentioned projects, Đorđević played a key role in connecting specialists in the Balkans from both sides of the Atlantic. The fact that during his professional career he was a member of the editorships of influential journals such as *East European Quarterly* (from 1970), *Historical Abstracts* (from 1972) and *Austrian History Yearbook* (1974–1978) was not only an acknowledgement of his reputation as a scholar but it also additionally facilitated his mediatory role between different historiographical traditions. Đorđević's endeavours produced manifold results regarding the inclusion of Balkan historiographies in the global historiographical strata and, thereby, regarding the deepening of historical knowledge of the Balkan societies.[59] However, it seems that the cooperation between Balkanic and American historians initiated by Đorđević was most fruitful in the field of historical theory and methodology: although the nation state still presents one of the basic units of historical research, Balkan historiographies, gradually accepting approaches of social and comparative history, managed to transcend (albeit not entirely) ethnocentrism as one of their most distinctive features from the time of their emergence in the middle of the nineteenth century.[60] Đorđević's influence on Serbian historiography could be compared with the role of Hans Rosenberg, an émigré historian from Nazi Germany who contributed considerably to the modernisation of West German historiography through his socio-historical approach.[61] Like Rosenberg, in the process of historiographical acculturation during the 1970s, Đorđević accepted the concepts of American social history, applying them to the research into Balkan history. By adoption and appropriation of these concepts, he achieved a synthesis of various intellectual traditions in his own methodological approach, retroactively influencing (although to a limited extent) Serbian historiography. The Serbian reception of Đorđević's socio-historical works coincided with the so-called *social turn* in Serbian historiography during the 1990s, which enabled its opening to different approaches of social history and/or history of society.[62]

Keeping the mentioned facts in mind, Đorđević's example confirms the thesis that many émigré historians, with their innovative concepts, played a decisive role in the transformation of the historiography practised in their native countries.[63] However, the émigré historians from the interwar period, as well as those from the 'second generation' of their descendants, regularly experienced social marginalisation and cultural up-rootedness, which significantly hindered their integration into the new environment.[64] Compared with these émigré historians' experiences, Đorđević's case was completely different and atypical. Having come from Belgrade to the 'heaven of an eternal spring in Santa Barbara',[65] Đorđević integrated himself into the community of American historians without major difficulties, built a successful career and earned the reputation of an internationally recognised specialist in Balkan history. Having found a new social environment within his large 'Balkan family'[66] – postgraduate and doctoral students – Đorđević significantly improved Balkan Studies in the US. Considering his contribution to the theoretical and methodological modernisation of Serbian historiography, Đorđević, through his transcultural communication, enriched both Serbian and American historical culture, which constitutes his worthiest intellectual legacy.

Notes

1. Fischer, 'Dimitrije Djordjevic', 1069. See also Bataković, 'Dimitrije V. Djordjević', 9–24.
2. Djordjevic, *Scars and Memory*, 349.
3. Đorđević, *Ožiljci i opomene*, vol. 3, 25.
4. Bourdieu, 'The Forms of Capital', 241–58.
5. Milićević, *Jugoslovenska vlast i srpsko građanstvo*, 413–16.
6. Ibid., 462–509.
7. The term 'Yugoslav historiography' was the common denominator for six Yugoslav historiographies (Slovenian, Croatian, Serbian, Montenegrin, Bosnian and Herzegovinian and Macedonian) organised within six Yugoslav republics. These historiographies followed their own dynamics, had different traditions and, despite some common Yugoslav historiographical institutions, they developed almost independently from each other. However, for practical purposes, the historiography developing in Yugoslavia was called simply Yugoslav historiography. See Antolović, 'Writing History', 49–73.
8. For the Yugoslav and Serbian historiography after World War Two, see Antolović, 'Writing History', 49–73; Banac, 'Historiography of the Countries of Eastern Europe', 1084–104; Brunnbauer, 'Historical Writing in the Balkans', 353–74; Stanković and Dimić, *Istoriografija pod nadzorom*; Nikolić, *Prošlost bez istorije*; Koren, *Politika povijesti u Jugoslaviji*.
9. Nikolić, *Prošlost bez istorije*, 28–29.
10. Marković,Ković and Milićević, 'Developments in Serbian Historiography', 278.
11. Höpken, 'Vergangenheitspolitik im sozialistischen Vielvölkerstaat', 210–43.
12. Banac, 'Historiography of the Countries of Eastern Europe', 1086.
13. Antolović and Šimunović-Bešlin, 'History as Vallis Aurea', 122–23.
14. Antonić, 'Vasa Čubrilović (1897–1990)', 139–65.
15. Đorđević, *Ožiljci i opomene*, 28.
16. See Šegvić and Branđolica, 'The Mediterranean', 367–81.
17. Đorđević, *Izlazak Srbije na Jadransko*.
18. Pavlowitch, 'Izlazak Srbije na Jadransko', 580–81.
19. Đorđević, *Carinski rat Austro-Ugarske i Srbije*.
20. Samardžić, *Pisci srpske istorije*, 234. See Vucinich, 'Dimitrije Đorđević', 354–55.
21. Đorđević, *Milovan Milovanović*.
22. Calic, *Geschichte Jugoslawiens*, 200–2; Lampe, *Yugoslavia as History*, 267–75.
23. For Jorjo Tadić and his relation to Braudel, see Šegvić and Branđolica, 'The Mediterranean', 372–73.
24. See Iatrides, 'Basil Laourdas', 474.
25. Đorđević, *Ožiljci i opomene*, 75.
26. Tzortzevits, *Historia tēs Servias*.
27. Erdmann, *Die Ökumene der Historiker*, 350–52.
28. Leften S. Stavrianos published his groundbreaking synthesis only a few years earlier. See Stavrianos, *The Balkan since 1453*.
29. See a discussion of the book in which twenty-one historians from Europe and the US took part, Mikoletzky, *XIIe Congrès International des Sciences Historiques*, 358–59.
30. Rath, *Nationality Problem*.
31. Đorđević, *Ožiljci i opomene*, 173.
32. Ibid., 146.
33. Djordjevic, *Scars and Memory*, 463.
34. De Baets, 'Exile and Acculturation', 320–21. Unlike the emigration of historians from Europe to the US in the interwar period, the emigration of historians during the Cold War is still not researched systematically. See Mandelíčková and Goddeeris, 'Living in the Past', 404–5.

35. See Schroeder, 'The Status of Habsburg Studies', 267–95; Fellner, 'The Special Case of Austrian Refugee Historians', 109–15.
36. De Baets, 'Exile and Acculturation', 316–49.
37. See, for example, Stearns, 'Social History', 890–96.
38. Đorđević, *Ožiljci i opomene*, 146.
39. Ibid., 145.
40. Djordjevic and Fischer-Galati, *The Balkan Revolutionary Tradition*.
41. Sugar, 'Dimitrije Djordjevic and Stephen Fischer-Galati', 1119.
42. Đorđević, 'The Impact of the State'.
43. Đorđević, 'An Attempt at the Impossible'; Đorđević, 'Agrarian Factors'; Đorđević, 'Balkan Revolutionary Organizations'; Đorđević, 'Agrarian Reforms in Post-World War One Balkans'.
44. Đorđević, 'The Role of the Military'.
45. Đorđević, 'Balkan versus European Enlightenment'; Đorđević, 'National Factors'; Đorđević, 'Foreign Influences'.
46. Đorđević, *Ožiljci i opomene*, 214.
47. Đorđević, 'Die Serben', 734–74.
48. Mitrović, *Istorija srpskog naroda*, 95–207. See also Djordjevic, 'Serbian Society 1903–1914', 227–39.
49. Djordjevic, 'Slobodan Jovanovic', 21–40.
50. Djordjevic, 'Stojan Novaković', 51–69.
51. Djordjevic, 'Vojvoda Putnik', 569–89.
52. Djordjevic, 'Vuk Karadžić', 37–50.
53. Boia, *Great Historians from Antiquity to 1800*, 85–88, 341–44; Boia, *Great Historians of the Modern Age.*, 783–798.
54. See editor's 'Acknowledgment' and 'Preface to the Series', in Király and Djordjevic, *East Central European Society*, ix–xii.
55. Djordjević, *The Creation of Yugoslavia 1914–1918*.
56. Király and Djordjevic, *East Central European Society*.
57. Đorđević and Samardžić, *Migrations in Balkan History*.
58. Đorđević, 'The Present State of Studies', 136.
59. For Đorđević's complete bibliography, see Bataković, 'Dimitrije V. Djordjević', 17–24.
60. Turda, 'Historical Writing in the Balkans', 349–66.
61. See Berger with Conrad, *The Past as History*, 302.
62. Marković and Milićević, 'Serbian Historiography', 157–58.
63. Tortarolo, 'Historians in the Storm', 377.
64. Ibid., 387. See also Lehmann and Sheehan, *An Interrupted Past*; Daum, Lehmann, and Sheehan, *The Second Generation*.
65. Miller, 'Scars and Memory', 467.
66. Đorđević was mentor for nineteen doctoral dissertations on various issues in the history of the Balkans and Eastern Europe. See Spence and Nelson, *Scholar, Patriot, Mentor*, 415–16.

Bibliography

Antolović, Michael. 'Writing History Under the "Dictatorship of the Proletariat": Yugoslav Historiography 1945–1991'. *Revista de História das Ideias* 39 (2021), 49–73. DOI: https://doi.org/10.14195/2183-8925_39_2.
Antolović, Michael, and Biljana Šimunović-Bešlin. 'History as Vallis Aurea: Đorđe Stanković and the Modernization of Serbian Historiography'. *Tokovi istorije* 3 (2018), 109–45.

Antonić, Zdravko. 'Vasa Čubrilović (1897–1990): Osnivač i prvi direktor Balkanološkog instituta SANU'. *Balcanica: Annuaire de l'institut des etudes balkaniques* 30–31 (2000), 139–65.

Banac, Ivo. 'Historiography of the Countries of Eastern Europe: Yugoslavia'. *American Historical Review* 97 (1992), 1084–104.

Bataković, Dušan T. 'Dimitrije V. Djordjević (1922–2009): Leading Serbian and Serbian-American Expert on Balkan History'. *Balcanica* 40 (2009), 9–24.

Berger, Stefan. *The Past as History: National Identity and Historical Consciousness in Modern Europe.* Basingstoke: Palgrave MacMillan, 2015.

Boia, Lucian (ed.). *Great Historians from Antiquity to 1800: An International Dictionary.* New York: Greenwood Press, 1989.

———. *Great Historians of the Modern Age: An International Dictionary.* New York: Greenwood Press, 1991.

Bourdieu, Pierre. 'The Forms of Capital', in J. Richardson (ed.), *Handbook of Theory and Research for the Sociology of Education* (Westport, CT: Greenwood, 1986), 241–58.

Brunnbauer, Ulf. 'Historical Writing in the Balkans', in Axel Schneider and Daniel Woolf (eds), *The Oxford History of Historical Writing*, vol. 5 (Oxford: Oxford University Press, 2011), 353–74.

Calic, Marie-Janine. *Geschichte Jugoslawiens im 20. Jahrhundert.* Munich: C.H. Beck, 2010.

Daum, Andreas W., Hartmut Lehmann and James J. Sheehan (eds). *The Second Generation: Émigrés from Nazi Germany as Historians.* Oxford: Berghahn Books, 2016.

De Baets, Antoon. 'Exile and Acculturation: Refugee Historians since the Second World War'. *The International History Review* 28 (2006), 316–49.

Djordjevic, Dimitrije. 'Slobodan Jovanovic', *Journal of Contemporary History* 8 (1973), 21–40.

———. 'Vojvoda Putnik, The Serbian High Command and Strategy in 1914', in Béla K Király and Nandor F Dreisziger (eds), *East Central European Society in the First World War* (Boulder: East European Monographs, 1985), 569–89.

———. 'Serbian Society 1903–1914', in Béla K. Király and Dimitrije Djordjevic (eds), *East Central European Society and the Balkan Wars* (Boulder, CO: Social Sciences Monographs; Highland Lakes, NJ: Atlantic Research and Publications, 1987), 227–39.

———. 'Stojan Novaković: Historian, Politician, Diplomat', in Dennis Deletant and Harry Hanak (eds), *Historians as Nation Builders – Central and South East Europe* (London: Macmillan, 1988), 51–69.

———. 'Vuk Karadžić: The Historian of the Serbian Uprising', in Robert Conquest and Dusan J. Djordjevic (eds), *Political and Ideological Confrontation in Twentieth-Century Europe: Essays in Honor of Milorad M. Drachkovitch* (New York: St. Martin's Press, 1996), 37–50.

———. *Scars and Memory: Four Lives in One Lifetime.* Boulder, CO and New York: Columbia University Press, 1997.

Djordjevic, Dimitrije (ed.). *The Creation of Yugoslavia 1914–1918.* Santa Barbara, CA and Oxford: ABC-Clio Press, 1980.

Djordjevic, Dimitrije, and Stephen Fischer-Galati. *The Balkan Revolutionary Tradition.* New York: Columbia University Press. 1981.

Đorđević, Dimitrije. *Izlazak Srbije na Jadransko more i Konferencija ambasadora u Londonu 1912.* Belgrade: Graf. Preduzeće "Slobodan Jović", 1956.

———. *Milovan Milovanović.* Belgrade: Prosveta, 1962.

———. *Carinski rat Austro-Ugarske i Srbije 1906–1911.* Belgrade: Istorijski institut, 1962.

———. 'The Impact of the State on Nineteenth-Century Balkan Social, Economic and Political Development', in *Mouvements sociaux et nationaux dans les pays du sud-est européen: traits communs et caractères spécifiques* (Bucharest: Office d'informations et documentations dans la sciences sociales et politiques, 1974), 70–83.

———. 'Balkan versus European Enlightenment: Parallelism and Dissonances'. *East European Quarterly* 9 (1975), 488–97.

———. 'An Attempt at the Impossible: Stages of Modernization of the Balkan Peasantry in the Nineteenth-Century'. *Balcanica* 8 (1977), 321–35.

———. 'National Factors in Nineteenth-Century Balkan Revolutions', in Belá K. Király and Gunther E. Rothenberg (eds), *War and Society in East Central Europe*, vol. 1 (New York: Columbia University Press, 1979), 197–214.

———. 'Agrarian Factors in Nineteenth-Century Balkan Revolutions', Belá K. Király and Gunther E. Rothenberg (eds), *War and Society in East Central Europe*, vol. 1 (New York: Columbia University Press, 1979), 163–82.

———. 'Die Serben', in Adam Wandruszka and Peter Urbanitsch (eds), *Die Habsburgermonarchie 1848–1918*, vol. III/1 (Vienna: Österreichische Akademie der Wissenschaften, 1980), 734–74.

———. 'The Role of the Military in the Balkans in the Nineteenth Century', in Ralph Melville and Hans-Jürgen Schröder (eds), *Der Berliner Kongress von 1878: Die Politik der Grossmächte und die Probleme der Modernisierung in Südosteuropa in der zweiten Hälfte des 19. Jahrhunderts* (Wiesbaden: Franz Steiner, 1982), 317–47.

———. 'Agrarian Reforms in Post-World War One Balkans: A Comparative Study', *Balcanica* 13–14 (1982–83), 255–69.

———. 'Balkan Revolutionary Organizations in the 1860s and the Peasantry', in Belá Király (ed.), *The Crucial Decade: East Central European Society and National Defense 1859–1870* (New York: Columbia University Press, 1984), 269–83.

———. 'The Present State of Studies of Nineteenth Century History of Balkan Peoples in the United States', in Radovan Samardžić (ed.), *Conference internationale des balkanologues. Belgrade, 7–8 septembre 1982* (Belgrade: Academie serbe des sciences et des arts, Institut des etudes balkaniques, 1984), 127–36.

———. 'Foreign Influences on Nineteenth-Century Balkan Constitutions', in K.K. Shangriladze and E.W. Townsend (eds), *Papers for the V. Congress of Southeast European Studies, Belgrade, September 1984* (Columbus, OH: Slavica Publishers, 1984), 72–102.

———. *Ožiljci i opomene*, vol. 3. Belgrade: SKZ, 2001.

Đorđević, Dimitrije, and Radovan Samardžić (eds). *Migrations in Balkan History*. Belgrade: Institute for Balkan Studies, Serbian Academy of Sciences and Arts, 1989.

Erdmann, Karl Dietrich. *Die Ökumene der Historiker: Geschichte der Internationalen Historikerkongresse und des Comité International des Sciences Historiques*. Göttingen: Vandenhoeck & Ruprecht, 1987.

Fellner, Fritz. 'The Special Case of Austrian Refugee Historians', in Hartmut Lehmann and James J. Sheehan (eds), *An Interrupted Past: German-Speaking Refugee Historians in The United States after 1933* (Washington, D.C.: German Historical Institute; Cambridge: CUP, 1991), 109–15.

Fischer, Bernd J. 'Dimitrije Djordjevic, 1922–2009'. *Slavic Review* 69 (2010), 1069–70.

Höpken, Wolfgang. 'Vergangenheitspolitik im sozialistischen Vielvölkerstaat: Jugoslawien 1944 bis 1991', in Petra Bock and Edgar Wolfrum (eds), *Umkämpfte Vergangenheit. Geschichtsbilder, Erinnerung und Vergangenheitspolitik im internationalen Vergleich* (Göttingen: Vandenhoeck und Ruprecht, 1999), 210–43.

Iatrides, John O. 'Basil Laourdas, 1912–1971'. *Slavic Review* 30 (1971), 474.

Király, Béla K., and Dimitrije Djordjevic (eds). *East Central European Society and the Balkan Wars*. Boulder and New York: Columbia University Press, 1987.

Koren, Snježana. *Politika povijesti u Jugoslaviji (1945–1960): Komunistička partija Jugoslavije, nastava povijesti, historiografija*. Zagreb: Srednja Europa, 2012.

Lampe, John R. *Yugoslavia as History: Twice There Was a Country*. Cambridge: Cambridge University Press, 2000.

Lehmann, Hartmut, and James J. Sheehan (eds). *An Interrupted Past: German-Speaking Refugee Historians in The United States after 1933*. Washington, D.C.: German Historical Institute; Cambridge: Cambridge University Press, 1991.

Mandelíčková, Monika, and Idesbald Goddeeris. 'Living in the Past: Historians in Exile', in Ilaria Porciani and Lutz Raphael (eds), *Setting the Standards: Institutions, Networks and Communities of National Historiography*. Basingstoke: Palgrave MacMillan, 2012, 394–411.

Marković, Predrag J., Miloš Ković, and Nataša Milićević. 'Developments in Serbian Historiography since 1989', in Ulf Brunnbauer (ed.), *(Re)Writing History – Historiography in Southeast Europe after Socialism* (Münster: Lit Verlag, 2004), 277–90.

Marković, Predrag J., and Nataša Milićević. 'Serbian Historiography in the Time of Transition: A Struggle for Legitimacy', *Istorija 20. veka* 25 (2007), 145–67.

Mikoletzky, Hans Leo. *XIIe Congrès International des Sciences Historiques, Vienne, 29 août – 5 septembre 1965: Actes. 5*. Vienne: Verlag Berger und Söhne, 1967.

Miller, Nicholas J. 'Scars and Memory: Four Lives in One Lifetime. East European Monographs, CDLXXI. Boulder, CO: Distributed by Columbia University Press, 1997', *Canadian Slavonic Papers* 40 (1998), 467–69.

Milićević, Nataša. *Jugoslovenska vlast i srpsko građanstvo 1944–1950*. Belgrade: INIS, 2009.

Mitrović, Andrej (ed.). *Istorija srpskog naroda*, vol. VI/1: Od Berlinskog kongresa do ujedinjenja 1878–1918 (Belgrade: Srpska književna zadruga, 1983), 95–207.

Nikolić, Kosta. *Prošlost bez istorije: Polemike u jugoslovenskoj istoriografiji 1961–1991*. Belgrade: ISI, 2003.

Pavlowitch, Stévan K. 'Izlazak Srbije na Jadransko more i Konferencija ambasadora u Londonu 1912. by Dimitrije Djordjević'. *The Slavonic and East European Review* 36 (1958), 580–81.

Rath, John R. (ed.). *Nationality Problem in the Habsburg Monarchy in the Nineteenth Century: A Critical Appraisal*. Houston, TX: Rice University, 1967.

Samardžić, Radovan. *Pisci srpske istorije*, vol. 4. Belgrade: Prosveta, 1994.

Schroeder, Paul W. 'The Status of Habsburg Studies in the United States'. *Austrian History Yearbook* 3 (1967), 267–95.

Šimetin Šegvić, Filip, and Tomislav Branđolica. 'The Mediterranean, Dubrovnik, Braudel', in Drago Roksandić, Filip Šimetin Šegvić and Nikolina Šimetin Šegvić (eds), *Annales in Perspective: Designs and Accomplishments* (Zagreb: CKHIS, FF Press, 2019), 367–81.

Spence, Richard B., and Linda L. Nelson (eds). *Scholar, Patriot, Mentor: Historical Essays in Honor of Dimitrije Djordjević*. Boulder, CO and New York: Columbia University Press, 1992.

Stanković, Đorđe, and Ljubodrag Dimić. *Istoriografija pod nadzorom: Prilozi istoriji istoriografije*, vol. 1–2. Belgrade: Službeni list, 1996.

Stavrianos, Leften Stavros. *The Balkan since 1453*. New York: Rinhart & Company, 1958.

Stearns, Peter N. 'Social History', in Peter N. Stearns (ed.), *Encyclopedia of Social History* (New York and London: Garland Publishing, 1994), 890–96.

Sugar, Peter F. 'Dimitrije Djordjevic and Stephen Fischer-Galati, *The Balkan Revolutionary Tradition*, New York: Columbia University Press. 1981'. *American Historical Review* 86 (1981), 1119.

Tortarolo, Edoardo. 'Historians in the Storm: Émigré Historiography in the Twentieth Century', in Matthias Middell and Lluis Roura (eds), *Transnational Challenges to National History Writing* (New York: Palgrave Macmillan, 2013), 377–403.

Turda, Marius. 'Historical Writing in the Balkans', in Stuart Macintyre, Juan Maiguashca and Attila Pók (eds), *The Oxford History of Historical Writing*, vol 4 (Oxford: Oxford University Press, 2011), 349–66.

Tzortzevits, Dimitrios. *Historia tēs Servias, 1800–1918*. Thessaloniki: Hetaireia Makedonikōn Spoudōn, 1970.

Vucinich, Wayne S. 'Dimitrije Đorđević, Carinski rat Austro-Ugarske i Srbije 1906–1911, Belgrade: Istorijski institut, 1962'. *Slavic Review* 23 (1964), 354–55.

CHAPTER 12

António Sérgio and José Ortega y Gasset

History, Theory and Experiences of Exile

Sérgio Campos Matos

In the twentieth century, the reflection on the historical experiences of the Iberian nations reached a high level, with essays by two important essayists and philosophers, marked by experiences of exile: the Portuguese António Sérgio (1883–1969) and the Spaniard José Ortega y Gasset (1883–1955).

Neither Sérgio nor Ortega was a historian, but they both produced relevant theoretical reflections on history and its social function, alongside critical interpretations of the past of their two nations – perhaps the most striking in the Iberian Peninsula in the twentieth century – that accentuated the contrast between the Peninsula and the rest of Europe. They both developed essays of a philosophical, scientific, social and political, economic, literary and pedagogical kind. They both experienced a cosmopolitan life, in European and South American cultural milieu. They were men of action (Ortega only until 1932), and they both had to go into exile. The central question is: what is there in common, or at odds, in the conceptions of history and the experiences of exile of these two intellectuals? How did their experiences of exile affect their production in the field of history?

I'll use a comparative method that aims to emphasise the affinities as well as significant divergences between the thought and the metaphors[1] related to exile and used by these two perfectly contemporaneous essayists, taking into account their different perceptions of life. My starting point is that the

Notes for this section begin on page 219.

conceptions of history of the two essayists as well as their philosophical positions are fundamental to understanding their diverse experiences of exile, as well as their contrasting profiles as public intellectuals.

Intellectual Trajectories and Experiences of Life: Convergences and Divergences

Sérgio and Ortega were both born in 1883, Sérgio in Damão (Portuguese India), into an aristocratic milieu; Ortega in Madrid, into an upper bourgeois milieu. They confronted largely the same problems, in similar historical contexts: they lived through a time of crisis in the Liberal system, the rise of totalitarianisms and a war-torn Europe – the time of the First World War, the Spanish Civil War and the Second World War.

They had, in part, a similar intellectual education – in rationalism and neo-Kantianism – and had studied some of the same philosophers, such as Plato, Descartes, Leibniz, Kant, Hegel, Nietzsche, and neo-Kantians from the Marburg School (Hermann Cohen and Paul Natorp) – in short, the rationalist Western tradition, although Ortega had become a critic of Kantian rationalism at an early stage.

They resisted the over-valorisation of the state above the individual, in a critical attitude that opposed not only totalitarianism but also narrow and backward-looking forms of nationalism and patriotism, consistent with cosmopolitan and European attitudes that placed the national within a transnational context.

Both regarded their nations as problematic – historically, socially, in terms of their elites, but also in mentalities: Ortega followed in the footsteps of the so-called Generation of 1898 (e.g. Pio Baroja, Miguel de Unamuno, Ángel Ganivet, Valle-Inclán), and Sérgio in those of the Portuguese Generation of 1870 (Antero de Quental, Oliveira Martins, Eça de Queiroz). For both essayists, the difficulties of their respective nations were in large part an educational and pedagogical problem – hence both saw education as an instrument for citizenship.[2] They both developed critical interpretations of the history of the two Peninsular nations – marked by Europeanism, theories of decadence and delay, emphasising the contrast between Iberia and Western Europe.

They both emphasised the importance of the social and cultural function of the elites as a condition for progress – a topic very much emphasised by sociologists such as V. Pareto and G. Mosca. Both nursed the hope of becoming intellectual mentors of the national elites. As engaged intellectuals, they were intent on intervening into public affairs.[3] They even held public office sporadically – Sérgio as Minister for Instruction (1923), and Ortega as a parliamentary deputy (1932). Both examined the role of the intellectual in modern society while holding different views on this topic. Already in 1924, during the dictatorship of Primo de Rivera, Ortega sustained that

> The intelligentsia should not aspire to command, nor even to influence and save men . . . It is not by becoming the first rank of society in the manner of the politician, the warrior, the priest, that it will best fulfil its destiny, but the other way around, by rectifying itself, darkening itself, retiring to more modest social lines.[4]

Sérgio, on the contrary, always made intervention in the public arena a priority in his activity, both during the democratic regime of the Portuguese First Republic (1910–26), under the Military Dictatorship (1926–33) and the Estado Novo (1933–74). For this, as with many other intellectuals and politicians, he was persecuted by the dictatorial regimes, being imprisoned five times.[5] On several occasions his publications were seized by the censors,[6] and he was forced into exile twice, to Madrid and Paris (1927–33) and again to Madrid (1935–36).

Ortega maintained an active public and political life until 1932, when he became disillusioned with what he considered to be the Spanish Second Republic radicalism and totally withdrew from political activity. He went into exile successively in Paris (1936–39), Buenos Aires (1939–42) and Lisbon (1942–45),[7] mainly to avoid the violence of the Spanish Civil War. His silence on that conflict was interpreted very negatively in Republican circles.

In contrast to the Spanish philosopher, Sérgio was always a man of action, and during his exile in Paris that impulse was strengthened. He conspired on successive occasions against the Portuguese Military Dictatorship, and against the Salazar regime (1932–68).

While António Sérgio was self-taught, an outsider to the academic world (though he had a scientific education at the Naval School in Lisbon), Ortega quickly entered academia –particularly the Universities of Madrid and Marburg. Unlike Sérgio, who was never accepted into the then closeted University of Lisbon, Ortega reached the top of his profession while still very young, at the University of Madrid (1910).

Conceptions of History

The two essayists have very distinct conceptions of history, seeing the relationship between past, present and future in very different ways.

Sérgio is heir to a belief in progress and the perfectibility of man, in a framework of optimism for the future, based on rejecting and overcoming "errors" of the past. This position is particularly evident in his critical diagnosis of the Portuguese cultural environment in the early decades of the twentieth century. In his view, there was an excess of the past and of tradition in the present – related to historism, an antiquarian and archivist mentality[8] that prevailed amongst historians at that time. In his perspective, in Portugal there was a heavy legacy of a historical deviation due to ideas and attitudes that he believed to be 'erroneous' – isolation from Europe, purification,[9] state dependency and parasitism – and not in harmony with a national universalistic vocation.

Sérgio cultivated an idealist view of the national trajectory. Portugal's historical mission was, in his view, cosmopolitan and universalist. For him, history is 'an instrument of humanist education . . . a way of freeing ourselves from the past . . . and from every kind of limitation'.[10] It is, then, a presentist conception: history only interests him in as much as it addresses the problems and needs of the present and illuminates our steps into the future.[11] His gaze upon the past is subordinated to the needs of the present and a rational view of a *Should Be*. Ortega, too, at least episodically, formulates this idea. As with Benedetto Croce or António Sérgio, for Ortega historical inquiry is located in the present, history is a 'systematic science of the radical reality that is my life. It is, then, the science of the most rigorous present'.[12] A presentist and pragmatic position that we also find in John Dewey.[13]

At a theoretical level, Sérgio develops a concept of social fact and data as intellectual construction; facts are constructs – as he liked to say. In this way, he develops a position very close to Lucien Febvre and Marc Bloch, the theoreticians of the *Annales*,[14] and philosophers such as Karl Popper: the idea of 'imagining hypotheses' – that is, the relevance of imagination in producing knowledge. He is also not far from the neo-Kantian Max Weber when he assumes that knowing is relating, integrating and building meanings. It should be noted that the German sociologist understood sociological explanation as 'apprehension of the significant set' and concepts as scientific constructions.[15]

If in Ortega history is also a construction[16] – an anti-Positivist idea comparable to Sérgio's – it is a fact that he accentuates the difference between reality and thought, between life and reason, which is contrary to Sérgio, for whom the perception of the real is indissociable from the human mind.

In contrast to the prospective rationalism of António Sérgio, Ortega combats abstract intellectualism and rationalism, handing the real primacy over to theory. Theory is rooted in real, concrete life. Ortega underlines the historicity of the act of thinking, of philosophising, of living, as a heritage of the past and rejects a conception of a universal man, gifted with permanent and abstract intellectual capabilities. In his critique of intellectualism, pure reason needed to be replaced by historical reason, by narrative reason.[17] Another fundamental difference from Sérgio (and Dewey) is that Ortega is basically concerned with situating facts, ideas and concepts in their historical context – their circumstances.

But the fundamental divergence between the two essayists could be summarised in the following: while the philosophical and historical position of A. Sérgio is commanded by an entrenched consciousness of a rational *Should Be* (*Dever Ser*) that leads him to cultivate an optimistic idea of the future – no matter how much the present seemed to deny that ideal – Ortega radically rejects a utopian reason that in his view is an abstract imposition on a reality that resists it.

Thus one understands the distinction that he established between beliefs and ideas. For him, the starting point was real, concrete life, men with their beliefs. For Sérgio, on the contrary, it was thought immanent to human consciousness that commanded the world. Perhaps in this way we can better understand the very diverse relationship of these two intellectuals within the public space. And even the very diverse languages they used – even metaphorically.

Metaphors

The most frequent metaphors in Ortega's works are those related to medicine and the organism. In 1922, he used in the title of an important book the qualification *invertebrate* to refer to Spain and saw in Spanish society a sickness.[18] He considered the concept of generation (imported from biology) the most important in the field of history.

António Sérgio also makes use of organic metaphors but less frequently and without making them structural: he is far from giving them a central place.[19] He upholds the theory of the nation having a conscience and a will (after the Portuguese historian Herculano) and rejects the thesis of an organic nation. Nevertheless, especially in his youthful texts, he uses terms such as *body, remedy, parasitism*.

However, the most frequent metaphors in Sérgio's works are maritime or concern light. The maritime metaphors are related to his experience in his youth as a naval officer and accentuate the idea of the freedom of thought and knowledge as an adventure on the high ocean. They are applied at times to an illuminating self-analysis. A rare but important example of this is the allusion to his difficult situation as an exile in Paris, unemployed and disheartened, in 1931, expressed in private correspondence to a friend: 'I feel the last years of lucidity escaping me, without the smallest hope of employment. My life has been all a *continuous shipwreck*, borne with an apparently cheerful resignation. There you have it.'[20] In difficult personal circumstances, the nocturnal and depressive António Sérgio is a spectator of himself, in complete contrast to the rationalist confidence in his ideas, in his elevation of spirit and a rational *Should Be*, which are located far above the circumstances he was living through.

In Ortega, by contrast, maritime metaphors are rare and when they occur often have an ontological and dramatic sense. For example: 'Man lives habitually *submerged in his life, shipwrecked in it*, dragged time after time by the *turbulent torrent* of his destiny . . .'[21]

Contrasting Experiences of Exile

Exile is always an uprooting experience. Edward Said put it well when he said that an exile is dislocated, he is eccentric, he lives in 'a discontinuous state of being'.[22] Sérgio and Ortega experienced exile in very different ways, in different historical contexts: Sérgio in 1926, at the start of the military dictatorship in Portugal, when authoritarian and totalitarian regimes proliferated in Europe; Ortega in 1936, when the polarisation of radical political positions intensified and the Second Republic was facing the military uprising led by Franco. Coincidentally, they were both in Madrid in the early months of 1936, during Sérgio's second period of exile; and again in Lisbon, when Ortega was there between 1942 and 1945, and during his later stays there. But as far we know they never met.

Their experiences of exile were both marked by great financial difficulties. And also existential difficulties. The distance from their home countries and the separation from their personal libraries imposed new and adverse conditions for intellectual work. By the end of 1929, Sérgio would confess to a friend: "My erratic life forces me to entrust everything to my head. I don't take a note; I limit myself to marking the books, but I almost never have them with me!"[23] Sérgio lived through hard times in Paris, forced to take on different activities to earn a living. He worked for the French publishing houses, for a cinematic company (Paramount), he made translations and gave private lessons on various subjects. The financial crash led him to periods of unemployment; in 1932 he even looked for work in Spain, where he gave an open course at the University of Santiago de Compostela (1933). In his correspondence, he characterises this way of life, classifying himself as proscribed and his situation as leading a wandering life in a wretched situation,[24] contrasting sharply with his confidence for the future and his optimism for a quick end to the military dictatorship in Portugal. In late 1927, he gave this account of his life in a letter to Valéry Larbaud: 'I have been here since February. I have thought of looking you up. But . . . I play here *the romantic part of the political émigré*, and even of the conspirator against the military dictatorship which has prevailed in Portugal for more than a year.'[25] In reality, Sérgio engaged in intense activity amongst the Portuguese exiles against the dictatorship, with the aim of alerting international public opinion to the situation in his country. To this end, he frequently collaborated with the progressive

Catholic press, and he was secretary of the Liga de Defesa da República, an organisation founded by political exiles that fought for democracy in Portugal (also known as the Paris League). Within this league, he was responsible for overseeing financial assistance to political émigrés. Unlike Ortega, Sérgio was a man of action, even if he did not consider himself particularly suited to political activity.[26] He tried to build a broad convergence against the Portuguese dictatorship between various sectors of intellectuals and politicians who had held prominent positions in the First Republic (1910–26). But deep political and strategic divergences as to how to overthrow the dictatorship ended up undermining the success of his action.[27]

The emigrants in Paris were kept under observation by the Portuguese political police, and Sérgio laid the blame on them when his office at the Editora Ibero-Americana was broken into.[28] The Portuguese censorship also put considerable limitations on freedom of expression, which led Sérgio to self-censor – something that was already clear by 1932, when he was included in an amnesty that year. Surveillance even included exiles' correspondence, and Sérgio complained on several occasions of interference with letters to his Portuguese friends.[29]

One might ask to what extent this political engagement, especially during his years in exile, shaped Sérgio's work and intellectual activity. In a letter to the former President, Bernardino Machado, dated to late 1932, he sums up those years of forced exile: 'My years in exile, completely lost, signify *a great hole in my life*. In sum: it is necessary to remain silent about that. So let us remain silent.'[30] In another letter to the same person, a few days later, he says: 'in six years of exile, I was only truly useful on the half-dozen days when I argued in Geneva for the defeat of the loan plan for the Dictatorship.'[31]

We can understand the frustration and annoyance he felt about those years when Salazar had just come to power, due, no doubt, more to the failure of his political activity than to the interruption to his work. However, if we look at his writings, it is clear that he published a great many things during those years, in various languages, most notably two volumes of essays (II and III, 1929 and 1932),[32] *A Sketch of the History of Portugal* (Lisbon, 1928), *História de Portugal* (Barcelona, 1929), and an *Antígone* (Porto, 1930) and *Le Portugal* (both privately published, s.l., n.d.). He published extensively in periodicals, particularly *Seara Nova* and the international press, and manifestos against the dictatorship. He also translated philosophical works such as Descartes's *Meditations* and Tolstoy's novel *The White Devil*. Within this output, the strong element of history stands out, and most particularly the role of the uprooted as agents of progress, in harmony with the deep vocation of the Portuguese nation. Sérgio had come to see himself as uprooted.

But to return to our topic: to what extent did day-to-day politics influence his work as an essayist? If we take the Introduction to his second book of essays, addressed 'to the young reader', it is clear that he has adopted a pragmatic aim hand in hand with a reflexive one: 'Making of my pen a plough, and not a chisel, I bring an objective of practical action. And this volume is a contribution . . . to the study of the reform of mentalities and the social education of the Portuguese.'[33] At this time, Sérgio saw himself as an 'agitator for ideas', surely the most prominent enabler of democratic propaganda against the dictatorship in Portugal. He became an exemplary fighter for the values of liberty and democracy. Though he had contacts with French intellectuals such as Paul Langevin, Léon Brunschvicg or Charles Gide, he did not integrate himself with Parisian cultural circles, let alone the universities, and continued to feel himself an expatriate.

The experience of political emigration marked his work, always varied in its topics, focusing more in these years on two main areas, the history of Portugal and politics. In history, he underlined his thesis that the formation of Portugal, in the Middle Ages, was an expression of maritime and European commercial movement, thus affirming its 'maritime and universalist' character.[34] The preponderance of a commercial and maritime bourgeoisie would have made Portugal a more cosmopolitan nation than its neighbour. He also emphasised the role of the navigators and the uprooted in the history of Portugal, going so far as to affirm that 'the great Portuguese tradition is exactly that of *uprooting*. The distinctive task of Portugal, namely the Discoveries, is the work of the *uprooted*; furthermore, Portugal owed its existence to the *uprooted* of other countries'.[35]

In referring to the uprooted, he was also highlighting the exiled liberal politicians of the period prior to the liberal revolution in Portugal and those who had been forced to leave on the formation of the military dictatorship. Here he would certainly have had in mind himself and his Portuguese friends Jaime Cortesão (an historian) and Raúl Proença (a political essayist), who were part of a network of Portuguese exiles in those years in Paris. Praising the role of the so-called *peregrinos* (*estrangeirados*) as a progressive Portuguese elite, obliged to leave their country on account of the lack of freedom and tolerance in Portugal in the seventeenth and eighteenth centuries, he further advanced his case for making a critical assessment of a past that, as we have seen, was in contradiction with the true vocation of the nation: a cosmopolitan, universalist vocation.

In the field of politics, the years in exile provided Sérgio with a distance that allowed him to reassess the political experiment of the First Republic, particularly to make a revaluation of the political practices centred on party divisions and on the primacy of personal differences over differences in ideas, of the way in which the parliament functioned, and proposals for reform, etc. In his third volume of essays, he develops a reflection on the failure of the democracy that the Republican regime of 1910 had aimed to install in

Portugal. How could he explain the change in political direction instituted by the military dictatorship? In his dialectical analysis of the problem, he writes:

> It seems that the periods of reaction are crises in the growth of the democracies, necessary amongst the peoples that are incapable of advancing in democracy by good processes – which are the peaceful ones of construction. It could be said, then, that in those same peoples the Spirit of Democracy generates its opposite, with the aim of overcoming it and overcoming itself.[36]

One of the fundamental reasons for that failure was the absence of an active and interventionist public opinion that could regulate the activities of politicians, meaning that a renewed political pedagogy was needed.

It is in this context that we should situate the advocacy for cooperativism to which Sérgio turned precisely in the last years of his exile. Initially inspired by Proudhon, he would add, during his years in Paris, readings and reflection on those theoreticians of cooperativism in France such as Charles Gide, Fabien France, Ernest Poisson and Fernand Corcos, making their texts available in the review *Seara Nova*, from 1932.[37] He saw in consumer and producer socialist cooperativism an anti-statist alternative both to Soviet-style state socialism and the authoritarianism of the Estado Novo. This cooperativist bent accentuates the social and economic character of Sérgio's ideal of democracy, further distinguishing him from the conservative liberalism of Ortega.

Let us look at Ortega's trajectory. Very critical of the political elite of the Restoration (the system instituted in Spain in 1875) and the dictatorship of Primo de Rivera (1923–31), he initially supported the Second Republic, serving for a time in the Agrupación al Servicio de la Republica and becoming a parliamentary deputy (though he refused to serve as a minister). But he quickly became disillusioned and distanced himself from the regime.[38] This led him to break off his contributions to the Spanish periodical press and to turn inwards, focusing on his philosophy. In July 1936, he refused to subscribe to a document in support of the threatened Republic. He felt himself under threat, and soon afterwards went into exile, in Paris. Like other liberal intellectuals, such as Marañon, Unamuno, Pérez de Ayala, Manuel García Morente, Xavier Zubiri etc., he distanced himself both from the revolutionary environment emerging from the Republic of the Popular Front and from the authoritarianism of the nationalists. Ortega's exile in Paris extended through the years of the Civil War (1936–39). The company he kept there with other exiles was not always to his taste, perhaps due to the heady atmosphere in a time of accentuated radicalisation. Ortega tried to keep an equal distance between the two sides, though without finding there a 'Third Spain'.[39] His unease in the rather incestuous atmosphere in Paris led him to brief stays in Holland (April–August 1937) and Portugal (February–

May 1939).[40] In that context, the social function of the intellectual was a topic on the agenda. Julien Benda[41] had denounced the mobilisation of intellectuals around practical interests related to the state, homeland or class at the expense of values such as justice or reason. The debate on the topic was not only European: it took place in Latin America and, in particular, in Argentina when Ortega was there.[42] In exile, the Spanish philosopher lived off loans from friends, collaboration in magazines such as the Argentinean *La Nación*, and courses that took place at the Asociación Amigos del Arte and at the Faculdad de Filosofia y Letras in Buenos Aires. Like Sérgio, the difficulties he experienced were not only economic but also psychological and moral, aggravated by the uncertainty of the future and the insecurity of living in exile.[43] But the attitudes of the two intellectuals towards these situations of adversity were quite different: if Ortega adopted a defensive behaviour retreating into retirement, on the contrary, Sérgio turned to international political combat.

If Sérgio saw himself as an agitator for ideas, an apostle, and a pedagogue, Ortega y Gasset, on the contrary, refrained from political activity, persistently refused to take sides, and took on the role of philosopher-intellectual in his ivory tower, concerned with contemplation and the search for truth. His political silence provoked perplexity and incomprehension both in Spain and Argentina, losing him many previous admirers. How did he justify himself?

In keeping with his rational vitalism, Ortega saw in life – or, more properly, the act of living – constant tension and training.[44] It is understandable that within that concept he should regard the simple fact of living as a compromise[45] – which involves a generalisation that is difficult to sustain. So much so that, in 1944, he identified as a function of the intellectual the need 'to correct public opinion and to bring men from the error that they are in to the truth that they need';[46] that is, he recognised in the *clerc* a former of public opinion. On the other hand, he downplayed political activity, regarding it as superficial in an age of extremisms.[47] However, he did submit those extremisms to a profound analysis, identifying their one-sidedness and simplified ways of thinking for the pragmatic purposes of mobilising the masses: 'Extremism is the way of life that aims to live only at one extreme of the field of living, at one essentially peripheral question or dimension or theme. One corner is frenetically affirmed and the rest is denied.'[48]

Evidently one could conclude that in this context of the hegemony of totalitarianism and dogmatism, the role of the intellectual, which Ortega had so clearly identified, would be more necessary than ever. But on the contrary, basing himself on Comte, Ortega considered the intrusion of intellectuals into the leadership roles degrading and advised them to withdraw and to 'focus themselves on their solitude, [a] "radical solitude . . . without anything, even yourself", the most perfect way of being an intellectual'.[49] Ortega thus justified living in his interior world beyond the world.[50] He characterised political life as 'inauthentic' and superficial, seeing in politics a secondary dimension in life and in history.[51]

We know that Ortega did not integrate himself into the places where he was in exile, living in a certain isolation – he remained a foreigner, uprooted, in a life apart. But he continued to work on the philosophical themes he had addressed before – in other fields, the same was the case with medieval historians Sánchez-Albornoz (also in Buenos Aires), Américo Castro (in the United States), and the prehistorian Bosch Gimpera (in Mexico).[52]

Ortega's stay in America was shorter than that of those scholars, but that did not stop him from pursuing themes related to his circumstances, such as the role of the intellectual and his relationship with those in power and with civil society, as if to justify his status as expatriate, on the margins of his community of origin. That did not stop him from sometimes delivering lectures and university courses, but of course he abstained from any direct political intervention, either in Buenos Aires or later in Lisbon. He saw in Argentina occasionally that 'margin of tranquillity'.[53] But, in fact, it wasn't.

He had had great success during earlier stays in that country (in 1916 and 1928), but later during his time as an expatriate he was disheartened and even depressed, facing the hostility of other exiles, financial hardships,[54] and problems with his editor, Espasa-Calpe, despite publishing several texts with them, such as 'Ensimismamiento y alteración' (1939), 'Ideas y creencias' (1940) and 'La razón histórica' (1944). In completing the first of these, which corresponded to the first lecture in the course held at the Asociación Amigos del Arte, he insisted on his negative view of politics:

> The level at which that discourse moves . . . is almost completely invaded by impassable passions spread over the planet by a huge conspiracy. We, on the other hand, *are going to distance ourselves from all that popular chatter, to stay away from the public square, the club, the committee, the drawing room*, descending vertically to a stratum where the myths don't reach and evidence begins.[55]

In reality, Ortega had come to disparage politics. In 1951, in a lecture in England, he would reduce it to a 'struggle to take hold of public power' and 'a sickness'.[56] If he defined life as a *faciendum*, it is also clear that, like Nietzsche, he saw in solitude and a withdrawal from public life the only environment favourable to discovering the truth. Solitude would be 'the most perfect way of being an intellectual'.[57]

In contrast with the forward-looking rationalism of Sérgio, Ortega has his eye on the present of modern man, which accentuates his sense of insecurity, unfittedness, loss and emptiness: 'The man of today starts to be disorientated in relation to himself, *expatriated*, he is outside his own country, thrown into a new circumstance that is *like an unknown land*.'[58] Man is a foreigner, an *expatriate*⁵⁹– a view that coincides exactly with his own situation in exile – which, in his opinion, only accentuates the need for history as a fundamental science. In his view, the *common man* who dominated his time was ignorant of history, which contributed to the disorientation that marked the present. In discussing this situation, he underlines the fact that the human condition is subject to permanent change: '[man] is constitutionally, radically, mobility and change'⁶⁰ – a change that could nevertheless include reversals. Ortega sees man as a problematic and adventurous being, a 'being in essence a drama', in risk of dehumanisation.⁶¹

In the last months of his exile in Argentina in 1941 and early 1942, Ortega's financial difficulties deepened dramatically due to problems with his publisher, Calpe. He even confessed, in a letter to his friend, Victoria Ocampo: 'I am going through the hardest period of my life.'⁶² He might well have said that in Buenos Aires he lived 'a sort of exile within exile'.⁶³ The Lisbon experience (1942–45) was more peaceful. He gave a short course in the Lisbon Faculty of Arts on historical reason (continuing his reflections on this topic). There he was connected with a restricted group of background intellectuals⁶⁴ but not with António Sérgio, whose work he certainly knew, though he never quoted it.

Exile, Human Condition and History

It would be difficult to find more contrasting conceptions of the human condition and of the place of intellectuals in public space than those of these two essayists and philosophers.⁶⁵ Sérgio and Ortega lived two deeply diverse experiences of exile that do not coincide in time: the Portuguese essayist between 1926 and 1933, and later in 1936; Ortega between 1936 and 1945. Firstly, it should be noted that these experiences followed the establishment of a dictatorial regime (in the case of Portugal): Sérgio was compelled to expatriate; Ortega went into a voluntary exile: with the approaching Civil War he felt threatened by republican radicalism. Sérgio gave primacy to conspiratorial action against the military dictatorship and the Portuguese New State. For his part, Ortega withdrew, adopted a radical political silence and distanced himself from the public space, focused as he was on his work. He distanced himself from opposition to Franco and was far from taking a stand against the Spanish dictatorship, even if he was at times a victim of the censorship adopted by the regime.

These different experiences of exile correspond to two very different concepts of the intellectual: the ideal of the romantic engagé intellectual (Sérgio), and the ideal of the contemplative intellectual (Ortega), who lives far from the crowd. From the 1920s to the 1940s, other intellectuals adopted comparable positions: Romain Rolland, Sartre, Paul Valéry.

However, both Sérgio and Ortega were elitist intellectuals disputing the cultural hegemony between the elites of their respective nations. Sérgio was an heir to the classical, humanist, rationalist and neo-Enlightenment tradition. His optimism for a future of progress was commanded by the categories of Good, Justice and rational *Should Be*. Of course, he did not apply this optimism to a past and present experience marked by adversity that he lived through in exile.

Ortega declared once that 'life "is neither material nor soul", but rather has a determinedly spatial and temporal perspective, contrary to all utopianism and uchronism', and that his output was 'a constant battle against utopianism',[66] that he relates to the ideology of reason and to revolution. His harsh experience of exile accentuated a dramatic dimension of life, the *expatriation* – man as foreigner in this world, expatriated.

Starting out from positions that had much in common in 1910 – neo-Kantism and anti-Positivism – the two essayists quickly diverged from several points of view.

At the level of conceptions of history, if Sérgio sketches a rationalist idea of progress through the exercise of reason and the fulfilment of a *Should Be* inscribed in the human conscience, it is also a fact that for him the future is not predictable: in the field of the human sciences there is an indeterminacy. By contrast, Ortega was a critic of Kantian rationalism and the belief in progress inherited from enlightenment philosophy. We do not find in his work the idea of a redemptive future but rather a dramatic view of the erosion of intellectualist belief in progress and a vision of man in fall. For him, there is an indeterminacy about the future, but, up to a point, men can sound out the tendencies that will make their future.

Sérgio's propensity for action is related to his platonic ideal of Good and Justice with a concept of civic nation and above all with a stoic and voluntarist attitude, through which *clercs* should have a social responsibility to intervene in the polis and to improve it. Ortega was, at times in tune with this position until 1932. From then on, disappointed with what he considered the radicalism of the Spanish Republic, he changed his orientation and withdrew from the public space.

At a political level during his years of exile, Sérgio deepened his theorisation of a renewed social democracy based on the elites but with broad participation of autonomous, interventionist and critical citizens. Liberal and Conservative Ortega agrees with an elitist vision of democracy, and from the 1920s comes to see it as the lesser evil. There is, however, a point of convergence between the two, namely an understanding of dictatorships as an inevitable result, or even a 'punishment', resulting from the failings of the previous political systems.[67]

Coherent with his universalist approach to human kind, Sérgio was perhaps the harshest and most systematic critic of ethnic determinism and the concept of race in Portugal, while Ortega frequently makes use of this concept, using it not only in a cultural but also a biological sense and applying it frequently to the Spanish people.

Sérgio actively praises the condition of *déracinement* (uprooted people), including amongst them exiles, peregrine people who had to emigrate in conditions of intolerance and a lack of freedom. Sérgio's experience of exile marked his historical vision of Portugal as a nation of uprooted people: the Portuguese who embarked on the maritime discoveries and a cosmopolitan experience, in contrast to a tendency towards isolation, rootlessness and an overemphasis on the role of the state.

His own experience of being uprooted deepened during his years in exile and also led him to concentrate on a reflexive analysis of the historical-political experience of the recent past: the First Portuguese Republic (1910–26). On the other hand, it was in France that he was able to deepen his knowledge of French cooperativism and the theorisation of democracy with the intention of accelerating the overcoming of the dictatorship. It was during exile that he published in Spain and England his *History of Portugal* (1929) and, already in Portugal, the first volume of a larger work with the same title – which would not go beyond the first volume (the *Geographical Introduction*, 1941), because it was banned by censorship.

From his side, Ortega accentuates the dramatic dimension of life, the *expatriation* in ontological terms – man as foreigner in this world, expatriated, exile in the world – a topic very close to Heidegger's *dasein*. His work expresses well the tragedy of a human condition that lived through two devastating wars and the Holocaust. In contrast to Sergio, the South American European and then European experience of exile led him to distance himself from political reflection and to concentrate on philosophical thought. For him, contemplation was superior to action; philosophy was superior to politics. On the contrary, Sérgio, who believed in an ethical conception of politics as a transformative action towards the Good, saw civic intervention as a fundamental imperative of the intellectual's conscience on behalf of the community. The attitudes of the two essayists, so different on this point, are inscribed in the dichotomy that is present in the Western philosophical tradition and that can already be found in Plato: the conflictual tension between philosophy and the polis.[68]

However, Ortega will not fail to learn from historical experience and from the work of historians (such as Toynbee, of whom he was very critical). If the bulk of his books reflecting on the Spanish historical experience

(*España Invertebrada*, 1921) and theory of history (*History as a system*, 1935) predate his years of exile, in his philosophical works during the Argentine and Portuguese exiles, the problem of historical reason and the place of the intellectual in society occupied a prominent place, justifying his disengagement from political life. On the other hand, concerning his vision of Spain one notes the emphasis on a ontological reflection on regional characters and on the national character – see the way he idealises the soul of the Andalusian – a vegetative and paradisiacal ideal of life, marked by laziness and non-doing – in contrast to the northern peninsular populations.[69] This is an essentialist vision of the exceptionality of a people, which is evident even in the use of concepts such as *race* and *soul* of the Andalusians. António Sérgio was alien to these identitarian generalisations although, as we have seen, he valued the cosmopolitan and universalist vocation of the Portuguese.

Sérgio's positive view of uprooting is based on a reading of history guided by an optimistic, neo-enlightenment conception of man, with his obsessive search for unity and a unifying life, whether by a rational pathway or by a mystical one, with his faith in the intelligibility of the world and of human problems. His complaints about the hardships experienced by the uprooted in exile only appear in his private correspondence – where he represents life metaphorically as a *continuous shipwreck* or a *great hole*, or even as a life 'in exile' in the interior of his own country.[70] On the contrary, for Ortega life was as a whole and from the beginning an irremediable shipwreck, even though a fall could be 'the great stimulus to man'. We could say that it was the nocturnal António Sérgio (who in the toughest conditions of his Parisian exile saw life as a continuous shipwreck) who came closest to Ortega's modernist metaphysics. And both Sérgio and Ortega experienced exile within exile, maintaining difficult relationships with other exiles.

Notes

1. Here I return to and broadly elaborate on a previous study, Matos, 'Dos teorias y lenguages de la historia'.
2. Bonilla, 'Los intelectuales y la crisis del Estado liberal en España', 374.
3. Amoedo, 'A intervenção cívica'.
4. Ortega y Gasset, 'Cosmopolitismo', 112.
5. Baptista, *António Sérgio de Sousa*.
6. For instance Sérgio, *Os diálogos*, 1–84 and Sérgio, *Introdução geográfico-sociológica*.
7. Ortega still lived intermittently between Madrid and Lisbon for years.
8. See Cunha, 'História e método', 56–57.
9. In the sense of inquisitorial blood-cleansing policies.
10. Sérgio, *Breve interpretação*, 146.
11. Sérgio, *Introdução geográfico-sociológica*, 18.
12. Ortega, *Historia como sistema*, 52.
13. Dewey, *Democracy and Education*, 221–22. See Graham, *Theory of History*, 140–42.

14. For instance, his use of the concept of civilization as a structure. Sérgio, *Introdução geográfico-sociológica*, 13.
15. Weber, *Économie et société*, 49–50.
16. 'History is not only to see, but to think the seen . . . it is always a construction', see Ortega y Gasset, 'Guillermo Dilthey', 182.
17. Ortega y Gasset, 'Ensimismamiento y alteración', 309 and Ortega y Gasset, 'La razón histórica', 237.
18. Ortega y Gasset, 'Ideas y creencias', 393, and Ortega y Gasset, *España Invertebrada*, 111.
19. Sérgio, *Breve interpretação*. Instead of *70 Generation*, Sérgio prefered to use terms such as *phalange* or *the unadapted*.
20. Sérgio, 'Letter to Carvalho, 29-06-1931', 996.
21. Ortega y Gasset, 'A razão histórica', 123.. [my emphasis].
22. Said, *Reflexões*, 50.
23. Sérgio, 'Letter to Carvalho, 21-11-1929', 961.
24. Sérgio, 'Letter to Carvalho, 29-11-1927', 958; Sérgio, 'Letter to Carvalho, 21-11-1929', 961; and Sérgio, 'Letter to Carvalho, 04-07-1932', 1003–4.
25. Rivas, 'António Sérgio en France', 75. [my emphasis].
26. Baptista, *Dois democratas*, 10.
27. On Sergio's political action and emigrant disagreements, see Clímaco, *Republicanos, anarquistas*, 126–66.
28. Baptista, *Dois democratas*, 154.
29. For instance, the letter to Bernardino Machado: Sérgio, 'Letter to Machado, 23-11-1932', 117.
30. Sérgio, 'Letter to Machado, 27-12-1932', 132 [my emphasis].
31. Sérgio, 'Letter to Machado, 2-01-1933', 136.
32. However, all the essays included in Sérgio, *Ensaios*, vol. II, 1st ed. 1929, were written before his exile.
33. Sérgio, 'Prefácio da primeira edição', vol. II, 19.
34. Sérgio, 'Um livrinho', 140.
35. Sérgio, 'Notas de política', annotation A, 235. My emphasis.
36. Sérgio, 'Prefácio da primeira edição', vol. III, 16 [my emphasis].
37. In a series entitled 'Em torno da democracia económica', begining in *Seara Nova* 288 (03.03.1932), 379.
38. Gracia, *José Ortega y Gasset*, 453–61.
39. The term 'Third Spain' was coined by Alcalá-Zamora in 1937 to designate a third position, the liberal one, which did not follow either the Spain of the Republic or the nationalist Spain that supported Franco. Giustiniani, 'El exilio de 1936'. But following his correspondence with his Luzuriaga, Ortega didn't believe in the possibility of this Third Spain. See Campomar, *Ortega y Gasset*, 82.
40. Giustiniani, 'El exilio de 1936'.
41. Benda, *La trahison*.
42. Campomar, *Ortega y Gasset*, 333–37 and 354–55.
43. Campomar, *Ortega y Gasset*, 165, 218, 223, 231.
44. Ortega y Gasset, *A rebelião*, 79.
45. Ortega y Gasset, 'Una interpretación', 216.
46. Ortega y Gasset, 'A razão histórica', 81.
47. Ortega y Gasset, 'La razón histórica', 203. We should be reminded that Ortega devalued the place of politics in history already in 1923, see Ortega y Gasset, *Obras Completas*, vol. III, 155.
48. Ortega y Gasset, 'En torno a Galileo', 112.
49. Ortega y Gasset, 'A razão histórica', 56, 59 and 79.
50. Ortega y Gasset, 'Ensimismamiento y alteración', 300–1.

51. Ortega y Gasset, 'La razón histórica', 204–5 and 217.
52. Sánchez-Albornoz, *Exilio e historia*, 3.
53. Ortega, 'Ensimismamiento y alteración', 313.
54. In Paris, Ortega lived off the payments of his publisher and the periodical *La Nación*, including a loan from the Asociación Amigos del Arte, from Buenos Aires. Campomar, *Ortega y Gasset*.
55. Ortega y Gasset, 'Ensimismamiento y alteración', 315 [my emphasis].
56. Ortega y Gasset, *A Rebelião*, 257.
57. Ortega y Gasset, 'A razão histórica', 56 and 79.
58. Ortega y Gasset, 'En torno a Galileo', 93 and Ortega y Gasset, *Obras Completas*, vol. I, 93. [my emphasis]. See also Ortega y Gasset, 'A razão histórica', 136.
59. Ortega y Gasset, 'La razón histórica', 218. [my emphasis].
60. Ortega y Gasset, 'La razón histórica', 237.
61. Ortega y Gasset, 'Ensimismamiento y alteración', 305.
62. Campomar, *Ortega y Gasset*, 394.
63. Medina, 'Ortega y Gasset, desterrado'.
64. Herrero, *O pensamento sócio-político*, 53–54 and Medina, *Ortega y Gasset no exílio português*, 22–24.
65. Furthermore, the criticisms that Sérgio made of Ortega are highly significant. See *Seara Nova* 430 (14.03.1935), 347–48, also in A. Campos Matos, *Diálogo*, 127–28. As far as we know, there is not any direct allusion in Ortega's works to A. Sérgio, nor in his library are there books of the Portuguese essayist. In contrast, in Sérgio's library, there are six Ortega titles profusely annotated with many critical allusions.
66. Ortega y Gasset, 'Prólogo para alemanes', 44.
67. In 1930, in a letter to Joaquim de Carvalho, Sérgio confesses: 'The dictatorship in Spain was perhaps the only pathway for the Republic; in Portugal, the only road to democratic regeneration. God works in mysterious ways, and so I accept that my hardships in exile are very well employed.' Sérgio, 'Letter dated 02-03-1930', 971. And in 1934, Ortega declared: 'When I announced ten years ago that there would be dictatorial situations in every part, that these were an irremediable sickness of the age and a worthy punishment for its vices, my readers felt very sorry for the state of my brains.' See in Ortega y Gasset, *España Invertebrada*, 21.
68. See Arendt, 'Qu'est-ce que l'autorité?', 145–58.
69. Ortega y Gasset, *Teoria de Andalucía*. http://www.juntadeandalucia.es/averroes/centros-tic/29009892/moodle2/pluginfile.php/2669/mod_resource/content/1/Teor_adeAndaluc_a_OrtegayGasset.pdf accessed the 21 March 2022
70. 'Resposta a um apelo', *República*, 3 November 1953.

Bibliography

Amoedo, Margarida. 'A intervenção cívica como cumprimento generoso de um dever em Ortega y Gasset e António Sérgio', n.d.
Arendt, Hannah. 'Qu'est-ce que l'autorité?', in *La crise de la culture* (Paris: Gallimard, 1972), 121–85.
Baptista, Jacinto. *Disse chamar-se António Sérgio de Sousa*. Lisboa: Ed. Caminho, 1992.
———. *Dois democratas contra a ditadura: António Sérgio/Bernardino Machado: Cartas (1928–1935)*. n.d.
Benda, Julien. *La trahison des clercs*. Paris: Grasset, 1975 [1927].
Bonilla, Javier Zamora. 'Los intelectuales y la crisis del Estado liberal en España: A propósito de la actuación pública de José Ortega y Gasset', in Manuel Baiôa (ed.), *Elites e poder: A crise do sistema liberal em Portugal e Espanha (1918–1931)* (Lisbon: Colibri, 2004), 353–80.

Campomar, Marta. *Ortega y Gasset: luces y sombras del exilio argentino*. Madrid: Biblioteca Nueva, 2016.
Campos Matos, A. *Diálogo com António Sérgio*. Lisbon: Colibri, 2019.
Clímaco, Cristina. *Republicanos, anarquistas e comunistas no exílio (1927–1936)*. Lisbon: Colibri, 2017.
Cunha, Norberto F. 'História e método em António Sérgio', in Actas do Colóquio realizado pelo Centro Regional do Porto da Universidade Católica Portuguesa (eds), *António Sérgio: pensamento e acção*, vol. I (Lisboa: INCM, 2004), 55–85.
Dewey, John. *Democracy and Education*. Carbondale: Southern Illinois University Press, 1980 [1916].
'Em torno da democracia económica'. *Seara Nova* 288, 3 March 1932, 379.
Giustiniani, Eve. 'El exilio de 1936 y la Tercera España: Ortega y Gasset y los "blancos" de París, entre franquismo y liberalismo'. *Circunstancia* 19 (2009). Retrieved 25 June 2019 from http://www.ortegaygasset.edu/publicaciones/circunstancia/ano-vii—n-19—mayo-2009/articulos/el-exilio-de-1936-y-la-tercera-espana–ortega-y-gasset-y-los-blancos-de-paris–entrefranquismo-y-liberalismo.
Gracia, Jordi. *José Ortega y Gasset*. Madrid: Taurus, 2014.
Graham, John T. *Theory of History in Ortega y Gasset*. Columbia and London: University of Missouri Press, 1997.
Herrero, Jesús. *O pensamento sócio-político de Ortega y Gasset*. Lisbon: Ed. Brotéria, 1980.
Matos, Sérgio Campos. 'Dos teorias y lenguages de la historia en perspectiva comparada: António Sérgio y Ortega y Gasset', in Javier Fernández Sebastián and Faustino Oncina Coves (eds), *Metafóricas espácio-temporales para la Historia: Enfoques teóricos e historiográficos* (Valencia: Pre-textos, 2021), 159–81.
Medina, João. *Ortega y Gasset no exílio português*. Lisbon: Centro de História, 2004.
Medina, José Lasaga. 'Ortega y Gasset, desterrado'. *Revista de Libros*. Retrieved 29 July 2019 from https://www.revistadelibros.com/articulos/ortega-y-gasset-luces-y-sombras-del-exilio-argentino.
Ortega y Gasset, José.'Artículos (1902-1913)" , in *Obras completas*, vol. I. (Madrid: Alianza Ed./ Revista de Occidente, 1983), 11-263.
———. 'El tema de nuestro tiempo", in *Obras completas*, vol. I. (Madrid: Alianza Ed./ Revista de Occidente, 1983 [1923]), 143-203.
———. 'En torno a Galileo', in *Obras completas*, vol. V. (Madrid: Alianza Ed./ Revista de Occidente, 1983 [1933]), 12–165.
———. 'Guillermo Dilthey y la idea de la vida', in *Obras Completas*, vol. VI. (Madrid: Alianza Ed./Revista de Occidente, 1983 [1933–34]), 165–214.
———. *Historia como sistema y otros ensayos de filosofía* (Madrid: Alianza Editorial, 1987 [1935])
———. 'Ensimismamiento y alteración', in *Obras Completas*, vol. V. (Madrid: Alianza Ed./ Revista de Occidente, 1983 [1939]), 293–315.
———. 'Ideas y creencias', in *Obras Completas*, vol. V. (Madrid: Alianza Ed./ Revista de Occidente, 1983 [1940]), 379–409.
———. *Teoria de Andalucía*. Madrid: Revista de Occidente, 1942. http://www.juntadeandalucia.es/averroes/centros-tic/29009892/moodle2/pluginfile.php/2669/mod_resource/content/1/Teor_adeAndaluc_a_OrtegayGasset.pdf
———. 'La razón histórica', in *Obras Completas*, vol. XII. (Madrid: Alianza Ed./ Revista de Occidente, 1983 [Buenos Aires, 1940]), 145-237
———. 'Una interpretación de la história universal', in *Obras Completas*, vol. IX. (Madrid: Alianza Ed./ Revista de Occidente, 1983), 33–218.
———. 'Prólogo para alemanes', in *Obras Completas*, vol. VIII. (Madrid: Alianza Ed./ Revista de Occidente, 1983), 11–59.
———. 'Cosmopolitismo', in *Historia como sistema y otros ensayos de filosofía* (Madrid: Alianza Editorial, 1987 [1924]), 105–13.

———. *A rebelião das massas*. Lisboa: Circulo de Leitores, 1989 [1929].
———. *España Invertebrada*. Madrid: Alianza Editorial, 1994 [1921].
———. 'A razão histórica', in Margarida Isaura Almeida Amoedo (ed.), *Ortega y Gasset em Lisboa: tradução e enquadramento de La razón histórica* [Curso de 1944] (Coimbra: IUC, 2017), 47–144.
'Resposta a um apelo e a uma pergunta de sua excelência o Ministro do Interior'. *República*, 3 November 1953.
Rivas, Pierre. 'António Sérgio en France'. *Arquivos do Centro Cultural Português* 20 (1984), 65–80.
Said, Edward. *Reflexões sobre o exílio*. São Paulo: Ed. Schwarcz, 2003.
Sánchez-Albornoz, Nicolás. *Exilio e historia*. Alicante: Biblioteca Virtual Miguel de Cervantes, 2017. Retrieved 17 July 2019 from http://www.cervantesvirtual.com/descargaPdf/exilio-e-historia-847204/.
Seara Nova 430, 14 March 1935, 347–48.
Sérgio, António. *Introdução geográfico-sociológica à História de Portugal*. Lisbon: s.n., n.d.
———. *A Sketch of the History of Portugal*. Lisbon: Seara Nova, 1928.
———. 'Em tôrno de um livrinho'. *Seara Nova* 201, 20.02.1930, 140–42.
———. 'Letter to Bernardino Machado, 23-11-1932', in Jacinto Baptista, *Dois democratas contra a ditadura: António Sérgio/Bernardino Machado: Cartas (1928–1935)*. n.d., 117.
———. 'Letter to Bernardino Machado, 27-12-1932', in Jacinto Baptista, *Dois democratas contra a ditadura: António Sérgio/Bernardino Machado: Cartas (1928–1935)*. n.d., 132.
———. 'Letter to Bernardino Machado, 2-01-1933', in Jacinto Baptista, *Dois democratas contra a ditadura: António Sérgio/Bernardino Machado: Cartas (1928–1935)*. n.d., 136.
———. *Breve interpretação da História de Portugal*. Lisboa: Sá da Costa, 1971 [Spanish ed. 1929].
———. *Os diálogos de doutrina democrática*. Lisbon: Sá da Costa, 1974 [1933], 1–84.
———. *Ensaios*, vol. II. Lisbon: Sá da Costa, 1977.
———. 'Prefácio da primeira edição', in António Sérgio, *Ensaios*, vol. II. Lisbon: Sá da Costa, 1977, 19.
———. 'Notas de política', in António Sérgio, *Ensaios*, vol. III (Lisbon: Sá da Costa, 1980), 141–239.
———. 'Prefácio da primeira edição' [1932], in António Sérgio, *Ensaios*, vol. III. (Lisbon: Sá da Costa, 1980), 5–23.
———. 'Letter to Joaquim de Carvalho, 29-11-1927', in Fernando Catroga and Aurélio Veloso, 'António Sérgio: cartas do exílio a Joaquim de Carvalho (1927–1933)'. *Revista de História das Ideias* 5(II) (1983), 958.
———. 'Letter to Joaquim de Carvalho, 21-11-1929', in Fernando Catroga and Aurélio Veloso, 'António Sérgio: cartas do exílio a Joaquim de Carvalho (1927–1933)'. *Revista de História das Ideias* 5(II) (1983), 961.
———. 'Letter dated 02-03-1930', in Fernando Catroga and Aurélio Veloso, 'António Sérgio: cartas do exílio a Joaquim de Carvalho (1927–1933)'. *Revista de História das Ideias* 5(II) (1983), 971.
———. 'Letter to Joaquim de Carvalho, 29-06-1931', in Fernando Catroga and Aurélio Veloso, 'António Sérgio: cartas do exílio a Joaquim de Carvalho (1927–1933)'. *Revista de História das Ideias* 5(II) (1983), 996.
———. 'Letter to Joaquim de Carvalho, 04-07-1932', in Fernando Catroga and Aurélio Veloso, 'António Sérgio: cartas do exílio a Joaquim de Carvalho (1927–1933)'. *Revista de História das Ideias* 5(II) (1983), 1003–4.
Weber, Max. *Économie et société*, vol. I. Paris: Plon, 1995.

CHAPTER 13

Émigré Portuguese Historians in France, 1945–1974

New Methods of Thinking and Writing Portuguese History

CHRISTOPHE ARAUJO

The Second World War is perhaps a late starting point when analysing Portuguese chronology during the Age of Extremes. In fact, Portugal was already an authoritarian Regime[1] from 1926: a coup against the dying First Republic installed a military dictatorship that slowly transformed into a civilian one. In 1933, the Constitution of the New State (*Estado Novo*) was validated by a plebiscite.[2] This New State was led by two academics, first – and above all – António de Oliveira Salazar, Prime Minister from 1932 to 1968, and then Marcelo Caetano, from 1968 to 1974. It was a conservative, nationalist government, firmly rooted in Catholicism, right-wing and regime-based. During the Second World War, Portugal stayed neutral, but 1945 marked a turning point. Indeed, the Portuguese affinities for the Axis powers were no longer relevant, and Portugal had to change, as the world was in a new era. Thanks to the quick onset of the Cold War, the old fight against communism[3] made Portugal a valuable ally for the Western Bloc. If Portugal had shown, after 1945, some signs of openness to escape accusation of being a rough dictatorship, it was only for the image abroad; for the population, there was no change, and the Portuguese scholars are an example of that.

Indeed, any application for a university position was subjected to ministerial approval, and they did not hesitate to ask the political police, the

Notes for this section begin on page 233.

PVDE/PIDE/DGS,[4] if the applicant had displayed political ideas contrary to the regime. This led to the exclusion, both in the academic and professional world, of a considerable number of intellectuals. While some observed the exile situation from the inside, like the Portuguese winner of the 1949 Nobel Prize for Medicine, Egas Moniz – who nevertheless admitted to feeling 'exiled in his own country' – others actually endured exile. In this regard, neighbouring Spain was favoured in the 1930s, but the end of the Second Spanish Republic compromised this solution, making Brazil and France the two main host countries for Portuguese.[5] The United States,[6] Great Britain,[7] Israel,[8] and France since the 1930s, were welcoming countries for exiled academics escaping from totalitarian and authoritarian regimes. Recent Portuguese historiography has mostly focused on Portuguese migrants in France[9] or in Brazil,[10] and only a few studies have been written on Portuguese academic émigrés, always using one scholar as an example or as a special focus. As a matter of fact, only a few Portuguese historians went abroad for a substantial period of time and for political reasons, whether to Brazil or France. Born at the end of the 1910s, António José Saraiva (1917–1993), Vitorino Magalhães Godinho (1919–2011) and Joaquim Barradas de Carvalho (1920–1980) were three historians that chose to leave Portugal for France after 1945. Other historians also left for France, such as José Gentil da Silva; however, it is unclear whether he kept links with the academic world, as there is a lack of information on what he did upon his arrival in France. Moreover, a few years after his arrival, he left the academic field. Miriam Halpern Pereira also came to France but not for personal political reasons and stayed less than a decade. In comparison with the three historians mentioned above, her situation and José Gentil da Silva's are different and do not fit this research's angle. Moreover, António José Saraiva, Vitorino Magalhães Godinho and Joaquim Barradas de Carvalho talked about their experience in many interviews or writings and as a result seem to be the most relevant cases to study and the only ones that stayed abroad for an extended period.

The three men's situations need to be considered. They were no refugees, as they were not under a death threat by the Portuguese State. If, then, they were not physically forced to leave Portugal after the Second World War, were they migrants or émigrés? A migrant is someone who moves from one country to another specifically to find work. As Godinho, Saraiva and Barradas de Carvalho had already graduated from the University of Lisbon and move abroad to work, they qualify as migrants. *Émigré* stemmed from the aristocrats during the French Revolution, who, due to political reasons, had to leave France and tried, from abroad, to put an end to the revolutionary process. Indeed, when facing a regime that represses a group for its political affiliation, the only solution can be to leave one's country and therefore to go into exile, becoming an émigré. Does it apply to our three historians?

Saraiva and Barradas de Carvalho were both activists within the Portuguese Communist Party,[11] and Godinho never concealed his left ideas, even if he did not belong to a political party when he left Portugal. Barradas de Carvalho is the closest to an émigré due to his involvement in a tentative coup in 1961; it was subsequently necessary to flee Portugal to escape prison. For their part and due to their political ideas, Saraiva and Godinho were forbidden, by the authoritarian power, to teach at university. This situation can fit the émigré category. Indeed, such a notion conveys more than just a political dimension and also encompasses economic issues.[12] The impossibility of a career in the Portuguese university for these three historians forced them to find another job in Portugal or to go to a foreign university. As a result, they can all be called émigré historians.

Leaving a country always leads to a 'double absence' as Abdelmalek Sayed[13] has shown: a migrant or an émigré is absent from his or her family and home country but can also feel absent in the host society, due to the difficulties of being accepted and integrated. Studying the consequences of the French exile of Barradas de Carvalho, Godinho and Saraiva brings us to focus on both home and host country. In the country that was left behind, these émigrés became special figures, as they had already begun to write history and were well-known authors. In the host country, their French experience offered them new opportunities and possibilities. Finally, the networks show how the oscillations between France and Portugal were constants in their professional life.

The Construction of the Figure of the Exiled Historian

For our three historians, their moments abroad are of significant importance to understand the consequences of their exile. Vitorino Magalhães Godinho[14] went to France in 1947 at the age of 29, joining the CNRS (the National Centre for Scientific Research) on his arrival and remaining in his position until 1960. He was then invited by the Minister of the Overseas Provinces, Adriano Moreira, to teach at the Higher Institute of Overseas Studies in Lisbon, before being dismissed in 1962 for his sympathies towards a strike movement. He worked in Portugal as an editor until 1970, before being appointed to the University of Clermont-Ferrand, in central France, a position he held until 25 April 1974, when he returned to Portugal at the age of 56. Over a period of 27 years, he spent a total of 17 years in exile. António José Saraiva[15] arrived in France in 1960 at the age of 43 with a grant from the Collège de France.[16] He quickly joined the CNRS until 1966 and then the École Pratique des Hautes Etudes until 1969. He left for the Netherlands in 1971 and returned back to Portugal in 1974 at the age of 57. Thus, he spent 14 years in exile, including 11 in France. Finally, our third historian, Joaquim Barradas de Carvalho,[17] arrived in France in 1961 at the age of 41 as the recipient of a scholarship from the French Ministry of Foreign Affairs. He then obtained a scholarship from the Calouste Gulbenkian Foundation before becoming a CNRS researcher. He left for Brazil in 1964 and returned to France in 1969, where he stayed until 1974, when he came back to Portugal at the age of 54. As a consequence, he stayed 13 years in exile, of which he spent 8 years in France. It can be seen that, with the exception of Vitorino Magalhães Godinho, who left for exile at a young age with regards to the rhythm of the University's environment, Saraiva and Barradas de Carvalho left at an older age.

This age difference may have caused a gap not only in the perception but also in the experience of exile. Indeed, Godinho left Portugal for France when he was still young, describing his departure in this way:

> I was grateful to the totalitarian Regime for the persecution that pushed me, despite the serious difficulties it caused me for five years, to work for publishers and to teach. Simple reason: it is from France that I was invited to cross the borders (without it being 'jumping'[18]) and to join the CNRS as a research fellow, under the direction of Lucien Febvre and Fernand Braudel. It is this opportunity that has saved my career as a researcher and a teacher. I was able to achieve what I wanted, thanks to France.[19]

His exile, therefore, was an opportunity, an opportunity that he knew how to seize at the right time. For those who remained in Portugal and appreciated his work and method, this situation was felt as a loss, part of a brain drain from the country. While he preferred to end his career at the CNRS to return to Portugal, his second resignation in 1962 was more of a sacrifice, which he made in solidarity with the striking students. His self-sacrifice was recognised by the Portuguese opposition, who saw him as a hero, as did other exiles. This is evidenced by an article written by Joaquim Barradas de Carvalho in the *Portugal Democrático*, a newspaper he ran when he was in exile in Brazil. The article focused on academics being pursued by the government. The author wrote the following:

> Finally, among the half-dozen that we have mentioned, Vitorino Magalhães Godinho, the greatest living Portuguese historian, who has already paid with his unshakeable civic courage for having been twice dismissed from his position as professor at the University of Lisbon.
> Among the youngest, a little younger than Vitorino Magalhães Godinho, some of whom were still his students, we remember Joel Serrão, Rui Grácio, José Augusto França, Victor de Sá, José Tengarrinha, Augusto da Costa Dias, Armando Castro, Alexandre Cabral, Alberto Ferreira, among those who have never had access to a place in Portuguese universities.[20]

We can therefore see how Godinho's situation is illustrative of many young researchers linked to the Portuguese left.[21] We note here the expression of a form of solidarity among the opposition circles – those in Portugal and those who had gone into exile – in the fight against political power.

But the experience of Godinho is also illustrative of difficulties that suggest the self-sacrifice of exiled individuals. Indeed, the exiled faced the difficulty of integration into a new country, finding housing and creating a network having left, for most of them, family and friends behind. António José Saraiva, particularly, would have felt this, having arrived in France in his forties – that is, after having had time to establish a life in full already, in Portugal. In his correspondence with his friend Óscar Lopes, he describes the suffering associated with his remoteness as follows:

> I hope it will be the last year in Paris, but I don't know if in the end I will be able to find the homeland . . . I would like to have a chair in Porto, with my children nearby, classes, students, people, human comfort. I was not made for this gypsy life, although I do not deny it, because it taught me many things and probably delayed my ageing . . . So far I suffered from all the disadvantages of being far from Portugal, without in exchange having found a way of integration.[22]

We can, therefore, clearly feel the gap between what he wants and the tearing reality he faces because of the impossibility of his return. It should of course be stressed that this is a letter written to a close friend and not a newspaper article; therefore, it does not amount to an ostentatious claim. But these confidences are all the more compelling to understand the consequences of exile for Saraiva. Thus, the different narratives of historians show sacrifice is implicit, for many, in the mere fact of being exiled.

Exiled Historians and New Historiographical Practices

To grasp the novelty of émigré historians in France's historiographical practices, we cannot avoid a presentation of the historiographical landscape they left behind. There is no shortage of qualifiers to belittle the history that was then written by historians holding a chair in the country's two literature faculties, Lisbon and Coimbra, or by the Portuguese Academy of History's members, an institution re-created in 1936 by ministerial decision and where conservative historians were the most prominent figures.[23] We can rely on a description made by Joaquim in *Portugal Democrático*, where he portrayed dissenting intellectuals. He outlines the Portuguese academic environment in his biography of Godinho when the latter taught at the University of Lisbon and when Barradas de Carvalho was still one of his students:

> There, he entered in 1941, causing a kind of earthquake in the old building of Arco de Jesus, the same faculty that Professor Manuel Rodrigues Lapa, a few years earlier, had said was the only school in the world where 'you enter

by descending'.²⁴ With the waters asleep, the cemetery that was the Faculty of Lisbon was shaken, and in order for the old building not to fall into ruins once and for all, it was necessary, two years later, to expel the embarrassing Professor Vitorino Magalhães Godinho. He had the audacity to prepare the courses, to present himself in front of the students with an updated bibliography, he had the extreme audacity to do scientific research, to publish the results of this research, and maximum crime, had the idea of creating study centres (historical and philosophical), where, in collaboration with the students, one sought to do historical or philosophical research. Here, the scandal was such that the Faculty Council felt that this Professor should be supervised in his classes by a History Professor, if he had not exposed students to demonic subjects . . . Not submitting to this police imposition, Vitorino Magalhães Godinho abandoned the old Arco de Jesus building, leaving it to its secular sleep.²⁵

Through this ironic description, we perceive the torpor and conservatism at work where an overly ambitious researcher aroused a certain mistrust, especially since he seemed to manifest left-wing ideas, without necessarily being a member of the PCP. In a letter to Fernand Braudel on 1 August 1950, Vitorino Magalhães Godinho also refers to the working conditions in the Portuguese archives while having already begun to develop habits in France: 'At the Torre do Tombo the working conditions have become worse: you can no longer even write in ink! [sic] always the same schedule – from 11:15 to 15:45, no catalogues; documents withdrawn from reading; etc . . .'²⁶ Here, the letter describes, in striking detail, the painful and very restrictive conditions to which historians' key work phase was subjected. Many other scientific accounts evidenced that some documents were not searchable, and the lack of a catalogue created tremendous difficulties. As a result, researchers were dependent on the goodwill of libraries' and archives' officials. Therefore, it was only once in France that the exiled historians would become clearly aware of the obstacles that existed in the exercise of their profession in Portugal. This newly acquired freedom of research amounted to a novelty for those historians' practices.

The novelty is also in the way history was written. In fact, in the very writing of history, these historians are characterised by a writing that moves away from Portuguese historiography made in universities. The latter was centred on a political and erudite study of the great royal figures and important characters, not hesitating to politically reinterpret certain facts, as did João Ameal when speaking of correcting the mistakes of Portuguese history in his books *From Dom João V to Dom Miguel: Errors in History of Portugal*.²⁷ In contrast, Vitorino Magalhães Godinho, who was strongly influenced by the work of Lucien Febvre and Marc Bloch, is considered to be one of the major figures in Portuguese economic and social history. His postgraduate thesis, 'Prices and Currencies in Portugal: 1750–1850', prefaced by Lucien Febvre, is the perfect illustration of this different practice in economic history. Barradas de Carvalho and Saraiva were also influenced by economic and social history, the mainstream written history in France, the highlight being the journal *Annales Économies, Sociétés, Civilisations*.

Furthermore, some historical themes were viewed with a new distance. To begin, the themes explored by exiled Portuguese historians remained strongly linked to subjects touching Portugal. Vitorino Magalhães Godinho worked mainly on Portuguese colonial expansion in the modern era but also on the end of the modern period. António José Saraiva focused on Portuguese modern history. He worked on literature and, besides, developed very important research on Jews converted to Catholics. Finally, Barradas de Carvalho wrote both on a nineteenth-century historian and on Portuguese colonial expansion. But the approach to these themes was very different. For example, in his book *Inquisition and New Christians*, António José Saraiva[28] studied the conversion of Jews as a research topic to criticise some common views shared by the Portuguese power, with the clear objective to undermine many certitudes at the time by focusing on the control exercised by the Inquisition over this social group. Some French works have remained untranslated into Portuguese, but most of them were, and some even had some editorial success. This indicates that a part of the population felt the need for historiographical renovation.

Portugal in Mind? Dynamics of the Émigré Historians' Networks

The historian's arrival in a new country when to remain in the country of origin seemed compromised implied integration into the host country's network of researchers. As evidenced above, such an integration did not necessarily translate to their research focus, as they opted for themes linked with Portugal. It was rather in their approach to research subjects and most of all via their network that such an integration took place: from correspondence with publishers, scholars and editing committees of journals and newspapers. French networks were seen as a complement to the vital[29] networks oriented towards Portugal.

Godinho is the perfect illustration of the researcher who easily managed to insert himself in national and host country networks. An element that I have not yet mentioned is that all these historians mastered French, which was preferred to English in the first half of the twentieth-century in the Portuguese educational system, and so the linguistic question was important but not necessarily a barrier that could not be overcome. Godinho had a very good command of French and wrote his two theses – the postgraduate thesis and the state thesis – in French without too much difficulty. Recruited at the CNRS, he quickly managed to establish a network among Hispanists and Portuguese teachers but also, and especially, with historians. Through

Godinho's correspondence with Fernand Braudel, we conclude that he had contact with Pierre Chaunu. Albert Silbert even lent him his apartment for several months in 1949, and Frédéric Mauro visited him at his home in Lisbon for a few months in 1950.[30] The important number of publications in Portugal and the fact that he was invited by the Minister to teach is a clear sign of his good insertion into Portuguese networks, as well.

Barradas de Carvalho and Saraiva's contacts included the most prominent historians specialised in the Iberian world at the time: Léon Bourdon, Albert Silbert and Marcel Bataillon. This network was very useful for sure, as French historians could be very considerate. For instance, while Barradas de Carvalho was still in Brazil, Fernand Braudel sent him a telegram a few months after the coup d'état, on 21 September 1964, in order to bring him back to Paris: 'BARRADAS CARVALHO UNIVERSIDADE CAIX POSTAL 8105 SAO PAULO BRESIL SUBMIT YOUR CANDIDATURE CNRS COMMISSION 27 BY PLANE REGARDS BRAUDEL.'[31] Some may have had difficulty forging relationships in a professional environment where opportunities for meeting could sometimes be limited. We can build on António José Saraiva, who confides to Óscar Lopes, 'I don't know if you know it, but the Parisian scene is unpleasant and tends to repel foreigners.'[32] Saraiva mainly benefited from the almost continuous support of Fernand Braudel but suffered from his enmities with some French researchers. Thus, his renewal at the CNRS was blocked by Marcel Bataillon, a Hispanic professor who was rather close to the one who in France became Saraiva's main opponent, Israel Salvator Révah. These two professors had long argued about the Marranos. Faced with this hostility, Saraiva concludes, 'finally, feudalism has survived, with its bosses and customers, bound by bonds of protection and personal loyalty. French higher education is an example of this.'[33] He also had difficulties with Léon Bourdon, the main teacher of Portuguese in France at the Sorbonne.

Saraiva and Barradas de Carvalho did not neglect the links with the Portuguese university network, in the eventuality of a return to Portugal. A solidarity existed, of course, between the exiled Portuguese who were in France. For instance, Barradas de Carvalho asked Fernand Braudel if he had the opportunity to help Mário Soares, who later became one of the great figures in Portuguese political history, by finding him an academic position in France:

> Dear Mr. Braudel...
> In a nutshell. I would like to remind you of the case of my friend Mário Soares, the only exiled member of the Marcelo Caetano Government. He submitted his application to the CNRS commission of Modern History, in order to finish a postgraduate thesis on Portugal's intervention in the War of 14–18 according to French, Italian and English diplomatic archives documents.
> Can I still hope you'll do for him ... what you can? Thank you in advance.

I am well aware that neither you nor F. Mauro belong to the Commission anymore. Frédéric Mauro promised to intervene with François Chevalier. Could you do the same with someone or some of your friends who belong to the Commission?[34]

Sometimes, more surprising links can be discovered. For example, Alexandre Marques Lobato, a Portuguese historian close to the ruling regime, thanked Godinho in a footnote for having given him details about consulting certain sources.[35] This demonstrates that communications were not broken between dissenting historians and those close to the regime, especially when taking into account that Portugal is a very small country where formation locations are very small and therefore where the university environment is limited.

However, the effects of distance can be strong, and some links with the departed country can be weakened, making certain vital elements of research activity more complex. Indeed, António José Saraiva explained to Óscar Lopes the difficulties he experienced in publishing. As we mentioned, leaving the PCP in 1962 had the effect of cutting him off from an entire part of the opposition that saw him as a 'social traitor'. Óscar Lopes remained his unwavering friend despite this. Dissenting newspapers or publishers, for their part, could have been harmed by publishing Saraiva:

> I have a bad relationship with Europa-América. Seara Nova refuses my articles, o Tempo e o Modo has never clearly invited me (despite suggestions from third parties). So that if you except o Comércio do Porto, I don't have a place to publish in Portugal? Strange fate of a 'successful' author![36]

We can therefore measure the difficulties that some have encountered in maintaining ties with the country of origin's network within a competitive academic environment.

To conclude, we were able to see through the trajectories of three historians who left for France – and two of them for other countries as well – what exile has meant for them. First, leaving Portugal for many years lead to a very specific image of the historian who is far from his homeland: this portrait was made by other historians and at the same time by the émigré historians, who stressed the difficult moments they lived through. Second, this life abroad had consequences for the history they wrote: liberated from any risk of censorship or forbidden themes, they could explore new historiographical practices, far from the Portugal they had left and closer to the socio-economic history of the 'Annales'. Finally, leaving a country led the three historians to develop new academic networks in the host country, to find support in the main institutions of research. At the same time, they all tried to maintain links with Portugal, as the history they wrote was on Portugal and the interested publishers were there, so too were the other historians of the opposition that remained and could help find a journal or a publisher.

After the authoritarian regime was overthrown on 25 April 1974, a revolution led to the resignation of some university professors while others, especially left-wing professors, were appointed. Barradas de Carvalho, Godinho and Saraiva very quickly returned to Portugal. Thus, as early as 1974, Godinho obtained a chair at the University of Lisbon, Saraiva at the New University of Lisbon and Barradas de Carvalho took a little longer but obtained a chair in 1977, also at the University of Lisbon. Years abroad and difficulties were finally part of the past in the new political Portuguese paradigm. They were at last able to be what they had not been allowed to be before: not only historians writing history but also teaching it.

Notes

1. For this case study, I refer to Portugal during 1926 and 1974 as an authoritarian regime, following the definition offered by Juan Linz in his works (such as, *Totalitarian and Authoritarian Regimes*, a book summing up his 1970s position on the Spanish dictatorship). In fact, since the fall of the regime, scholars have been divided on whether Portugal qualifies as having been a fascist country during the dictatorship. The 2012 historiographical polemic on Rui Ramos' study of the New State is an illustration of this heated debate (for a summary of this so-called Hot Summer, see Meneses, 'Slander, Ideological Differences, or Academic Debate?', 62–77).

   I opted not to use the term 'fascism', as it would have brought a debate that happens to be removed from this book's focus. To have a clear vision of the division among scholars, see Sena, *O Fascismo catedrático*, 453.

2. It was legally called a referendum and took place on 19 March 1933. The results, published by the Government, showed that 99.52% of the voting population approved the text. As a result, it is more relevant to name it a plebiscite. For the official results, see *Diário do Governo*, I(83), 11 April 1933.

3. From its beginnings, the Portuguese regime was fighting against the communist doctrine, and the Portuguese Communist Party was prohibited. Under the Statute n°27 003 of 14 September 1936, every civil servant had to sign a declaration stating that they were not communist. Being a communist was sufficient reason to be removed from university.

4. In 1945, the PVDE turned into the International Police of Estate Defence (PIDE). It became a very powerful police force, gaining efficiency. It later, in 1969, became the General Directorate for Security (DGS). For the history of the PIDE, see Pimentel, *A história da PIDE*.

5. As it was shown by Cristina Clímaco, Paris was a city that had welcomed exiles since the beginning of the authoritarian regime. See Clímaco, *Republicano*.

6. The United States became the main refuge for academics and even more for those born abroad and trained in the United States, see Daum, Lehmann, and Sheehan, *The Second Generation*.

7. The history of the so-called Continental Britons has been described by Alter, *Out of the Third Reich*.

8. See chapter 2 Aschheim, *Beyond the Border*, 45–80.

9. Pereira, *La Dictature de Salazar*.

10. Heloisa, *Aqui também é Portugal*.

11. Joaquim Barradas de Carvalho was a member of the PCP during the entire period covered by this chapter; António José Saraiva left the PCP in 1962, remaining close to the left but out of the main opposition party to the regime. This situation put Saraiva in a hard

position, since exiting the PCP, for him, meant a double exclusion: an exclusion from Portuguese society as he was abroad and an exclusion from the powerful communist networks. A similar situation had been endured by Flausino Torres, a Portuguese historian who left the PCP after witnessing the intervention of the Russian army in Prague in 1968 (see Bento, *Flausino Torres*).

12. Conversely, economic issues can be linked to political reasons, such as the Portuguese who came to work in France when there was a significant need for labour, a situation that allowed them to escape military service in Africa after the outbreak of the colonial war in 1961. See Dreyfus-Armand and Groppo, 'Objectifs de la journée d'études'.

13. Sayad, *La double absence*.

14. All the biographical information about the three historians can be found in the online dictionary of Portuguese historians edited by Sérgio Campos Matos. See Magalhães, 'Vitorino Magalhães Godinho'.

15. Guerreiro, 'António José Saraiva'.

16. For further information about this institution, see https://www.college-de-france.fr/ [accessed 19 January 2021].

17. Magalhães, 'Joaquim Barradas de Carvalho'.

18. The Portuguese word is 'a salto': it was a reference to the illegal way of crossing the border with Spain, mainly during the night, to get to France, in the same decade, the 1960s. See Pereira, *La Dictature de Salazar*.

19. Godinho, *A crise da História*, 8.

20. *Portugal Democrático* 111 (October 1966). All the references from *Portugal Democrático* relate to Joaquim Barradas de Carvalho and can be found in the PIDE archive, in the Torre do Tombo in Lisbon (Archive PIDE/DGS Série: CI(2) N°Proc: 79 NT: 6958, sheet 294 for these extract), but they were also gathered in a book published a few months after the end of the dictatorship. See Carvalho, *O Obscurantismo Salazarista*.

21. For the main study of the historians outside the regime positions, see Torgal, chapter 8 'Portuguese Historiography', 313–98. The communist historians are also referred to in the fourth part of the seminal work of Neves, *Comunismo e Nacionalismo*.

22. For this excerpt, see Neves, *António José Saraiva e Óscar Lopes*, 69. The book contains the letters sent by Saraiva from France and the Netherlands to Lopes.

23. Very few works mention the historians close to the Portuguese regime and even less write about the Portuguese Academy of History, due to the bad image of the authoritarian regime after 25th April 1974. See Torgal, Chapter 7 'History during the "Dictatorship"', 273–311.

24. Until the 1960s, the Faculty of Letters was in the Convent of Nossa Senhora de Jesus, built in the seventeenth century. In fact, to enter the cloister, there is a stairway to join the ground floor due to the topography of the site of the Convent. But for opponents, it was the symbol of a regressive way of entering a place of knowledge.

25. The article was written by Joaquim Barradas de Carvalho, number 94 of *Portugal Democrático* (1965). See Archive PIDE/DGS Série: CI(2) N°Proc: 79 NT: 6958, sheet 336.

26. Excerpt from the file 'Vitorino Magalhães Godinho', sheet 7, personal archive of Fernand Braudel in the Institut de France (MS 8510).

27. João Ameal (1902–1982) was trained in Law and became a journalist and also a historian recognised by the regime: he received many official prizes and wrote several books about Portuguese history. After 25th April 1974, he gained a bad reputation due to his very partisan history. See Ameal, *De D. João V a D. Miguel*.

28. Saraiva's book was a great success in Portugal and saw several editions during the 1960s, showing the curiosity of a certain public. See Saraiva, *Inquisição e Cristão Novos*.

29. By using the word vital, I mean that it was vital to their public and academic existence in Portugal to maintain the link with Portugal, even if material living conditions were assured by their work in France.

30. Reported in a letter sent from Lisbon on 2nd March 1949, sheet 2 of the file 'Vitorino Magalhães Godinho', personal archive of Fernand Braudel in the Institut de France (MS 8510).
31. File 'Joaquim Barradas de Carvalho', sheet 10, personal archive of Fernand Braudel in the Institut de France (MS 8510).
32. Letter sent during the summer 1961, see Neves, *António José Saraiva e Óscar Lopes*, 64.
33. Letter sent 1st March 1966 see Neves, *António José Saraiva e Óscar Lopes*, 142.
34. File 'Joaquim Barradas de Carvalho', letter written 5th May 1971, sheet 20, personal archive of Fernand Braudel in the Institut de France (MS 8510).
35. Lobato, *A Expansão portuguesa*, 389.
36. Letter from António José Saraiva to Óscar Lopes in June 1968, see Neves, *António José Saraiva e Óscar Lopes*, 180.

Bibliography

Alter, Peter (ed.). *Out of the Third Reich, Refugee Historians in Post-War Britain*. London: I.B. Tauris, 1998.
Aschheim, Steven E. *Beyond the Border: The German-Jewish Legacy Abroad*. Princeton-Oxford: Princeton University Press, 2007.
Bento, Paulo Torres. *Flausino Torres (1906–1974): Documentos e Fragmentos Biográficos de um Intelectual Antifascista*. Lisbon: Edições Afrontamento, 2006.
Carvalho, Joaquim Barradas de. *O Obscurantismo Salazarista*. Lisbon: Seara Nova, 1974.
Clímaco, Cristina. *Republicanos, Anarquistas e Comunistas no exílio (1927–1936)*. Lisbon: Edições Colibri, 2017.
Daum, Andreas W., Lehmann, Hartmut, and Sheehan, James J. (eds). *The Second Generation: Émigrés from Nazi Germany as historians*. New York: Berghahn Books, 2016.
Dreyfus-Armand, Geneviève, and Groppo, Bruno. 'Objectifs de la journée d'études'. *Matériaux pour l'histoire de notre temps*, issue named 'Exilés et réfugiés politiques dans la France du XXe siècle', 44 (1996).
Godinho, Vitorino Magalhães. *A crise da História e as suas novas directrizes*, 3rd edn. Lisbon: Imprensa Nacional-Casa da Moeda, 2013.
Guerreiro, Luís Ramalhosa. 'António José Saraiva', in Matos, Sérgio Campos (ed.), *Dicionário de Historiadores Portugueses, da Academia Real das Ciências ao final do Estado Novo*, on-line dictionary. Retrieved 26 January 2021 from http://dichp.bnportugal.pt/historiadores/historiadores_saraiva.htm.
Heloisa, Paulo. *Aqui também é Portugal: A colónia portuguesa do Brasil e o Salazarismo*. Coimbra: Quarteto, 2000.
Linz, Juan. *Totalitarian and Authoritarian Regimes*. London: Lynn Rienner Editions, 2000.
Magalhães, Joaquim Romero. 'Joaquim Barradas de Carvalho', in Matos, Sérgio Campos (ed.), *Dicionário de Historiadores Portugueses, da Academia Real das Ciências ao final do Estado Novo*, on-line dictionary. Retrieved 26 January 2021 from http://dichp.bnportugal.pt/historiadores/historiadores_barradas_carvalho.htm.
———. 'Vitorino Magalhães Godinho', in Matos, Sérgio Campos (ed.), *Dicionário de Historiadores Portugueses, da Academia Real das Ciências ao final do Estado Novo*, on-line dictionary. Retrieved 26 January 2021 from http://dichp.bnportugal.pt/historiadores/historiadores_godinho.htm.
Meneses, Filipe Ribeiro de. 'Slander, Ideological Differences, or Academic Debate? The 'Verão Quente' of 2012 and the State of Portuguese Historiography'. e-JPH [online] 10(1) (2012), 62–77.
Neves, Leonor Curado (ed.). *António José Saraiva e Óscar Lopes: Correspondência*. Lisbon: Gradiva, 2004.

Neves, José. *Comunismo e Nacionalismo em Portugal: Política, Cultura e História no Século XX*. Lisbon: Tinta-da-china, 2011.
Pereira, Victor. *La Dictature de Salazar face à l'émigration: L'État portugais et ses migrants en France (1957–1974)*. Paris: Presses de Sciences Po, 2012.
Pimentel, Irene Flunser. *A história da PIDE*. Lisbon: Círculo de Leitores, 2007.
Sayad, Abdelmalek. *La double absence: Des illusions de l'émigré aux souffrances de l'immigré*. Paris: Seuil, 1999.
Sena, Jorge Pais de. *O Fascismo catedrático de Salazar, das Origens na I Guerra Mundial à intervenção militar na guerra civil de Espanha, 1914–1939*. Coimbra: Imprensa da Universidade de Coimbra, 2011.
Torgal, Luís Reis. 'History during the "Dictatorship"', in Catroga, Fernando, Mendes, José Maria Amado, and Torgal, Luís Reis (eds), *História da História em Portugal, séculos XIX–XX*, vol. 1 (Lisbon: Temas e Debates, 1998), 273–311.
———. 'The Renovation of the Portuguese Historiography', in Catroga, Fernando, Mendes, José Maria Amado, and Torgal, Luís Reis (eds), *História da História em Portugal, séculos XIX–XX*, vol. 1 (Lisbon: Temas e Debates, 1998), 313–98.

Sources

Ameal, João. *De D. João V a D. Miguel. Erratas à História de Portugal*. Porto: Livraria Tavares Martins, 1939.
Diário do Governo, I(83), 11 April 1933.
File 'Vitorino Magalhães Godinho', letter sent from Lisbon, on 2nd March 1949, sheet 2, personal archive of Fernand Braudel in the Institut de France (MS 8510).
File 'Joaquim Barradas de Carvalho', letter written 5th May 1971, sheet 20, personal archive of Fernand Braudel in the Institut de France (MS 8510).
File 'Joaquim Barradas de Carvalho', sheet 10, personal archive of Fernand Braudel in the Institut de France (MS 8510).
File 'Vitorino Magalhães Godinho', sheet 7, personal archive of Fernand Braudel in the Institut de France (MS 8510).
Lobato, Alexandre Marques. *A Expansão portuguesa em Moçambique de 1498 a 1530. Livro I: Descobrimento e ocupação da Costa, 1498–1508*. Lisbon: Agência Geral do Ultramar, coleção 'Estudos moçambicanos', 1954.
Portugal Democrático 111 (October 1966), PIDE archive in the Torre do Tombo in Lisbon, Archive PIDE/DGS Série: CI(2) N°Proc: 79 NT: 6958, p. 294.
Portugal Democrático 94 (1965), PIDE archive in the Torre do Tombo in Lisbon, Archive PIDE/DGS Série: CI(2) N°Proc: 79 NT: 6958, p. 336.
Saraiva, António José. *Inquisição e Cristão Novos*. Porto: Editorial Inova, 1969.

Conclusion

New Perspectives on Émigré Scholarship and What Remains to be Done

STEFAN BERGER AND PHILIPP MÜLLER

The current volume that we present here pursues a number of related themes that fit into the historiography of émigré scholarship that we reviewed in the introduction to this volume. First, it investigates how émigré scholars were at the mercy of diverse institutional policies. Secondly, it also traces how these scholars helped to shape and change such institutional policies. Thirdly, it examines the various scholarly personae with which emigrants were confronted and how these encounters shaped the active self-fashioning of émigré scholars. These constructed personae had a major impact on their scholarship. The notion of the 'scholarly persona'[1] first appeared in studies of the new history of sciences that focused on researchers, who for lack of institutional scientific autonomy adopted non-scientific entities as sources of epistemic power.[2] In recent years, studies looking into the development of the persona have shed light on the personae in their various forms and in their historicity.[3] The term describes – in a positive and almost idealistic sense – the bundle of specific values and virtues that characterise a scientific profession. Moreover, the values and virtues are directly linked to character traits and also implicit expectations of the respective actors. Furthermore, they are subject to the semi-public negotiations of the scientific community. In the course of exile and emigration, scholars' encounters in foreign countries had a profound impact on their personae, yet this is a topic that needs to be studied far more. The studies of Jo Tollebeek and Herman Paul in this book make first crucial steps in this direction.

Notes for this section begin on page 246.

The established perspective on the scholarly persona also needs to be expanded to include a gender historical perspective. All too often, the scholarly persona has so far been seen as exclusively male. Accordingly, attributes attached to the scholar's persona presume a quasi-natural-seeming privilege of the male scholar that tacitly presupposes the 'unpayable love services' of wives, mothers and sisters.[4] Yet women have played a central, though publicly hardly acknowledged, role in scholarly research, including in the historical sciences. Peter Schöttler was the first to draw attention to a female émigré historian, by highlighting the work and career of Lucie Varga.[5] The Vienna-born historian was already engaged in a lively intellectual exchange with Marc Bloch and Lucien Febvre prior to the annexation of Austria in 1938, when she left for Paris to escape the racist and political persecution of the National Socialists, in order to cooperate with the founders of the Annales.

The scholarly persona of Varga was not only shaped by her gender but also by what we might term scholarly micropolitics. Social networks abroad repeatedly proved to be a central resource for émigré historians like Varga. They benefited in many other cases from social networking and the mediation and advocacy of third parties. Thus, as Christophe Araujo shows in his contribution, contacts with Fernand Braudel enabled Portuguese historians to escape persecution in their home country and to find refuge in France. On the basis of their own social capital and that of their network, émigré historians were more likely to obtain temporary residence or even (temporary) employment. The émigré historians' networks and contacts also determined who they selected for support and positions, as the example of Alvin Johnson, the founder director of the New School in New York, clearly shows.[6]

The role of intermediaries and brokers, their specific practice and social interdependence and, above all, their constitutive significance have not yet been systematically researched. Here, the volume picks up on an important observation of recent studies in the history of the sciences.[7] They have highlighted the institutional precondition of patronage, which was indispensable for early modern natural sciences. They also showed the relevance of academies for networking in the early modern era. And they underlined how necessary the promotion by brokers and intermediaries was for research in archives in the nineteenth century.[8] Overall, in recent studies in the history of knowledge and science, intermediaries have repeatedly crystallised an exceptionally important, albeit long-neglected group of people in research that was of central importance for scientific transactions. Although this group of people usually acted in the background and the individual persons usually did not receive any public recognition in their time, more recent research shows that they provided valuable services. These included, for example, advocacy, the provision of locally specific knowledge, publicity and circulation, scientific research, monetary resources, and other social linkages that made concrete research in the natural sciences and humanities possible in the first place. The question of social networks is all the more important, as the possibility of refuge, migration and professional reintegration of emigrated historians was directly linked to the support of brokers and intermediaries.[9] It is precisely in this sense that Iryna Mykhailova refers in her study to Paul Oskar Kristeller, who wisely noted that academic careers in the United States are made in two ways, either with money or with contacts. However, he only had an address book at his disposal. Scholarly micropolitics of the sort mentioned here was a central resource, but it was also scarce and contested.

The making of scholarly personae often went hand in hand with the construction of political personae. Be it advising politicians, working for secret services, or providing historical input and commentary in popular mass media, political matters played a key role in the intellectual and social world of scholars in the age of extremes, as we noted when reviewing the historiography above. The contributions to this book show that the entanglement of the political and intellectual deserve new attention given the renewed and intensified research on political dimensions of cultural matters. Scholars integrated political ideas into their intellectual designs; they developed them further and made themselves advocates of this or that political idea.[10] What is more, the implementation of political ideas in concrete political practice rendered them even more appealing to many intellectual scholars. In the course of flight and emigration, political concepts did not lose their intellectual meaning or their political weight. Even after the successful escape abroad, intellectuals and scholars continued to be a thorn in the side of the authorities, whose clutches they were trying to escape. As Antoon De Baets shows in his chapter, the authorities of dictatorships came up with a whole raft of measures to persecute and pursue émigrés beyond the political borders of their own territory.

What is more, given their first-hand experience of political crises and struggles, émigré scholars promptly raised questions about the how and the why of recent political trends and thus an intensified intellectual engagement with history followed. In a foreign country, their own political orientation played no small part in their career prospects. The case studies presented in this book show, independently of each other, that some liberal and conservative-minded scholars were able to establish themselves relatively quickly and successfully at leading universities in the United States, for example, whereas other historians who were intellectually akin to Marxist ideas and concepts often fared less well.[11] Famous are also the many examples of learned scholars who openly took sides in political conflicts, such as Francis L. Carsten (subsequent to his professional training as a historian in Oxford),[12] and Béla Iványi-Grünwald, Jr., who is the topic of Vilmos Erős' chapter. But even beyond the present political situation, they did not limit themselves to being active as memory agents. In day-to-day political business, they took up activities as advisors or engaged themselves in military and political conflicts in order to contribute to the 'right cause'. Kai Johann Willms focuses in his analysis of Polish émigré scholarship on scholars who were engaged in political matters at the highest level. The Polish historian Oskar Halecki worked as an advisor of the Polish government after the Second World War; the political scientist Zbigniew Brzeziński acted as a consultant for the campaign of John F. Kennedy and Hubert Humphrey and later worked as National Security Advisor to President Jimmy Carter.

Others were involved in aiding immigrants. Fernand Braudel, in the 1930s, made the Annales School a point of contact for scholars fleeing from National Socialist Germany and, a few years later, those from annexed Austria, but also for historians who had left behind dictatorships in Portugal and Spain. Some scholars committed themselves to providing aid for foreign colleagues in distress, by engaging in relief organisations and associations. They were not necessarily entirely free in their actions and had social reservations and prejudices of their own, including sentiments of antisemitism and racism, as we learn from Joseph Malherek's study in this book. For others, the political proved to be an all too delicate subject that was generally to be avoided. Branimir Janković highlights in his study how a group of historians who fled from the Soviet Union deliberately avoided political topics and began to deal with historical topics that were distant in time, precisely because more recent topics would have been too political and therefore would have affected their own lives and professional advancement negatively. It is true that emigrants, often forcibly expelled and fleeing in haste to save their lives, were exposed to political violence and its disastrous consequences. But at the same time, contributions in this book reveal that émigré scholars did not only react to changing political circumstances; in many cases, they were already involved in the political and social processes and, equally important, they often played an active role in shaping them in their later course of flight and emigration.

The relevance of political concepts and categories for the performance and thinking of scholars can also be observed in the disputes and discussions that went on between different scholars and groups within the scientific community. Often national and political categories that went unquestioned guided their perceptions and value judgements. After the end of the Second World War, West German historians recognised that the accessibility of German archive material, in the possession of the United States, to non-German scholars would eventually make it difficult for German historians to construct the dominant interpretations of the German past.[13] For Gerhard Ritter and other German historians, Germany's past should be primarily rendered available for German research. The linking of scholarly research to the auctoritas of the archives has a long tradition in the study of history,[14] but arguing in favour of national exclusivity and the idea to limit the inspection of records cannot be understood without taking the nationalist and military conflicts in the twentieth century into account. In the decades after the Second World War, as Philipp Stelzel points out in his chapter, German historians continued to adhere to nationalist notions of scholarship, as they viewed scholarly contributions on contemporary German history by emigrated historians with suspicion. They doubted the ex-pats' patriotic sentiment and loyalty and questioned, therefore, their scholarly authority, before an increasing internationalisation of sciences began to change the image of the foreign and the self.[15]

Many contributions in this volume underline how difficult it was for emigrants to resettle in unfamiliar and often hostile new environments. Yet the latter could also offer new opportunities.[16] For those who succeeded in making an unforeseen diagonal career path – transnational in the true sense of the word[17] – it opened the possibility for new insights. Michael Antolović shows how the Serbian historian Dimitrije Đorđević developed new perspectives on the history of his homeland because of his experiences as an émigré historian. António Sérgio and José Ortega y Gasset were capable of doing the same for the histories of Portugal and Spain respectively, as Sérgio Campos Matos demonstrates in his chapter. The Portuguese historians Vitorino Magalhães Godinho not only found refuge in France but also a new intellectual home. Here he became familiar with economic and social history, which he eagerly took up and adopted for his own historical research. For historians like Godinho, the fortune of their successful escape as well as their luck in terms of professional success were inevitably inscribed into their (self-)portrayal and (self-)assessment and remained inseparably linked, in retrospect.

However, for others there was no need to alter their intellectual concepts. In an astounding way, some émigré scholars held fast to their premises and assumptions and exercised a kind of intellectual resilience towards their new academic environment. Here it is worthwhile to work with the concept of generation, which has already been introduced into research on émigré scholarship, as we noted above.[18] The independent studies in this book show very clearly that it could make a huge difference whether émigré historians had just passed their exams and then continued their studies abroad with a doctoral thesis and at the same time were scientifically reoriented, or whether they were already established scholars who often held on to notions of the 'lost homeland'. As Iryna Mykhailova emphasises in her analysis of Paul Oskar Kristeller, his steadfast adherence to concepts he developed before his exile was an intellectual manifestation of the violent experience of flight and the loss of home. Oskar Kristeller's intellectual resilience did not, however, harm his career. On the contrary, like many other émigré scholars from Germany, he benefited from the international esteem and prestige that German intellectual history and philosophy still enjoyed at the time. This was an advantage that was not available in this form to émigré historians from neighbouring Central European countries – despite their intellectual kinship in principle – who therefore had less cultural capital at their disposal to draw on.

For female émigré historians, competition was much harder given the principally gendered formation of the historical discipline, as Judith Szapor shows in her contribution on Laura Polanyi. Lucie Varga is another case in point here. Varga proved extremely vulnerable as a woman in a professional field dominated by men; and it was her particular gender-specific vulnerability as an émigré historian that made her advancement significantly more difficult and prevented her from progressing. Research on émigré women scholars in exile remains a task that must be deepened and expanded.[19] But records, where they do exist, reflect structural discrimination, making research on female émigré historians very difficult.[20] The precariousness of their professional circumstances was not conducive to documenting their lives, hence a lot of the history of emigrated historians has been left to oblivion.

Outlook: Practices of Historical Research

In the history of historiography and in the history of scholarly knowledge production more generally, the importance of knowing more about the actual practice of generating that knowledge has of late been emphasised by a variety of different scholars.[21] In their analyses, these studies shed new light on the making of scholarship that goes beyond the established research concepts of narrative and idea, and therefore they have proven productive in asking new questions concerning the highly gendered nature of the historical discipline, the imagination of archival bodies or the materiality of archival historical research. This is also true for research on exile and emigration. The yearbook *Exilforschung*, edited by Claus-Dieter Krohn, has long since drawn attention in a very impressive way to a wide range of thematic aspects of exile, including gender, publishers and media, autobiographies and metropoles of exile.[22] The question of historical practice, however, goes beyond this. A thematic expansion here is rather the effect of a question that places the practice of historical research at the centre of the analysis and asks about the preconditions, the actors involved, the processuality and the consequences and changes of science and its knowledge.

The question of historical practice and its role for émigré scholarship is all the more urgent in view of the fact that in their design various and independent studies repeatedly refer to essential resources of structural significance for scholarly work, and they emphasise their significance for the establishment of science and the generation of knowledge. This refers primarily to the scholar's private home, the epistemic objects on the basis of which observations are made, the media and techniques for organising and storing knowledge, and the aforementioned resource of social contacts employed in the scholarly micropolitics. These resources are deliberately attacked in their integrity and coherence by means of political violence, and they are also deliberately stolen and/or destroyed, and if something can be salvaged in the course of flight and migration, it is only under very difficult circumstances.

The scholar's private home established a domestic culture of research, which is not only to be observed in the historical sciences in the nineteenth and twentieth centuries but far back into the early modern era, throughout other areas of the humanities and also in the natural sciences.[23] The entanglement of this private institution and the performance of scientific work was a key prerequisite for women's participation in scientific work processes, their management and communication, while the role of women in the public sphere was substantially limited due to gender-specific attributions, and thus their versatile and comprehensive performance was neither recognised or appreciated. Discrimination and persecution dissolved these social orders of the private home by force, and in the course of flight and expulsion it must have been very difficult to restore this domestic order. Against this background, the question arises all the more urgently: how did the existential hardships and fears of exile burden and overshadow the scholars' historical work? What were the consequences of flight and migration for research practice? How did established routines change? How did they affect the roles of women and men and their research practice?

Other research resources were no less threatened in their existence. Under National Socialism, private book collections of Jewish individuals and political opponents as well as the holdings of scientific institutes were often deliberately looted, sold or destroyed.[24] Current research is dominated by the question of the provenance and restitution of these holdings. By contrast, the concrete working contexts in which they were embedded, and the consequences of robbery and loss, are hardly addressed in recent studies.[25] In most cases, loss is only referred to in individual cases, which ultimately made further work impossible. At best, we know about the timely dispatch and safekeeping that secured the valuable collection of books at the Aby Warburg Library in Hamburg, whose holdings were shipped to London in

December 1933.[26] In view of recent studies, the question arises as to whether smaller systems of knowledge organisation proved to be more manageable than the heavy mass of book collections in these imponderable and unstable situations. Already Walter Benjamin observed that a book is merely a transitional medium between two card boxes.[27] Prior to the introduction of digital technology, note-taking and systems of paper slips were widespread technical means of recording and organising data in writing. The mode of organising and using data varied, but as recent studies show, it was directly linked to pragmatic requirements, professional purposes in teaching as well as to methodological considerations.[28]

Finally, another subject concerns the question of epistemic things: What kind of objects are considered relevant and appropriate in the eyes of researchers in order to establish facts? In the history of science, therefore, questions concerning the history of epistemic objects, their conception and selection, and the question of collection and access have received increasing attention.[29] It is only recently that scholars have considered it appropriate and necessary to make statements and produce observations with the explicit consent and cooperation of their informants and their sources. It was common practice to realise research agendas without taking into account the concerns and interests of the persons involved, as in the example of Karl and Charlotte Bühler. The political, financial and also spatial connection of the Vienna Psychological Institute to the city of Vienna and its social-democratic government guaranteed Charlotte Bühler privileged access to children and young people, an essential resource for her empirical psychological studies. Given the political support she and her husband had enjoyed from the Social Democrats as well as her Jewish origin, Charlotte and Karl Bühler were subject to increasing political persecution subsequent to the 'Anschluss' of Austria, and they were forced to leave Vienna. In the United States, Charlotte Bühler had to improvise, and so she set up a back room in a Soup Kitchen in New York to advance her research with the children of waiting mothers.[30] Other émigré scholars working in the sciences, such as Paul Lazarsfeld, were more fortunate and were able to continue their research, or even to set up new laboratories and develop their research more easily.[31]

The research of émigré historians basically required working with source material. One can only assume the loss of immediate proximity to institutions with thematically relevant archive holdings must have immeasurably increased the value of secured material collections – the scholars' 'own archives', comprising of notes, transcripts and copies. It would be very interesting to see how scholars reacted to the loss of valuable working materials. What alternative acquisition and research strategies did émigré historians develop, and how did new projects take shape with other, hitherto unknown but available material collections?

One dimension that comes to the fore in this context is the archival imaginations of historical researchers.[32] Legendary are the dreams of a large archive that would unite all important collections – but primarily the material that oneself recognised as important, unique and therefore as a privileged medium of historical observation and knowledge. The imagined 'Archivkörper',[33] the body of the archive, took on a female form, given the gendered perspective of 'men of science', and the male scholars dressed their material finds, their work with the coveted sources in an erotic and sensual language. The objects of their studies, the great men of history, were also framed in emphatic and emotional terms.[34] It has recently been pointed out that the language of scholarly historians in the twentieth century could not have taken on a less expressively passionate form, especially in the context of questions concerning patriotism and national loyalty of émigré scholars.[35] Following on from the studies on the nineteenth and early twentieth centuries, it would be worthwhile to pursue the question as to how the imago of the 'archive body' was transformed and, in this context, how the (erotic) and sensual discourse of source material in the twentieth century altered in general – not least against the background of changing gender relations in the historical discipline. What material experiences did émigré historians have with unusual historical traditions, and how did they further embrace them? What impulses did their novel material experiences give to their established perspective on source material. What new kind of 'Quellenblick' did they develop?[36]

Émigré scholarship is and will remain an exciting subject for historical research. The international expansion is proving to be extremely productive. This is all the more important due to the national traditions of historical scholarship in Europe and its powerful ramifications up to the present day. Especially in the field of historiographical research, a field in which traditionally national developments are reviewed and studied, these histories are hardly acknowledged or even heard of. Yet, a truly international perspective allows us to relate, compare, connect and, ultimately, to challenge our established views. Therefore, a broader international perspective will deserve even more attention in the future. This is also true for the central question concerning the dynamics of emigration and its repercussions for scholarship. The concrete consequences of political violence and persecution, the question of institutional politics and the appropriation of these politics by émigré scholars, the role of micropolitics and the question of the émigrés' personae in a foreign world – these are all essential elements of émigré scholarship, and above all they played a crucial role in the production of historical knowledge. What is more, a recent strand of studies that have focused on issues such as practices and materiality of historical research warrants new questions. One methodological challenge that remains, however, is that of asymmetrical documentation. Successful émigré historians often left behind extensive documentation, and some of them were actively fashioning their scholarly persona during their lifetime, which contributed to their general fame and encouraged certain directions of interpretation. Much more difficult is the study of less known émigré scholars, who have left fewer material traces – female historians and amateur researchers but also the numerous male researchers who were less successful abroad. In this case, bequests usually do not exist or have been lost, and because of immediate existential and material needs, they were not able to do extensive research during their lifetime – one more reason to advance our historical studies and our methodological reflection.

Notes

1. Daston, 'Die wissenschaftliche Persona', 109–36.
2. Biagioli, 'Galileo the Emblem Maker', 230–58; Shapin, 'The House of Experiment', 373–404.
3. Paul, 'Self-Images of the Historical Profession', 157–71; Saxer, *Quellenblick*; Klausnitzer, Spoerhase and Werle, *Ethos und Pathos der Geisteswissenschaften*; Paul, *How to be a Historian*.
4. Saxer, *Quellenblick*; Smith, *Gender of History*; Tollebeek, 'Salon Vert'; Tollebeek, 'A Stormy Family', 58–72.
5. Schöttler, *Lucie Varga*; idem, 'Lucie Varga', 100–20; Davis, 'Women and the World of the Annales', 121–37.
6. Krohn, *Wissenschaft im Exil*, 71 f.
7. Biagioli, *Galileo, Courtier*; Von Oertzen, *Strategie Verständigung*.
8. Müller, *Geschichte machen*, 602–32.
9. With regard to artists and intellectuals, see Schreckenberger, *Networks of Refugees from Nazi Germany*.
10. Keßler, *Deutsche Historiker im Exil*; Keßler, *Exilerfahrung in Wissenschaft und Politik*.
11. Similar observations can be made in the emerging fields of psychology and sociology when comparing the career paths of scholars Karl and Charlotte Bühler, Paul Lazarsfeld, Egon Brunswick and Marie Jahoda, originally based in Vienna. See Fleck, *Etablierung in der Fremde*; idem, *Transatlantische Bereicherungen*.
12. Berghahn, 'Francis L. Carsten 1911–1998', 504–10, see also Meinschein, *Geschichtsschreibung in der Emigration*.
13. Eckert, 'Notwendige Kooperation', 133–52.
14. Müller, 'Doing Historical Research', 80–103; Nippel, 'Das "forschende Verstehen"', 337–92; Müller, 'Histoire, recherche et politique', 625–56; Berger, 'National Archives'.
15. Stelzel, 'The Second-Generation Émigrés', 287–303; Cornelissen, 'Deutsche Geschichtswissenschaft nach 1945', 17–33; Etzemüller, *Sozialgeschichte*.
16. Ash and Söllner, 'Introduction', 1–19.
17. Thelen, 'The Nation and Beyond', 965–97.
18. Daum, Lehmann, and Sheehan, *The Second Generation*.
19. See the studies by Ute Lemke about the historian Margarete Rothbarth (1887–1953): Lemke, 'Völkerbundinstitut für geistige Zusammenarbeit', 51–59; Lemke, 'La femme', 45–59.
20. Walther, 'Hedwig Hintze', 197–222.

21. Hagner, *Ansichten der Wissenschaftsgeschichte*; Serres, *Eléments d'histoire des sciences*; Biagioli, *The Science Studies Reader*; Müller, 'Geschichte machen', 415–33; Shapin, *Never pure*; Tollebeek, 'L'historien quotidien', 143–67; Friedrich, Müller, and Riordan, *Practices of Historical Research*; Füssel, *Wissensgeschichte*.

22. The yearbook *Exilforschung: Ein internationales Jahrbuch* (1983 ff.) is published by the renowned publisher Text + Kritik and edited by Claus-Dieter Krohn; see for example themed issues on 'Frauen und Exil' Volume 11 (1993), 'Kulturtransfer' Volume 13 (1995), 'Metropolen des Exils' Volume 20 (2002), and most recently 'Archive und Museen' Band 37 (2019).

23. Regarding historical studies: Smith, *Gender of History*; Saxer, *Schärfung des Quellenblicks*; Tollebeek, 'Writing History in the Salon Vert', 35–40; idem, *A Stormy Family*; Passerini and Voglis, *Gender in the Production of History*. With regard to the history of sciences: Schiebinger, 'Maria Winkelmann at the Berlin Academy', 174–200; Lindsay, 'Intimate Inmates', 631–52; Wobbe, *Frauen in Akademie und Wissenschaft*; idem, *Zwischen Vorderbühne und Hinterbühne*, 84–107.

24. Bertz and Dorrmann, *Raub und Restitution*; see especially: Reifenberg, 'NS-Raubgut in deutschen Bibliotheken', 157–60; Grimstead, 'Geplünderte jüdische Archive in Osteuropa', 179–87.

25. But see Krohn, *Bibliotheken und Sammlungen*.

26. The Warburg Institute Library still holds the books from 1930 for research purposes, see Gombrich, *Aby Warburg*.

27. Benjamin, 'Einbahnstraße', 93.

28. Trüper, 'Das KleinKlein der Arbeit', 82–104; idem, 'Unordnungssysteme'; Trüper, *Topography of a Method*.

29. Rheinberger, *Experiment, Differenz, Schrift*; Te Heesen and Spary, *Sammeln als Wissen*; Müller, 'Quellen sammeln'.

30. Benetka, *Psychologie in Wien*; Rollett, 'Charlotte Bühler', 25 f. See for similar observations about Anna Freud's empirical work with children: Zahra, *The Lost Children*, 18, 63 f.

31. Fleck, *Etablierung in der Fremde*; Fleck, *Transatlantische Bereicherungen*.

32. Further stimulating perspectives have been developed in recent studies on the scholar's appearance, see Etzemüller, *Der Auftritt*, as well as by studies on discourses concerning the scholarly body, see Schnicke, *Die männliche Disziplin*.

33. Wimmer, *Archivkörper*. See also Farge, *Le goût de l'archive*; Lüdtke and Nanz, *Laute, Bilder, Texte*.

34. Smith, *Gender of history*, Saxer, *Quellenblick*; Wimmer, *Archivkörper*; Schnicke, *Männliche Disziplin*.

35. See Stelzel, 'Second-Generation Émigrés'.

36. Daniela Saxer coined the term 'Quellenblick' in her fascinating study and defined the concept as the result of three interlinked practices: the practice of ordering, the technique of critique and the discursive description of historical source material. See Saxer, *Quellenblick*.

Bibliography

Ash, Mitchell G., and Alfons Söllner. 'Introduction: Forced Migration and Scientific Change after 1933', in Mitchell G. Ash and Alfons Söllner (eds), *Forced Migration and Scientific Change: Emigré German-Speaking Scientists and Scholars after 1933* (Cambridge: Cambridge University Press, 1996), 1–19.

Asmus, Sylvia, Doerte Bischoff, and Burcu Dogramaci (eds). 'Archive und Museen des Exils'. *Exilforschung* 37 (2019).

Benetka, Gerhard. *Psychologie in Wien: Sozial- und Theoriegeschichte des Wiener Psychologischen Instituts 1922–1938*. Wien: WUV, 1995.

Benjamin, Walter. 'Einbahnstraße', in Walter Opitz (ed.), *Walter Benjamin: Ein Lesebuch* (Frankfurt am Main: Suhrkamp, 1996), 75–139.

Berger, Stefan. 'The Role of National Archives in Constructing National Master Narratives in Europe'. *Archival Science* 13 (2013), 1–22.

Berghahn, Volker. 'Francis L. Carsten 1911–1998'. *Geschichte und Gesellschaft* 25 (1999), 504–10.

Bertz, Inga, and Michael Dorrmann (eds). *Raub und Restitution: Kulturgut aus jüdischem Besitz von 1933 bis heute.* Göttingen: Wallstein Verlag, 2009.

Biagioli, Mario. 'Galileo the Emblem Maker'. *Isis* 81 (1990), 230–58.

———. *Galileo, Courtier: The Practice of Science in the Culture of Absolutism, Science and its Conceptual Foundations.* Chicago: University of Chicago Press, 1993.

Biagioli, Mario (ed.). *The Science Studies Reader.* New York: Routledge, 1999.

Cornelissen, Christoph, 'Deutsche Geschichtswissenschaft nach 1945: Zwischen nationalen Traditionen und transnationalen Öffnungen', in Ulrich Pfeil (ed.), *Die Rückkehr der deutschen Geschichtswissenschaft in die 'Ökumene der Historiker': Ein wissenschaftsgeschichtlicher Ansatz* (München: Oldenbourg, 2014), 17–33.

Daston, Lorraine. 'Die wissenschaftliche Persona: Arbeit und Berufung', in Wobbe, Theresa (ed.), *Zwischen Vorderbühne und Hinterbühne. Beiträge zum Wandel der Geschlechterbeziehungen in der Wissenschaft vom 17. Jahrhundert bis zur Gegenwart* (Bielefeld: Transcript, 2003), 109–36.

Daum, Andreas W., Hartmut Lehmann, and James J. Sheehan (eds). *The Second Generation: Émigrés from Nazi Germany as Historians.* Oxford: Berghahn Books, 2016.

Davis, Natalie Z. 'Women and the World of the Annales'. *History Workshop Journal* 33 (1992), 121–37.

Eckert, Astrid. 'Notwendige Kooperation: Westdeutsche Zeitgeschichte als transnationales Projekt in den 1950er Jahren', in Ulrich Pfeil (ed.), *Die Rückkehr der deutschen Geschichtswissenschaft in die Ökumene der Historiker nach 1945: Ein wissenschaftsgeschichtlicher Ansatz* (München: Oldenbourg, 2008), 133–52.

Etzemüller, Thomas. *Sozialgeschichte als politische Geschichte: Werner Conze und die Neuorientierung der westdeutschen Geschichtswissenschaft nach 1945.* München: Oldenbourg, 2001.

———. *Der Auftritt: Performance in der Wissenschaft.* Bielefeld: Transcript, 2019.

Farge, Arlette. *Le goût de l'archive.* Paris: Seuil, 1989.

Fleck, Christian. *Transatlantische Bereicherungen: Zur Erfindung der empirischen Sozialforschung.* Frankfurt am Main: Suhrkamp, 2007.

———. *Etablierung in der Fremde: Vertriebene Wissenschaftler in den USA nach 1933 Frankfurt am Main.* New York: Campus Verlag, 2015.

Friedrich, Markus, Philipp Müller, and Michael Riordan (eds). 'Practices of Historical Research in Archives and Libraries from the Eighteenth to the Nineteenth Century'. *History of Humanities* 2 (2017).

Füssel, Marian. *Wissensgeschichte.* Stuttgart: Franz Steiner Verlag, 2019.

Gombrich, Ernst Hans. *Aby Warburg: An Intellectual Biography.* Chicago, IL: University of Chicago Press, 1986.

Grimstead, Patricia K. 'Geplünderte jüdische Archive in Osteuropa: Kriegsbeute aus dem ehemaligen Sonderarchiv in Moskau', in Inga Bertz and Michael Dorrmann (eds), *Raub und Restitution: Kulturgut aus jüdischem Besitz von 1933 bis heute* (Göttingen: Wallstein Verlag, 2009), 179–87.

Hagner, Michael (ed.). *Ansichten der Wissenschaftsgeschichte.* Frankfurt am Main: Fischer, 2001.

Keßler, Mario. *Exilerfahrung in Wissenschaft und Politik: Remigrierte Historiker in der frühen DDR.* Köln: Böhlau, 2001.

Keßler, Mario (ed.). *Deutsche Historiker im Exil (1933–1945): Ausgewählte Studien.* Berlin: Metropol, 2005.

Klausnitzer, Ralf, Carlos Spoerhase, and Dirk Werle (eds). *Ethos und Pathos der Geisteswissenschaften: Konfigurationen der wissenschaftlichen Persona seit 1750.* Berlin: De Gruyter, 2015.

Krohn, Claus-Dieter. *Wissenschaft im Exil. Deutsche Sozial- und Wirtschaftswissenschaftler in den USA und die New School for Social Research*. Frankfurt am Main: Campus Verlag, 1987.
Krohn, Claus-Dieter (ed.). 'Metropolen des Exils'. *Exilforschung* 20 (2002).
Krohn, Claus-Dieter, Erwin Rotermund, and Lutz Winckler (eds). 'Frauen und Exil: Zwischen Anpassung und Selbstbehauptung'. *Exilforschung* 11 (1993).
―――. 'Kulturtransfer im Exil'. *Exilforschung* 13 (1995).
―――. 'Bibliotheken und Sammlungen'. *Exilforschung* 29 (2011).
Lemke, Ute. 'Das Pariser Völkerbundinstitut für geistige Zusammenarbeit und die aus Deutschland geflüchteten Intellektuellen', in Anne Saint Sauveur-Henn (ed.), *Fluchtziel Paris. Die deutschsprachige Emigration 1933–1940* (Berlin: Metropol, 2002), 51–59.
―――. 'La femme, la clandestine de l'histoire. Margarete Rothbarth: Ein Engagement für den Völkerbund'. *Lendemains: Études comparées sur la France* 37 (2012), 45–59.
Lindsay, Debra. 'Intimate Inmates: Wives, Households and Science in Nineteenth Century America'. *Isis* 89 (1998), 631–52.
Lüdtke, Alf, and Tobias Nanz (ed.). *Laute, Bilder, Texte: Register des Archivs*. Göttingen: Vandenhoeck & Ruprecht, 2015.
Meinschein, Birte. *Geschichtsschreibung in der Emigration: Deutschsprachige Historikerinnen und Historiker in Großbritannien*. Berlin, 2020.
Müller, Philipp. 'Geschichte machen: Überlegungen zu lokal-spezifischen Praktiken in der Geschichtswissenschaft und ihren epistemischen Konsequenzen: Ein Literaturbericht'. *Historische Anthropologie* 12 (2004), 415–33.
―――. 'Doing Historical Research in the Early Nineteenth Century: Leopold Ranke, the Archive policy, and the Relazioni of the Venetian Republic'. *Storia della Storiografia* 56 (2009), 80–103.
―――. 'Histoire, recherche et politique en Mitteleuropa 1800–1850'. *Annales: Histoire, Sciences Sociales* 74 (2019), 625–56.
―――. *Geschichte machen: Historisches Forschen und die Politik der Archive*. Göttingen: Wallstein, 2019.
―――. 'Quellen sammeln, Geschichte schreiben: Zur Materialität historischen Wissens im 19. Jahrhundert'. *Historische Zeitschrift* 311 (2020), 602–32.
Nippel, Wilfried. 'Das "forschende Verstehen": Die Objektivität des Historikers und die Funktion der Archive: Zum Kontext von Droysens Geschichtstheorie', in Stefan Rebenich and Hans-Ulrich Wiemer (eds), *Johann Gustav Droysen (1808–1884): Philosophie und Politik, Historie und Philologie* (Frankfurt am Main: Campus, 2012), 337–92.
Passerini, Luisa, and Voglis Polymeris (eds). *Gender in the Production of History*. Florence: EUI, 1999.
Paul, Herman. 'Self-images of the Historical Profession: Idealized Practices and Myths of Origin'. *Storia della storiografia* 59 (2011), 157–71.
―――. *How to be a Historian: Scholarly Personae in Historical Studies 1800–2000*. Manchester: Manchester University Press, 2019.
Reifenberg, Bernd. 'NS-Raubgut in deutschen Bibliotheken', in Inga Bertz and Michael Dorrmann (eds), *Raub und Restitution: Kulturgut aus jüdischem Besitz von 1933 bis heute* (Göttingen: Wallstein Verlag, 2009), 157–60.
Rheinberger, Hans-Jörg. *Experiment, Differenz, Schrift: Zur Geschichte epistemischer Dinge*. Marburg an der Lahn: Basilisken-Presse, 1992.
Rollett, Brigitte. 'Charlotte Bühler: Porträt einer anspruchsvollen Wissenschaftlerin', in Lieselotte Ahnert (ed.), *Charlotte Bühler und die Entwicklungspsychologie* (Göttingen: V&R Unipress, 2015), 19–29.
Saxer, Daniela. *Die Schärfung des Quellenblicks: Forschungspraktiken in der Geschichtswissenschaft 1840–1914*. München: Oldenbourg, 2014.
Schiebinger, Londa. 'Maria Winkelmann at the Berlin Academy: A Turning Point for Women in Science'. *Isis* 78 (1987), 174–200.

Schnicke, Falko. *Die männliche Disziplin: Zur Vergeschlechtlichung der deutschen Geschichtswissenschaft 1780–1900*. Göttingen: Wallstein, 2015.

Schöttler, Peter. 'Lucie Varga: A Central European Refugee in the Circle of the French 'Annales' 1934–1941'. *History Workshop Journal* 33 (1992), 100–20.

Schöttler, Peter (ed.). *Lucie Varga: Les autorités invisible: Une historienne autrichienne aux Annales dans les années trente*. Paris: Cerf, 1991.

Schreckenberger, Helga (ed.). *Networks of Refugees from Nazi Germany: Continuities, Reorientations, and Collaborations in Exile*. Leiden: Brill, 2016.

Serres, Michel (ed.). *Eléments d'histoire des sciences*. Paris: Bordas, 1989.

Shapin, Steven. 'The House of Experiment in Seventeen-Century England'. *Isis* 79 (1988), 373–404.

———. *Never Pure: Historical Studies of Science as if it was Produced by People with Bodies, Situated in Time, Space, Culture, and Society, and Struggling for Credibility and Authority*. Baltimore: Johns Hopkins University, 2010.

Smith, Bonnie G. *The Gender of History: Men, Women and Historical Practice*. Cambridge, MA: Harvard University Press, 1998.

Stelzel, Philipp. *History after Hitler: A Transatlantic Experience, Philadelphia*. University of Pennsylvania Press, 2019.

———. 'The Second-Generation Émigrés' Impact on German Historiography', in Andreas W. Daum (ed.), *The Second Generation: Émigrés from Nazi Germany as Historians* (New York: Berghahn Books, 2015), 287–303.

Te Heesen, Anke, and Emma C. Spary (eds). *Sammeln als Wissen: Das Sammeln und seine wissenschaftsgeschichtliche Bedeutung*. Göttingen: Wallstein Verlag, 2001.

Thelen, David. 'The Nation and Beyond: Transnational Perspectives on United States History'. *Journal of American History* 86 (1999), 965–97.

Tollebeek, Jo. 'A Stormy Family: Paul Fredericq and the Formation of an Academic Historical Community in the Nineteenth Century'. *Storia della storiografia* 53 (2008), 58–72.

———. 'Writing History in the Salon Vert'. *Storia della Storiografia* 46 (2004), 35–40.

———. 'L'historien quotidien: Pour une anthropologie de la science historique moderne'. *Revue Suisse d'Histoire* 61 (2011), 143–67.

Trüper, Henning. 'Das KleinKlein der Arbeit: Die Notizführung des Historikers François Louis Ganshof'. *Österreichische Zeitschrift für Geschichtswissenschaften* 18 (2007), 82–104.

———. 'Unordnungssysteme: Zur Praxis der Notizführung bei Johan Huizinga', *Zeitenblicke* 10 (2011).

———. *Topography of a Method: François Louis Ganshof and the Writing of History*. Tübingen: Mohr Siebeck, 2014.

Von Oertzen, Christine. *Strategie Verständigung: Zur Transnationalen Vernetzung von Akademikerinnen 1917–1955*. Göttingen: Wallstein, 2012.

Walther, Peter T. 'Hedwig Hintze in den Niederlanden 1939–1942: Ein Werkstattbericht', in Mario Keßler (ed.), *Deutsche Historiker im Exil 1933–1945: Ausgewählte Studien* (Berlin: Metropol, 2005), 197–222.

Wimmer, Mario. *Archivkörper: Eine Geschichte historischer Einbildungskraft*. Konstanz: KUP, 2012.

Wobbe, Theresa (ed.). *Frauen in Akademie und Wissenschaft: Arbeitsorte und Forschungspraktiken 1700–2000*. Berlin: Akademie Verlag, 2002.

———. *Zwischen Vorderbühne und Hinterbühne: Beiträge zum Wandel der Geschlechterbeziehungen in der Wissenschaft vom 17. Jahrhundert bis zur Gegenwart*. Bielefeld: Transcript, 2003.

Zahra, Tara. *The Lost Children: Reconstructing Europe's Families after World War II*. Cambridge, MA: HUP, 2011.

Index

A History of Modern Germany (1934), 115
A Sketch of the History of Portugal (1928), 211
Aby Warburg Library, 243
Academic Assistance Council, 8, 76, 80
Across Cultural Borders (2002), 15n
Aczél, Tamás, 161
Adorno, Theodor, 103
aestheticism, 48, 163
Africa, 9, 10, 234n
 Southern, 10
Age of Extremes (1994), 25
age of extremes 4, 173, 184, 188, 224, 239
Alföldi, András, 157, 163, 195
Altamira, Rafael, 6
America, American, 27, 45, 49, 51, 74, 76–80, 83, 94–96, 102–03, 112, 114, 117–18, 125–33, 141–43, 146–51, 194–99, 211, 215
 California, 12, 64, 67, 188, 194–95
 Chicago, 11, 24, 50–51, 64
 New York, 9, 12, 24, 125, 129, 142, 238, 244
 Santa Barbara, 115, 188, 194–96, 199
 society, 83, 127, 130, 132
 Wisconsin, 67
 See also United States of America
American Council on Germany, 4
American Historical Association, 4, 49, 118
American Historical Review, the, 52

American Jewish, 30
American Office for War Information, 4
American Philosophical Association, 97, 104n
American philosophy, 99
American Slavic Studies, 195
anarchist, 63, 66
Andics, Erzsébet, 156
Annales, 35, 130, 191, 208, 232, 238, 240
Annales Economies, 230
anthropology, 143
anti-foreignism, 75, 79, 86
antisemitism, 27, 29, 74–76, 84–86, 111, 119, 146, 151, 240
Archive of Czechs and Slovaks Abroad in Chicago, 7
archives, 8, 14, 60, 62, 148–49, 196, 229, 231, 238, 241
Argentina, 9, 214–216
Armenian genocide, 68
Arndt, Ernst Moritz, 158
Aronson, Stanisław, 1
artists, 75, 77, 111, 131, 145–46
Aryamanesh, Kourosh, 63
Aryans, 74–75
Aschheim, Steven, 113, 118
Ash, Mitchell G., 46
Asia, 9, 10, 36, 162, 174
assimilation, 29, 69, 132, 146, 183
Association of Feminists, 147
Atlantic community, 130

Auschwitz, 36, 63, 67
Australia, Australian 3, 101,
Austria, 75, 142, 148–49, 191, 238, 240
  Vienna, 26–31, 98, 128, 140–42, 146–47, 193, 238, 244, 246n
Austrian History Yearbook, 198
Austro-Hungarian empire, 128, 146
authoritarianism, 213
autobiographies, 25, 28, 139, 144, 150, 242

Bainton, Roland H., 96
Bakhmeteff Archive at Columbia University, 7
Balkan patriotism, 180
Balkan Studies, 179–80, 188, 192–95, 198–99
Balkan Wars –1912/13, 191
Balkans, 174–77, 184, 192–98
Baltic states, 3
Baráth, Tibor, 156, 162
barbarism, 13, 37
Baron, Hans, 14, 50, 94
BBC, 159–61, 164
Becker, Carl, 33
Beethoven, 46
Belgium, 12
  Brussels, 10, 159
Bell, Susan Groag, 25
Below, Georg von, 48
Benjámin, László, 161
Benjamin, Walter, 66, 244
Bentham, Jeremy, 158
Berdiaieff, Nikolai, 158
Berger, Stefan, 1, 108, 237
Bergson, Henri, 158
Berlin's Hochschule für Politik, 4
Beveridge, William, 76, 80–81
biographies, 23, 47, 118, 125, 147, 149–50, 173
biologism, 158
Bismarck, Otto von, 28, 111, 158
Björk, Ragnar, 14
Blanc, Louis, 9
Bloch, Marc, 208, 229, 238
Bobula, Ida, 156, 162
Bogyay, Tamás, 157
Bohemia, Bohemian, 13, 25, 28, 30
Boia, Lucian, 198

Bolgár, Elek, 156
bourgeois
  family, 128, 141
  Serbian, 188
  social strata, 53, 159, 188–89, 206
  Bourgeois Experience: Victoria to Freud, the (1984), 37
bourgeois feminist movement, 141
Bourgeois Radical Party, 141
Braudel, Fernand, 192, 227, 229, 231, 238, 240
Brazil, 225, 227, 231,
Britain, British, 3, 5, 7– 8, 10, 14, 24, 26, 28, 68, 76, 81–82, 111, 142, 160
  See also England, United Kingdom
Brooklyn College in New York, 12
Brzezinski, Zbigniew, 131
Bühler, Charlotte, 244
Bühler, Karl, 244
Bulgaria, 174, 183
Burckhardt, Jacob, 52, 104, 163
Burke, Peter,
  'double deprovincialization', 14, 124
Byzantine studies, 176–180, 182–184

Caetano, Marcelo, 224, 231
Cambridge University, 24, 34, 38, 193,
Canada, 7, 25, 132
Carsten, Francis L., 195, 239
Carter, Jimmy, 132, 240
Castro, Americo, 6, 215
Catholicism, 5, 48, 128, 161, 211, 224
Cedrón, Jorge, 67
Central European University, 28
Chae-ho, Sin, 63
China, Chinese, 8, 11, 34, 58–59, 62–63, 68
  Cultural Revolution, 68
  Kuomintang, 8
Christian humanists, 164
Christian personalism, 158, 161, 164
civil wars, 2
Civil Rights Movement, 34
CNRS (Center national de la recherche scientifique), 226–27, 230, 231
Cohn, Alfred E., 80
Cold War, 2, 3, 7, 33, 125, 127, 131, 133, 195, 224
Collegium Carolinum in Munich, 7

Columbia University, 78, 113, 127, 129, 133, 147
communism, communist, 3, 6–9, 13, 33–35, 59, 64, 111, 127, 161–63, 166n, 180–83, 188–92, 233n
anti-Communism, 11, 13
Comte, August, 158, 214
concentration camps, 63, 68, 72n, 127, 194
conservatism, 5, 36, 102, 111, 229
conventionalism, 53
cooperativism, 213, 218
Cornell University, 67, 80
cosmopolitanism, cosmopolitan, 23, 26, 30, 36, 51, 76, 205–06, 208, 212, 218–19
Crisis of German Ideology, the (1964), 35, 116
Croatia, 174, 181, 184
Croce, Benedetto, 6, 164, 208
Cuba, 24
Culianu, Ioan, 64
culture, cultural 11, 26–31, 33, 37, 54, 76, 95, 102–03, 124–26, 131, 160, 162, 164, 165n, 176–77, 183, 189, 199, 243
cultural anxieties, 79
cultural capital, 46, 51, 189, 242
cultural critic, 66
of knowledge, 134
Czechoslovakia, 13, 25, 33, 63, 130, 150 174, 178, 180
Prague, 6, 7, 13, 31, 33, 173, 175, 179, 234n

d'Olwer, Lluís Nicolau, 4
da Silva, José Gentil, 225
Daum, Andreas, 47
De Baets, Antoon, 3
de Carvalho, Joaquim Barradas, 225, 227
Deák, István, 195
decolonisation, 3
Deér, József, 157, 162, 163
dehumanisation, 216
democracy, democratic, 34, 59, 111, 126, 207, 212, 244
anti-, 117
English, 160, 163, 164
depression, 63, 67, 68
Déry, Tibor, 161

diaspora, 26, 68
black African, 10
historiography, 3
dictatorship, 6, 9–10, 14, 59, 64, 69–70, 111, 145, 163–64, 189, 207, 210–13, 216–18, 224, 233n, 234n, 239, 240
Die Habsburger Monarchie 1848–1918 (1973), 197
Dilthey, Wilhelm, 104, 158
diplomatic protests, 61
discrimination, 1, 13, 34
gender, 5
structural, 242
diversity, 6, 28, 29, 30–31, 38, 110, 115, 119, 128
dogmatism, 48, 214
Dominican Republic, 63
Đorđević, Dimitrije, 188–99, 241
Dragnich, Alex N., 196
Dubnow, Simon, 63
Duggan, Stephen, 74–86

East European Quarterly, 198
Eckel, Jan, 50
Einstein, Albert, 81
Einstein, Carl, 66
Emergency Committee in Europe, 82
emigration, 1–2, 6, 23, 59, 76, 80, 95, 97, 110–11, 117, 132, 141, 143, 150–51, 153n, 156–65, 166n, 174–75, 177, 182, 184, 188, 195, 212, 237, 239, 240, 242, 245
Russian, 125, 174
empiricism, 33, 97
Encyclopedia of the Social Sciences (1935), 76
Encyclopedia of Historians and Historical Writing (1999), 176
England, 23, 24, 27, 81, 114, 141, 147, 148, 159, 160, 166n, 193, 215, 218
See also Britain, United Kingdom
English
civil war, 8
working classes, 159
Enlightenment, 33–38, 113, 197–98, 217
Enlightenment, the (1973), 34
Epstein, Catherine, 36, 143, 145, 150
Epstein, Klaus, 114, 116,17
Erdmann, Karl Dietrich, 116
Estonia, 3, 71n

ethnic minorities, 131–32
ethnocentrism, 193, 199
Eurasianism, 12
Europe
  central, 6, 10, 27
  east Central, 130, 198
  eastern, 7, 126–33, 164, 193–95
  southeastern, 174, 176, 180
  western, 15, 128, 176, 192–93, 206
European War – 1914, 191
Europeanism, 206
exclusion, 5, 9, 33, 225, 234n
exile
  historiography, 3–4, 6, 8, 10, 14
  scholarship, 3, 7, 9, 59
extremisms, 214
École Russe de Hautes Études Sociales, 9

fascism, fascist, 3, 6, 8, 63–64, 66, 79, 113, 126, 140, 144, 157, 180–81, 183, 233n
Fay, Sidney B., 115
Febvre, Lucien, 208, 227, 229, 238
Feldman, Gerald, 118
feudalism, 231
films, 61–62, 67
First World War, 9, 12, 78, 175, 190–91, 193, 197, 206
Fischer-Galati, Stephen, 195–96
Fischers, Fritz, 115
Foucault, Michel, 37
France, 3, 6, 8, 9, 62–63, 66, 82, 125, 129, 174, 178, 213, 218, 225–32, 234n, 238, 241
  Paris, 6, 8, 9, 10, 62–64, 66–67, 81, 125, 127–29, 159, 175, 207, 209–13, 228, 231, 233n, 238
  Sorbonne, 145, 231
Francisco Franco Historia de un mesianismo (1964), 62
Francoism, 6
Frankfurt School, 78
Free University Berlin, 109, 111–12
French Revolution, 67, 225
Freud, Sigmund, 37
Fuchs, Walther Peter, 109

Gasset, José Ortega, 205–20, 241
Gay, Peter, 23, 31–32, 36, 110, 113–14, 144

Geistesgeschichte, 103, 157–58, 160, 162–64
gender, 2, 4–5, 142–43, 145, 151, 238, 242–43, 245
genocides, 2
geography, 15n
Georgescu, Vlad, 64
German Historical Association, 110–11
German Historical Institute, 144–45
Germany, German, 4–5, 6, 10–15, 23–24, 27–28, 30–37, 49, 50, 52, 54, 63, 66, 67–68, 74–75, 77, 80, 94–96, 102–04, 110, 112–18, 125, 129–30, 142, 144, 146–47, 151, 179–80, 199, 240, 242
  Berlin, 4, 6, 24–32, 34, 46, 52–53, 95–98, 102, 112–13, 115, 141, 146, 175
  Bundestag, 110
  East, 33, 110
  Gestapo, 63, 66
  Göttingen, 32– 33, 98, 112
  Hamburg, 24, 36, 27, 115, 243
  Heidelberg, 96, 99
  Marburg, 95, 96, 207
  Munich, 25, 29, 64, 159
  Nuremberg Laws, 75
  Weimar Republic, 24, 36, 51, 146, 150
  West, 5, 12, 110–11, 113, 117
German Conception of History, the (1968), 35– 36
German Opposition to Hitler, the (1961), 114
Geschichte in Wissenschaft und Unterricht, 116
Gilbert, Felix, 6, 23, 46, 49–50, 52, 94, 113
Gimpera, Pere Bosch, 6, 215
globalisation, 2
Gobetti, Piero, 63
Godinho, Vitorino Magalhães, 225–27, 229, 230
Goethe, Johann Wolfgang, 28, 46
Golden Age, 190–91
Görres, Joseph, 158
Great Depression, 13, 75
Great Historians from Antiquity to 1800 (1989), 198
Great Historians of the Modern Age (1991), 198
Greece, Greek, 11, 102, 106n, 130, 174, 178–79, 192–193
Gross, Feliks, 128, 132
Gross, Jan T., 195

Guerricabeitia, José Martínez, 62
Gumplowicz, Ludwig, 158

Habsburg empire, 10, 194, 197
Halecki, Oskar, 126, 128–131, 180, 240
Hamerow, Theodore, 110
Harvard University, 62, 115, 133
Harvard-Ukrainian Research Institute, 7
Hatvany, Lajos, 156
Hauser, Arnold, 156
Háy, Gyula, 161
Heavenly City of the Eighteenth-Century Philosopher, the (1932), 33
Hebrew University in Palestine, 77
Hegel, Wilhelm, 206
hegemony, 30, 111, 214, 217
Heidegger, Martin, 37, 95–96
Heller, Emmy, 5
Hempel, Carl, 97–98
Herder, Johann Gottfried 35–36
heritage, 26, 36, 117, 126–27, 130, 208
heterodoxy, 38
Higher Institute of Overseas Studies in Lisbon, 226
Hilberg, Raul, 25, 113
Hilferding, Rudolf, 63, 66
Hintze, Hedwig, 67
historians
  American, 10, 46, 114, 116, 139, 180, 199
  Basque, 10, 62–63
  bourgeois, 6–7, 190
  Catholic, 48
  communist, 9, 234n
  Croatian, 174
  cultural, 124
  German, 12–13, 46, 48, 51–53, 109, 110, 113–19, 144–45, 240–41
  Hungarian, 143, 161, 195
  Islamist, 5
  Jewish, 5, 63, 66–67
  labour, 5
  migration, 46
  nationalist, 47
  non-Muslim, 5
  Polish, 195, 240
  protestant, 5
  rightwing, 156
  social, 3, 118–19
  Spanish, 8, 60, 67

women, 5, 145–46
Yugoslav, 174, 183
Historical Abstracts (1972), 198
historical novelists, 62
historicism, 2
historicity, 208, 237
historiography, 45, 239
  American, 47, 196, 198
  ancient, 11
  Anglo-American, 197
  Austrian, 197 British, 17n
  Croatian, 183–84, 198
  diaspora, 3
  European, 47
  of exile, 6, 13
  German, 17n, 35, 51–52, 115
  Greek, 11
  history of, 15, 36, 242
  Hungarian, 156
  Marxist, 162, 190, 196
  National Socialism, 119
  nineteenth-century, 53
  Polish, 128
  Portuguese, 225, 229 postwar West German, 5 Serbian, 189, 190, 197–99
  Soviet, 196
  traditional, 190
  West German, 199
  Western, 130
  Yugoslavian, 189, 194
Historische Zeitschrift, 117
historism, 35–37, 208
history
  American, 112
  American social, 199
  Balkan, 188, 191, 193, 198–99
  Black, 10
  cultural, 24, 110, 113, 157
  economic, 141, 157, 182, 196, 229, 232, 241
  European, 1, 112, 128, 157, 196
  German, 28, 110–18, 120n, 241
  Hungarian, 157, 163, 166n, 167n
  intellectual, 24, 52, 118, 157, 165n, 242
  Italian, 6
  labour, 25
  of philosophy, 103
  of sexuality, 113
  Polish, 8, 128, 130

public, 163, 164, 167n
Slavic, 177
social, 35, 37, 47, 118, 130, 162, 180, 192, 196–97, 199, 229, 241
Spanish, 6
teleological, 12
women's, 143, 151
History and Theory – journal, 101
History as a system (1935), 219
history of philosophy, 96, 97
History of Russia, the (1929), 180
Hitchins, Keith, 195
Hitler, Adolf, 32, 36, 63, 66, 75–76, 111, 115–17, 140, 143, 146–47, 151, 159, 179–81
Hobsbawm, Eric J., 24, 26, 35, 37
Hoffmann, Peter, 117
Holborn, Hajo, 4, 23, 46, 109, 112, 114, 117–18
Holland, 213
Holocaust, 1, 36, 113, 218
Home Army, 1
home country, 60–61, 65, 68–69, 110, 151, 226, 238
homeland, 3, 10–14, 125, 145, 151, 164, 175, 214, 228, 232, 241
homogeneity, 30
Hong Kong, 62
Horváth, Mihály, 156
human rights, 3, 35–36, 65, 70
humanism, 94, 96
humanities, 8, 102, 126–27, 142, 174–77, 181, 239, 243
Humboldt, Alexander von, 28
Hume, David, 37
Humphrey, Hubert, 131, 240
Hungarian
  historians, 139–42, 145, 147–49, 151, 156–57, 159, 160–64
  revolution, 160
Hungary, 15, 140–42, 146–50, 157, 159–60, 162, 164, 191
  Budapest, 28, 37, 140–42, 146, 160, 165n
Huttenbach, Henry, 27
hypernationalisms, 2

Iberian nations, 205
Iberian Peninsula, 15, 205

ideological instrumentalisation, 4
Igersheimer, Georg Gerson, 25
Iggers, Georg, 13, 23, 32, 34, 37
Iggers, Wilma, 13, 25, 28–30, 33, 38
Iglesia, Ramón, 60, 67
illiberalism, 74
Illustrious Immigrants: The Intellectual Migration from Europe, 1930–41 (1968), 144
Illyés, Gyula, 161, 162
imperialism, 158
India, 68, 206
'insider/outsider' dichotomy, 27, 31
Institute for Advanced Study in Princeton, 81, 113
Institute for Balkan Studies in Belgrade, 194
Institute of International Education, New York, 76
intellectualism, 208
intellectual isolation, 50
International Federation of Human Rights, 3
internationalism, 14, 75, 76
Iran, 58, 63, 64
  Ayatollah, 64
  Islamic Republic of Iran, 5
Iranian Revolution, 63
Ireland, Irish, 49
Iron Curtain, 7, 33
irrationalism, 37
Islam, Islamic
  nation states, 5
Israel, Israeli, 63, 225, 231
  Mossad, 63
  Tel Aviv, 1
Italy, Italian, 6, 13, 27, 49, 63–64, 94, 96, 104n, 144, 150–51, 164, 231
Iványi-Grünwald Jr., Béla, 157, 159–60, 162, 164, 239

Jajko, Walter, 132
Janson, Horst Woldemar, 27
Janssen, Johannes, 48
Japan, Japanese, 2, 63, 129, 162
Jaspers, Karl, 95, 158
Jászi, Oszkár, 156, 160
Jefferson, Thomas, 158
Jelačić, Aleksije, 176, 180–82, 184

Jelavich, Barbara, 195
Jew, Jewish, 1, 5, 6, 8, 25–31, 36, 49, 63–64, 66–67, 74–75, 77, 81, 84–86, 94–95, 98, 118–19, 126, 129, 140, 145–46, 148, 150–52, 159, 165n, 243–44
Hungarian-Jewish, 142
Johns Hopkins University, 52
Johnson, Alvin, 76, 86
Joós, Tibor Badiny, 156
Journal of Contemporary History, 113, 197
Journal of Philosophy, 98–99
journalism, journalists, 7, 60, 62, 75, 103, 163–64, 167n

Kant, Immanuel, Kantian, 95, 100, 103–04, 206, 217
Neo-Kantian, 95, 98–99, 206, 208, 217
Kassák, Lajos, 161
Kater, Michael H., 47
Kayyali, Abdul-Wahhab, 63
Kazhdan, Alexander, 195
Kennedy, John F., 131, 240
Kerényi, Jr Károly, 157, 163
Király, Béla, 195
Klemperer, Klemens von, 24, 116–17
Kondakov Institute in Prague, 7, 173, 179
Korea, 63
Koselleck, Reinhart, 12
Kotschnig, Walter, 76, 80, 82
Krieger, Leonard, 110, 118
Kristeller, Paul Oskar, 23, 94–04, 104n, 239, 241–42
Kucharzewski, Jan, 126
Kukiel, Marian, 4
Kultura journal, 127, 131, 133

labour movements, 190, 192
Lamberti, Marjorie, 78, 143
Lampe, John R., 196
Lamprecht, Karl, 48
Lange, Oskar, 126
Laqueur, Walter, 24, 113, 145, 197
Latin America, 6, 9–10, 26, 214
Latvia, 3, 63
League of Nations, 75, 82, 128
Lebonon
  Beirut, 63
  Palestinian diaspora, 63

Lelewel, Joachim, 10
Lerner, Gerda, 25, 143, 150–51
Lessing, Theodor, 63
Levin, Isaac Osipovich, 63
liberalism, 36, 74, 102, 158, 213,
liberal values, 86
Liebreich, Aenne, 66
literature, 15, 47, 67–68, 77, 127, 143, 145, 152n, 158, 160, 162, 165n, 191, 196, 228, 230
  on suicide, 68
Lithuania, 3
  Polish-Lithuanian Commonwealth, 128
Liu, Henry, 64
Logical positivism, 97, 98
London School of Economics, 76, 129
Lukács, György, 156, 164

MacKenzie, David, 196
Maier, Charles, 118
Malagón, Javier, 6
Malinowski, Bronisław, 126, 129
Málnási, Ödön, 156
Mannheim, Karl, 156
Marburg School, 206
Marczali, Henrik, 147
Maritain, Jacques, 158
Marks, Shula, 60
Marx, Karl, 9, 100, 158, 196
Marxism, 98, 100, 190, 196
materialism, 158, 189
Max Horkheimer circle, 101
Max Planck Institute for History in Göttingen, 112
Mayer, Arno, 110, 118
Mayer, Gustav, 5, 50
McCarthy, Joseph, 59
Meinecke, Friedriche, 4, 27, 36, 46, 49, 51–52, 112, 118
Méray, Tibor, 161
Mexico, 4, 64, 67, 215
Michelet, Jules, 8, 28
Mickiewicz, Adam, 8
micropolitics, 2, 238–39, 243, 245
Middle Ages, 66–67, 195, 212
migration, 1–3, 51, 54, 124, 143, 174, 185, 239, 243
Miskolczy, Gyula, 157, 163
Modern Germany (1956), 114

modernisation, 7, 12, 146, 193, 197, 199
modernism, modernists, 35, 113, 120n
Mommsen, Hans, 50, 102, 117
Mommsen, Theodor, 67
Mommsen, Wolfgang J., 47, 113
Montalembert, Charles de, 158
moral relativism, 35
morality, moralism, 35, 48, 36–37, 39
Mošin, Vladimir, 176, 178–79, 182–83
Mosse, George, 24, 110, 113, 116, 117–18, 144
Mounier, Emmanuel, 158
Müller, Philipp, 2, 108, 238
multiplicity, 26
Murrow, Edward R., 79, 80, 83
Museum of Russian Culture in San Francisco, 7
Mussolini, Benito, 63, 144
My German Question (1998), 36

National Association for the Advancement of Colored People, 34
national historical master narratives, 6, 10
National History and New Nationalism in the Twenty-First Century (2021), 15n
National Socialism, Nazi, 4–7, 10–14, 23–25, 30, 32, 36–37, 52, 63–64, 68, 74–75, 77, 84–85, 94, 96, 111–14, 116–19, 125, 129, 146, 199, 240, 243
nationalism, 3, 29, 36, 158, 193, 197, 206
  anti-, 30
  Balkan, 193
  Jewish, 30
nationalists, 5, 8, 10, 26, 30, 37, 47, 52, 63, 110–11, 133, 224, 241
Nations and Nationalism since 1780 (1990), 30
nativism, 74, 75, 78, 85
natural sciences, 98, 99, 102, 238–39, 243
Nekrich, Alexander, 195
Netherlands, 67, 114, 226, 234n
new history of sciences, 237
New School for Social Research in New York, 76, 101
New School in New York, 9, 238
New York Times, 79
Nietzsche, Friedriche, 4, 37, 206, 215
NKVD (People's Commissariat for Internal Affairs), 1

Nobel Prize, 225
nostalgia, 23, 30, 31, 68, 103, 124
Notgemeinschaft Deutscher Wissenschaftler im Ausland (1933), 8
novelists, 7

October Revolution, 6, 34, 174, 176, 180–81
Office of Strategic Services (OSS) in the USA, 4
optimism, 111, 207, 210, 217
oral history, 95, 191
organic nation, 209
organism, 209
Orientalists, 144
original theory of history, 95
Ostrogorsky, George, 176, 179, 181–82, 190
Ottoman empire, 8
Oxford University, 38, 160, 193, 239,

Padányi, Victor, 157, 162
Palestine, 81–82
Past & Present (journal), 35
Past as History, the (2015), 15n
Parga, Ramón Iglesia, 67
Park, Robert E., 45
Passmore, John, 101
patriotism, 206, 245
peaceful coexistence, 29, 131
pedagogics, 140
Peradze, Grigol, 63
Pereira, Miriam Halpern, 225
Petrovich, Michael B., 196
Pflanze, Otto, 110
philology, 48, 96, 102–03, 162, 177
philosophy, 35, 94–97, 99–01, 104n, 146, 213, 217–18, 242
  analytic, 97
PIASA (Polish Institute of Arts & Sciences of America), 7, 125–33, 134n
Ping-Ti Ho, 11
Pinson, Koppel, 114
Pirenne, Henri, 12
Plato, 95, 104, 206, 218
Platonism, 96
'pleasure in history', 48
Plekhanov, Georgi, 181

Poland, 10, 15, 26, 125–33, 180
  Kraków, 126, 128–29
  Lodz, 1
  Warsaw, 10, 28
Polanyi, Laura 139–51, 242
Polanyi, Karl, 147–48
Polish Institute and Sikorski Museum in London, 7
Polish Instytut Historyczny in Rome, 7
Polish Review, the, 7
Polish studies, 131
Polish University in Exile, 4, 125, 129
political parochialism, 52
political science, 128
political violence, 1, 240, 243, 245
politics, 3, 9, 35–39, 50, 52, 65, 95, 100, 102, 117, 140–41, 160, 163, 179, 182, 184, 190–91, 197, 211–12, 215, 218, 245
Politics of Cultural Despair, 116
Popkin, Jeremy D., 28
Popper, Karl, 98, 208
Portugal, 8, 129, 208, 210–13, 216, 218, 224–33, 234n, 240–41
  Coimbra, 228
  Lisbon, 207, 210, 215–16, 225, 228–29, 233
Portuguese chronology, 224
Portuguese Communist Party, 226, 233n
positivism, 99, 158, 190, 196
  anti-, 217
positivists, 98–100
Poverty of Historicism, the (1957), 98
Primitive Rebels (1959), 38
professional self-images, 47
progress, 33, 35–36, 206–207, 211, 217
Progressive, the (1929), 117
Protestantism, 5, 16n, 48
protests, 61, 102
provincialism, 74
Prussia, 10
psychology, 143, 146, 246n
Pulszky, Ferenc, 156

Rabinbach, Anson, 113
race, racism, racial, 2, 4, 6, 29, 34, 75, 81, 84, 96, 162, 218–19, 240
  racial segregation, 34
radicalism, 3, 38, 207, 216–17
Ramírez, Luís, 62

Ranke, Leopold von, 2, 47–48, 51–52, 104, 157
rationalism, 33, 206, 208, 215, 217
Ravignani, Emilio, 9
refugees, 5, 7, 9, 10, 28, 31, 58, 63, 75, 79, 82–83, 142, 144, 146, 174–76
  intellectual, 140
  Jewish, 27
relativism, 95, 100–02
  moral, 130
religion, 5, 28, 33, 64, 86, 101
  orthodox, 175
religiosity, 161
Remak, Joachim, 115
Révai, József, 156
Review of Politics, 117
Rickert, Heinrich, 95, 98–01, 104
Riess, Ludwig, 2
Rise and Fall of the Third Reich, the (1960), 117
Ritter, Gerhard, 109–12, 114–16, 240
Rivera, Primo de, 207, 213
Romania, 64, 151, 174, 179
romanticism, 116, 158
Romero, José Luis, 9
Rónai, Jácint, 156
Roniger, Luis, 9
Rosenberg, Arthur, 9
Rosenberg, Hans, 12, 46–47, 49, 52–54, 109, 111, 113, 115–16, 199
Rosselli, Carlo, 63
Rosselli, Nello, 63
Rothfels, Hans, 4, 11, 23, 46, 50, 109–10, 114, 117
Rudé, George, 3
Russia, 3, 10–15, 58, 63, 81, 125, 130, 175–77, 180,183–84
  Moscow, 13
  St. Petersburg, 13
Russian Civil War, 174
Russian émigré scholars, 173–85
Russian empire, 10
Russian Historical Archive Abroad, 7
Russian Research Center at Harvard, 133
Russian Revolution, 180–81, 184
Russian University in Prague, 6

Sabalingham, Sabaratnam, 64
Said, Edward, 124, 210

Salazar, António de Oliveira, 224
Salvemini, Gaetano, 6
Sánchez-Albornoz, Claudio, 4, 6
Saraiva, António José, 225–26, 228, 230–32
Saudi Arabia, 58
Scandinavia, 14
scepticism, 113, 126
Schäfer, Dietrich, 48
Scheler, Max, 158
Schieder, Theodor, 117
Schiller, Friedrich, 46
Schlosser, Friedrich Christoph, 48
Schoeps, Hans-Joachim, 110
scholarly persona, 23, 45–46, 50–51, 53, 237–38, 246
Scholem, Gershom, 30
Schorske, Carl, 118
Schwartz, Philipp, 77, 81
Second World War, 3, 4, 7, 10, 49, 66, 82, 109, 112, 116, 125, 156, 157, 164, 179–82, 188–90, 192, 195, 206, 224–25, 240–41
Serbia, 15, 175, 184, 190–91, 193, 197
    Belgrade, 173, 175, 179, 182, 188, 190–92, 199
Sérgio, António, 205, 207–09, 216, 219, 241
Shariati, Ali, 63
Sheehan, Jim, 118
Shirer, William, 117
Skëndi, Stavro, 195
Slav Library, 7
Slavic ideology, 176
Slavic studies, 177, 180, 182
social anthropology, 126
Social Democrats, 6, 114, 244
social justice, 34
social sciences, 52, 77, 99, 102, 119, 127–28, 174–76
socialism, socialist, 6, 9, 12, 113, 158, 189, 213
    German, 114
Society for the Protection of Science and Learning, 8, 82
sociologists, 45, 50, 99, 114, 128, 130, 206, 208
sociology, 100, 131, 143, 146, 153n, 157, 161–62, 246n
Söllner, Alfons, 46

Solovjev, Aleksandar, 176, 182
South Africa, 10, 60
South America, 81–82, 205, 218
Souvarine, Boris, 9
Soviet Union, USSR, 3, 6–8, 12–13, 34, 59, 64, 125, 129, 130, 141, 147, 159, 163, 180–82, 189, 195, 240
    Bolshevik regime, 125
    Sovietisation, 127
Spain, 6, 8, 10, 60, 62–63, 66–67, 129, 209–210, 213–14, 218–20, 225, 234n, 240–41
    Madrid, 82, 206–07, 210
    Second Spanish Republic, 225
    Spanish Civil War, 6, 67, 206, 207
Sri Lanka
    Tamil Tigers, 64
    Velupillai Prabhakaran, 64
Stalin, Josef, 1, 7, 64, 180, 182
State University of New York, 24
Stern, Fritz, 24, 110, 113, 115–16, 118, 144
Stokes, Gale, 196
Stricker, Laura Polanyi, 139
Suárez, Jesús de Galíndez, 63
Sugar, Peter, 195
suicide, 63, 66–70
Switzerland, 8, 67, 81, 129, 182
    Geneva, 76, 81, 182, 211
    Zurich, 77, 81
Sybel, Heinrich von, 48
Szalay, László, 156
Sznajder, Mario, 9

Taiwan, 8, 63–64
    Chiang Ching-kuo, 64
Tanzania, 10
Thukydides, 8
Tiananmen massacre – 1989, 62.
Tito, Josip Broz, 181–82
Tokyo Imperial University, 2
totalitarianism, 130, 206, 214
Toynbee, Arnold, 218
transnational biographies, 2
transnationalism, 14
Treitschkes, Heinrich Gotthard, 49
Trotsky, Leon, 64, 70
True History of the Conquest of New Spain (1967), 60
Turanist, 157, 162

Turkey, Turkish, 58, 77, 81, 162, 179
Turner, Henry, 118
Two Lives in Uncertain Times (2006), 25, 38

uchronism, 217
United Kingdom
  London, 24, 26–27, 63, 79, 80–82,
    125–26, 129, 159, 191, 243
  See also Britain, England
United States of America, 5, 7–8, 10–14,
  23–31, 45–47, 53, 59, 62, 74–79,
  81–85, 94–98, 101–04, 104n, 110–18,
  125–29, 131–32, 139, 141–48, 151,
  174, 179, 182, 192–95, 199, 215, 239,
  240, 244
  See also America, Americans
University of California in Berkeley, 12
University of Belgrade, 181, 194
University of Bonn, 117
University of Chicago, 5, 11, 111
University of Cologne, 111
University of Istanbul, 77, 84
University of Lisbon, 227
University of London, 24
University of Santa Barbara, 194
University of Toronto, 116
University of Tübingen, 50, 110
University of Warsaw, 128
University of Wisconsin, 113
Uruguay, 9
USSR, *see* Soviet Union
utopianism, 217

Varga, Lucie, 5, 238, 242
Venturi, Franco, 6
Vietnam War, 13, 34, 194

Vinogradoff, Pavel, 9
Volksgeschichte, 5
Voltaire, 37
Vucinich, Wayne, 196

Wagner, Richard, 46
Waitz, Georg, 48
Washington University, 112
Weber, Max, 67, 208
websites, 60
Wehler, Hans-Ulrich, 109
Weidlein, János, 156
Weimar culture, 31, 33, 113
  See also Germany
Wenqian, Gao, 62
Westernisation, 12
White, Hayden, 35
Wieruszowski, Helene, 23
Windelband, Wilhelm, 98
Women of Prague (1995), 13, 31
World War *see* First World War, Second
  World War
Writing History in Exile (2016), 17n

xenophobia, 69

Yale University, 4, 129
Yugoslavia, 130, 173–85, 189, 192, 194–95,
  198

Zilsel, Edgar, 67
Zionism, Zionist, 29, 30

This index was compiled by Ramesha Jayaneththi.

Lightning Source UK Ltd.
Milton Keynes UK
UKHW020628100223
416712UK00004B/61